# THE SEVERED WORD

# THE SEVERED WORD

OVID'S *HEROIDES*

AND THE *NOVELA SENTIMENTAL*

*Marina Scordilis Brownlee*

PRINCETON UNIVERSITY PRESS

PRINCETON, NEW JERSEY

*LIBRARY OF CONGRESS CATALOGING-IN-PUBLICATION DATA*

BROWNLEE, MARINA SCORDILIS.

THE SEVERED WORD : OVID'S HEROIDES AND THE NOVELA SENTIMENTAL /
MARINA SCORDILIS BROWNLEE.

P.   CM.

INCLUDES BIBLIOGRAPHICAL REFERENCES AND INDEX.

ISBN 0-691-06809-7 (ALK. PAPER)

1. SPANISH FICTION—TO 1500—HISTORY AND CRITICISM.   2. EPISTOLARY FICTION,
SPANISH—HISTORY AND CRITICISM.   3. OVID, 43 B.C.–17 OR 18. HEROIDES.
4. OVID, 43 B.C.–17 OR 18—INFLUENCE.   I. TITLE.

PQ6253.B76   1990   863'.209—DC20   90-37413 CIP

PUBLICATION OF THIS BOOK HAS BEEN AIDED BY THE PROGRAM FOR
CULTURAL COOPERATION BETWEEN SPAIN'S MINISTRY OF CULTURE AND
UNITED STATES' UNIVERSITIES

THIS BOOK HAS BEEN COMPOSED IN GALLIARD TYPEFACE

PRINCETON UNIVERSITY PRESS BOOKS ARE PRINTED ON ACID-FREE PAPER,
AND MEET THE GUIDELINES FOR PERMANENCE AND DURABILITY
OF THE COMMITTEE ON PRODUCTION GUIDELINES
FOR BOOK LONGEVITY OF THE COUNCIL
ON LIBRARY RESOURCES

PRINTED IN THE UNITED STATES OF AMERICA BY
PRINCETON UNIVERSITY PRESS, PRINCETON, NEW JERSEY

1   3   5   7   9   10   8   6   4   2

*For Kevin, Madeleine, and Nicholas*

# CONTENTS

# ACKNOWLEDGMENTS

I T IS A PLEASURE to acknowledge here several colleagues to whom I am indebted. My thanks to James Burke and Stephen Nichols for the erudition and insight they generously shared with me in reading the manuscript. They have contributed significantly to it. The friendship and intellectual companionship of Howard Bloch, John D. Lyons, Beatriz Pastor, and James Tatum have been very important to me in this project, as in many others. The relentless humor of Richard Axel has provided me with much appreciated levity, putting ivory-tower pursuits into their proper perspective. I thank the National Endowment for the Humanities for a twelve-month fellowship that enabled me to complete this book much sooner than would otherwise have been the case. Thanks must also go to Roy Thomas for his meticulous and intelligent editing of the manuscript.

However, the greatest pleasure is to acknowledge the role of the three people to whom this book is dedicated: to Kevin Brownlee, who contributed immeasurably to the intellectual evolution of this book, and to our daughter Madeleine and our son Nicholas, for their delightful distractions from it.

Philadelphia
25 June 1990

# THE SEVERED WORD

# PROLOGUE
## TWO THEORIES OF UTTERANCE


NOMINALISM acknowledges the discontinuity between words and things. Originating in the twelfth century, the expression of this linguistic sign theory culminated two centuries thereafter with the work of the speculative grammarians.[1] Yet the effects of this skeptical attitude toward language have continued to manifest themselves in both philosophical and literary discourse at different times and in various ways since it was first articulated.

A privileged locus for studying the implications of nominalism during the liminal period of the late Middle Ages is the rather ambiguously designated "novela sentimental" or "sentimental romance" of fifteenth-century Spain. This series of roughly seven texts was first described as a unified literary corpus in 1905 in a way that has remained virtually unchallenged despite the contradictions inherent in its postulation.[2] Having first invented the term *novela sentimental*, Marcelino Menéndez Pelayo went on to specify that it designates a generic hybrid, "a mixture of chivalric and [Italian] erotic literature, a combination of *Amadís* and the *Elegia di madonna Fiammetta*."[3]

The insufficiency of this definition arises, first of all, from the fact that chivalric literature is decidedly erotic—more erotic, in fact, than Fiammetta's solipsistic, retrospective account of unrequited passion. There is always an amorous motivation behind the deeds of knightly prowess, not to mention intimate encounters both verbal and physical.

Yet a more serious reservation to Menéndez Pelayo's classic formulation stems from the fact that *Amadís* and the *Elegia* exhibit two radically different discursive environments—namely, romance and novel respectively. His definition ignores the fact that the formal and semantic dimensions of a text must each be scrutinized separately before their combined effect and its generic expression can be determined. Cautioning the reader against an analogous form of discursive oversimplification, Hans-Robert Jauss wryly remarks: "One puts a princess in a fairy tale next to a princess in a novella, and one notices the difference."[4] In other words, it is not only the subject matter itself but the discursive environment constructed by the author that is crucially important. The verbal system implied by the novel is as alien to romance as the novella is to the fairy tale. And it is precisely this type of critical differentiation of discourses—based on linguistic referentiality—that must be acknowledged and explored within the context of the *novela sentimental*.

Part of the problem involved in defining this literary form results from the notorious terminological imprecision of the word *novela* in the Spanish lexicon, its usage to designate both novel and romance.[5] As such, *novela* participates in the same kind of generic ambiguity as *roman* in French and German, a term used to designate all long narratives, either novelistic or romance in nature. With a similar lack of precision, English, meanwhile, employs "novel" to indicate any long prose fiction. Yet the difference is decidedly qualitative rather than quantitative.

Definitions of the novel and novelistic discourse are equally heterogeneous. Literary historians attempt to define a diachronic progression for this elusive type of fiction, while theorists posit ahistorical distinctive features (formal, semantic, sociological, etc.). Nonetheless, amid this plurality of approaches and perspectives one feature remains constant—namely, the novel's status as Other, as oppositional discourse, as the noncanonical genre par excellence.

A protagonist's failure to conform to mythic paradigms of behavior (such as those celebrated by epic and romance) is one way of identifying the novel.[6] And this distinction between myth and novel expresses itself not simply in actantial terms, but in a consistent attitude toward language per se: "The novel and myth [are] two 'genres' that . . . constitute the opposite poles of the intertextual continuum. Myth implies a transparency of language, a coincidence of words and things; the novel starts out with a plurality of languages, discourses, and voices, and the inevitable awareness of language as such; in this sense, the novel is a basically self-reflexive genre."[7] The inability for heroic self-fulfillment corresponds to the shift in focus from the successful physical adventures of the outer world of romance to the fragile novelistic inner world of the individual human psyche. It is, for example, this movement that differentiates *Amadís* from the *Elegia*.

In discursive terms, Bakhtin conceptualizes this shift by contrasting the monologism of epic and romance with the dialogism of the novel, where idealized literary discourse becomes undermined by its contact with the nonliterary, unheroic discourses of quotidian reality.[8] Romance, like epic, is "monologic" in nature, that is, it offers a univocal, transcendent model of referentiality that is exemplified by a single discursive system. The signifying potential of words is never questioned within such monologic genres. By contrast, novelistic discourse is "dialogic"—a confrontation of different discourses that inevitably has the effect of questioning the authority of each one. Clearly, these two genres represent two very different types of utterance—indeed, two opposing attitudes toward language and its performative capacity.

Elaborating this distinction with respect to literary canonicity, Walter Reed observes that: "the novel is distinctive in the prominence and autonomy it gives to forms which are unliterary or uncanonical. . . . The novel explores the difference between the fictions which are enshrined in the institution of literature and the fictions, more truthful historically or merely more familiar, by which we lead our daily lives."[9] It is this seminal difference that the *novela sentimental* both exposes and thematizes.

Numerous theorists of the novel have labored to discern its first manifestation, some bestowing the distinction on *Don Quijote*, others on *Lazarillo de Tormes*, *Jehan de Saintré*, the *Elegia*, or even the *Vita Nuova*. This four-hundred-year disparity of attribution stems from the fact that no continuous novelistic tradition exists. As literary history bears witness, this genre appears and disappears according to the discursive climate of a given historical epoch.

Beyond the intermittent appearance of the long, realistic fictional form that we conventionally call the novel, however, there exists novelistic discourse not contained within a novel, resulting from the dialogic confrontation of other forms. A notable example is provided by the fourth century in the so-called Greek romance exemplified by Heliodorus and Achilles Tatius, which exploits a wide gamut of diverse genres ("the love elegy, the geographical novel, rhetoric, drama, the historiographic genre"), fusing them into "a new—specifically novelistic—unity."[10]

An equally novelizing potential exists in the composition of letters. Epistolary discourse is one of the most enduring and complex forms of communication, able to express clinical objectivity as well as extreme subjectivity. Ovid's *Epistulae Herodium* (referred to herein as *Heroides*) explores this discursive range, the letter's potential for subjective, novelistic discourse, for the first time and in a way that exerted a lasting effect on the Middle Ages and Renaissance.

It is highly significant that epistolarity is one of the defining features of the *novela sentimental*.[11] And while literary histories consistently acknowledge this formal aspect, they fail to perceive its novelistic potential for deconstructing the referentiality implied by romance in general—and these fifteenth-century Spanish texts in particular.[12] In fact, this protonovelistic form exploits the epistolary medium with a degree of sophistication normally attributed to eighteenth-century France and England.

Since the time of Menéndez Pelayo's initial formulation of the *novela sentimental* as a fusion of chivalric and Italian erotic literature, a second and third school of critics has emerged, finding the epistolary aspect of the *novela sentimental* to be an indication that either Ovid's *Heroides* or Boccaccio's *Elegia*, and perhaps also Piccolomini's *Historia de duobus amantibus*, are its principal subtexts.[13] Such scholars focus on these texts not simply because of the erotic element they share with the Spanish texts, but also because the *novela sentimental* exhibits a first-person autobiographical narrative which the author inscribes within a global letter structure, as well as intercalated exchanges of letters. Those who posit these model texts, however, do not distinguish between the unmediated elegiac missives of Ovid, the substantially different diary form that Fiammetta's confession takes, and the embedded letters of Piccolomini's third-person account. Yet in discursive terms the difference between them is great, as the chapters to follow will illustrate. In general, moreover, critical writing devoted to the epistolary dimension of the *novela sentimental* has failed to recognize that the inclusion of letters—like the insertion of verse into prose (another of the genre's discursive properties)—denotes, in structural terms, "the writer's distance from his own and other texts."[14] Intercalation implies the self-conscious creation of a metacritical distance that is fundamentally different from the unmediated (uncritical) authorial stance of romance discourse.

A fourth vein of *novela sentimental* criticism places greater emphasis on its extensive use of allegorical discourse (replete with allegorical castles and representations of "the erotic hell"), viewing this literary production as a late manifestation of the Ovidian dream-narrative tradition mediated through French models.[15] Allegoresis is decidedly important to this literature, but not merely as a perpetuation of the accustomed dream vision. Rather, it constitutes a departure from other medieval manifestations in that it is consistently deconstructed by the Spanish texts. In this case allegory, like epistolarity, is exploited as a nominalistic tool whereby the status of language itself is called into question.

The fifth major critical trend sees the *novela sentimental* instead as being the product of third-person chivalric romance narrative in combination with first-person *cancionero* lyric. César Hernández Alonso represents this attitude when he writes: "The Spanish sentimental or courtly novel originates with the *Siervo libre* as the fusion of *cancionero* lyric and chivalric narrative. This sentimental environment results from the commingling of these two worlds; it is a new form, entirely different from either one of its constituent parts."[16]

While the *novela sentimental* makes use of the various generic forms enumerated by Hernández, their simultaneous presence signals a hybrid dialogic environment. On the one hand, he acknowledges this by saying that the outcome is something entirely new. If, however, this is the case, then Hernández logically contradicts himself by viewing them at the same time as "reconciled" and participating in a "continuous permeability." Generic integrity cannot be maintained while simultaneously producing something entirely new. In this particular instance, *cancionero* poetry cannot be reconciled with chivalric romance. The lyric form represents an aesthetic of discontinuity (a fragmented encyclopedia of lovers) whereby the lover is effaced by the writer/compiler of the collection. It is "an ethic of totalization, but an aesthetic of discontinuity."[17] Moreover, this is an elegiac poetry, an unanswered expression of lament, and as such it represents a type of performative inefficacy that is quite alien to romance. In effect, such poetry represents the novelistically rooted discourse of affective failure.

In the last analysis, it is not productive to argue for either the *cancionero* or the *Elegia* as the subtext for the *novela sentimental*. For as Pamela Waley astutely observes:

> Sanvisenti, Menéndez Pelayo, Farinelli and others in their wake have claimed that the early *novelas sentimentales* were inspired by Boccaccio's *Elegia*, basing these claims on the concern of their authors with the emotions of love, and in particular with emotion expressed in the first person, and with an elementary "psychology" based on observation of emotional reaction to external circumstances. The same themes however are commonly found in the poetry of the fifteenth-century *cancioneros*, deriving from Provençal, French, Italian and Galician-Portuguese lyric poetry.[18]

To this observation must be added the fact that this concern with an anatomy of love rooted in the first person originates in Ovid's *Heroides*. The *Elegia* has been accurately described as "an expanded heroid."[19] Like the *cancionero* poetry, the *Elegia* is an extended lyric meditation. So are the *Heroides*, and it is a translation of these Ovidian letters (the *Bursario*) that directly precedes the writing of the first *novela sentimental*. Moreover, rather than *cancionero* poetry, it is clear that epistolarity constitutes a far more extensive concern of the Spanish authors.

At the same time, it is extremely important to note that the insertion of *cancionero* poetry within the *novela sentimental* serves—like epistolarity and the subversion of the allegorical system—to represent and to problematize the referentiality of language per se. It is, I maintain, no accident that we find all three features contained within *novela sentimental* composition, for they serve individually and collectively to erode the linguistic optimism of romance. Thus, by contrast with previous studies, I see all three formal features as part of an epistemological continuum, as contributing to the nominalistic undermining that is the consistent linguistic concern of this form. Nonetheless, since epistolarity is the most extensively developed of the three, it serves as the prime focus of the study that follows.

## Epistolary Anatomy

The first section of this study establishes the fundamental features of epistolary discourse as exemplified by the *Heroides*. From this point of departure, the threefold impact of Ovid's text—its implications for translation, the expanded heroid structure, and the device of embedded letters in the Middle Ages—is examined.

Regardless of their origins or thematic particularity, myths are totalizing structures that invariably reduce the complexities of individual subjectivity. Ovid's *Heroides* dramatizes this distinctive feature of mythic discourse (the adversarial relationship between individual and universal) by presenting a series of individual authors, legendary females, each of whom voices her own subjective interpretation of the myth to which she pertains. Here, rather than encountering a third-person narrative of the external actions which made these women famous (or infamous), we see them exclusively through interior monologues—a totally different dimension of their accustomed, official psychological profiles, and now viewed for the first time as psychologically complex individuals, not as totalized, monolithic abstractions.

The metaliterary import of the *Heroides*, the originary status of this discourse and its radical implications for mythographic discourse, was concretely understood by Ovid, for by the act of hollowing out his "heroines' " magical, transcendent identities, Ovid's discursive gesture unravels the phenomenology of myth itself. He effects this mythographic innovation on its most basic level, by voyeuristically betraying a side of heroines such as Medea, Penelope, Dido, and Phaedra in the individual letters they and other illustrious women send to their absent lovers.

More is at issue, however, for the disposition of these epistolary monologues is such that they are meant to be read collectively as well as individually, that is, syntactically as well as semantically. This double structure is crucial in its implications for subjective discourse in general and epistolary discourse in particular. We see that while each letter writer is a self-proclaimed victim of abandonment by her lover, she is at the same time a consummate artist, a verbal artificer who reveals the inescapably deceptive nature of language. It is by this problematization of language found in the fifteen epistolary self-portraits that the *Heroides* establishes a kind of novelistic letter discourse that is entirely original. And, as a result of his epistolary innovation, Ovid may be justifiably included in the Foucauldian distinction between authors and those writers whom he identifies as "founders of discursivity." To illustrate this latter category he identifies innovators such as Galileo, Marx, Freud, and Saussure—each one an initiator of a discursive practice that resulted in nothing less than a new way of looking at the world. Galileo, for example, "made possible not only those discourses that repeated the laws that he had formulated, but also statements very different from what he had said."[20] Similarly, models of generative grammar could not have been constituted without the prior existence of Saussure's method of structural analysis. It is, as we shall see, the discursive innovation of the Ovidian epistle, its new attitude toward language, that forms the basis of the medieval Spanish *novela sentimental* by serving to problematize the linguistic integrity implied by romance.

If Ovid programmatically dismantles the exemplary, paradigmatic function that had initially accorded his heroines their legendary status by showing them to be all too humanly vulnerable, the Middle Ages effected a reversal of this hermeneutic procedure. Unlike the epoch in which it was written, medieval readers no longer viewed Ovid's text as a politically and discursively subversive artifact, but instead as its opposite. Indeed, rather than reading it as the immediate cause of his exile from Augustan Rome, they interpreted the *Heroides* (not the *Ex Ponto*) as the principal work he wrote in order to be pardoned, to revoke his exile.

Wishing to leave nothing to chance, medieval exegetes make explicit what for them constitutes the extradiegetic, ethical exemplarity of the *Heroides* in a number of ways. That is, while Ovid's original compilation of first-person epistles contains no third-person critical apparatus, extensive commentary of this kind abounds in its medieval transformations. Global prefaces constructed according to the dictates of the medieval *accessus* now introduce the letter collection, while more specific didacticism detailing the positive or negative valence to be attached to each of the legendary females is indicated in the form of individual rubrics that precede each of the letters.

Quite alien to the Ovidian *mentalité*, this new hermeneutic environment characterizes the traditional reception of the *Heroides* in the Middle Ages. Nonetheless, it is axiomatic that for every example there exists a counter-example. And Spain provides just such a notable exception to the normative reading in Juan Rodríguez's fifteenth-century rewriting entitled *Bursario o las Epístolas de Ovidio*, a work that at the same time constitutes the earliest vernacular rendering of the entire Ovidian collection in Europe.

Because it relies on Alfonso X's partial translations, it is consistently invoked as an example of the enduring influence of Alfonsine prose. And while this subtextual affiliation is irrefutable, it has led to the misperception that Rodríguez engaged in a merely scribal activity, a kind of uncreative transmission. Such an appraisal of the *Bursario* represents a myopic interpretation that ignores Rodríguez's creative *translatio* of his subtext. For the *Heroides*, the *Bursario*, and the Alfonsine chronicle that mediates between the two epistolary anthologies represent three very different attitudes toward language.

The transmission and translation of the *Heroides* in Spain was effected by Alfonso X in his universal history during the second half of the thirteenth century. However, in both formal and semantic terms his representation of the Ovidian text is a fragmentary one. That is, of Ovid's twenty-one epistles, Alfonso presents only eleven, virtually half of the Ovidian total. Even more revealing of his fragmentary representation is the fact that Alfonso looks to the same heroines as objective "proofs," universal examples of his extraliterary (decidedly imperial) public values. In so doing, he seeks, in effect, to return the legendary women to the heroic, external, public world of male values from which Ovid had liberated them. Rather than juxtaposing the semantic and syntactic dimensions of the text so as to question the status of language itself, Alfonso offers an impersonal, second-person plural reporting of "authoritative" history which is rendered even more official by the inclusion of embedded portions of selected heroids.

Objectivity, precisely the opposite discursive reality from that which Ovid sought to generate, is now the goal. In his universal history Alfonso effects a *translatio* that is cultural as well as linguistic, one that is intended, in its broadest terms, to promote the legitimacy of his own discourse. What emerges from a reading of the Ovidian epistles in their thirteenth-century historiographic recontextualization is their use as an authoritative source for the preservation of a collective memory that is filtered through Alfonso's own axiological system. In other words, if Ovid was bent on illustrating the primacy of *discours* in the communication of his *histoire*—its considerable potential for distortion—Alfonso's concern is to have the subjective *discours* be coterminous with objective *histoire*.

The mid-fifteenth-century *Bursario* is quite another matter. In place of Alfonso's occasional intercalation of selected *epístolas* dispersed throughout many hundred pages of historiography, we find a reinstatement of the initial Ovidian structure of unembedded, consecutive letters. Rodríguez includes all of the original letters except Sappho's (a text that had not yet been rediscovered by the Middle Ages). In this way, the semantic/syntactic tension of the Ovidian text is restored, but with a significant difference. Missives exposing the subjective torments of the legendary figures are now being juxtaposed not (as in Ovid) by an implicit editor, but by an explicit one. Indeed, a revealing progression can be discerned in these three presentations of the *Heroides*: from Ovid's voyeuristically private context to Alfonso's public context, further transformed in the *Bursario* by a clever juxtaposition of the two anterior perspectives. Taking the form of a didactic rubric that precedes each of the letters, this critical apparatus represents a hermeneutic mechanism present throughout medieval redactions of the *Heroides*. Despite his ostensible continuation of this generalized practice, however, Rodríguez actually exploits the rubric convention in order to dismantle the authority of its extratextual framework by means of which the Middle Ages had obscured the metadiscursive breakthrough achieved by the Ovidian original.

Paradoxically, it is from an ostensible imitation of the medieval exegetical readers of the *Heroides* that Rodríguez transforms the letters in such a way as to recuperate their original epistemological value as novelistic discourse. Yet, while this discursive recuperation is of paramount importance, it must be stressed that Rodríguez's aim is not simply restorative. For having effected this Ovidian recontextualization, he will go on to juxtapose its novelistic discourse with medieval romance discourse in the mid-fifteenth-century *Siervo libre*.

Before discussing the *Siervo libre* itself, the two prose texts consistently evoked as its immediate predecessors bear consideration in this study, for it is no accident that they too rely both visibly and in a sustained manner on Ovid's heroidean model. Boccaccio's *Elegia di madonna Fiammetta* (1344), often referred to as the first modern European novel, constitutes an expanded heroid. Specifically, it takes the form of a letter written by an abandoned female, the eponymous Fiammetta, who offers a first-person epistolary elegy which is most reminiscent of the second heroid, that of Phyllis to Demofoon. Beyond this resemblance, Fiammetta overtly models herself on a number of additional letter writers from the *Heroides*, as well as citing lengthy passages from their letters virtually verbatim. Both texts are pseudoautobiographies of females written by men, both contain narrators who are elegiacally lovelorn females.

In terms of the addressee, however, there is a crucial difference that points to Boccaccio's highly original recasting of his predecessor. For while the Ovidian women each address themselves to their respective absent lovers, Fiammetta's inscribed readers are explicitly designated as the anonymous "*donne innamorate*" (enamoured ladies). What becomes clear in the unfolding of her existential dilemma, however, is that she cannot reveal her situation by writing such an open letter. She must console herself with a strictly confidential diary which can be read by no one other than herself. This epistolary paradox, which she generates by addressing a reader whom she must never allow to read her words, is, moreover, essential to an understanding of Boccaccio's discursive innovation.

Recognized as the progeny of the *Elegia* and traditionally invoked as the other important narrative model for the *novela sentimental* is Piccolomini's *Historia de duobus amantibus* (1444). Although separated by one hundred years, these two texts are conventionally paired because they both detail the predictable effects on the adulterous wife who is seduced and abandoned by a lover who has sworn eternal fidelity. Both despair as the lovers announce their departure, Lucretia dying of grief while Fiammetta recedes into madness. In addition, epistolarity is a fundamental issue within each text. While Boccaccio turns the Ovidian epistle into a solipsistic written reverie, Piccolomini takes the exploration of epistolarity one step further by embedding ten of the love letters exchanged by Lucretia and Euryalus within his third-person narrative. Despite these undeniable similarities between the two texts written in Italy, however, the epistolary discourse of the *Historia* reveals the epistemological chasm that in fact separates Lucretia from Fiammetta.

That the problematic relationship of words and deeds is carefully charted by Piccolomini is evident in the symmetrically configured speech acts that characterize the letters of the amorous pair. This symmetrical disposition of the letters provides the author with an opportunity to illustrate a number of paradoxes inherent in letter communication, and to thematize the ultimately irreducible distance separating word from deed. Once both lovers have articulated their mutual desire, mediated words (theory) are replaced by unmediated action (praxis) which might or might not correspond to them.

## The Allegorical Paradox

Allegory (as its etymon "allos" implies) necessarily involves a linguistic paradox whereby signifier and signified are provisionally disassociated from one another. Their separation is a temporary pedagogical strategy which prevails until the text's heuristic trajectory has been completed for the reader, at which time the consubstantiality of these two factors of referentiality is celebrated. Each of the three texts treated in this section, three early examples of the *novela sentimental* (written in the 1440s and 1450s), will pointedly question the epistemological relevance of this procedure.

The heroidean letter structure in Juan Rodríguez's writing is by no means confined to the *Bursario*. For his *Siervo libre*, which initiates the *novela sentimental* corpus, also consists of a lover's extended epistolary monologue characterized by retrospective psychological probing. As with Boccaccio and Piccolomini, however, Rodríguez effects a radical transformation of the Ovidian speech situation in his medieval rewriting. Of fundamental importance for his narrative configuration is the fact that unlike the *Heroides*, the *Siervo libre* is a letter addressed not to a lover whose reciprocated love is sought at the present time of writing, but to a male confidant, and it narrates only completed actions and emotions in the past. It is not attempting either to persuade a beloved or to elegiacally lament the writer's fate. Instead the lover opts out of the accustomed discourse of desire entirely, and in so doing Rodríguez boldly remotivates the speech situation initiated by the *Heroides*.

Analysis reveals that beyond its dependence on the epistolary form, the *Siervo libre* relies not, as is often claimed, on Boccaccio but on Dante for a conceptual framework that will be initially recalled in order to transform it into something entirely new. More precisely, the *Siervo libre* makes extensive use of certain thematic concerns and narrative configurations (particularly that of the poet/lover/beloved) established by Dante in the *Vita Nuova* and elaborated thereafter in the *Commedia*. Indeed, Rodríguez establishes Dante as his only vernacular *auctor* in order to redeploy him for his own metadiscursive purposes, to "unravel" Dante's literary tapestry, as it were, in order to illustrate not the potential of human love (as emblematized by Beatrice), but rather its overwhelming limitations. Rodríguez replaces Dante's positivistic discourse with his own novelistic discourse. Moreover, this unraveling is achieved by questioning the discourse of desire in an eminently heroidean manner—exposing its polysemously novelistic nature, hence its performative inefficacy.

The *Siervo libre* is the first of three *novelas sentimentales* that rely heavily on allegorical discourse for their structure. The second text is the *Satira de felice e infelice vida* and the third is *Triste deleytaçion*. What becomes immediately apparent from this enumeration is the fact that their titles are consistently oxymoronic: *The Free Servant of Love* (or *The Servant Freed of Love*), *The Satire of Felicitous and Infelicitous Life*, and *Sad Delectation*. And this coincidence is not accidental. Rather, the titles reflect the epistemological contradiction at issue in their subversive treatment of allegory. The separation of signifier from signified offered by medieval allegory is traditionally presented as being merely provisional, as a necessary stage in the educative progress of the reader. In these three texts, however, this separation is definitive, representing a new way of portraying the problem of subjective discourse, of the linguistic referentiality initiated by the Ovidian epistle.

We have already noted the inefficacy of courtly discourse in the *Siervo libre* as expressed by Rodríguez's rewriting of the Dantean model of Christian allegory. The *Satira*, on the other hand, looks to the courtly allegorical figures of Jean de Meun's *Roman de la Rose* for its initial inspiration. We find a lover who has been in love for five years with a lady who does not reciprocate his passion.

As the narrative begins, he experiences a vision in which he is confronted by a series of personifications with whom he must debate. Yet while the *Rose* incorporates a gallery of Ovidian myths within its personification allegory, Don Pedro's text seeks to separate clearly myth and allegory. These are, significantly, the two principal discursive modes of the Middle Ages (myth corresponding to *histoire* as defined by Emile Benveniste's distinction and allegory to *discours*).

The most visible means by which he effects this separation is in an extensive exegetical apparatus of more than one hundred glosses to the text. Introduction of this type of interpretive mechanism in an amorous allegory represents a significant departure, for it signals the intrusion of an extratextual dimension in the courtly system that is in its very nature necessarily intratextual, subjective, hermetic. Yet the implications of this innovation extend still further. For by consistently (and obtrusively) juxtaposing the subjective states of the lovelorn protagonist with the impersonal historicity of the glosses, the tension of self and other, Don Pedro replaces the anticipated lyric structure with a novelistic one.

Just as allegorical discourse fails, so does the discourse of the glosses. Rather than offering information and orientation to the reader, they are prolix, often inaccurate, and overwhelmingly narrative rather than interpretive in nature. And as a consequence of this programmatic presentation, the *Satira* calculatedly succeeds in undermining the function of exegesis itself. The exemplary mechanisms of allegory and gloss are shown to be unable to combat the irrationality of love. The nominal rather than real coexistence of signifier and signified has been recognized and as a result, the positivistic function of words is definitively eroded. Thus the modes of allegory and exegesis behave in the same discursively skeptical way that epistolarity functions.

The ontology of language also serves as the focus of *Triste deleytaçion* (c. 1460). Like all *novelas sentimentales*, it is inscribed within a letter. And like the works discussed thus far, it too relies heavily on a subtextual framework it will radically transform. In the case of this work, written by the anonymous "F.A.D.C.," it is the axiology of the *novella* initiated by Boccaccio's *Decameron* that underlies the imaginary universe constructed by *Triste deleytaçion*. In fact, F.A.D.C. exploits no fewer than twelve of the *Decameron's novelle*, virtually all of them from Day 5 (the day, significantly, in which the discursively problematic Fiammetta reigns). Once again we find a distraught lover who projects the familiar courtly romance topoi and devices. They are, however, consistently displaced, rendered obsolete by the cynical empiricism of *novella* discourse.

Indicative of the uncourtly ethos that overtakes the anticipated courtly system in this text is the suggestion made by the lover's friend, that if his lady will not oblige him he should simply find another one who will. This would, of course, be unthinkable in a courtly romance, but even more alien to the discourse of *fin' amor* is the lover's suggestion that the friend seduce the lady's stepmother for the sake of expediency, so that the affair may proceed more smoothly. Nonetheless, this is exactly what happens. After a number of misogynistic and misandrist perspectives have been articulated and valorized by the cynical characters themselves, we find the familiar *novella* situation of the deceived husband spying on his wife and, in this case, murdering her. It goes without saying that this prosaic emphasis on conjugal domesticity and the perils that adultery implies are anathema to the courtly idyll, which dwells instead on the exquisite torments of desire. After receiving word of the murder, the lover flees the city without seeing his lady, motivated by the very unidealistic impulse of fear. And with a comparable degree of cynicism, motivated by expedience rather than true religious vocation, the lady becomes a nun in order to escape the life-threatening reprisals of her father.

The last third of the text abruptly shifts into verse for the narration of an allegorical journey to the Otherworld in which we find the protagonist traveling through Hell and Purgatory, ultimately reaching Paradise in a greatly modified version of the Afterlife offered by the tripartite spatial configuration of Dante's *Commedia*. Quite unlike the *Siervo libre's* somber rewriting of Dante (and as a response to it), *Triste deleytaçion* presents a comical rewriting in which the axiology of the Dantean system is once again, as with the *Siervo libre*, subverted.

In a decided departure from the *Commedia*, we now find only lovers in F.A.D.C.'s extraterrestrial landscape. The lover (who entered into Hell purely by accident) is likened to Hippolytus (a traditional avatar of Christ), a mythographic association that is also evoked in the *Commedia*. Because of his own journey into death, Dante makes the additional identification of himself with Hippolytus, and it is no doubt for this reason that F.A.D.C. parodically expands the subtextual compass to include himself as well. This detail is offered as one of many indications of the irreverence that lies at the core of this rewritten Afterlife. The lover moves from Hell to Purgatory to Paradise, we are told, because Fortune has decreed that the God of Love will save him. The geographic placement of the various figures is, moreover, arbitrary. We find Boccaccio situated in Hell, and Torrellas, the notorious misogynistic poet, quite illogically (but humorously) placed in Heaven. Equally unlikely candidates for this amorous Paradise are the figures of Virgil, Helen of Troy, and Rodríguez (whose biography as well as the *Siervo libre* unambiguously confirm his definitive rejection of courtly love). Finally, we see the traditional medieval allegory procedure, an initial dream followed by an interpretive, teleological gloss, being overturned in *Triste deleytaçion*. The elaborate, unrealistic (versified) vision is preceded by a (prose) gloss that has the effect of diminishing the authority of allegorical discourse per se—because it artificially oversimplifies the problematic, novelistic axiology that has prevailed until virtually the end of the text.

## Linguistic Transgressions

This section deals with the late fifteenth-century *novelas sentimentales* (published in the 1490s), two written by San Pedro and two by Flores. No longer interested in exposing the limitations of allegory in an extended fashion, these texts relegate it to the periphery of their fiction, focusing instead on related problems of "realistic" discourse.

San Pedro's *Arnalte y Lucenda* and the *Cárcel de amor*, published only one year apart (in 1491 and 1492 respectively), have been interpreted as part of a genetic progression, that the former work served as a kind of first draft for the latter. And in thematic terms they do share an undeniable affinity. Yet a discursive analysis shows these two texts to be fundamentally different, offering two distinct but mutually complementary meditations on linguistic usage.

In the case of *Arnalte*, it is the principle of metaphoric exchange first articulated in Aristotle's *Poetics* that is at issue. We routinely speak of the "poetic economy" of a given text, and San Pedro offers bold confirmation of such "verbal economics" by having each of his four characters construct an extensive network of currency and exchange in which words, clothing, money, and sex are repeatedly transferred.

Arnalte, Lucenda, Belisa, and Yerso individually participate in this type of semantic distortion in order to promote their subjective desires, and they do so by engaging in a series of euphemistic exchanges involving the words "love," "honor," and "friendship." It is important to note, however, that some of the proposed exchanges succeed, while others fail. To give one example, Belisa manages to persuade Lucenda to accept her highly incongruous proposal (the exchange of her *philos* for *eros* directed at Arnalte) because of the nature of the particular friendship these women share. That is, Lucenda wants above all to please Belisa, Arnalte's sister, viewing the risk to her friendship as being far greater than the risk to her honor. The exchange of letters between Arnalte and Lucenda offers further corroboration of this principle, at the same time providing a corollary to Piccolomini's system of epistolary response, whereby only a shared common interest results in epistolary exchange.

San Pedro's other *novela sentimental*, the *Cárcel de amor*, approaches the problem of referentiality from a substantially different perspective, though it arrives at similar conclusions. Recognized as the epitome of its genre, the *Cárcel* is conventionally regarded as an assemblage of rather disparate parts: an allegorical prelude which inexplicably fades away, an epistolary tale of love, a chivalric combat, a profeminist encomium, etc. Beyond the rhetorical value of its structure, the work is, on a thematic level, viewed as an illustration of the insoluble existential conflict of courtly values (represented by Leriano) and chivalric values (steadfastly upheld by Laureola), mediated by a fictional author figure who serves as go-between. This view constitutes an oversimplification, however, since Laureola herself subverts the chivalric ethos by refusing to accept the favorable verdict of Leriano's adjudicated duel on her behalf, just as Leriano subverts the courtly system by publicly rescuing her from imprisonment.

The *Cárcel* is considerably more nuanced than either of these interpretations would suggest. It is rather at the level of the illocutionary act that San Pedro's blueprint for the *Cárcel* becomes visible. Only at that level does a programmatic structure emerge that strategically deviates from the discursive conventions of a number of medieval genres. More precisely, we find a relentless violation of the "appropriateness conditions" (the contextual presuppositions and expectations) implied by each of the genres San Pedro evokes. A veritable gallery of disparate speech situations culminates as Leriano's failure to communicate with Laureola prompts him to shred the love letters, consuming them with water in a venereal reenactment of the Eucharist, whereupon he expires.

In a very real sense, Leriano's eating of the words serves as an emblem of a "dead end" speech situation. In this exclusively epistolary relationship, words are presented as sterile graphic markers rather than mechanisms for communication. Laureola's words and their communicative function are reduced to the status of a metonym for Laureola herself—one that displaces communication—leading to death, that is, silenced words.

Written in the 1480s, the texts of Flores, *Grimalte y Gradissa* and *Grisel y Mirabella*, expose the ambiguity of discourse in still another manner. *Grimalte* presents itself as an explicit continuation of the *Elegia*, picking up the narrative thread left hanging when Fiammetta considered disguising herself as a pilgrim to search through the world for Panfilo. Yet this continuation does not merely advance the Boccaccian intrigue, for Flores distinguishes his text from his subtext by inverting the focus—i.e., by focusing on the implications of action (rather than speech, as was the case in the *Elegia*). Indeed, he offers his readers as programmatic a rewriting of the *Elegia*'s metalinguistic concerns as Boccaccio does of the *Heroides*.

Not one but two couples populate Flores' text: Fiammetta and Panfilo and Grimalte and Gradissa—all avid readers of the *Elegia*. In fact the text thematizes the act of reading and its effects to such a degree that it is frequently compared to Cervantes' obsessive concerns with the power of reading in *Don Quijote*. Flores explores the inherent subjectivity of language in an original way, for by replacing the *Elegia*'s first-person structure with a second-person dialogic structure as well as an epistolary one, *Grimalte* permits a simultaneous multiplicity of interpretations of Fiammetta's affair.

Realizing that Boccaccio's Fiammetta had only two options—either perpetual madness or suicide—Flores offers a different course. There is a movement out of the secrecy contained within Fiammetta's chamber to the world at large. Similarly, the paralytic inaction of the Italian work is replaced by a profusion of activity in the Spanish continuation. Also by way of distinguishing *Grimalte* from its model text, we discern a notable absence of mythological discourse in the Spanish continuation.

As with the other *novelas sentimentales*, linguistic alienation forms the principal concern of *Grimalte*, yet it is treated here in two strikingly original ways. Grimalte succeeds in overcoming the inescapable problem of referentiality only by fleeing society entirely, restoring linguistic integrity by joining Panfilo to live out what remains of his life as a hermit in the desert. While this constitutes an extreme solution to the problem, the fate of Fiammetta is even more extraordinary. Having been consigned to Hell, she appears to Grimalte and Panfilo three times a week in a ghastly vision, tormented by devils who force her to suffer in actions the words of malediction she had so deceptively articulated in the *Elegia*, threats that she had no intention of realizing. In this way Flores finally punishes Fiammetta's linguistic counterfeit, forcing her for the first time to make her words accord with her actions. Paradoxically, it is his continuation that definitively effects closure on the *Elegia*'s openendedness and it does so in a way that both continues and further complicates Boccaccio's theory of language.

*Grisel* continues the exploration of language (especially legal discourse) begun in *Grimalte*. More precisely, while *Grimalte* explores law in the (private, individual) amorous register, *Grisel* further problematizes the discourse of desire by placing it in the (public, universal) context of society. For in essence, *Grisel* examines the relationship between natural and judicial law as they pertain to the discursive authority of their guarantor—the king.

Echoing *Grimalte's* subtextual strategies, *Grisel* is also based on a rewriting of Boccaccio, the model in this case being the first tale in Day 4 of the *Decameron*. Yet the importance of this subtext tends to be minimized, deemed unessential to an understanding of *Grisel*, which is valorized either for its innovative debate structure or for its interest in fifteenth-century feminism. Both issues, however, stem from Boccaccio's discursive postulation of nominalism. *Grisel*, like its subtext, is about language, about naming, about the legitimacy of discourse per se.

Flores remotivates the predictable discursive contamination of the king's incestuous inclination and its effects in several significant ways, however. The first occurs in the prefatory remarks he makes to his own lady. Rather than the anticipated praise for her beauty, for her role as (passive) muse figure, he praises her intellect, soliciting her active editorial collaboration to such a degree in fact that he instructs her to destroy his text if she feels it is without merit.

It is significant that the only exception to the linguistic perversion that plagues the kingdom is an extradiegetic one, namely the couple represented by Flores and his lady. They perpetuate the philosophy of language projected by Grisel and Mirabella in an enduring verbal artifact—the eponymous text on which they collaborate. In this way the discourse of dismemberment generated by the verbally incestuous monarch is finally ended, replaced by a linguistic integrity that exposes the devastating implications of such discourse.

Finally, by the role accorded to the extradiegetic couple in his literary love letter, Flores attempts to rectify the linguistic alienation initiated by the *Heroides*, to reinstate referentiality. Yet at the same time, given the editorial emphasis of Flores' letter, it projects the somber implication that the creation of such linguistic integrity is largely unattainable.

## Epilogue: Physical and Verbal Violence

This section offers a brief meditation on additional forces that contribute to the breakdown of referentiality in these texts. The tension of alien discourses, visible throughout the *novela sentimental*, is heightened by a particular kind of geographical alienation. While eroticism and exoticism very often coexist, in this group of texts the preponderence of unfamiliar, re-mote (often savage) landscapes serves instead to project a different form of alienation, but one that reinforces the intensity of the verbal estrangement. The repeated linguistic violence quite literally leads, in every case, to physi-cal violence (suicide, murder, mutilation, madness, etc.). Whereas the am-biguity of the sign had been articulated in fourteenth-century Spain (most notably by the *Libro de buen amor*), it is the fifteenth-century *novela senti-mental* that fully grasps the existentially and novelistically dire conse-quences of this ambiguity.

Finally, this consistent attitude toward language suggests the fundamen-tal importance of the *novela sentimental* for *La Celestina*, the most influen-tial text of fifteenth-century Spain. On the basis of its findings, this study seeks to advance a new interpretation of this intertextual relationship, at the same time demonstrating the undeniable discursive disparity separating the romance of chivalry and the *novela sentimental*, which are traditionally paired. In both cases, the nature and function of epistolarity is paramount.

# PART ONE

## EPISTOLARY ANATOMY

# ONE

## VICTIM AS ARTIST

### (*EPISTULAE HERODIUM*)

MYTHS—in Ovid and in general—are universal structures. Irrespective of their particular nature, they invariably reduce the complexities of individual consciousness to a mere function of themselves. Ovid's *Heroides* dramatizes this distinctive feature of mythic discourse, the conflict between individual and universal. What confronts us in the text is a series of individual authors each voicing her own subjective interpretation of the myth to which she pertains. Individualized, hermetic portraits by legendary women of their subjective states each correspond to one exclusive interpretation of her own existential circumstances. Penelope, for example, discourses on her unique form of abandonment to Ulysses, as does Phaedra to Hippolytus and Medea to Jason. By their respective accounts we see, first of all, a side of these legendary lovers that differs—in an important sense—from their normal associations as the creatures of myth. That is, they each initially attained mythic stature for their notable actions: Penelope for resisting would-be suitors during Ulysses' twenty-year absence; Phaedra for her incest; and Medea for her sorcery and infanticide. Here, rather than seeing them through a narration of their external actions, we view them for the first time through their interior monologues in all their psychological complexity, and not as paradigmatic abstractions.

The significance of this new form of Ovidian metamorphosis cannot be overstated. For in essence, Ovid displaces the legendary women he treats from their accustomed demiurgic status, revealing them in their intimate humanity. In so doing, Ovid subverts the phenomenology of myth itself. For if, as Northrop Frye explains, myths are endowed with authority "because of cultural forces impelling them to do so,"[1] we can understand the added metaliterary, societal threat posed by the composition of the *Heroides*. As Florence Verducci puts it, "In the *Heroides* Ovid subjects traditionally lofty subjects to the 'middle level' of style, and the result proves 'very dangerous' to his subject, a subject by definition in the arena of 'the passions and the sublime.' "[2]

Realizing the far-reaching implications of his mythographic innovation, Ovid proclaims his originality in no uncertain terms when in the *Art of Love* he states that he invented the heroid genre "Ignotum hoc aliis ille novavit opus" [he first invented this art, unknown to others].[3] This sweeping assertion requires closer scrutiny, for there did exist before Ovid amorous complaints both fictional and authentic written by abandoned females. In fact, his subtextual dependence is considerable. Penelope (Epist. 1) and Briseis (Epist. 3) are drawn from Homer; Hypsipyle (Epist. 6) and parts of Medea (Epist. 12) stem from Apollonius and his Roman imitators; other dimensions of Medea and Phaedra (Epist. 4) are indebted to Euripides; Deianeira (Epist. 9) to Sophocles; Ariadne (Epist. 10) to Catullus; and probably Laodamia (Epist. 13) and Hypermnestra (Epist. 14) to Horace.[4] At the same time, there was certainly an elegiac tradition and an epistolary one as well—represented by the letters of Cicero, Plato, Epicurus, and Propertius.

Given these facts of literary history we may justifiably question Ovid's self-proclaimed invention. In the process of doing so, however, we see that his claim is a valid one. Such is the case because the elegiac tradition before Ovid did not conceive of a series of texts that were meant to be read collectively as well as individually—syntactically as well as semantically, to borrow the terminology of Fredric Jameson.[5] As analysis will make clear, this double structure is radical in its implications for the establishment of subjective discourse. And it is Ovid's departure from the norm—even from his own narrative strategies in the *Amores*—focusing for the first time on the woman's affect rather than on that of the poet-lover, which is at the root of his originality. Finally, he must be credited with inverting the accustomed direction of the elegiac form: "he has chosen to modernize a heroic situation instead of heroizing an everyday erotic situation."[6]

Despite this fundamental transformation wrought on the legendary heroines, it does not constitute a devaluation of heroic myth, as Howard Jacobson explains: "Ovid's treatment is not a denigration of heroic myth. In one sense, it is an elevation of it; or better, it is a translation of it into a completely different dimension."[7] Likewise, the current feminist concern with female abandonment and orphanhood is subsumed under the primary concern with an anatomy of discursive subjectivity.[8] As the next chapter will make clear, the double letters of Paris–Helen, Leander–Hero, and Acontius–Cydippe reveal Ovid's concern with the orphanhood wrought by desire to be non-gender-specific. Ovid's women are not antiheroic, they are (in accord with the concerns of the elegiac tradition) unaware of the heroic ethos which obtains in epic. It is precisely from this relocation of epic characters in the diction and axiological criteria proper to elegy that the originality of the *Heroides* emerges.

The full implications of this radical discursive conflation emerge with even greater clarity in the ideological context of Augustan Rome: "The *Heroides* set all-importance in the individual, the seemingly insignificant individual who is obscured by the dazzling glare of massive events and great principles. . . . Historically, this view takes on extra importance when we place the *Heroides* against the backdrop of Augustus and Vergil's

*Aeneid*, a world in which the individual is a mere sacrificial lamb on the altar of community and principle."[9]

Irreverence toward the official mythology of Augustan epic in fact characterizes Ovid's artistic output in general. His rhetorical ideal pointedly rejects hierarchy, as Richard Lanham notes: "The point is not to hierarchize—there are no hierarchies here. . . . [Ovid] leaves his form open, aleatory, waiting to be realized."[10] In his study of Plato and Ovid as representatives of the two dominant (and polar) conceptions of reality (the serious and the rhetorical), Lanham offers an appropriate spatial analogue to their philosophies of language: "Ovid's strategy in both the love poetry and in the *Metamorphoses* stands opposite to Plato. Plato sought an externally sanctioned center beyond language; Ovid writes poems that have holes in the middle."[11] His interest in recasting the perspectives on these heroines is decidedly discursive—an interest that runs through his entire output.

"Aleatory" is the adjective used by Lanham to describe Ovid's poetics in general. It is a term that is chosen advisedly, and whose appropriateness is nowhere more visible than in the *Heroides*. Indeed, the relevance of this term here is not fortuitous, for as Roland Barthes explains, the lover's discourse is always supremely aleatory: "Dis-cursus—originally the action of running here and there, com-ings and goings, measures taken, 'plots and plans': the lover, in fact, cannot keep his mind from racing, taking new measures and plotting against himself. His discourse exists only in outbursts of language, which occur at the whim of trivial, of aleatory circumstances."[12] Each of the fifteen single letters exhibits just such chaotic, mercurial discourse.

In his study of the reading process as an act of construction, Tzvetan Todorov remarks that "two types of causal constructions seem most frequent (as Aristotle [has] already noted): [an] event is perceived as the consequence (and/or the cause) either [1] of a[n individual] character trait or [2] of an impersonal or universal law."[13] Supremely aware of this distinction, Ovid offers us individual psychologies rather than psychological paradigms—the latter being the usual identification we make of these heroines as unwavering universal archetypes: Penelope as an exemplum of uxorial fidelity, Phaedra of incest, and Medea of treachery.

The first type of causal construction is "iterative" in nature[14]—an event perceived as the consequence of a unique character trait, pertaining, in the Ovidian text, to the mode of *signification* as Todorov defines it—direct evocation through speech: "Signified facts are *understood*: all we need is knowledge of the language in which the text is written."[15]

Ovid offers us a new dimension of these exemplary women through their direct discourse to their absent lovers, their silent inscribed readers. This use of direct discourse is highly significant since it is the only way to eliminate the difference between narrative discourse and the world it evokes. In this way, each of the letter writers possesses absolute control over her discourse—a hermeneutic circumstance that differs radically from her third-person presentation in the *Metamorphoses* or the *Odyssey*, for example, and the resultant spectrum of interpretations to which they are subject. As a result, while in each case the letter writer is a self-proclaimed victim, she is (although she would vehemently deny the association) also an accomplished, aleatory artist.

The creative potential afforded by this discursive environment is considerable—so great, in fact, that it provokes skepticism in the reader, as Florence Verducci has noted: "The epistolary fiction imposes upon the reader a kind of vigilant scrutiny very different from the kind of attention exacted by the monologue or soliloquy in the theater: the reader can never be certain whether the authoress is telling the truth as it was, or the truth as she saw it or remembers it, or the truth as she has adjusted it to the rhetorical motive forced upon her by her circumstances. Indeed, sometimes the epistolary revelation will conceal more than it reveals and raise more questions than it answers."[16] Also indicative of the epistle's inherent ability to relativize the truth is Janet Altman's observation regarding the *Heroides*: "Given the letter's function as a connector between two distant points, as a bridge between sender and receiver, the epistolary author can choose to emphasize either the distance or the bridge. When Ovid began to explore the letter's narrative potential in the *Epistulae Herodium*, he was already aware of both aspects of the letter's intermediary nature."[17]

But Ovid does even more in the *Heroides* than offer an innovative elegy because of its transposition from a third- to a (notably unreliable) first-person structure. For he juxtaposes the *signified* evocation at the level of each individual letter writer with the (often radically different) *symbolized* evocation that confronts the reader. That is, these unique first-person psychological character studies are unavoidably juxtaposed both with each other and with their third-person (impersonal) mythic (hence exemplary) associations as a consequence of the *dispositio* of the text. Quoting Todorov: "*Symbolized* facts are [indirectly] *interpreted* [extrapolated by the reader from the text]; and interpretations vary from one subject to another."[18]

Aware of this intersubjective disparity, Ovid structures his text so as to dramatize the epistemological gulf separating the signified and symbolized levels of interpretation, the difference between "objective" event and subjective discourse. More precisely, he does so by treating the same event or myth from a number of perspectives. The Trojan matter, for example, is viewed from at least six different perspectives. And in so doing, Ovid, as it were, relativizes myth. "By treating many events or myths more than once in the course of the *Heroides*, Ovid compels us to see that a myth or an event must be understood not as an absolute entity in itself but as the sum of the individual perspectives that bear upon it."[19] An awareness of the overpowering nature of the subjective self and its epistemologically problematic corollary—a novelistic awareness of the inescapably deceptive relativity of language—thus emerges from Ovid's collection.

While the letter's ability to create ambiguity and the *Heroides*' manipulations of myth have received substantial commentary in recent years, the text's establishment of a new kind of (novelistic) discourse has not. Ovid has been termed "a baroque spirit before his time,"[20] and it is this admixture and conflict of alien discourses that is consummately novelistic. It is also important to note that the *Heroides* offers a lucid illustration of Bakhtin's fundamental distinction between novelistic and mythic discourse. For him novel and myth are two discursive extremes,[21] since the novel denies the relationship between words and things. Bakhtin's definition of the novel is avowedly idiosyncratic. And while no one would be tempted to identify the *Heroides* as novels, they do incarnate the "decomposition of stable verbal and ideological systems" that is the hallmark of novelistic discourse.[22] Moreover, as we shall see in the pages to follow, it is this perception of the opacity of language arrived at through epistolary mediation that forms the axiological basis of the *novela sentimental* as well.

Dido's letter (*Her.* 7) exposes the innovative nature of the Ovidian love letter, at the same time illustrating its function as a powerful political document—an extended, subversive critique of Augustan Rome and the Virgilian values it revered. The politics of empire—specifically the subjugation of the individual which they imply—are crystallized by the rewriting of Virgil's Dido. Such political subversiveness, in fact, is a permanent fixture within Ovid's poetic *mentalité*:

> You cannot leave Dido behind. She will not oblige by sacrificing the private life, the life of the feelings, to the greater glory of Rome. She will curse you, come after you. Accommodate the life of feeling or you will end up with daughters and granddaughters like Augustus's two Julias. Ovid, then, points to the central Roman weakness, to the lack of a full and balanced interiority, of a rich self. All Ovid's poetry before the exile explores this split, this gap in the center, in one way or the other. It was his obsessive great subject and he embraced it all his poetic life.[23]

Not only was the critique of empire a persistent feature of Ovid's writing, it is claimed by some scholars that the *Heroides*' portrayal of *impius* Aeneas was the direct cause for his exile.[24] The relevance of the Bakhtinian perspective in this context could hardly be more striking, for in essence, novelistic discourse is generated in epochs of weakening political centralization. As Bakhtin explains:

> The embryos of novelistic prose appear in the heteroglottic and heterological world of the Hellenistic era, in imperial Rome, in the process of disintegration and decadence of the verbal and ideological centralism of the medieval Church. Similarly, in modern times the flourishing of the novel is always

connected with the decomposition of stable verbal and ideological systems, and, on the other hand, to the reinforcement of linguistic heterology and to its impregnation by intentions, within the literary dialect as well as outside of it.[25]

In the seventh heroid, Ovid transforms the frenzied, suicidal Virgilian queen into a woman-artist figure. From the very first words she utters we see her poetic abilities at work as she invokes the familiar swan song—the song immediately preceding death. What follows directly thereafter illustrates a series of paradoxes inherent to any epistolary communication. By its very existence, a letter simultaneously signifies absence and presence. Were the addressee not both spatially, temporally (and often psychologically) absent, there would be no need for communication by letter. At the same time, the letter reflects an awareness of absence; the letter writer works to eliminate it by manipulating time. Epistolary discourse in fact guarantees its own relevance by consistently manipulating both space and time in order to overcome these barriers, to make communication psychologically relevant (rather than anachronistic) in the moment at which the addressee reads the letter. In temporal terms, from a present perspective, the letter seeks to control the future based on past information.[26]

Accordingly, Dido uses the present tense in addressing Aeneas: "Nec quia te nostra sperem prece posse moveri, / adloquor—adverso movimus ista deo; / sed merita et famam corpusque animumque / pudicum / cum male perdiderim, perdere verba leve est" [Not because I hope you may be moved by prayer of mine do I address you—for with God's will adverse I have begun the words you read; but because, after wretched losing of desert, of reputation, and of purity of body and soul, the losing of words is a matter slight indeed].[27] In addition, she, like all the heroines in Ovid's gallery, presents herself as in the process of writing—as *scribentis imago*. The implications of this portrayal are narratologically significant, indicative of her artistic autonomy. For as William Anderson remarks, "Her words provide the sole means Ovid employs to give his character being; no background details, no dramatic introduction, commentary or epilogue in any way may fill the portrait."[28] In other words, the accustomed *histoire* is, as we shall see, being represented by a highly idiosynchratic *discours*.[29]

Ostensibly written as a suicide note, the seventh heroid actually serves to delay the act of self-annihilation—to defer, to postpone the finality of the moment. This interest in deferral is typical of the lover, since a lover's discourse logically seeks, above all, to avoid closure.[30] A lover seeks instead to perpetuate his or her life in the presence of the beloved. Thus in typically contradictory fashion, while claiming that she does not write because she hopes to convince Aeneas to return, Dido's letter attempts to do just that. And it is that aspiration, of course, that makes suicide a self-defeating gesture. Unlike Virgil's heroic, despairing Dido, Ovid's heroine is still hope-

ful, clinging to the illusion that her words may be convincing. We as readers of Ovidian mythology, of course, know otherwise—that the letters will
actually have no effect on the men they are intended to persuade.

In an uncomprehending complaint against the ideal of empire, Dido
rebukes Aeneas saying, "facta fugis, facienda petis; quaerenda per orbem
/altera, quaesita est altera terra tibi" (*Her.* 7.13–14) [What is achieved, you
turn your back upon; what is to be achieved, you ever pursue. One land has
been sought and gained, and ever must another be sought, through the
wide world (Showerman, 83)]. We see by these words that her intent to
convince Aeneas to return could not be more concrete.

At the same time, as Barthes has observed on a theoretical level and as
the other heroids themselves attest, the lover plots against him or herself,
unable to "keep his mind from racing."[31] The lover's discourse, in other
words, is profoundly contradictory. Dido is the very embodiment of such
contradiction. In one breath she asserts her unconditional suicidal resolve,
and in the next she implores her lover's return. This argumentation, ranging from abandonment to reunion, is followed even more precipitously by
a move from cynicism and rejection to the other extreme of idealistic love.
Dido first acknowledges that she is not unique, but the victim of a universal
female affliction, namely masculine duplicity: "scilicet alter amor tibi restat
et altera Dido; / quamque iterum fallas altera danda fides" (7.17–18) [I
suppose a second love lies in store for you, and a second Dido; a second
pledge to give, and a second time to prove false]. In spite of her lover's
faithlessness, however, Dido confesses that she is "uror, ut inducto ceratae
sulpure taedae" (7.23) [all ablaze with love, like torches of wax tipped with
sulphur]. Evocation of the familiar *odi et amo* topos takes on a paradoxically
causal relationship here—for the more she complains of his lack of faith,
the more she loves.

Having reproached Aeneas because of his affective mutability, Dido
proceeds to underscore her own powers of contradiction through verbal
repetition. That is, she begs him to *be* mutable, to return to his initial amorous discourse. Indeed, like her sisters in the other fourteen epistles, Dido
ranges through the entire spectrum of possible affective states: seduction,
betrayal, abandonment, exile, solitude, denial, hope, and so on. After blam-
ing Aeneas for her plight, she blames her own irresponsibility in giving him
everything—her kingdom as well as herself. And in return for her generos-
ity, she is left all alone, threatened by foreign invasion, and very likely pregnant: "Forsitan et gravidam Dido, scelerate, relinquas, / parsque tui lateat
corpore clausa meo. / accedet fatis matris miserabilis infans, / et nondum
nato funeris auctor eris" (7.133–36) [Perhaps, too, it is Dido soon to be
mother, O evil-doer, whom you abandon now, and a part of your being lies
hidden in myself. To the fate of the mother will be added that of the
wretched babe, and you will be the cause of doom to your yet unborn
child].

An additional feature of the love letter which Dido's missive projects is its dual function as metaphor and metonym of desire. Not only does it "replace" or "transfer" the sentiment of love, it forms an integral part of that love. Writing figures of the body in the sense that the sender wishes she could substitute herself for the missive, imagining herself in its stead, at the desired destination, being touched by the beloved.[32] For the same reason, we often see the letter of a beloved being treated as if it were the beloved him or herself—kissed, fondled, treated with corporeal passion, etc.—as anything but a neutral parchment.

Whatever the context, the discourse of love is necessarily an alien discourse, because it is, by definition, obsessed with the Other. This is why it expresses itself by means of polar oppositions: love-hate, affection-abandonment. It is consummately dialogic, presenting a counterpoint of ideologies in conflict, rather than a single, coherent resolution. And, the metadiscursive implications of this discursive reality are quite revealing. Drawing on the observations of Barthes and Bakhtin, Kauffman explains that: "Every discourse of desire is therefore simultaneously a critique of language. The lover is a critic who has been described as a linguistic orphan in philosophical solitude."[33] This pluralistic perception of language leads unavoidably to the question of referentiality—to the "auto-criticism of language" that defines novelistic usage.

Because language emerges as "orphaned" its amorous enunciators attempt to endow it with authority by exploiting, among other things, the devices of legal oratory. Ovid's heroines, like Boccaccio's Fiammetta (indeed like all the lovers in the pages to follow), will attempt to be sternly legalistic in order to guarantee the reciprocity of the beloved. In this context, Bakhtin understood the intimate relationship between amorous discourse in any age and judicial discourse, more precisely its role in the generation of pathos:

> Novelistic pathos always works in the novel to restore some *other* genre, genres that, in their own unmediated and pure form, have lost their own base in reality. In the novel a discourse of pathos is almost always a surrogate for some other genre that is no longer available to a given time or a given social force—such pathos is the discourse of a preacher who has lost his pulpit, a dreaded judge who no longer has any judicial or punitive powers, the prophet without a mission, the politician without political power, the believer without a church.[34]

Of the novel's attempt "to restore some other genre," Kauffman specifies that "the genre for which it is a surrogate is that of amorous epistolary discourse in general and the *Heroides* in particular."[35] Yet this assertion is open to considerable debate. For example, neither the novel of adventure nor the picaresque—two of the genre's most prominent forms—seeks to restore amorous epistolary discourse, much less the particular speech situation of the *Heroides*.

Kauffman takes issue with Bakhtin, imputing to him the equation of pathos as being "peculiarly novelistic . . . quite unlike that found in poetry." She counters the validity of his claim by saying that pathos and poetry are precisely the defining features of the *Heroides*. Two points must be made in this regard, however. The first is that when Bakhtin claims that "novelistic pathos [is] quite unlike that found in poetry," he is speaking with a high degree of temporal specificity—referring to the discursive systems operative during the age of the Baroque—i.e., the Baroque novel as opposed to Baroque poetry. And this distinction is essential. But much more serious is her misreading of his postulation of pathos. Evidence that Bakhtin clearly envisions the possibility for the coexistence of pathos and poetry is, in fact, offered only a few sentences beyond the fragment cited above, when he draws a sharp distinction between the novel's generation of pathos through "borrowed" forms in contradistinction to poetry's "authentic pathos": "Novelistic pathos does not have discourses that belong to it alone—it must borrow the discourses of others. When *authentic* pathos inheres in a subject, it can only be a poetic pathos."[36] In other words, he distinguishes between the generically artificial (hence synthetic) borrowed pathos of the novel, which arises from the dialogic collision of alien discourses, with the (generically homogeneous) authentic pathos of poetry generated by the speaking subject. As such, the *Heroides* can be said to exhibit both forms of pathos—the lyric, elegiac pathos of an abandoned woman, as well as the novelistic pathos that results from the juxtaposition of epic, erotic, and maternal discourses—each alien to the other.

The philosophy of language projected by novelistic discourse in Bakhtin's conception is in full accord with that of Ovid. The pathos inherent in and implied by the novel is synonymous with the crisis of language—the realization that words lack referentiality, transcendence. Such novelistic perception is repeatedly affirmed by Ovid's heroines as one by one they subvert the authority of their own contradictory discourses, a cyclical progression claiming first mutual love, then hate, despair followed by renewed hope, etc.

If we compare the way in which the women comment upon one another, we see Ovid's fascination with the subjective status of language in even greater relief. Letters 6 (by Hypsipyle) and 12 (by Medea), both to Jason, offer a unique basis for such a comparative reading since they are—unlike the rest of the heroids—written to one and the same man. More precisely, Hypsipyle's rendering of Medea and Medea's own self-portrait dramatically expose the mechanisms that underlie human subjectivity and its extensiveness, a perception that is realized through the intense subjectivity of their discourse.

Medea begins her missive by recalling that it was Jason—not she—who initiated the relationship, seeking her out because of her art (in *Her.* 12.2). This claim to uniqueness, however, to her unique alchemical ability, is soon displaced, replaced by her perception of Jason's betrayal as a virtually universal phenomenon: "hoc illic Medea fui, nova nupta quod hic est" (12.25) [There, I, Medea, was what here your new bride is]. We recall that the specific occasion for this missive is Jason's marriage to Creusa, which results in Medea's enforced exile. Medea's considerable mythopoetic abilities are revealed by the deceptive details she chooses to include in her portrayal of herself as a jilted lover. She speaks of herself as a *puella simplex* (12.89–90) [a simple maid], which is anything but the horrifying association that led to her legendary status. In order to convey this self-perceived vulnerability, she recalls her sense of terror when Jason sowed the fields with poisoned teeth: "arva venenatis pro semine dentibus inples, / nascitur et gladios scutaque miles habens. / ipsa ego, quae dederam medicamina, pallida sedi, / cum vidi subitos arma tenere viros" (12.95–98) [The ploughed fields you sow full with envenomed teeth in place of seed; and there rises out of the earth, with sword and shield, a warrior band. Myself, the giver of the charmèd drug, sat pallid there at sight of men all suddenly arisen in arms].

Of this extraordinary self-depiction, Verducci notes an additional characteristic that is narratologically significant: "There is no other letter in the *Heroides* whose organization is so dominated by the narrative of past events recalled from the vantage of the present; and there is no other account of the present memory of past events so colored in the telling by present emotion or so insistently confronted by allusions to the present condition of the speaker."[37]

The irony of Medea's portrait of herself as an impressionable, tender maiden here is obvious. For she is transfering the responsibility for and awesome effects of her witchcraft onto Jason. Insisting on her *virginitas*, her maidenly innocence, Medea can fault herself on only one account. Reminiscent of Dido's self-criticism, Medea also chastises herself for her inordinate trust in her lover: "meritas subeamus in alto, / tu fraudis poenas, credulitatis ego!" (12.119–20) [Let the penalty that is our due overtake us on the deep—you for your treachery, me for my trustfulness!]. By such details we see that her *ars* is not simply material alchemy, but verbal alchemy as well, whereby she totally transforms her real identity. Justification for her complaint is, she reminds us, evident by virtue of their marriage oath, witnessed and guaranteed by the presence of Juno. Even more powerful testimony of their love exists, however, namely, their children: "per meritum et natos, pignora nostra, duos" (12.192) [by the two children who are our mutual pledge]. With this expression of maternal devotion the reader is shocked given the consistent mythic association of Medea with uncompromisingly bloodthirsty behavior, especially since much of her infamy results from the murder of these same children (*Met.* 7.396).

Comparison of Medea's letter to Jason with Hypsipyle's letter, the sixth heroid, is quite revealing of the pervasiveness of subjectivity and the victim's notable abilities as artist. Impatient at the lack of communication from Jason, Hypsipyle complains that he should have written to her by now. Yet, not wanting to admit rejection, she excuses the delay saying that "ventos non habuisse potes" (*Her.* 6.6) [the winds might have failed you]. With a similar capacity for denial, she affirms her love despite the rumors claiming that he has embraced the love not of a *puella simplex* (12.89–90), but of a *barbara venefica* (6.19) [barbarous poisoner]. Reminding Jason of his binding contractual obligation to her—the day they were joined in wedlock by Juno—Hypsipyle is invoking precisely the same connubial authority as Medea (12.87). For her part, Hypsipyle reveals an additional complication, a vow made to the gods on behalf of Jason's safety. The words of her oath are now meaningless, however, since he has fallen prey to Medea's witchcraft. Indeed, it is not just the alchemy of herbs and grasses in which her rival engages, but sinister voodoo as well: "devovet absentis simulacraque cerea figit, / et miserum tenuis in iecur urget acus— /et quae nescierim melius" (6.91–93) [She vows to their doom the absent, fashions the waxen image, and into its wretched heart drives the slender needle—and other deeds 'twere better not to know]. To this description Hypsipyle adds a threat to Jason's masculinity—that Medea intends to dwarf his accomplishments by her own.

Neither beauty nor lineage nor dowry does Medea possess, as Hypsipyle reminds her estranged lover. And, like Dido and Medea, she too saves the incentive of progeny (twins, in fact) as a final unassailable argument to effect Jason's return. By contrast, Hypsipyle graphically explains that Medea is ruthless and that, if given the chance, she herself would exact bloody vengeance on the sorceress: "paelicis ipsa meos inplessem sanguine vultus, / quosque veneficiis abstulit illa suis! / Medeae Medea forem!" (6.149–51) [as for your mistress—with my own bloody hand I would have dashed my face with her blood, and your face, that she stole away with her poisonous arts! I would have been Medea to Medea!].

This passionate letter (a lucid illustration of the polarities of intense love and intense hatred) ends with Hypsipyle's double curse. The first is directed at Medea—that she, like Hypsipyle herself, be an exile, utterly alone "aera temptet; / erret inops, exspes, caede cruenta sua!" (6.161–62) [let her make trial of the air; let her wander, destitute, bereft of hope, stained red with the blood of her murders!]. The second extends to Jason as well: "vivite, devoto nuptaque virque toro!" (6.164) [Live on, a wife and husband, accursed in your bed!].

What Ovid effects by this pair of letters in characterological terms is truly extraordinary, for Medea and Hypsipyle, by the end of their respective letters, have, in effect, exchanged identities. Hypsipyle shows that she is more vengeful than Medea herself, who in turn depicts herself as the impressionable young maiden. Medea's unblemished self-portrayal serves, among other things, to highlight the deceptive selectivity of myth—the fact that a myth reduces the being it represents to one salient feature, offering a highly idiosyncratic, paradigmatic presentation. The *Heroides* boldly overturns that phenomenology, overturning in the process the relationship of word to deed as well. Words no longer serve the merely representational function of describing deeds, but to question the validity of such representation—the axiologically and experientially reductive nature of myth itself.

Literary history of the *Heroides'* reception provides an additional perspective on the text as signifying system. Each of the interpretations of this protean composition have, with varying degrees of success, attempted to account for the disturbing mixture of explicit pathos on the part of the heroines as well as Ovid's wit, his implicit but highly visible indecorous exposé of them. Some critics have chosen to emphasize the amusing, manipulative nature of Ovid's rewriting, thus playing down the pathetic dimension of these self-portraits in favor of their artificer's deft manipulations of them. Accordingly, these interpreters regard the pathos as a serious "flaw" in Ovid's poetics that, in their view, mars the clearly parodic intent of the *Heroides*.

Others contend that Ovid designed these epistles to be taken seriously, as ironic, unquestionably tragic, elegies. But a difficulty arises with this interpretation as well. For how then does one account for the poem's inherent and obtrusive levity—Ovid's toying with the dignity of these legendary figures? Why would Ovid compromise the tragic valence of these heroines in such a sustained manner? If one tries to read these letters as exempla of pathos, as E. K. Rand has remarked: "One waits in vain for the thrill of tragic pity and fear." To view the heroids as unrelieved portraits of tragedy one must construe the poet's parodic impulse as "unintentional and infelicitous."[38]

Howard Jacobson sees the *Heroides* in such tragic terms in order to foreground their epistemological implications as an index of human subjectivity:

> The *Heroides* are subjective poetry as perhaps no other work of antiquity. . . .
> When we consider all the philosophical schools of antiquity which in one way
> or another disputed the existence of a stable reality or distinguished between
> the real and the seemingly real or denied that knowledge was possible (e.g.,
> Heraclitus, the Eleatics, Plato, the Academics), it is not surprising to find in
> Ovid an awareness of the problem.[39]

While Jacobson's location of Ovid's work within the intellectual climate of antique philosophy is compelling, his dismissal of the *Heroides'* playfulness reveals his interpretation to be insufficient in explaining the work as a whole.

Most recently, Florence Verducci advances a different—rhetorical—reading that views the two earlier interpretations (the parodic and the tragic) as doing violence to the text because they privilege either the pathos of the heroine or Ovid's own wit, unable to accommodate both discourses. Finding Jacobson's recuperative argument to be alien to Ovid's poetic enterprise, she is led to remark that "What is most disconcerting in Jacobson's recuperation of the *Heroides* is not so much the manner in which he establishes their status as 'serious' literature by attributing it largely to the unorthodox epistemology their unorthodox use of perspective presumably implies. Rather, it is the fact that Ovid *is* recuperated."[40] In addition it represents an anachronistic reading, according to Verducci: "In its epistemological implications (particularly for the relative, inaccessible, or unreal nature of Truth, Reality, or Coherent Meaning), the result of Ovid's method becomes a value-laden variant on a contemporary orthodoxy."[41]

In contradistinction to her predecessors, she argues vigorously against imputing "higher truths" to literature. And as a result of her formalist attitude, Verducci does not attempt to resolve or look for unity in the disequilibrium that defines the *Heroides*, viewing such an enterprise as inherently misguided:

> The rule of Ovid's *Heroides* is the rule of indecorum, of wit in conception no less than in language, a wit which is not his heroine's own but the token of the poet's creative presence in the poem. Its dispassionate, intellectual, emotionally anesthetizing presence is a constant reminder of how far we, in a sympathy for a heroine, have departed from the traditional view of her situation, and it is a constant goad to the dissociation of emotional appreciation from formal articulation.[42]

To support her formalist belief in the autonomy of poetic language, Verducci invokes T. S. Eliot's contempt for a poem's "meaning"—calling it "the piece of meat the burglar throws the watchdog" to distract his attention in an anodine manner.[43] In what she terms "canine criticism" the analogy refers to the critics' misguided theft of a poem's true identity as autonomous verbal system, and its distortion by imputing to it anything other than its ultimate autonomy.

Yet this formalist approach is reductive in a way that is different from the first two—but equally distortive. For rather than privileging one semantic dimension of the text at the expense of either pathos or wit, she denies both. The formalist reading, which accounts for the pathos of the letter writer and the manipulative nature of the poet by refusing to interpret them, ignores the essential difference between language and discourse: "The fundamental difference between discourse and language [is] the existence of a common horizon between speaker and listener."[44] As Bakhtin has lucidly demonstrated, language is not a hermetic code that can be studied in isolation, a form that can be surgically extricated from a particular context. Rather, it is by nature a communicative system that is endowed with meaning only by the interaction of speaker and listener, writer and reader. In and of themselves words are neutral, but as soon as they are placed in any particular context they lose their neutrality.

Given—as Verducci herself admits—that the *Heroides* is constructed out of two markedly different registers (the pathetic and the playful) they must both be accounted for in a coherent fashion. They are an example, on the broadest level, of the generic dialogism exploited by Ovid throughout the forging of his text. It is not qualitatively different from the axiological extremes that the letters themselves entail: from love to hate, reproach to imploration, thoughts of suicide to reveries of amorous delectation.

Above all, these extremes have the effect of questioning the discourse of each heroine qua enunciating subject, unlike their previous epic identity. Bakhtin crystallizes this novelistic effect by contrasting it to the epic in general theoretical terms: "The idea of testing the hero, of testing his discourse, may very well be the most fundamental organizing idea of the novel, one that radically distinguishes it from the epic."[45]

The *Heroides'* ability to generate subjective, psychological, skeptical—novelistic—discourse is the hallmark of its discursive innovation. Verducci ultimately rejects this identification of Ovid as "the father of epistolary, sentimental and psychological fiction" on the grounds that the Ovidian collection of love letters "seems to have expired, as it was born, with the *Heroides*."[46] This is a specious argument, however. For if one measures poetic innovation on the basis of immediate progeny, then we would have to similarly question the originality of the *Metamorphoses*.

From this consideration of the text's critical reception what emerges is the validity of discourse analysis because, unlike previous methodologies applied to the *Heroides*, it is able to account for the text in its discursively complex totality. While an undeniably indecorous assemblage of perspectives made possible by Ovid's epistolary innovation, it is at the same time a semantic and syntactic whole. It exposes the discursive, subjectivizing potential of the letter form and its ability to sever signifier from signified, word from deed. It is this metalinguistic achievement—the creation of subjective epistolary discourse—that, in a variety of ways, forms the basis of each of the texts to follow.

# TWO

## EXEMPLARY COUNTERFEIT

### (*EL BURSARIO*)

**M**EDIEVAL READERS of the *Heroides* reversed its perception
as potentially and discursively dangerous, seeing it instead as
ideologically exemplary. Indeed, rather than reading it as the
immediate cause of his exile from Augustan Rome, the *Heroides* (not the *Ex
Ponto*) is interpreted as the work Ovid wrote in order to be pardoned—to
revoke his exile:

> Ovidius, morans ibi, sustinebat multa incommoda scilicet famem, sitim et
> nuditatem; et incepit inde cogitare qualiter posset exire, et qualiter earum
> amicitiam recuperare posset, qui sicut incusacione earum venerat, ita earum
> prece eriperetur. Et tunc composuit hunc librum in quo multum commendat
> mulieres castas et pudicas, et reprehendit incestas et impudicas.[1]

> While Ovid lingered there, he endured many hardships, namely, hunger,
> thirst and nakedness; and he therefore began to think of how he might escape
> and how he might regain the women's friendship; for just as he had been sent
> there because of their accusations, so he could be taken away through their
> entreaties.

This account is indicative of the radically new hermeneutic context in
which the Middle Ages situated the *Heroides*. Wishing to leave nothing to
chance, these medieval interpreters make explicit the extradiegetic, ethical
exemplarity of the heroids in a number of ways. Global prefaces constructed according to the dictates of the medieval *accessus* now introduce
the letters. In fact, as A. J. Minnis observes in speaking of the medieval
*accessus* tradition, "this technique [of analysis] was at its most sophisticated
in introductions to Ovid's *Heroides*."[2] As such, we find sections devoted to
the *materia, intentio authoris, utilitas*, and *philosophiae suppositio*. More
specific didacticism is indicated in the form of individual rubrics which
precede each letter, detailing the positive or negative valence to be attached
to each heroine. Thus no longer does each writer enjoy the freedom of
her own spontaneous, unmediated self-depiction. She has once more been
imprisoned within the evaluative hierarchy of an alien discourse. Specifically, it is the (for them) wholly anachronistic discourse of Christian
axiology. In short, allegory replaces mimesis.

It is axiomatic that for every example there exists a counterexample. And Spain provides just such an exception to the medieval reception of the *Heroides* in Juan Rodríguez's translation entitled *Bursario o las Epístolas de Ovidio*.[3]

The *Bursario*'s importance has been interpreted in one of two ways. Because it relies on Alfonso X's translations, it is invoked as an example of the enduring influence of Alfonsine prose, as María Rosa Lida has noted.[4] And, while the validity of Lida's observation is irrefutable, it has led to the misperception that Rodríguez engaged in merely a scribal activity, to the attitude that Rodríguez "is utterly devoid of creative ambitions in his version of the *Heroides*—the *Bursario*."[5] At the same time, one of the three letters of Rodríguez's own invention that he appends to the Ovidian letters, and presented as the work of Ovid himself (the "Carta de Madreselva a Manseol"), is considered to be highly significant in the development of the *novela sentimental*. Indicative of this appreciation is Martin Gilderman's remark that for the modern reader, "the *Bursario*'s interest resides almost exclusively in the epistle of Madreselva to Manseol, because it is a sentimental novel in miniature."[6]

Both of these critical perspectives ignore the importance of the *Heroides* in its semantic individuality and syntactic collectivity, the true mark of its originality as we saw in Chapter One. Yet only through an initial understanding of the metaliterary concerns addressed by Ovid's unique discursive network can we begin to adequately assess the *Bursario*. For the *Heroides*, the *Bursario*, and the Alfonsine chronicle, which mediates between the two epistolary anthologies, represent three disparate speech situations—three appreciably different attitudes toward language.

Discrepancies between language and its referentiality characterize Ovid's fifteen epistolary monologues, as we have seen. Such is also the case with the three pairs of heroid letters (correspondence between Paris and Helen, Leander and Hero, and Acontius and Cydippe), which Ovid perhaps wrote later than the first fifteen. Whether or not these "double letters" were composed at the same time as the first fifteen is not of central importance for the purposes of the present study since all twenty-one letters were transmitted to the Middle Ages as one unified work.[7] And, although these last six letters constitute dialogues—answered letters dealing with reciprocated love in its initial stages—rather than monologues of abandonment, they too serve to dramatize the potential and constraints of epistolary discourse.

The transmission and translation of the *Heroides* in Spain was effected by Alfonso X in his universal history during the second half of the thirteenth century.[8] And because the *Bursario* relies heavily upon the wording found in the Alfonsine history, it is assumed that Rodríguez is engaged in a largely unoriginal literary enterprise in that the *Bursario* constitutes a "mere translation"[9] in Olga Impey's words. She detects not only extensive verbal borrowings from Alfonso in Rodríguez, but axiological similitude as well:

> Alfonso's influence on Juan Rodríguez is not limited to the verbal level: it extends to the deepest stratum of meaning. More precisely, Juan Rodríguez adopts in the *Bursario* Alfonso's ideological, ethical, and sometimes aesthetic interpretations of the *Heroides*. The praise of marriage, chastity, loyalty, and nobility, the emphasis on inner debate and on the pathetic mood, the profound insights into the emotional life that . . . Alfonso underlined in his version of the *Heroides*, reverberate again in the *Bursario*.[10]

Only the mode of presentation is acknowleged by Impey as different, that Rodríguez "sums up in a few lines [the prefatory rubric] material that often takes up one or more chapters of Alfonso's work."[11]

The problem with this interpretation is that it ignores the semantic and syntactic interplay that defines the discursive structure of the *Heroides*—and of the *Bursario* as well—which is alien to Alfonso's historiographic exploitation of the letters. While Ovid includes a total of twenty-one heroids (the fifteen single and six double epistles), Alfonso utilizes only eleven of them, virtually half of the Ovidian total. By contrast, Rodríguez offers translations of twenty of the original letters, leaving out only the Sappho epistle—either because it had not yet been rediscovered or correctly attributed.[12] To the Ovidian translations Rodríguez adds three that he himself composed (a pair exchanged between Troilus and Briseida, as well as a single, unanswered letter written by Madreselva to Manseol). The fact that Rodríguez attributes these, his own letters, to Ovid serves, among other things, as an opening signal that alerts us to the fact that he is engaged in a blatant act of literary counterfeit. As such, his text must be carefully scrutinized at every level, for the literary forgery consists not only of his fictitious attribution of the last three letters, but extends to the overtly exemplary axiology of the collection as a whole. For, as analysis will show, his metalinguistic strategy is much closer to Ovid's problematizing of discourse than to Alfonso's political and linguistic positivism.

Alfonso seeks to generate unproblematic discourse both in general and in his particular appropriation of the *Heroides*. He has no interest in juxtaposing semantic individuality and syntactic collectivity in such a way as to make his audience question the truth-status of his words, of language itself. He pursues the opposite objective. That is, rather than showing the politically and linguistically subversive side of the individual psyche as reflections of the "hole at the center" of both language and empire,[13] Alfonso looks to the same heroines as objective "proofs," universal examples of his extraliterary (decidedly imperial) public values. To Verducci's aptly worded observation that "the rule of the *Heroides* is the rule of indecorum," one can append an Alfonsine corollary. Namely, that the rule of Alfonso's *Heroides* is the rule of decorum personified.[14]

Presentation of a conventionally masculine world from a female perspective—the private, affective erotic microcosm—constitutes the achievement of Ovid's innovation, as we saw in the first chapter. By contrast, Alfonso minimizes the subjective dimension by returning the legendary women to the heroic, external, public world of male values (in the embedded letters that make up the *Libro de las duennas*) in his chronicle of universal history—the *General historia*.

For this purpose, he discards the Ovidian structure that juxtaposes a series of subjective authors with the implied (objective) editor who compiles and organizes the letters, betraying, at the same time, the privacy of the letter writers. That is, the letters were obviously intended by their fictional writers for the eyes of their estranged lovers only. It is important to note also that each of the *Heroides* fails in its function as "directive," to bring about a change on the part of the man to whom the letter is addressed. Mythological substantiation bears out this fact, as we know from the outcome of these heroines' lives.

What replaces this narrative structure in the chronicle is the impersonal, second-person plural reporting of history within which are embedded portions of selected heroids. Objectivity—precisely the opposite discursive reality from that which Ovid sought to generate—is now the goal.[15]

Translation, according to Ortega y Gasset, follows one of two possible trajectories: "o se trae el autor al lenguaje del lector, o se lleva el lector al lenguaje del autor" [either the author is (re)cast into the language of the (modern) reader, or the reader is transported back to the language of the author].[16] Alfonso's choice, his medievalizing intent, is clear. And Impey has convincingly demonstrated the consummately medieval cultural significance that the Ovidian portraits exert in Alfonso's vast historiographic enterprise. The *translatio* in question is cultural as well as linguistic.

The second heroid—the letter written by Phyllis to Demofoon, who has abandoned her after swearing total fidelity—offers a characteristic example of the distance separating Alfonso's perspective on the story from Ovid's. At the conclusion of Phyllis's letter in Part 2 of the *General estoria*, there follows a chapter of exegesis (chapter xx) which details the didactic valence we are meant to ascribe to the unfortunate affair:

La entençion de Ouidio en esta epistola fue dar enxenplo e castigo a las donzellas de alta guisa, e avn a quales quier otras que su castigo quisieren tomar que non sean ligeras de mouer se para creer luego los dichos de los entendedores, por que se non fallen mal dello despues commo fizo esta Fillis que creyo a este Demofon, e la enarto el, e se fallo ende muy mal por que se fue e finco ella desanparada. E entiende otrosi Ouidio en esta epistola trauar a los varones en los engannos que contra las mugeres que los creen e fazen por ellos lo que ellos quieren, e que lo non deuen fazer; ca es mal estança e pecado grande que al cabo, o al cuerpo o al alma, aduze a ome a pena qual meresçe que faze falsedat a quien le cree.[17]

Ovid's intention in this letter was to give an example and warning to maidens of high standing and to any others wishing to heed his warning that they not easily believe the words of suitors, so that they not find misfortune thereafter as happened to Phyllis who believed Demofoon, who in turn tired of her and abandoned her, to her great suffering. In this letter Ovid also warns men against the deceptions they perpetrate on women who believe them and are malleable, cautioning them not act thusly; for it is a bad practice and a great sin that ultimately results in well-deserved harm to a man's body or soul if he acts falsely to one who believes in him.

Women should be skeptical of men's promises if they wish to fare better than Phyllis. Likewise, for their part, men should refrain from deceiving women in this way. It is a sin ("pecado") and the person who engages in such irresponsible behavior deserves the torment that will be the inevitable result for his doomed soul. The exemplary intent of this heroid for Alfonso's audience could hardly be more vivid. It serves as an *exemplum ex negativo* designed to affirm, above all, decorum—traditional ethical values.

At times Alfonso embellishes this general didactic interest with a different type of allegorical exegesis, such as his borrowing from John of Garland to explicate the theft of the Golden Fleece. Here the allegorical detail is not of an ethical nature, rather it is a poetic embellishment that serves to make the mythological narrative even more powerful:

E maestre Johan dize otrosi que por el cuero dorado del carnero que se entiende Medea misma; e por el oro robado, la esposa por que leuo Jason a Medea; e por el dragon e los toros que eran guarda de la virgen e los vençio Jason que se entiende que el ganando la uirgen por el arte della que le ayudo, commo es contado, vençio el todas las cosas fuertes que alli estauan encantadas, e leuo a ella e al velloçino dorado, e fuese con todo para Greçia commo es dicho, vençedor e rico e bien andante. (2.2.72)

And Master John also states that the Golden Fleece represents Medea herself; and the stolen gold represents the wife whom Jason abandoned for Medea; and the dragon and the bulls which guarded the virgin and which Jason defeated through the help of the virgin's magic, as is recounted; he defeated all his adversaries that were under a spell and he thus carried off both her and the Golden Fleece, thereafter heading for Greece, as the story says, triumphant, rich, and fortunate.

Neither the first (ethical) kind of gloss, nor the second kind entailing further narrative elaboration, is found consistently throughout Alfonso's presentation, however.

It has also been claimed that in his medievalizing zeal Alfonso excises the erotic matter of the *Heroides*, replacing it with the discourse of Christian wedlock and fidelity. Two points should be made in this regard. First, as the analysis of the letters in Chapter One makes clear, the legendary women themselves spoke in terms of loyalty, marriage (overseen by Juno), and maternity as well. Hypsipyle and Medea, as we saw, exhibit these features and have recourse to each of them as arguments to persuade their estranged husbands to return. Moreover, eroticism is not eliminated in the letters included in the *General estoria*. Phaedra's letter of incestuous love for her stepson Hippolytus (*Her.* 4) offers in Alfonso's version declarations such as the following: "Enamorada so e tengo en los pechos llaga ciega que me fizo por ti el amor" (*Gen. est.* 2.1.447) [I am in love and I have in my breast a blind wound which made me fall in love with you]. A more transgressive eroticism is hard to imagine.

Despite these inconsistencies, however, it must be stressed that Alfonso's authorial intentionality does not attempt to suggest any degree of deconstructive undermining. Rather, what emerges from a reading of the Ovidian epistles in their thirteenth-century historiographic recontextualization is a consistent twofold function. They serve, firstly, as one authoritative source among many, which is being "accurately" transmitted. Thus we find, for example, at the end of various letters claims such as that which concludes Medea's letter to Jason: "non le dixo en [la epístola] mas de quando nos avemos contado aqui, segunt que lo Ouidio en el *Libro de las duennas*" (2.2.87) [She said no more to him in the epistle than what we have narrated here, according to Ovid's *Book of the Ladies*]. Similarly, with the fourteenth heroid written by Hypermnestra to Linceus, the chroniclers are quite explicit in pinpointing where her letter leaves off: "Et acaba aqui Ypermestra su epistola; mas si la saco dent Lino o si non, non lo dize Ouidio que cuenta esto al, pero dizen las otras Estorias que la saco dent so padre, el rey Danao, e despues de sos dias que fue ella reyna e so marido rey daquel reyno de Argos" (2.1.143) [At this point Hypermnestra ends her letter; but whether Linceus liberated her (from prison) or not, Ovid does not say. Nonetheless, the other histories recount that King Danaus, her father, freed her and after his death she was queen and her husband king of the kingdom of Argos]. The faithful transcription of the letters, moreover, functions in a way analogous to Dares's and Dictys's claim of superiority over Homer's account of the Trojan war by virtue of their presentation of eye-witness accounts. In this sense transcription of the *epístolas* constitutes a kind of *auctoritas* that is superior to their Alfonsine context, an experientially unmediated account of the events they present. More than ethics or thirteenth-century medievalizing, it is the authenticity of historical narrative of antiquity that the *Heroides* provides. The authority of this narrative, of course, serves to further underscore the authority of Alfonso's own text. Beyond their value as venerable, authoritative sources, the letters offer first-person dramatic monologue which is a welcome contrast to the second-person plural (impersonal) chroniclers' voice. And in this capacity, their contribution to the telling of an engaging story, an "accomplished *estoria*," is considerable.[18]

If Ovid was bent on illustrating the primacy of *discours* in the communication of his *histoire*—its potential for distortion—Alfonso's concern was to have the subjective *discours* be coterminous with objective *histoire*. Yet the *Bursario* is an entirely different matter. Or rather, it treats the same matter in a radically different manner. Although, as Impey has conclusively demonstrated, Rodríguez relies extensively upon Alfonso's translations, the hermeneutic basis—and even the superficial formal presentation—reveals that the *Bursario* is constructing a markedly different imaginary universe from the *Libro de las duennas*.

Visible and immediate substantiation of this fact exists in that Alfonso's occasional intercalation of selected *epístolas* throughout many hundreds of pages of prose is replaced by the initial Ovidian structure of twenty unembedded, individual, consecutive letters—all but the lost letter written by Sappho, number 15 of the *Heroides*. In this way, the semantic/syntactic tension of the Ovidian work is restored, but with a significant difference. Missives exposing the subjective torments of the legendary figures are now being juxtaposed not (as in Ovid) by an implicit editor, but by an explicit one. Indeed, a revealing progression is at issue: from Ovid's private to Alfonso's public context, further transformed in the *Bursario* by the juxtaposition of these two anterior perspectives.

This juxtaposition takes the form of a didactic rubric which precedes each one of the letters. As such, it reflects a hermeneutic mechanism operative throughout medieval redactions of the *Heroides*. A few examples of this epigraphic practice documented by Heinrich Sedlmeyer in his critical prolegomenon to the text will suffice to illustrate the didacticism with which Ovid's texts are imbued from the perspective of the medieval reader. Our reading of the first heroid is oriented as follows: "Auctor vero intendit ipsam (Penelopen) et omnes consimiles a legitimo et casto amore commendare" [In truth the author intends to praise this one (Penelope) and all who are like her for legitimate and chaste love]. Similarly, Phyllis's letter to Demofoon is read as an exemplum of foolish love: "Intentio auctoris est ipsam (Phyllida) stulti amoris reprehendere" [The intention of the author is to reproach this one (Phyllis) for foolish love]. The letter from Phaedra to Hippolytus is recorded because: "Intentio auctoris est ipsam (Phaedram) illiciti et nefandi sceleris arguere et omnes consimiles" [The intention of the author is to argue against the illicit and wicked deeds of Phaedra and of all those who are like her].[19]

It is this general practice that Rodríguez ostensibly continues with the added inclusion of a brief biographical sketch of the legendary figure. Accordingly, Penelope's letter is glossed as follows: "La intincion del actor es de loarla del líçito amor, por que quiso guardar castidat a su marido, profiriendole a todos los que la solicitavan" [The author's intention is to praise her for her licit love because she wanted to remain faithful to her husband, preferring him to all the men who pursued her].[20] Such clarity of purpose—the praise of chaste love and the reprehension of illicit love—is belied, however, as early as the prologue to the work as a whole, indeed even by the contradictory gloss concerning the work's title.

Three successive (and conflicting) attributions are made by way of explaining the uncommon title of *Bursario*. The first refers to the similarity between the text and a pocketbook: "Segund la propiedat del uocablo, *bursario* es deriuado o ha naçimiento de *bursa*, uocablo latyno que quiere dezir en nuestro romançe, bolsa; por que asy como en la bolsa ay muchos pliegues, asy en este tratado ay muchos *oscuros vocablos* y *dubdosas sententias*" [According to the meaning of the word, *bursario* is derived from *bursa*, a Latin term which in the vernacular is the equivalent of *bolsa*, because just as the pocketbook contains many folds, so too in this treatise there are many *obscure words* and *doubtful sententiae*].[21] The apparent clarity of the epigraphs is thus called into question by this self-proclaimed "obscurity" and the "doubtful" sententiousness.[22]

Proof that the author is manipulating the reader's expectations for lucid exemplarity by generating ambiguity comes in the continuation of the same sentence cited above in an attempt to define the work's title. Having explained the complexity of the work—the many "dark folds and creases"—Rodríguez goes on to indicate that we can call it *bursario* because it is so brief in length (*tan breue compendio*) that a man can carry it in his pocket (*bolsa*) (*Bur.*, 197). This (formal) reasoning of size conflicts with the preceding (semantic) reason given, namely, the abundance of "dark" passages. It conflicts even more notably, however, with the appreciably different claim made immediately thereafter that a copious treatment is being offered: "es dicho bursario, por que en la bolsa, conuiene a saber, en las çelulas de la memoria deue ser refirmado con grand diligençia, por ser mas copioso tratado que otros" (*Bur.*, 197) [It is called *bursario* because in the pocketbook, that is to say, in the chambers of the memory, it should be reaffirmed with great diligence because it is a more copious treatment than others]. Here then, it is not brevity but its opposite, its protracted treatment, which is being upheld as the work's defining feature.

As to its instructional purpose, we are informed in a rather mechanical manner that: "La materia deste tratado es de amor liçito e illiçito, honesto y deshonesto, cuerdo y loco" (*Bur.*, 198) [The subject of this treatise is licit and illicit love, honest and dishonest, wise and foolish]. And although he praises Penelope's chaste love for Ulysses, Rodríguez takes both Hypsipyle and Oenone to task—for two forms of transgression that contain no moral valence in and of themselves: Hypsipyle is criticized because of her love for Jason since, as the *auctor* attests, "certus in hospitibus non est amor" (*Bur.*, 198) [there is no certain love in a traveler or guest]. Ulysses himself, of course, is the archetypal traveler. With equally dubious judgment, Oenone is condemned for loving Paris since: "son los niños inconstantes por la su variable hedat" (*Bur.*, 198) [children make inconstant lovers as a result of their age]. This claim is similarly problematic, for it was, as we know, Paris's infatuation with Helen, not his age, that led to his abandonment of the sea nymph. At the same time, other heroids—that of Hero and Leander, for example—will belie the fickleness that Rodríguez's forematter imputes to youth. Thus it is surprising, to say the least, that these initial words of caution regarding the love of travelers and youths in fact represent the substance of the brutally simplistic lessons afforded by the rubrics that precede the individual letters.

The rubrics are, as Charles Kany accurately observed, "far fetched," to say the least.[23] Unfortunately, he does not elaborate on this lucid appraisal and subsequent readers of the *Bursario* have not addressed it, accepting the misappropriated didacticism at face value, viewing it as indicative of the pedagogical concerns for ethical decorum expressed by the Middle Ages.[24]

As a reading of the rubrics will reveal, their didacticism is calculatedly counterfeit. Indeed, Rodríguez is interested in dismantling the overt and literarily trivializing accretions of medieval extradiegetic guidance. And in so doing he recuperates the unevaluative narrator of the Ovidian original. Moreover, the editorial voice revealed by the *Bursario* exhibits the three defining features of literary counterfeit that Gérard Genette exposes in *Palimpsestes*, basing himself on the arch literary counterfeiter of our age— Borges. Briefly stated, a literary forger presents (1) an encyclopedic treatment of his subject matter, in which there exist (2) conflicting interpretive signals conveyed by means of (3) laconic detail.[25]

That the *Bursario*'s treatment of the *Heroides* is encyclopedic is evident by its comprehensive translation of all the letters except the lost fifteenth one. Also encyclopedic is the critical apparatus that precedes each of the Ovidian translations in the form of an epigraphic rubric. The conflicting interpretive signals, as we shall see, consist of the discrepancy generated by the didactic rubric by comparison with the letter itself, as well as in occasional contradictions among the rubrics. The laconic nature of Rodríguez's manipulations is evidenced both by the simplistic oversimplification of the rubrics and by the contradictions which, while implicit, are very protrusive.

The first heroid, as noted above, is placed in the context of exemplary love—Penelope's fidelity despite Ulysses' twenty-year absence. While Penelope's fidelity is laudable, her jealous suspicion that Ulysses' delay in returning may be the result of his involvement with another woman, is not (*Her.* 1.75–77): "haec ego dum stulte metuo, quae vestra libido est, / esse peregrino captus amore potes. / forsitan et narres, quam sit tibi rustica coniunx, / quae tantum lanas non sinat esse rudes" [While I live on in foolish fear of things like these, you may be captive to a stranger love—such are the hearts of you men! It may be you even tell how rustic a wife you have—one fit only to dress fine the wool]. Penelope's letter ranges between fear that he may have abandoned her and reproach for not tending to his aged father Laertes and young son Telemachus, as well as herself—Ulysses' three helpless charges (1.97–99). Finally, she paradoxically anguishes over the reunion she so fervently desires because after the twenty-year separation she will doubtless seem an old woman, even if he were to return immediately (1.115–16).

Rodríguez augments the unexemplary jealousy felt by Penelope in a notable rewriting (*Bur.*, 200). In the Latin original she explained that: "usque metu micuere sinus, dum victor amicum / dictus es Ismariis isse per agmen equis" (1.45–46) [My heart leaped with fear at every word until I was told of your victorious riding back through the friendly lines of the Greeks with the coursers of Ismarus]. However, the *Bursario* version states that: "Los mis pechos tiemblan continua mente porque, seyendo vençedor, dizen que eres ydo con la compañera amigable delos ysmanios a tomar los cauallos de Traçia que de Reso avian robado" (*Bur.*, 200) [My heart trembles constantly because, they say, since you are victorious, you have gone with the friendly Ismanian woman to take the Thracian horses stolen from Resus]. The accent is thus on Penelope's jealousy and complaint. For this reason the unqualified praise accorded to her patient fidelity seems inappropriate since it is dwarfed by laments concerning her empty bed, the long nights, her suspicion, and so on.

Written by Phyllis to Demofoon, the second epistle, if we are to believe the rubric, exemplifies *loco amor* because she has chosen to love a guest, a traveler. We recall from the work's prologue that such love of a *huésped* is categorically denigrated. Nonetheless, this value judgment breaks down not only because of Ulysses' association as the paradigmatic traveler in the first heroid, but with a surprising evaluation offered of the third heroid, composed by Briseis to Achilles.

The rubric devoted to her letter indicates that the author's intention is to praise her—"loarla de castidat por que no queria conoçer sy no a Archiles que primera mente amo" (*Bur.*, 206) [to praise her for her chastity in not wanting to love any man but Achilles, the first man she ever knew]. Of this characterization several remarks should be made.

In the first place, why praise Briseis for being faithful to the first man she ever knew when Phyllis has just been condemned for the same kind of fidelity to her guest, Demofoon? Indeed, this contrast points to Briseis' very ignoble love—and not simply by comparison with her predecessor in the second heroid. That is, Briseis loves not only a traveler or a guest but an enemy, which makes her a traitor. Verducci rightly singles out Briseis' oath (*Her.* 3.103–10) as by far the strangest of the nine oaths to be found in the entire *Heroides*:

> Briseis' oath, sworn upon the bones of her dead husband, upon the souls of her brothers, and upon Achilles's sword, which tasted the flesh of those brothers and that husband, would have been entirely appropriate in a vow professing hatred and threatening retribution. It is entirely inappropriate as an avowal of sexual fidelity, especially since within the body of her oath Briseis names the man for whom she has been kept inviolate as the same man who is most properly her mortal enemy.[26]

In an attempt to modify the incongruity somewhat, Rodríguez alters the oath by having Briseis swear on Achilles' bones instead (*Bur.*, 209), in other words that the intensity of her love is such that she will be faithful to him even were he to die.

She thus betrays her brothers' and husband's memory in a most indecorous and unethical manner. Her fidelity, moreover, results not from choice but from her status as slave whereby she functions merely as commodity, as a material transaction, and this is an identity of which she is all too painfully aware. The fact that Achilles does not desire her return may arouse pathos, but if so such a reaction is dissipated as we see her groveling in a most servile manner, offering to be his concubine: "sy no quieres que te sigua, como sigue muger a marido, siguate yo como prisionera sigue a su vençedor" (*Bur.*, 208) [If you do not wish that I follow you as a legitimate wife, let me follow you as a prisoner follows his conqueror]. She has no rights, no dignity. To quote Verducci, "In short, Briseis' position—as slave and as lover—is an affective paradox."[27] Thus her servile identity as slave and the fidelity for which she is not responsible make the rubricator's words of high praise questionable to say the least. Still greater skepticism concerning both Briseis' words and those of the evaluative *actor* will ensue from the twenty-first and twenty-second letters of the *Bursario*—the exchange between Briseis and Troilus. Even at this early stage, however, the distance separating word from deed in the individual letters and the laconic, "farfetched" rubrics is clear.

The fifth and sixth heroids betray a similar inconsistency. As we might expect, Phaedra is condemned for the incestuous desire she has for Hippolytus, who is referred to as a *moço* (*Bur.*, 213). He, meanwhile, is praised for chastely disdaining the stepmother's transgressive desire. It is striking, therefore, that in the next letter Oenone is condemned for *loco amor* because she fell in love with a *moço*, namely Paris: "Ca los tales, como es dicho, suelen ser inconstantes" (*Bur.*, 216) [Since they are, as it is said, inconstant]. Hypsipyle's letter to Jason is intended as a complaint against Jason's disloyalty. According to the explanatory introduction, by contrast, she is reprehended for loving a guest—as if her relationship to Jason were nothing more than a one-night stand. Yet the introductory history of the affair indicates that this is by no means the case, that in fact "ella lo reçibio graçiosa mente en su reyno con toda su gente, y Jason tardo ally por espaçio de dos años" (*Bur.*, 221) [She received him graciously in her kingdom, along with all the other inhabitants, and he remained there for the duration of two years]. The result of the rubric is to reveal it to be—like the others before and after it—an inaccurate oversimplification.

Dido is condemned of foolish love by the author without giving any reasons for this negative judgment, which constitutes a departure from the practice observed in the other rubrics. In keeping with the exegetical machinery that has preceded the seventh letter, we would expect the motive for the reproach to be the fact that Aeneas is a foreigner, a traveler, a guest. What is revealed instead is simply that "ella lo resçibio benigna mente" (*Bur.*, 226) [she received him warmly] and that it was difficult for Aeneas to leave her.

The rubric that introduces Hermione's letter to Orestes speaks for itself. Its counterfeiting of the word—here *lícito amor*—is highly visible as we are told that she wrote with the intention of convincing him "que la robase, asy como Paris avia robado a su madre Elena. La intinçion del actor es loarla de liçito amor" (*Bur.*, 231) [that he abduct her as Paris did Helen. The intention of the author is to praise her for chaste love]. Yet Paris's love (referred to in letter 15) is expressly termed "illicit" (*Bur.*, 262), as is Helen's (268).

This type of contradiction contributes further to the reader's skepticism. With an equal degree of inconsistency, Leander's letter to Hero (heroid 17) is prefaced by a condemnation of his *loco amor*, since he risks his life each time he swims across the treacherous waters of the Hellespont to see her. Imperiling one's life is not a criticism made thus far in Rodríguez's collection. Our generic expectations, however, are strained even further in that we would have anticipated praise for his *liçito amor* since his fidelity is impeccable. At this point we would naturally expect a rebuke of Hero—for imperiling her lover's life. Indeed, Leander's letter (279) does register precisely this complaint. Yet, true to Rodríguez's manifold manipulations, we find instead praise for her fidelity (279). The fact that he is a foreigner (282), as well as a youth (283)—the two initial criteria for judgment according to the prologue to the letters—are not mentioned in the author's evaluation. By such glaring inconsistencies, the *Bursario* undermines the authority of its didacticism still further.

A hermeneutic interlude of a different sort takes place at the conclusion of Hero's epistle. For now we are confronted not by another proemial fragment of exegesis, but by a brief poem and its lengthy—and subversive—gloss. Attributed to the pen of Pero Guillén,[28] the poem reads as follows:

> Las sombras impiden Leandro ser visto
> ally do navegan las ondas marinas,
> e quando derraman las nueras sobrinas
> por sus ricos lechos la sangre de Gisto.
> La graue crueza del caso tan misto
> la sola Ypermesta a Lino reuela;
> la casta matrona desaze su tela
> por su deseado marido bien quisto.
>
> (*Bur.*, 285)

The shadows prevent Leander from being seen / there where the waves of the sea navigate, / and when the daughters-in-law who are cousins / shed Aegyptus's blood on their richly adorned beds. The grave cruelty of this chaotic scene is revealed only by Hypermnestra to Linceus; / the faithful matron unravels her thread on behalf of her beloved husband.

Rodríguez explains that the poet beheld a vision which occurred at midnight, resulting in the composition of this poem that treats three of the *Heroides* narratives: those of Hero and Leander (17–18), Hypermnestra to Linceus (14), and Penelope to Ulysses (1).

Specifying that Leander swam to Hero at midnight since he could not do otherwise ("que de otra manera ni en otro tiempo no podria" [*Bur.*, 286]), the author refers his readers to the letters of the two lovers for further explanation of this temporal necessity. Nowhere, however, is midnight specified either in Leander's letter or in Hero's. Indeed, a wide range of nocturnal references is made: "septima nox" (18.25) in Ovid, "siete noches" (274) in Rodríguez, "nox erat incipiens" (18.54), "la noche primera" (275), etc. Not only Ovid , but Rodríguez as well, specifies in Leander's letter that the lovers remain together in each other's arms until dawn, when "el luzero demostraua el naçimiento del alua" (277). Thus, far from being privileged, midnight is not even evoked. Similarly, while this gloss is offered to explain the first verse of the poem relating to Leander ("Las sombras impiden Leandro ser visto"), its inaccuracy renders it exegetically useless.

Midnight is also identified with Hypermnestra's aborted murder of Linceus, and with the successful murders committed by her forty-nine sisters of their respective husbands. Textual detail refutes this temporal specificity, as it did in the first case. References occur to "la noche corrompida con sangre" (258) [the night corrupted by blood] and to twilight ("la hora llamada crepusculo, que es comienço de la noche" [259]), but midnight is conspicuously absent in this letter. Rodríguez further teases his reader by concluding this gloss with an address to *los discretos* whom he invites to determine whether Hypermnestra was obligated to carry out her father's wish, whether she sinned by not doing so (286). Not only is this reference to a Christian axiology unanticipated because sin has not been an issue in the *Bursario*'s presentation of this gallery of overwhelmingly transgressive love, but also because it makes us question the authority of the unqualified rubric that preceded her letter, where she was praised for her compassion: "La entinçion del actor es loarla de piedat, porque no quiso ser cruel a su marido por mandado de su padre" (258). This is another type of laconic detail that exposes the calculated counterfeit of the *Bursario*'s exemplarity.

As we might have anticipated, Penelope's unraveling of her tapestry is also pinpointed as occurring at midnight, like the poet's *fiçión* (286). Again, the temporal reference obviously contradicts the text of the letter. Yet, reminiscent of Alfonso's claim to veracity, Rodríguez persists in affirming that each of the three relationships has been recounted accurately: "Hasta aqui va todo por las ystorias" (287), at which time he moves on to an allegorical exegesis of the poem's *moralidat*.

Leander, we recall, had been condemned for risking his life each time he swam across the treacherous waters to be reunited with his beloved (273). Now, however, "las sombras impiden . . . " is interpreted not as the literal, physical shadows that threaten him because he swims at night, but as metaphors of "sin": "las sombras, que son los pecados, impiden o embargan que sea visto y visitado de la gracia de Dios" (287) [the shadows, representing sin, prevent him from benefiting from God's grace]. The allegory extends even further. Not only are the shadows equivalent to Leander's sins, but there is a global application to be gleaned from his narrative, namely, that man imperils his life each time he sins, and for each "mortal sin" (*pecado mortal*) he must fast for seven years in expiation during his life, or atone for the same duration in purgatory.

Greater still is the interpretive liberty taken with Hypermnestra's tale. For having indicated that Aegyptus (Gisto) represents virtue personified, and his brother Danaus (Danao) evil, the glossator invokes Boethius's *Consolatio Philosophiae* to indicate that an evil man can be the brother of a benevolent man, since we are all descended from Adam.[29]

The multiple murders enacted by Danaus's daughters are seen as a metaphor for "character assassination"—turning one's "buena fama" into "mala fama" (*Bur.*, 287). The literal spilling of blood of Aegyptus's sons in their "ricos lechos" (verse 4) turns, very unexpectedly, into a meditation on "ricos amigos" for which the authority of Seneca is borrowed: "Como dize

Seneca, que no hay cosa mas rica ni mejor quel buen amigo, que con sus buenas obras y virtudes la buena fama con los amigos ganado avia" (287) [As Seneca says, there is no richer possession than a good friend, who with his good deeds and virtue won a good reputation among his friends]. In this case we see a very negative image inexplicably replaced by a wholly laudatory one. And this evident lack of connection makes the allegoresis if not derisory, unconvincing at the very least.

Verse five, "La graue crueza del caso tan misto" is taken to mean that evil constantly tries to "stir up" (i.e., to disturb) good. This in turn undergoes an additional leap of logic whereby it is specified that "Tollerabiliores sunt qui bona nostra diripiunt, quam qui famam" (288) [it is a greater sin to rob a man's good reputation (*fama*) than his property]. This particular *sententia* is culled from Saint Ambrose. Having just averred that evil constantly does evil, we are now informed—implicitly yet definitively—that such is not always the case: "no todas las obras del malo son malas" (*Bur.*, 288) [not all the deeds done by evil men are necessarily evil]. Proof of this wisdom is offered by Hypermnestra, the virtuous offspring of a decidedly wicked man. Once more, such blatant contradiction results in the reader's inability to accept the exegete's didacticism.

Consistent with the preposterous allegories of the first two narratives, Penelope is read now as the soul of anyone who tries to unravel his or her personal "thread" (i.e., the thread of life). The thread/life equivalence is a standard literary topos; however, its further articulation as symbolizing three infamous weavers—the temptations of the world, the Devil, and the Flesh—is not. The virtuous souls must constantly unravel their perfidious tapestry, and this activity is to be done only at the specified time—namely, midnight. It is at that time that one should dwell on his or her sins, on behalf of Christ, who will come on the Day of Judgment to indicate the virtuous souls. Thus the *casta matrona* (verse 7) is the soul of any virtuous Christian.

If this interpretation strains our credibility, the reference to midnight at this point does even further damage since it has—until now—been associated only with evil: Leander's "mortal sin" and the carnage wrought by Danaus's daughters. Two other mentions of this temporal reference, outside of the poem's gloss, refer to the poet's *fiçion* (286), that is, to the hermeneutic interlude as a whole. As a result, the reader is unavoidably surprised by the Christian reading in the (deprivileged) context of the negative diegetic associations and—at most—the neutral extradiegetic associations of the poet's *fiçión* as having occurred at midnight.

Skepticism generated by this allegorical reading is augmented by the final sentence of the gloss which confidently proclaims its success in clarifying the matter: "E asy pareçe estar bien declarada la escura copla, que por las epistolas prescriptas mejor la podes entender, avnque con mayor prolixidat e trabajo" (*Bur.*, 288) [In this way the obscure verses are clarified, which can be better understood by the preceding letters, although with greater prolixity and effort]. The claim that the letters afford a "better" understanding is important since they do not refer to a Christian axiology. Likewise their prefatory rubrics are so contradictory and/or oversimplified as to be unconvincing indeed.

What Rodríguez does by generating so many inconsistencies in his overtly didactic framework—the context in which the Middle Ages had imprisoned the *Heroides*—is to deconstruct it. In so doing he seeks to restore the letters to their original context unencumbered by the accretions of weighty and simplistic allegorical baggage which had been detrimentally imposed on them. Proof that his interest lies in generating a counterfeit didacticism occurs in the clever rubrication that follows the allegorical interlude as well.

Briefly stated, with reference to the letter of Acontius and Cydippe, the author's intention, we are told, is both to praise and to condemn: "reprehenderlo a el del engaño y loarlo de sabieza" (289) [to condemn him for his deceit and praise him for his cleverness]. This is a noteworthy claim for two reasons. First, because it admits greater complexity—the possibility of more than one interpretation—to the protagonist's behavior. More importantly, however, the praise of Acontius's *sabieza* stems from a decidely unexemplary impulse. The cleverness in question is precisely the *engaño*, his underhanded coertion of Cydippe, as the rubric itself explains. He forged a marriage oath, inscribing it onto an apple: "Yo, Çedipe, juro a ty, Acunti, por las sacradas virtudes de Diana, que yo sere tu compañera y tu muger" (289) [I, Cydippe, swear to you, Acontius, by the sacred virtues of Diana, that I will be your companion and wife]. Having gone to the temple to pray in her accustomed manner, Cydippe finds the inscription with her name on it and reads it aloud, thus, in effect, swearing allegiance to Acontius through total deception. Already affianced to someone else, she falls ill, consenting to marry this new suitor only out of fear "por miedo de Diana" (295).

If we had any doubts as to the witty manipulation Rodríguez effects in his stated judgment of Acontius, it is disclosed even more blatantly in the preface to Cydippe's letter. Because the maiden is willing to marry her wily suitor "for fear of Diana," the author praises her for her religious commitment (which amounts to fear resulting from the unlaudable motive of coertion). In a similarly perverse interpretation, this rubric specifies that Acontius, for his part, deserves praise for *liçito amor* (295) because he was intent on marrying legitimately!

A different form of counterfeit occurs in the next letter—the twenty-first—which is presented as forming part of Ovid's original collection, although it is clearly not. The letter in question, the "Carta de Madreselva a Manseol" appears unadorned by any prefatory explanation to guide the reader. And the importance of this omission cannot be overstated, for by its absence it indicates the kind of reading advocated by Rodríguez all along, i.e., one that is unencumbered by protrusive oversimplification and irrelevant ethical concerns.

Finally, the last two epistles—also spuriously attributed to Ovid—continue the decidedly unedifying, mischievous tone of the rubricator. Unlike the letter of Madreselva, they contain no evaluative judgments, being entirely descriptive rubrics instead—refusing to offer any didactic perspective on the narrative.

In this way Rodríguez exploits each of the three techniques of the counterfeiter's art enumerated by Genette in his deconstruction of the medievalizer's didactic apparatus in a highly original way—by turning it into an oversimplified, indeed extraneous, commentary. Unencumbered by the evaluative framework, the primacy of the letters themselves is restored.

Yet the issue of counterfeit in the *Bursario* intends even beyond its clever programmatic dismantling of the ponderous interpretive machinery that the medieval exegetes had grafted upon the *Heroides*. Namely, the final three epistles invented by Rodríguez and attributed to Ovid paradoxically show (like the twenty genuine translations) both his originality and his profoundly Ovidian poetics, an attitude toward language that will characterize the *novela sentimental* which he created.

In this context the important work of Impey should be acknowledged. For she has analyzed letters 21, 22, and 23 with insight and in a way that highlights their identity as proto–*novelas sentimentales*.[30] At the same time, since the principal thesis of her study is to demonstrate the *Bursario*'s dependence upon Alfonso X, an inevitable distortion results. For Alfonso entirely excludes Ovid's paired letters (the exchange between Paris and Helen, Leander and Hero, and Acontius and Cydippe) from his universal history, while Rodríguez, as we have seen, does not. Yet it is not simply the inclusion of these in the *Bursario* that is significant, but Rodríguez's exploitation of their qualitatively different poetics in his own invented epistles, which is crucially important. Much of what Impey claims to be his own innovation stems in fact from his reading and translation of these paired epistles.

The "Carta de Madreselva a Manseol" is a clear case in point. While acknowledging that it, like the final two letters, are "strewn with quotations from and allusions to the *Heroides*,"[31] she ignores the striking subtextual similarities it owes to Ovid's Acontius and Cydippe exchange.

Writing from prison, where she has been confined by her mother as a result of her clandestine love for Manseol, Madreselva complains to the man she loves. Through his cunning, Madreselva succumbed to his love and he is sentenced to death as a consequence. Yet through an even greater treachery, Artemisa—Madreselva's rival—falsely swears that Manseol had raped her in order to take him away from Madreselva. As a result of this false accusation, instead of being executed Manseol is married to Artemisa after she convinces the jury that restitution for her "perdida fama" can only be effected if Manseol is allowed to live as her lawful husband.

Much is made by Impey of Madreselva's chastity and of the moderation exhibited by both her and her beloved: "The most salient feature of their conduct is, in my opinion, the *amor mesurado*, the decorum they display in their love affairs. As a consequence, the sensual and adulterous atmosphere so characteristic of Ovid's epistles disappears completely."[32]

Granted, the love is chaste and there is, as Impey indicates, an insistence on marriage "syn quebrantar la fe ala casta Diana" (*Bur.*, 297). However, to contrast these concerns with Ovid's sensuality is to ignore the textual *realia* of letters 20 and 21. Nonetheless, the desire to remain faithful to Diana is, we recall, the issue around which the affair of Acontius and Cydippe revolves as well. Cydippe is already engaged to be married and it is her desire to behave decorously—with *amor honesto*—and within the bonds of lawful matrimony, which causes the torment of the Ovidian heroine. Acontius too insists on the need for a proper marriage. What becomes apparent is that the insistence on marriage and Madreselva's status as a "casta doncella" derive from the Ovidian figure of Cydippe, just as Manseol's cunning knowledge of the *artes amandi* has an obvious precursor in Acontius.

The originality of Rodríguez's rewriting of the Ovidian narrative has to do with the fact that we do not have the benefit of a reply by Manseol. Is Madreselva's love reciprocated or not? We recall that each of Ovid's three epistolary pairs represent reciprocated love, unlike the first fifteen where fidelity poses a key question. Will Madreselva's claim that a marriage by coertion is not binding ("No vale el matrimonio por fuerça otorgado" [302]) prevail? Such is certainly her hope. Is his new alliance really the result of Artemisa's Medea-like magic (299), a change of heart, or simply cowardice? Madreselva imagines him explaining "por saluar la mi vida, a mi fue forçado de te falleçer" (300) [in order to save my life I was forced to abandon you]—a possibility she briefly considers and then rejects. Suspense is generated by the lack of a response by Manseol, a feature Rodríguez borrows from the first fifteen *Heroides*.

The unresolved affair ends as Madreselva, like her Ovidian sisters, describes herself in the act of writing: "Començada enla pauorosa carçel, ala media noche . . . no puedo alcançar ala muy alta finiestra por mirar sy es de dia, y saber la hora" (302) [Begun in the frightful prison at midnight . . . I cannot reach the very high window to ascertain whether it is daytime and what hour it is]. This literal prison suggests the metaphorical *cárcel de amor* of her psychological, affective bondage. Except for the literal prison, Cydippe's situation is fundamentally the same. Moreover, both letters end with the striking image of the maidenly writer in anguish as she finishes her missive. Thus, while Madreselva's letter may be viewed as a proto–*novela sentimental* in terms of its psychological probing, its Ovidian origin is indisputable. With this letter Rodríguez succeeds in generating the kind of interpretive polysemy that is at the root of his recuperative reading of the *Heroides*, the dismantling of the medievalizers' reductive positivism in terms of true and foolish love.

The exchange between Troilus and Briseida likewise addresses this consistent hermeneutic preoccupation. We notice, first of all, that unlike the conspicuous absence of a judgmental authorial rubric to guide the reader in his appreciation of Madreselva's letter, in each of these final two letters rubrics are included yet they are exclusively descriptive. And it is important to note that this lack of evaluation constitutes a departure from all the previous texts of the *Bursario*.

Both Troilus's letter and Briseida's reply are attributed to Ovid, and this constitutes a different dimension of Rodríguez's counterfeit. For the only missive included in the *Heroides* concerning Briseis is the third heroid—her letter of complaint to Achilles in which, as we saw, she implores him to take her back, although he has no desire to do so. As a consequence of these final two letters we see yet a different kind of innovation effected on the Ovidian subtext. That is, while the *Heroides* offers a single example of letters by two women written to the same man (Hypsipyle and Medea both to Jason), here we have the same woman writing to two different lovers (Briseis to both Achilles and Troilus). Confronted by the last two letters, the reader's curiosity leads him to refer back to the third heroid in order to compare Briseis' presentation then and now.

The extradiegetic claim made in the third letter is that she is to be praised as an example of laudable love because she chose to remain faithful to Achilles, the first man she ever loved (*Bur.*, 206). No mention whatever is made of Achilles as lover of Briseis in this final epistolary exchange, either in the prefatory rubric or in the body of the letters. And, this glaring omission irreparably damages the author's authority—the truthfulness of his discourse—by making his judgments seem arbitrary and unstable. The referentiality of word and deed is seriously jeopardized here in a new way, but one that complements the narrator's arbitrary designation of *lícito e ilícito amor* throughout the letters.

This inverted pair is original not simply because it is the product of Rodríguez's own invention, offering us the possibility of one woman's love for two men, not found in Ovid, but also because of its subject, namely, disloyalty. As we have seen, claims of infidelity characterize the first fifteen epistles, but Ovid's paired letters lament not the issue of fidelity (they are all reciprocal lovers) but the obstacle of physical separation. Here, by contrast, Rodríguez combines the thematic of the fifteen monologic letters with the dialogic format of the last six. A further consequence of this new semantic and formal contribution is that the *Bursario* offers the discourse of the orphaned, alienated lover in the voice of a male speaking subject—an unprecedented existential circumstance in the *Heroides*.

Thus the discourse of abandonment—which Barthes characterizes as female—is here poignantly expanded in terms of gender.[33] The repeated lament that we have come to identify with Ovid's heroines is now reversed, as Troilus complains to his beloved:

> Do son agora, Breçayda, las innumerables promesas, juras y sagramentos que tu a mi me hazias por el dios de Apolo al que nos llamamos Febo, y otrosy Neptuno, dios delas aguas . . . infinitas vezes todos dias no çesantes me heziste, prometiste y juraste? (*Bur.*, 303)

> Where are now, Briseida, the innumerable promises, oaths and vows that you used to make to me by the god Apollo whom we call Febus, and also by Neptune, the sea god . . . the oaths you made unceasingly every day?

Like his female predecessors, Troilus resorts to all the rhetorical weapons he can think of in his overwrought state, including the verbatim reporting of words exchanged, and emotions recalled. Evoking the intense awareness of time, the coming of daybreak at which point the lovers must reluctantly part, Troilus reminds Briseida of her former devotion to him, and their shared concern for the passage of time. As she laments that it is almost day, the time at which they must part, he informs her "que era la hora dela media noche, quando el mayor sueño tenia amansadas todas las criaturas" (304) [it was midnight, the time when sleep subdues all creatures]. She is ecstatic at this reprieve. Moreover, this reference to midnight recalls the attribution of that time to the poet's activity during the hermeneutic interlude, leading us to wonder whether an overt allegorical framework is being set up here as well.

While our expectations are thwarted by not encountering any such exegesis in Troilus's letter, they are soon satisfied by the allegory that Briseida provides of her dream foretelling not her disloyalty to Troilus, but his disloyalty to her. In it an allegorical battle is enacted between the Empress of the Rock of Good Love (representative of Venus), her *alférez* (the lover's heart), and five knights (the lover's five senses)—all fighting on the same side. Opposite them we find "el desamante amado" (the unloving beloved) and with him two dueñas (Lady Forgetfulness and Lady Disloyalty). The goal of the battle is to take possession of the Rock which represents Troilus's love ("la voluntat firme del leal amador" [312]). In this *psychomachia* Troilus wins—thus signifying that he is no longer in love with Briseida. Impey rightly acknowledges that this psychomachic dream anticipates similar occurrences in the *novela sentimental*, beginning with Rodríguez's *Siervo libre*. Yet the device of an allegorical dream foretelling the outcome of a relationship can also be found in the *Heroides*. Witness, for example, Hero's dream of the dead dolphin (representative of Leander) washed up on the shore (*Her.* 19.195–202):

> namque sub aurora, iam dormitante lucerna,
> somnia quo cerni tempore vera solent,
> stamina de digitis cecidere sopore remissis,
> collaque pulvino nostra ferenda dedi.
> hic ego ventosas nantem delphina per undas
> cernere non dubia sum mihi visa fide,
> quem postquam bibulis inlisit fluctus harenis,
> unda simul miserum vitaque deseruit.

For, just before dawn, when my lamp was already dying down, at the time when dreams are wont to be true, my fingers were relaxed by sleep, the threads fell from them, and I laid my head down upon the pillow to rest. There in vision clear I seemed to see a dolphin swimming through the wind-tossed waters; and after the flood had cast it forth upon the thirsty sands, the wave, and at the same time life, abandoned the unhappy thing.

What is remarkable about Briseida's dream is that she implores Troilus to disprove her dream: "esfuerçate en amor y membrança de mi, quebrantando la fe alos sueños, demuestra tus fuerças por me recobrar" (*Bur.*, 313) [Exert yourself in your love and memory of me, disproving the dreams. Show your strength in winning me back]. Given her spurning of Troilus for Diomedes, she has as little right to expect this as she did to expect Achilles to take her back. By this erroneous self-presentation we are reminded of still other fictitious epistolary self-portrayals such as Medea's and Phaedra's. Again, it is Ovid's intense concern for the potential chasm separating a word from its referent—the indeterminacy of signs—that Rodríguez is most drawn to.

In this connection Impey points out Briseida as an example of "the redemptive nature of literary writing."[34] This heroine does indeed speak of the act of writing as a means of restoring her tarnished reputation as a loyal lover ("la saluacion de la denegrida fama") by means of her "rudo calamo" (305). The eponymous hero of the *Siervo libre*, as Impey notes, will also attempt to redeem himself through his text.[35] Yet, as with so many features of Rodríguez's text, this form of attempted redemption manifests itself first in his heroidean subtext. Moreover, as we will see in chapter 5, the *Siervo libre* will be doing something radically different from Briseida by rejecting the discourse of amorous desire altogether. What should be emphasized instead of the redemptive power of writing is Briseida's identity as explicitly proclaimed victim and—something that she would never admit—as verbal deceiver, as consummate artist.

# THREE

## VOYEURISTIC BETRAYAL

### (*ELEGIA DI MADONNA FIAMMETTA*)

W ITH A characteristically cryptic paradox Borges remarks that "every writer creates his own precursors."[1] In other words, intertextuality is inherently counterfeit in that it always involves a two-stage procedure—production of the new text by reinterpretation of the old. The relevance of this insight is readily apparent in the case of the *Elegia di madonna Fiammetta*, which constitutes an expanded heroid, as Vincenzo Crescini observed one hundred years ago.[2]

This generative function of the subtext has been profitably recognized in *Decameron* studies: Boccaccio is understood to be recasting preexisting narratives for new literary as well as metaliterary purposes. This all-important interplay of semantic and syntactic levels, so central to recent advances in *Decameron* criticism, however, remains to be explored in the *Elegia*, an equally experimental and hermeneutically significant text in the development of Boccaccio's language theory. The relevance of this text for the present study is twofold. First, it reveals the same skeptical attitude towards language as Ovid's epistolary elegies and, second, it has been consistently posited as a model text in the development of the *novela sentimental*.[3] In terms of its critical reception, the *Elegia* (dating from 1343–1344) tends to be evoked in two contexts. First, the work is rightly singled out as a notable departure, both formal and semantic, from Boccaccio's earlier writings, works in which Fiammetta served as his muse—the beloved for whom he wrote, whose love he cultivated: the *Filocolo* (1336–1338?), the *Comedia* (1341–1342), the *Rime* (c. 1340–1375), the *Teseida* (1339–1341), the *Commedia delle ninfe fiorentine* (1341–1342), and the *Amorosa visione* (1343).[4] In the *Elegia* the tables are reversed—the lady rejected. As Thomas Bergin puts it: "We can only marvel at the gulf that separates the character of the work from the nature and style of its immediate predecessors in the Boccaccian canon. We have here no allegorical mosaic in Dantean *terza rima*, no seductive nymphs whose rosy flesh and tempting limbs are draped in vestments of ethical symbolism; here is no romanticized would-be classical epic. Instead the scene is contemporary society, the protagonist an upper-class woman of that society, calling for our comprehension and compassion, needing no allegorical interpretation."[5]

This assessment is misleading, however; for while Boccaccio has left behind the allegorical third-person narrative for the mimetic first-person discourse of a distraught medieval woman, her discourse is, in fact, overwhelmingly mythological—both in its subtextual evocations and in its equally mythological high-flown rhetorical style. In fact, it is precisely the protrusiveness of myth—its status in the *Elegia*—that has perennially bothered critics, leading them to focus on the importance of the text's first-person psychological discourse to the unwarranted exclusion of the mythological discourse. Indeed, the *Elegia* competes in the annals of literary history with the *Vita Nuova*, the *Jehan de Saintré*, and *Don Quijote* for recognition as the first modern psychological novel.[6] In addition to echoing this long-standing identification of the *Elegia* as the first modern psychological novel, Vittore Branca further specifies its elegiac classification as deriving from the definition of elegy found in Dante's *De vulgare eloquentia* (because of its subject matter): "The title itself is Dantean: 'per elegiam stilum intelligimus miserorum' [elegy is to be understood as having the style of the miserable ] (Book II, Chapter iv, Part 6)—elegy is thus a sad tale about unhappy people."[7] The *Elegia* certainly conforms to this thematic distinction; however Dante defines the elegy in terms of diction as well, and he does so as follows: "si autem elegiace, solum humile oportet nos sumere" (2.4.6) [if (the subject is) suitable for the elegiac style, then we should employ only the low (i.e., humble) vernacular]. And *pace* Branca, the style of Boccaccio's *Elegia* is anything but humble.

Voicing skepticism concerning Branca's interpretation of the *Elegia* vis-à-vis the *De vulgare*, Hollander remarks that: "It seems difficult to believe that [Boccaccio] hoped that his readers would find his sad lady a morally positive creature. Whatever the strength of his desire to create an elegy, to exhibit his talents in still another genre, it seems foolish not to expect him to have been aware of the irrational quality of his heroine's conduct."[8]

In accord with this thinking, and as a logical extension of Boccaccio's pseudoautobiographical framework, I would argue that it is only the deluded Fiammetta herself who seriously interprets her text as elegy.

It is precisely the disparity between the high-flown (mythological) rhetoric of the text and its novelistic psychological probing of Fiammetta's inner world that perplexes its modern readers. Almost invariably, the positive assessment of the *Elegia*'s novelistic dimension is countered by a denigration of the mythological matter that obsesses its eponymous heroine, because it seems strangely incongruous in a novel. It tends, unfortunately, to be treated in evaluative terms—as "prolix" and "stilted"—rather than in its poetic function.[9]

As a consequence of various formal features that it exhibits, a critical consensus exists concerning the *Elegia*'s initial inspiration in Ovid's *Hero-*

*ides*. Both texts are pseudoautobiographies of females written by men, both contain narrators who are elegiacally lovelorn females. In the case of the Ovidian verse epistles, the legendary women each address themselves to their respective absent lover, whereas Fiammetta's inscribed readers are— significantly—the anonymous "donne innamorate" ("enamoured ladies"). Briefly stated, the *Elegia* is considered to be a vast *amplificatio* of the heroid genre—a microscopically detailed anatomy of love. More precisely, in its argument the *Elegia* most closely resembles the second heroid—that of Phyllis and Demofoon. Finally, it is recognized that Boccaccio copies into his text more or less verbatim lengthy passages from Ovid's epistolary elegies. Despite these very tangible features shared by Ovid and Boccaccio on the formal level, the semantic level—the gallery of Greek and Trojan myths that the *Heroides* supplies to Fiammetta—tends to be systematically minimized.

It is not simply the desire to interpret the *Elegia* as a novel that makes readers reluctant to valorize the integral function of myth to the medieval text. Boccaccio himself has contributed to this distortion by explicitly stating in his Prologue that we will find recounted in the *Elegia* neither "favole greche ornate di molte bugie, né troiane battaglie sozze per molto sangue" [Grecian fables depainted and set forth with plausible lies, nor Trojan wars foul and loathsome by deadly gore].[10] Just such remote fables pervade his text, however. The distance separating word and deed, what is said from what is done, could not be more blatant. We are meant, I submit, to view this prefatory statement as profoundly paradoxical—a trap for the unsuspecting *literal* reader, as we realize very early in the work when Venus (having just produced a lengthy catalogue of allusions to the Ovidian tales) remarks to Fiammetta: "Ma perché ci fatichiamo noi in tante parole?" (Segre, 962) [But wherefore do we trouble ourselves with recital of so many examples? (Hutton, 35)].

Clearly Boccaccio is calling our attention to the unreliability of his initial claim, doing here what he does on so many pages of his *opere*, i.e., explicitly enunciating one thing on the semantic level, thereafter blatantly contradicting it on the syntactic level in order to expose one of the mechanisms of deception inherent in language. Witness the opening sentence of Day 1 of the *Decameron*, where Boccaccio explicitly affirms: "quanto voi naturalmente tutte pietose siate"[11] [how compassionate (women) all are by nature[12]], only to undermine thereafter the authority of this judgment in actions and discourses carried out by a great many uncompassionate females who populate his encyclopedic text. In so doing, he dramatizes the epistemological fissure between enunciation and reference, *signans* and *signatum*, which consumed the attention of philosophers, theologians, and poets in the late Middle Ages.

A second (related and equally significant) unreliable assertion appears in the Prologue of the *Elegia*. For Fiammetta claims to be writing for the "donne innamorate," a generalized female audience, yet she writes a diary, which by its nature precludes disclosure of her text. She is not simply writing a journal, but a diary—and that is a qualitatively different activity. As Janet Altman explains, "The analogue to the theatrical monologue is the diary novel."[13] In other words, the diary is an epistolary monologue, and as such it lacks mechanisms for communicative reciprocity. Even when it appears to be intended for someone other than the writer himself, it is not. A salient example of this discursive feature of the diary is offered by Gerald Prince:

In *Journal de Salavin*, for instance, the protagonist, who wants to escape the mediocrity of his existence, decides to keep a diary which will record his struggle for transcendence. Though he often claims to be writing strictly for himself, he is constantly thinking about possible readers: his wife, his mother, his colleagues, his boss. He gradually finds out that no one is willing or able to understand his ambition, that no one constitutes a good reader. He comes to the point where he cannot read what he writes. He terminates his diary.[14]

Although her reasons for concealment are somewhat different (namely, fear of losing her reputation), Fiammetta too must keep her diary a secret. And, as we shall see, this epistolary paradox that she generates by addressing a reader whom she must never allow to read her words, is essential to interpretation of the *Elegia*.

With these epistemological discrepancies in mind, let us now turn to a consideration of the semantic and syntactic dimensions of the *Elegia*. Structurally speaking, Boccaccio's elegy is divided into a Prologue and nine chapters. Fiammetta and Panfilo (known only by these pseudonyms invented by the couple in order to protect their reputations [966]) fall in love and consummate their passion all in chapter 1. He abandons her in chapter 2 and never returns, the last seven chapters being devoted to Fiammetta's solipsistic reveries ranging from hope of amorous delectation to suicidal despair. It is important to note, however, that Fiammetta was initially hesitant to consummate her adulterous love until Venus appeared to her—a commonplace device in medieval erotic literature. What is unanticipated, however, is the argument advanced by Venus in order to convince Fiammetta to yield to Panfilo—one that immediately reflects Fiammetta's intimate identification of herself with the mythological deities: "Che mattamente fuggi? Se tanti iddii . . . da questo son vinti, tu d'essere vinta da lui ti vergognerai?" (Segre, 963) [What dost thou foolishly fly? —If so many divine Gods . . . have been conquered by (the God of Love), wilt thou then think it a shame to be overcome? (Hutton, 38)]. In an equally atypical mode of venereal argumentation (because of its domestic frame of reference), Venus adds: "Essi medesimi mariti amano le piú volte avendo moglie: riguarda Giasone, Teseo, il forte Ettore e Ulisse" (963) [Husbands themselves for the most part love other women, when they have wives of their own, as Jason for example, Hercules and wise Ulysses (39)].

Both the discourse of Venus here and that of Fiammetta throughout the work are, moreover, legalistic, based explicitly on laws—old and new. Again, if we consider the hermeneutic assumptions of myth, we recall that it too is, at its core, legalistic to the degree that it exemplifies universal laws of cognition and behavior.

The old law in this case refers to the first age of the world, the Golden Age as expressed in the mode of the *beatus ille*. Fiammetta invokes this familiar "good old days" topos as follows:

> Oh, felice colui il quale innocente dimora nella solitaria villa, usando l'aperto cielo! . . . Ohimè! niuna è piú libera né senza vizio o migliore che questa, la quale li primi usarono e che colui ancora oggi usa, il quale, abandonate le città, abita nelle selve. Oh felice il mondo, se Giove mai non avesse cacciato Saturno, e ancora l'età aurea durasse sotto caste leggi! Però que tutti alli primi simili viveremmo. (1022, 1023–24)

> Oh, how happy is [he] who dwelleth in the solitary village, enjoying only the open air! . . . There is no life (alas) more free, nor more devoid of vice, or better than this: the which our first fathers enjoyed, and with which also he is this day of all others best contented who, abandoning the opulent and vicious Cities, inhabiteth the private and peaceable woods. Oh, what a world had it been if Jupiter had never driven Saturn away, and if the Golden Age had continued still under a chaste law, because we might all live like to our primitive parents of the first world. (198, 202)

By way of contrast with the putatively harmonious old law of the mythological time frame, Fiammetta introduces the so-called "new laws"—which refer to her unreciprocated love for Panfilo and to her married state in the context of the God of Love (i.e., to her self-perceived uniqueness). In point of fact, both the old laws as well as the new pose serious problems for Fiammetta. While she would like to project the myth of the Golden Age to which she alludes above, the examples of lovers she offers (drawn primarily from the *Heroides* and *Metamorphoses*) all attest to the untenability—hence fallaciousness—of the old law even for the deities.

It is highly significant that Fiammetta shows herself to be equally contradictory when she alludes to the "new laws." Her first allusion to them underscores, once more, her deluded perception of herself as unique. Here they are evoked regarding the violence of her infatuation:

Ohimè! che Amore cosí come ora in me usa crudeltà non udita, cosí nel pigliarmi nuova legge dagli altri diversa gli piacque d'usare! Io ho piú volte udito che negli altri i piaceri sono nel principio levissimi, ma poi, da' pensieri nutricati, aumentando le forze loro, si fanno gravi: ma in me cosí non avvenne, anzi con quella medesima forza m'entrarono nel cuore, che essi vi sono poi dimorati, e dimorano. Amore il primo dí di me ebbe interissima possessione. (955)

Alas that love is not only content to use such a strange, and too severe kind of cruelty towards me, but in subduing me to his might, to prescribe new Laws, clean variant from others. I have oftentimes heard that love in others at his first entrance is but light, but by nourished thoughts augmenting his force is made greater. But so it fared with me: for he entered into my heart with that same force, wherewith he continued ever afterwards, as one who at the very first assault had most entire and free possession of me. (17)

The second usage of the "new law" (Segre, 975) refers to her unrequited love for Panfilo—that he swore an oath of eternal devotion, yet left her seduced and abandoned. The third usage, which Fiammetta ascribes to the "new law," refers to the law of marriage and her status as adulteress. In one breath (in chapter 8), she reviles herself for her infidelity to her loving (and oblivious) husband (1,071)—reasoning (quite irrationally) that perhaps because of it she is being morally punished by the pagan God of Love (to whom she has always been faithful); yet in the next breath she rejects this hypothesis, claiming that she is not, by any means, unique in her transgression of the sacred laws of wedlock: "E in questo io non sono prima, né sarò ultima, né sono sola, anzi quasi tutte quelle del mondo ho in compagnia, e le leggi contro alle quali io ho commesso, sogliono perdonare alla multitudine" (Segre, 1,071) [As I am not the first that hath committed such a friendly fault, so am I not alone, and shall not be the last, but having almost all Women in the world my companions in this excusable error, I am not so greatly to be condemned for the same (Hutton, 328–29)].

Fiammetta's problem is thus not an ethical but an existential one. More precisely, she cannot admit two things—first, she cannot admit to having been rejected by Panfilo, and second, she is unwilling to have her liaison become public out of the (very unheroic) impulse of fear. Feigning religious devotion for public consumption (as a mask for her true narcissism), she explains:

Io, piú peccatrice che altra, dolente per li miei disonesti amori, però che quelli velo sotto oneste parole, sono reputata santa; ma conoscelo Iddio, che, se senza pericolo essere potesse, io con vera voce di me sgannerei ogni ingannata persona, né celerei la cagione che trista mi tiene; ma non si puote. (1,027–28)

Myself a greater sinner than any other, and sorrowful for my dishonest loves, yet couching them under the Veil of honest words, am reputed holy: but the just Gods know that (if I could without danger of my honor and good name) with true reports I would make satisfaction to everyone whom in fictions, speeches and gestures I have deluded. (212–13)

Fiammetta is incapable, in the last analysis, of action, of the symbolized event that accorded legitimacy to the signified utterances of the mythological heroines whom she attempts to emulate. It is no accident that Medea is the role model whom Fiammetta invokes more frequently, by far, than any other because she functions as a reflection of Fiammetta's own deep-seated inadequacy in the realm of action. In this context it is important to note that Medea is recalled not according to her primary association—the notoriety that resulted from her bloodthirsty revenge—but rather in the context of amorous affect.

Like other readers of the *Heroides*, Fiammetta discerns a number of interpretations of Medea (five, to be precise). Unlike them, however, Fiammetta's views all reflect her own inability to act. We see her transposing Medea into her own inactive but amorously tormented identity. She is first presented as healer (because of her medical prowess in rejuvenating her father-in-law, Aeson, to further her own amorous designs [Segre, 974]); then as abandoned lover (forsaken by Jason [1,045]); as "survivor" (because of her subsequent involvement with Egeus [1,045]); as seducer of Jason (from Hypsipyle's point of view [1,045]); and, finally, as masochist ("cosí crudele divenisse contro di sé, come contro lo 'ngrato amante" (1,076) [(being) no less cruel to herself than malicious against her ungrateful lover (Hutton, 344)], namely Jason.

Because she is afraid, above all, of compromising her public name (that is, her comfortable social status), she maintains her affair in secret—spending virtually all her time cloistered in her bedroom, vacillating between the two extremes of hope and despair. She is cut off from society, effectively unable to convince herself for more than a few moments at a time either of being unique or exemplary. Indeed, at the end of her lengthy elegiac confession she is as unresolved to action as she was at the beginning. (After her brief and uncharacteristic suicide attempt in chapter 6—in which she was easily thwarted—she is the same as before it, living out a circular progression from hope to despair and back again.) This uncharacteristic act, in fact, results from a moment of frenzied hysteria, immediately before which she has argued, first, that she should not kill herself for her husband would be greatly saddened (Segre, 1,048), thereafter adding that killing herself would foreclose the possibility of being reunited with Panfilo (1,048). Immediately following her failed attempt she argues, in an even more contradictory manner, that: "Egli non è virtú il chiedere la morte" (1,053) [It is not a point of virtue to require death, and to call upon it (Hutton, 282)].

This circularity is, moreover, the progression that characterizes lyric, as Sharon Cameron observes in her study of lyric time: "the contradiction between social and personal time is the lyric's generating impulse, for the lyric both rejects the limitation of social and objective time, those structures that drive hard lines between past, present, and future, and must make use of them."[15] Also significant in this context is the fact that no dates are given in the *Elegia* from which we could calculate either the historical time frame of the work or even the length of the ex-lovers' separation. It is only by occasional references to the seasons (especially springtime, the lyric season *par excellence*) that we understand the separation to have lasted for at least one year. Fiammetta is thus no Don Quijote or Emma Bovary— each of whom first embrace and then reject the clarity of the world of books, each of whom came to realize the linear (rather than cyclical) trajectory inherent in the novel.

Commenting on the necessarily linear development of the novel, Eugenio Donato aptly crystallizes the Girardian view that it "has to take into account both the journey of the character through the domain of desire and at the end of his distancing from it to establish the epistemological privilege of the subject's claim to hold a discourse which is not a discourse *of* desire, but a discourse *about* desire and about the [disenchanting] truth of desire."[16]

The teleology of Fiammetta's autobiography is quite different. Considering the misfortunes suffered by the gallery of Ovidian heroines whom she recalls as imperfect analogues to her own situation, Fiammetta concludes as follows at the very end of chapter 7: "Se chi porta invidia è piú misero che colui a cui la porta, io sono di tutti li predetti de' loro accidenti, meno miseri che li miei reputandoli, invidiosa" (1,077) [If he that beareth envy is more miserable and more wretched than he to whom he doth bear it, then of all the forenamed persons I am the most miserable and unhappy woman. Because I do greatly emulate and not a little envy their ordinary accidents (as opposed to her extraordinary fate), accounting them not so grievous nor so full of such great misery as mine are (345)]. Her final words continue to echo each of the extremes of hope and despair with which the work had begun:

> Di tacere omai dilibero, faccendovi manifesto non essere altra comparazione dal mio narrare verissimo a quello che io sento, che sia dal fuoco dipinto a quello che veramente arde. Al quale io priego Iddio, che o per li vostri prieghi, o per li miei, sopra quello salutevole acqua mandi, o con trista morte di me, o con lieta tornata di Panfilo. (1,077)

There is no more comparison of my shadowed discourse to those substantial dolours, which I feel indeed, than there is of painted fire, to that which doth burn indeed: the which I pray all the Gods that either by your meritorious prayers or else by my earnest and effectual orisons, they would with some liquor of comfort extinguish, or with speedy death quite abolish; or else with the joyful return of my Panphilus assuage and moderate the same. (346–47)

Epistolarity confirms Fiammetta's incapacity to act. For unlike the women of the *Heroides*, she does not intend for the eyes of anyone else to pass over her extended letter. It is a diary novel, not an epistolary one, and this difference is paramount. Writing a diary "becomes a way of giving time a shape, of conferring a rhythm upon a formless and seemingly interminable present," as Prince observes.[17] The fact that Fiammetta's diary is a solipsistic activity, an artifact not intended for others, is obvious, since her overriding concern is to maintain her "honor and good name," which precludes the disclosure of her affair. Here too we see the circularity of her argument, the conflicting irrationality of her discourse. Perhaps the most dramatic display of this circular discourse is the last chapter, in which Fiammetta addresses her book: "Nel quale madonna Fiammetta parla al libro suo, imponendogli in che abito, e quando e a cui egli debba andare, e da cui guardarsi; e fa fine" (1,078) [In which lady Fiammetta addresses her book, instructing it in what mode of dress, and when, and to whom it should travel, and whom it should avoid; and then she puts an end to her book (my translation)].

Fiammetta begins the address to her book in a way that clearly suggests her irrational state. Having affirmed throughout her text that Love's "laws" are no longer viable (a transparent excuse for her failed relationship to Panfilo), she now assumes that they are in fact operative: "se Amore non ha mutate leggi poi che noi misera divenimmo. Né ti sia in questo abito cosí vile come io ti mando, vergogna d'andare a chiascheduna" (1,078) [If Love hath not changed his laws since I became a miserable Lover, let it be no shame for thee in so vile a habit (as I send thee) to go to every Lady and Gentlewoman (349)]. While appearing to be a radical departure, however, this altered perception of the laws indicates two related constants that have been operative since the first page of her text—her instability, and the need to perpetuate her narcissistic (circular) discourse. She wants to utter the words of an enamoured heroine but only within the confines of her bedchamber, that is, without imperiling her public image.

Also significant in this regard is the physical description here of the book as a figure of herself. It is a surrogate for the wretchedly clad pilgrim wandering in search of Panfilo (evoked in chapter 6), which she herself would have been, were she capable of matching her actions to her words. This substitution of discourse for action is quite explicit: "Tu dei essere contento di mostrarti simigliante al tempo mio, il quale, essendo infelicissimo, te di miseria veste, come fa me" (1,078) [Thou must be content to figurate my life, myself and my times (which being most unfortunate) make thee apparelled with misery as me appalled with mishap (349)]. Like its author, the book is physically disheveled: "non ti sia cura d'alcuno ornamento, sí come gli altri sogliono avere, cioè di nobili coverte di colori varii tinte e ornate, o di pulita tonditura, o di leggiadri minii, o di gran titoli; queste cose non si convengono. . . . Tu dei essere contento di mostrarti simigliante al tempo mio, il quale, essendo infelicissimo, te di miseria veste, come fa me. . . . Lascia e queste e li larghi spazii e li lieti inchiostri e l'impomiciate carte a' libri felici; a te si conviene d'andare rabbuffato con isparte chiome, e macchiato e di squallore pieno" (1,078) [Take thou no care for that which other books (whose subjects are contrary to thine) are wont to have, which are, sumptuous coverings garnished with curious and costly works. . . . Leave these aside (my woeful Book), and the great margins also, and ruled spaces, the brave kinds of coloured inks, and the great characters, placed in the beginning of happy Books. . . . It doth become thee best, with torn and ruffled leaves, and tached full of blots and blurs, to go thither (349–50)].

This *envoi* also has an important Ovidian resonance, not to the *Heroides*, but to another epistolary collection written by Ovid in exile, the *Tristia*. The similarities are quite striking:

> Parve—nec invideo—sine me, liber, ibis in urbem.
> ei mihi, quod domino non licet ire tuo!
> vade, sed incultus, qualem decet exulis esse;
> infelix habitum temporis huius habe.
> nec te purpureo velent vaccinia fuco—
> non est conveniens luctibus ille color—
> nec titulus minio, nec cedro charta notetur,
> candida nec nigra cornua fronte geras.
> felices ornent haec instrumenta libellos;
> fortunae memorem te decet esse meae.
> nec fragili geminae poliantur pumice frontes,
> hirsutus sparsis ut videare comis.
> neve liturarum pudeat; qui viderit illas,
> de lacrimis factas sentiet esse meis.[18]

Little book, you will go without me—and I grudge it not—to the city. Alas that your master is not allowed to go! Go, but go unadorned, as becomes the book of an exile; in your misfortune wear the garb that befits these days of mine. You shall have no cover dyed with the juice of purple berries—no fit colour is that for mourning; your title shall not be tinged with vermilion nor your paper with oil of cedar; and you shall wear no white bosses upon your dark edges. Books of good omen should be decked with such things as these; 'tis my fate that you should bear in mind. Let no brittle pumice polish your two edges; I would have you appear with locks all rough and disordered. Be not ashamed of blots; he who sees them will feel that they were caused by my tears.

As she has claimed from the very beginning, Fiammetta, in theory, offers her book as an exemplum of the deceitfulness of men. While reiterating this intention at the end of her text, she simultaneously indicates that it will convince Panfilo to return to her (Segre, 1,079–80). We see thus that the same two discourses of novel and romance persist with a total lack of resolution.

This schizophrenic contradiction is highlighted by a kind of anaphoric structure (the repeated use of the words "but if") that Fiammetta employs in the context of her hypothetical readers. Instructing her book on its proper comportment during its pilgrimage, Fiammetta indicates that a mocking reader among the enamored ladies should be reminded of the mutability of Fortune (1,078)—that her happiness will turn to grief. But if a sympathetic woman is found, she should be instructed to pray for the lovers' reunion (1,079). If the book reaches Panfilo's new lady (her rival), it should flee "come di luogo iniquo" (1,079) [fly incontinently from thence as from an infectious place (353)]—unless in reading it she feel compelled to restore Panfilo to Fiammetta. A logical discrepancy arises here since Fiammetta wants the book to be read only if it will be received favorably, yet reader response obviously cannot be determined a priori.

In a similarly problematic manner, she categorically tells her book "gli occhi degli uomini fuggi" (1,079) [shun the eyes of men (353)], stipulating further that if it reaches Panfilo, it should address him saying "fuggi di qui, e noi con le tue mani non violare" (1,079) [fly from hence, and do not violate me with thy unworthy and polluted hands (354)]. Unless, of course, by reading the book he will return to Fiammetta (1,079–80). In addition, this mention of Panfilo as a possible reader violates the audience posited in the Prologue and maintained throughout the work—that she is writing exclusively for the benefit of enamored ladies in order to warn them of male duplicity.[19]

A different kind of audience, this time the editorially critical female reader, is cited next. Fiammetta asks her to be indulgent, but this too is simply a pretext for articulating her existential dilemma: "di' che quelle ne mandi via. . . . E però piuttosto dirai che prenda ammirazione come a quel poco che narri disordinato, bastò lo 'ntelletto e la mano, considerando che dall'una parte amore e dall'altra gelosia con varie trafitte in continua battaglia tengono il dolente animo" (1,080) [Tell her that that which is unpolished and unpleasant for her fine conceit she may (if she please) overslip and let pass. . . . And therefore thou shalt say unto her, that she may a great deal sooner fall in admiration, how my troubled wit, my tired pen, and pains did last out but for that little which thou dost tell out of order, considering that fervent love on the one side, and burning jealousy on the other, with divers conflicts, held my sorrowful soul in continual battles (355)].

The last type of reader evoked by Fiammetta is the most hypothetical (indeed nonexistent) woman, who is more miserable than Fiammetta's book: "se pure piú misero di te si trovasse, che no 'l credo, il quale quasi a te come a piú beato di sé la portasse, làsciati mordere" (1,080) [If perchance thou shalt find any (which I think thou never canst) that, being more miserable than thyself, might emulate thee (as one more happy and not so wretched as herself), then patiently suffer thyself to be bitten (355)]. Unlike Don Quijote or Emma Bovary, Fiammetta is incapable of the linearity required by the novel—unable to mirror in her symbolized actions the substance of her signified utterances, unable to attain the individuality of a novelistic character or the exemplarity of a mythic archetype.[20] She is, in the last analysis, etymologically faithful to her name—not an all-consuming *fiamma*, but rather merely its diminutive form, a *fiammetta*.

Fiammetta's circular vacillation remains consistent to the end. Her book is a specular image of herself—her epistolary monologue—which she has no intention of making public. It is, rather, Boccaccio who voyeuristically betrays Fiammetta's intimate writing just as Ovid does with that of his imagined heroines.

# FOUR

## MEDIATED DISCOURSE

## (*HISTORIA DE DUOBUS AMANTIBUS*)

T HE *NOVELA SENTIMENTAL* is—consistently and significantly—epistolary. Because of this formal feature not only the
*Heroides* and the *Elegia*, but Aeneas Sylvius Piccolomini's *Historia
de duobus amantibus* as well is perennially invoked as an influential subtext
in its development. Nonetheless, the unique performative function of epistolary discourse within this novelistic form remains to be articulated. The
prevailing critical equation of epistolarity with emotive expression and/or
a concern for verisimilitude is clearly insufficient, offering only a limited
appreciation of the mechanisms of letter discourse—both formally and
semantically.

Indeed, the letter is a metalinguistic medium that comments upon the
status of language itself: from the relationship of word to deed in a specific
text to the ontology of literature in general. As Jacques Derrida observes:
"la léttre, l'épitre . . . n'est pas un genre mais tous les genres, la littérature
même."[1] In other words, the letter provides a *mise en abîme* of the writer/
reader relationship, with all the complexities and indeterminacies that the
activities of reading and writing entail.

Aeneas Sylvius Piccolomini's *Historia* is recognized, along with Boccaccio's *Elegia,* as being seminal both to the history of European fiction in
general and to the development of the Spanish *novela sentimental* in particular. Moreover, although separated by one hundred years, the *Elegia* and
the *Historia* are consistently paired by critics because both narratives detail
the predictable effects upon the adulterous wife who is "seduced and abandoned" by a lover who had sworn eternal fidelity.[2] More concretely, both
women fall in love, consummating their desire, which grows even greater
as a result. Both despair as the lovers announce their departure, Lucretia
dying of grief, while Fiammetta goes mad.[3]

At the same time, however, critics differentiate these works either on
formal or thematic grounds. Armando Durán, for example, finds the *Elegia*
to be *ficción erótica* (because Fiammetta betrayed a husband whom she
loved—hence her love fulfilled an illegitimate sexual drive rather than an
emotional need). By contrast, the *Historia*, in his view, exemplifies *ficción
sentimental* (because Lucretia betrayed a husband whom she did not love).
As such, she was seeking to fulfill a legitimate emotional need, rather than

merely a libidinous inclination. This dichotomy based on "la oposición presencia / ausencia de lazos afectivos entre Fiammetta y Lucrecia con sus respectivos esposos"[4] is a false one, however. For, as Keith Whinnom observes, the *Historia* "contains passages which border, at the very least, on the pornographic."[5]

Antonio Prieto, on the other hand, distinguishes the *Historia* from the *Elegia* in the narratological terms of narrative distance—the time of writing and the time of the narrative:

> La *Historia* de Enea Silvio Piccolomini ofrece una *perspectiva* narrativa respecto a la *Fiammetta*. No es ya el cambio de la primera persona narrativa a la tercera sino el tiempo del narrador. La *Fiammetta* como sucederá con el *Siervo libre* o la *Cárcel de amor* está escrita en el tiempo de amar de Boccaccio mientras que en su *Historia* (en la *Carta* proemial) Piccolomini especifica encontrarse en esa edad cercana a los cuarenta años en la que ya se estaba *fuera* del amor.[6]

> Piccolomini's *Historia* offers a narrative perspective on the *Elegia*. It is not a question of the shift from first- to third-person narrative, but of the narrator's temporal frame of reference. The *Elegia*, like the *Servo libre* or the *Cárcel*, is written while the narrator is in love, whereas in his *Historia* (in the prefatory letter) Piccolomini specifies that he is nearly forty years of age and, therefore, no longer a lover.

Hence the distinction between the *sujeto protagonista* (first-person discourse) of the *Elegia* and the third-person discourse of the *sujeto-testigo* in the *Historia*. For Prieto, the importance of the *Historia*'s more mature narrator ("ya viejo según los tratados") is that he can cast his narrative within the framework of a *tratado*—an exemplary treatise.[7] The letter to Marianus—his inscribed reader—does indeed express just such an exemplary intent. Witness the initial invocation in which Aeneas Sylvius sternly condemns his friend's request for a love story: "Rem petis haud convenientem aetati meae, tuae vero et adversam et repugnantem. Quid enim est, quod vel me, iam pene quadragenarium, scribere, vel te quinquagenarium, de amore conveniat audire?"[8] [You ask a thing ill-suited to my years, to yours both offensive and disgusting. For how can it become me, who am nearly forty, to write of love, or you, that are in your fifties, to read of it?[9]].

In fact, this uncompromisingly didactic attitude toward Marianus extends even further as Aeneas Sylvius indicates the beneficial effects that his narrative will no doubt produce on the young:

> Nam cum puella, quae in argumentum venit, amatore perdito, inter plorandum, moestam et indignantem exhalaverit animam, alter vero posthac nunquam verae laetitiae particeps fuerit: commonitio quaedam iuvenibus erit, his ut abstineant nugis. Audiant igitur adulescentulae et, hoc edoctae casu, videant, ne post amores iuvenum se eant perditum. Instruit haec historia iuve-

nes, ne militiae se accingant amoris, quae plus fellis habet quam mellis; sed omissa lascivia, quae homines reddit insanos: virtutis incumbant studiis, quae possessorem sui sola beare petest. (3)

For, while the lady that comes into this tale, lost her lover, and, amid lamentations, breathed out her sad, indignant spirit; he too, from that time, never had any part in true happiness: and this will be a kind of warning to the young, to shun such trifles. So let all maidens attend and, profiting by this adventure, see to it that the loves of young men send them not to their perdition. And this story teaches youths not to arm themselves for the warfare of love, which is more bitter than sweet; but, putting away passion, which drives men mad, to pursue the study of virtue, for she alone can make her possessor happy. (xx–xxi)

Such categorically pedagogical claims certainly conform to Prieto's interpretation of the work as exemplary treatise. However, this reading is invalidated by further extradiegetic detail. Speaking precisely of "those who are made happy by the study of virtue," the narrator says that they don't really exist:

Dicunt quidam, nihil esse, quod in sapiente queat fortuna. Hoc ego his sapientibus concedo, qui sola virtute gaudent, qui et pauperes et aegroti et in tauro Phalaris clausi, vitam se credunt possidere beatam; quadem nullum adhuc vel vidi, vel fuisse putarim. (33–34)

Some say, chance has no power over wisdom, and I admit it of those that are wise enough to take pleasure only in virtue, who whether poor or sick or shut up in the bull of Phalaris, can believe their life is happy. But I have never met anyone like that, and I don't think they exist. (83–84)

So that we do not miss the point of Aeneas Sylvius's unexemplary narrative, he explicitly derides the so-called *sabios* even in the dedicatory letter to Gaspar Schlick which precedes the letter to Marianus. Specifically, it is the irrelevance of their book learning to daily life (a traditional humanistic theme) that is the focus of the attack:

Stupuit Paglarensis et furti villicum accusavit, qui suem fetam undecim porcellos, asinam unam duntaxat enixam pullum retulerat. Bonitius Mediolanensis gravidum se putavit, diuque partum veritus est, quia se uxor adscendit. Hi tamen iuris maximum lumen habiti sunt. (1)

Paglarensis gaped, and accused his steward of theft who told him that one ass travailed for a single foal, while his sow had a litter of eleven. Bonitius of Milan thought he was with child and long went in fear of a delivery, because his wife had mounted him. Yet these men were considered the chief light of the law. (xiv–xv)

Aeneas Sylvius thus problematizes the relationship between word and deed. What he claims—the didactic function of his prose—and what he does are two radically different, in fact mutually contradictory, things. A further consequence of this disparity is that his conflicting words take on the power of action by transforming him into an unreliable figure. Indeed, blatant contradiction characterizes the narrator's asides to Marianus. To take one more striking example, at the end of the dedication, Aeneas Sylvius remarks as follows: "Qui nunquam vere sensit amoris ignes, aut lapis est, aut bestia" (Dévay, 2) [He who has never truly felt the flames of love is but a stone, or a beast (Grierson, xvi)], while thereafter, in speaking of Euryalus the lover, he affirms the opposite by recalling the Ovidian depiction of all lovers as "fieri ex hominibus aut bestias scribit, aut lapides, aut plantas" (25) [men that have become beasts (Ovid writes), or stones, or plants (60)]. In a similarly contradictory fashion, Euryalus claims that he wishes he were a flea so that he could gain entry to Lucretia's room (Dévay, 17)—a positively charged amorous image, despite its unheroic nature. But shortly thereafter (21) the narrator denigrates women misogynistically, saying that they are as easy to guard (in terms of their potential for infidelity) as it is to guard a swarm of fleas in the blistering sunlight.

This conflicting discourse is one of two techniques by which the narrator establishes himself as pedagogically untrustworthy . The other technique is that of the non sequitur. Having, for instance, just articulated in the letter to Marianus the value of his text as exemplum, Aeneas Sylvius introduces Menelaus as: "praediviti viro Menelao nupta; indigno tamen, cui tantum decus domi serviret, sed digno, quem uxor deciperet et, sicut nos dicimus, cornutum quasi cervum redderet" (5) [a wealthy man, but quite unworthy that such a treasure (as Lucretia) should look after his home; deserving rather that his wife should deceive him or, as we say, give him horns (2– 3)]. Hence, from the very beginning the diegetic level is presented as being decidedly unconcerned with serving as a cautionary tale. In a comparably incongruous moment, Euryalus misguidedly blames Lucretia, claiming that she does not love him, but rather merely toys with his emotions, taunting him like a stag in a net (Dévay, 27). (Significantly, this analogy constitutes an inversion of the Virgilian simile whereby Dido likens herself to an ensnared stag.)[10] This is, moreover, the first in a series of subversions of the Virgilian subtext that are essential to interpretation of the *Historia*—and to an understanding of the epistemological chasm that separates Lucretia from Fiammetta. At this juncture in his text, the narrator intervenes with an incongruous antifeminist remark on women's ability to deceive men: "Vide audaciam mulieris! I nunc et feminis credito Nemo tam oculatus est, ut falli non possit. Is duntaxat non fuit illusus, quem coniunx fallere non temptavit. Plus fortuna, quam ingeno, sumus felices" (28) [See the shamelessness of woman! Go now and trust the sex. No one has eyes so sharp that he cannot be cheated. Only he is safe, whose wife has not tried to deceive him. If we are fortunate, it is by good luck rather than good management (67)]. Similarly, Menelaus nails a window shut because, the narrator tells us, that:

> Nam, etsi nihil conscius erat illi, vexatam tamen feminam . . . non ignorabat et animum cognoscebat mulieris instabilem, cuius tot sunt voluntates, quot in arboribus folia. *Sexus enim femineus novitatis est cupidus, raroque virum amat, cuius copiam habet.* (37; italics added)

> though he had discovered nothing, he . . . knew the variable nature of women, that they have as many desires as a tree has leaves. *For the female sex is eager for novelty, and seldom loves a man whom she can freely possess.* (93; italics added)

This misogynistic advice is obviously invalidated by the example of Lucretia, the motivation for Menelaus's action. The narrator's unjust treatment of Lucretia, in evidence here and elsewhere, is another device, serving to underscore her laudable behavior as a supremely loyal lover.

In tandem with the reproach of Marianus's request as "repugnant," Aeneas Sylvius promises to oblige his friend with a truly sensual narrative: "Ero morigerus cupiditati tuae et hanc ingvinis aegri canitiem prurire faciam" (3) [I'll indulge your desire; I'll make the grey hairs of your sickly lust to itch (xix)]. This unanticipated capitulation to salaciousness is followed by an even more surprising admission by Aeneas Sylvius of his own corruptibility. In justifying his choice of subject matter, he explains: "Sed alienos, quam meos, amores attingam, ne, dum vetusti cineres ignis evolvo, scintillam adhuc viventem reperiam" (3) [I shall touch on other loves than mine, lest as I rake the ashes of some old fire, I find a spark still burning (xx)]. These two admissions by the narrator obviously undermine his initial claim to be writing a didactic treatise. His credibility is seriously called into question by the diametrically opposed narrative impulses of licentiousness and morality. Moreover, these two irreconcilable concerns characterize his extradiegetic digressions not simply in the preface, but throughout the text, so that the moral valence of his words is definitively negated. (The additional fact that Aeneas Sylvius repudiated the *Historia* once he became Pope Pius II further testifies to its lack of exemplarity.)[11]

The unreliability of Aeneas Sylvius is further emphasized by his claim—very reminiscent of Boccaccio's prefatory claim in the *Elegia*[12]—that he will not resort to classical examples: "Nec vetustis, nec obliteratis utar exemplis, sed nostri temporis ardentes faces exponam. *Nec troianos, nec babylonios, sed nostrae urbis amores audies*" (Dévay, 3; italics added) [(I shall not) make use of old forgotten types, but I'll bring forth torches that burned in our own days. *You will not hear the loves of Troy or Babylon*, but of our own city (Grierson, xx)]. Like Boccaccio, Aeneas Sylvius here makes a claim that he will blatantly contradict, since his text abounds in notable classical examples.

In the case of the *Historia* it is characters from the Trojan war and the *Aeneid* who serve as analogues—in addition to the raped Lucretia, whose uxorial fidelity has been immortalized by Livy.[13] Principal among the numerous figures from antiquity, in addition to the female protagonist Lucretia, is Menelaus the Greek, ruler of Sparta and husband of Helen—the wife whose elopement with Paris led to the Trojan war. In the *Historia* the Italian Menelaus is a bourgeois Sienese businessman who (rather than declaring war) is oblivious to his beautiful wife's involvement with Euryalus—although Aeneas Sylvius as well as Lucretia compare her affair repeatedly to that of Helen and Paris (Dévay, 4, 5, 7, 46, 48). In addition, the lovers are likened to Dido and Aeneas twice (17, 51). The fact that we are meant to compare the classical and modern figures who are linked by onomastic association is evident by additional correspondences. To take another example, we find that the brother of Menelaus, both the antique Greek and the fifteenth-century Italian, is Agamemnon. This celebrated king of Mycenae and commander in chief of the Greeks at Troy becomes, in his Italian reincarnation, a relentlessly suspicious and vigilant man obsessed with spying on Lucretia and with securing multiple bolts on the door to his brother's house to prevent the surreptitious entry of any potential philanderers. By comparison with their epic Greek namesakes then, these urban Italian figures are notably unheroic. Here, too, it is a question of the relationship between word and deed that is at issue.

Aeneas Sylvius, moreover, juxtaposes these recast Greek heroes with equally ignoble recast Trojan counterparts in the figures of Euryalus and Nisus, the devoted friends whose remarkable valor is epitomized by Books 5 and 9 of the *Aeneid*. In the Renaissance version of these two friends, while still soldiers by vocation they comport themselves as cowardly courtiers. Indeed, the programmatic epic subtext, as we shall see, is exploited by Aeneas Sylvius for novelistic purposes, to demonstrate the humanistic recognition of man's inability to conform to mythic paradigms of behavior. As such, the narrative of love between Euryalus and Lucretia, the diegetic level of the *Historia*—like the extradiegetic authorial digressions—contradict the didacticism claimed by Aeneas Sylvius in his prefatory letter.

One further remark should be made concerning the prefatory epistle, namely, the question of its extent. Critics traditionally indicate that the introductory letter serves to express the reluctance of Aeneas Sylvius to relate the lusty events of his *Historia*, which he writes only out of friendship for his inscribed reader. Critical attention has tended to focus only on the love letters written by the two protagonists. Commenting on the importance of the *Historia* in the development of the epistolary novel in Europe, Charles Kany, for example, observes that "Aeneas Sylvius is one of the first prose storytellers in modern literature to use the letter device."[14] He adds also that in the space of only fifty pages we find ten complete letters, as well as numerous allusions to still others which are exchanged by the lovers, but whose precise wording is not given. Finally, he underscores the importance accorded to the letter by Aeneas Sylvius as witnessed by the fact that the "complete wooing of the lady up to the point when she finally declares herself won, is accomplished by letters (as is the dénouement)."[15] Kany, and others, ascribe this intense interest in the epistolary mode to the prevailing interest with social realism: "Ladies were kept so closely guarded that the least difficult and often only approach possible was through missives smuggled to them with the utmost secrecy."[16] Robert Day observes an additional function of the letters, namely that "The [passionate] vehemence of the letters is emphasized all the more by the rather dry and objective manner in which the straight narrative is written and by the comparatively unemotional dialogue."[17] Yet all of these analyses fail to notice the important fact that the entire tale of Lucretia and Euryalus is inscribed within the letter from Aeneas Sylvius to Marianus. Thus, despite prevailing critical opinion, as a result of this extended letter structure, the text is not in fact structured according to the two extremes of narrative fiction—third-person chronicle and first-person dialogue. It is not simply a question of one more letter but—on the global, extradiegetic level—an entire text that, like the *novela sentimental*, constitutes a sustained example of epistolary communication.

The significance of this structural configuration is paramount, offering a double *mise en abîme* of letter discourse—the diegetic level of Lucretia and Euryalus, and the extradiegetic one of Aeneas Sylvius and his mute addressee (i.e., Marianus—and us). The value of this *double* structure is that it makes the hermeneutics of epistolarity all the more apparent. We are meant to react to the narrator's letter, its mechanisms and its indeterminacies, in a way that parallels the manner in which Euryalus and Lucretia react to each other's missives. It is, I maintain, this overtly metaliterary structure that differentiates the *Historia* most markedly from the *Elegia* on a structural level.[18]

Letter discourse is markedly different from third-person objective reporting and from dialogic discourse as well; it is unlike spoken dialogue (which is spontaneous and unmediated) and unlike third-person impersonal written narrative (which is also unmediated, although unspontaneous). Indeed, every letter entails an *histoire* (actions) which is necessarily mediated by a *discours* (words) calculated to manipulate its addressee. As Ronald Rosbottom explains:

Each letter has to recognize the existence of the Other, and each judgment has to take into account the relativity of values. Every letter is a rhetorical piece, designed to convince the recipient of the validity of the writer's point of view, and *every letter is as ambiguous as is the relationship between the sender and the receiver of the letters.*[19]

Aware of this discursive property inherent in epistolary communication, Aeneas Sylvius overtly structures his letter to Marianus according to the irreconcilable axiologies of eroticism and didacticism. His purpose in doing so is to ensure that the reader will be unable to reconcile this problematic pair of values, questioning instead the conflicting nature of the discourse itself. As such, the *Historia* thematizes one of the most significant properties of epistolary communication—its unavoidably *un*objective nature.

Moreover, this metaliterary concern is symptomatic of the letter form in general. As Janet Altman observes:

Epistolary fiction tends to flourish at those moments when novelists most openly reflect upon the relation between story-telling and intersubjective communication and begin to question the way in which writing reflects, betrays, or constitutes the relations between self, other, and experience. At those crisis moments the letter form foregrounds—in its very consciousness of itself as a form—questions that are basic to all literature.[20]

The *Historia* thematizes this writer/reader relationship inherent in correspondence (its potential and its constraints) with a remarkable degree of sophistication.

Indicative of the metacritical dimension of epistolary fiction in general, and the *Historia* in particular, is the existence of four types of readers, as Rosbottom observes: (1) the inscribed addressee(s) (in this case, Marianus); (2) the nonfictional reader(s) (namely, us); (3) the accidental readers (here they are the students, the old women, and Menelaus); and, underlying them all, (4) the fictional editor who determines the selection, arrangement, and publication of the letters (in this case, Piccolomini).[21]

It is important to note that in the *Historia* we have an additional level of mediation—that of the omniscient narrator. In addition to serving as scribe/redactor (the normative activity of the epistolary editor) Aeneas Sylvius functions *simultaneously* as an obtrusive omniscient narrator. He does not simply transcribe and organize a sequence of letters, he also knows the characters' innermost thoughts. While the role of redactor lends a dimension of empirical verisimilitude to the work, that of omniscient narrator achieves the opposite effect.[22] Like the conflicting lessons of lust and morality that the narrator blatantly juxtaposes, here too he juxtaposes two diametrically opposed narrative perspectives, and he does so for metacritical purposes—to comment on the unique nature of the epistolary author and addressee.

Yet, this paradox of authority, whereby the editorial fiction seeks to present itself as truth, is in fact only one of many paradoxes inherent in the epistolary form. Paradoxically, a letter simultaneously signifies both *absence* and *presence*. There are in fact three kinds of absence that are possible and/or inescapable, namely, spatial, temporal, and psychological distance. Epistolary communication indicates that the letter writer is absent to some degree from his addressee and from the events to which he refers. In addition, epistolary communication always implies a degree of spatial isolation. If there were no spatial distancing, the interlocutors would be engaging in spontaneous dialogue. Likewise, temporal disjunction is a constant of epistolarity, no matter how closely the exchange of letters occurs. Writing, as Ginés de Pasamonte reminds us, can never be simultaneous with the event itself.[23] Despite the temporal and spatial discontinuities, however, epistolary discourse consistently manipulates both space and time in order to overcome these barriers, thus making the communication psychologically relevant (rather than anachronistic) in the moment at which the addressee reads the letter. The letter freezes us in a *present* time that seeks to control the *future* based on *past* information: "Each letter halts us in a present time where the future is uncertain and yet where the characters have attempted to control that future by threats or vows."[24]

The first letter written by Euryalus to Lucretia offers us a clear example of just such explicit analysis of past events in the present in order to shape the future. He tries to guarantee a favorable reading from her (in the future) by citing (in the present) her favorable (visual) semiotic communication (in the past): "Nec durior erga me verbis esto, quam fueras oculis, quibus me colligasti" (Dévay, 14) [Be no crueller to me with your words than you have been with your eyes, with which you bound me to you (Grierson, 27)]. Indeed, such plotting of the future by invoking the authority of the past characterizes each of the five letters by Euryalus to Lucretia whose text we are given either verbatim or in paraphrased form. They all pertain to the illocutionary category of "directives": "illocutionary acts designed to get the addressee to do something, e.g., requesting, commanding, pleading, inviting, daring."[25]

By contrast, the five letters composed by Lucretia to Euryalus are all representatives: "illocutionary acts that undertake to represent a state of affairs, whether past, present, future, or hypothetical, e.g., stating, claiming, hypothesizing, describing, predicting, telling, insisting, suggesting, or swearing that something is the case."[26] More precisely, the epistolary exchange exhibits the following configuration:

L 1 = *Directive*: Euryalus asks Lucretia to save him from death by accepting his love service (Grierson, 26–27).

L 2 = *Representative*: Lucretia explains to Euryalus that she is unmoved by his request: "no love can reach me that is impure" (31).

L 3 = *Directive*: Euryalus asks Lucretia to grant him an interview (32–33).

L 4 = *Representative*: Lucretia indicates that even if she wanted Euryalus to visit, it is impossible: "you had need to be a swallow to find me alone. My house is high, and all its gates are well guarded" (33–34).

L 5 = *Directive*: Euryalus asks that Lucretia return his love: "Say that you love me, and I am happy" (34–36).

L 6 = *Representative*: Lucretia says that to love Euryalus would signal her destruction (since he will not remain in Siena forever) (36–39).

L 7 = *Directive*: Euryalus asks Lucretia to write to him saying that she loves him (39–45).

L 8 = *Representative*: Lucretia writes to Euryalus, explaining that she has capitulated to his love (45–46).

L 9 = *Directive*: Lucretia asks Euryalus to take her with him—invoking the example of the abduction of Helen by Paris (123–24).

L 10 = *Representative*: Euryalus tells Lucretia it is unfeasible to do so (125–28).

Aeneas Sylvius alludes to a number of additional letters, but without including their text. This is so, I would argue, because he elaborates the contents of the letters only when they serve as directives—as devices calculated to eliminate psychological distance (Euryalus' willingness / Lucretia's unwillingness). When it is simply a question of emotional outpourings, "illocutionary acts that express only the speaker's psychological state—i.e., 'expressives,' "[27] Aeneas Sylvius does not rely on the epistolary medium, but on dialogue.[28] Once both he and she have articulated the same desire, trysts arranged by faithful servants replace the mediated discourse of the letter. In this way the epistolary presence/absence paradox is resolved, and the need for letters is eliminated. Mediated *words* (theory) are replaced by unmediated *action* (praxis)—which might or might not correspond to them.

The relationship between words and deeds is thematized by Aeneas Sylvius throughout his text. With his first letter, Euryalus attempts to guarantee a favorable response from Lucretia by invoking her action, the "oculorum radii" (Dévay, 13) [glances of (her) eyes (Grierson, 27)], which have totally subdued him and made him Lucretia's prisoner. Similarly, he recalls his own action as observed by Lucretia: "te puto latere mei ardorem laesi pectoris. Index tibi potuit esse vultus meus, saepe lachrimis madidus et quae, vidente te, emisi suspira (13) [I think the passion in my wounded breast has not escaped you. For you must have read it in my face (26)]. In order to convince her that his words are coterminous with his actions, Euryalus sends his beloved a jewel—the token of his affection. He further elaborates the equation of words and deeds by endowing Lucretia's words with the power of action, since her words (her attitude toward him) will determine whether he lives or dies.

The bawd who delivers the first letter to Lucretia is also concerned with the link between word and deed. When Lucretia threatens to tear her letter to pieces, we are informed that: "Timuisset alia mulier; sed haec matronarum noverat mores et intra se ait: 'nunc vis maxime, quia te nolle ostendis'" (15) [The woman had expected worse than this, but she knew the ways of married ladies, and said to herself, "Yes, now you want him most, because you pretend to be most unwilling" (29)]. Her assessment of Lucretia's affect is accurate indeed. Fearing that the bawd will read her passion correctly, Lucretia tears up the letter and throws it into the ashes. However, as soon as the messenger has left, Lucretia retrieves the fragments of the letter, piecing them together so that she can read it. Not only is she not insulted by the letter, but "postquam milies egit, miliesque deosculata est, tandemque involutum sindone: inter pretiosa iocalia collocavit" (15) [When she had (read) it a thousand times, and kissed it as often, at last she wrapt it in a piece of muslin, and laid it among her most precious jewels (30–31)]. Thus we see the letter functioning both as metaphor and metonym.

Additional actions that contradict the words they accompany provide further insight into the *Historia*'s sustained interest in this phenomenon. The fact that Lucretia answers Euryalus' letter is a signal that she is keenly interested. Were she not, she would have left his letter unanswered, as the narrator reminds us: "hunc in modum dictatatam epistolam misit (15) [it showed him by what means their correspondence might be continued (31)]. Even more incriminating evidence exists in the fact that Lucretia does not return the jewels Euryalus included with that first letter, or with his successive letters either. In her second letter of reply, Lucretia gives a very transparent reason for having kept the jewels: "Munera tua suscepi, quia oblectavit me opus illorum. Sed, ne quid tuum gratis apud me sit, neve hoc pignus videatur amoris: remitto ad te annulum, quem matri meae vir dedit, ut apud te, quasi pretium sit venditorum iocalium" (16) [I will keep your gifts, because I like their workmanship, but that I may not take anything from you, and lest this should seem a pledge of love, I send in return a little ring, which her husband gave to my mother, and you must accept it as the price of the jewels you have sold to me (34)]. Although she continues to protest, Lucretia not only accepts the jewels she is sent, but in addition she herself sends jewels to Euryalus—hence, a total contradiction of words and deeds. Because this contradiction is quite apparent to Euryalus, he reinforces Lucretia's passion by reiterating that her words have total control over his actions as well as his words : "Facilius tu me verbis interimeres, quam alius quivis gladio" (17) [It would be easier for you to kill me with your words, than for anyone else with the sword (35–36)]. It is highly significant that shortly thereafter Euryalus endows Lucretia's words with a far weaker (in fact, precisely opposite) potential: "Verba sunt tantum, quibus rogas, ut amare desistam" (18) [Those are but words, with which you ask me to stop loving you (40–41)].

The description of Lucretia's capitulation to her love reveals a further dimension of the relationship between word and deed. Relying upon an uncharacteristically lengthy simile, Aeneas Sylvius employs the powerful images of martial destruction to indicate her act of surrender to Euryalus' words: "Vt turris, quae fracta interius, inexpugnabilis videtur exterius si vero aries admotus fuerit, mox confringitur: sic, Euryali verbis Lucretia victa est" (20) [As a tower, that is destroyed within, looks outwardly impregnable, but when the battering-ram is turned against it, straightaway collapses, so Lucretia fell to Euryalus' words (45)]. Word and deed are invoked immediately thereafter by the smitten Lucretia as she implores Euryalus to make his actions conform to his words: "Vide, ut serves, quae scripsisti" (21) [See that you observe what you have written (45)].

A different perspective on the word/deed dichotomy is offered by Pacorus, a Hungarian soldier who mistakenly interprets an action by Lucretia (a neighborly smile) as a smile of amorous inclination. Because of what he perceives to be her meaningful action he expresses his love in words, more precisely in the form of a love letter which he conceals in the stem of a violet. However, since Lucretia is totally absorbed by her interest in Euryalus, she carelessly hands the letter-laden flower to one of the girls near her, who in turn hands it to a pair of mischievous students. Realizing that the violet in fact conceals a purloined letter (in the etymological sense of "diverted" rather than "stolen"),[29] they deliver the love poem to Menelaus, who is predictably irate. Had Lucretia been interested in Pacorus of course, she would never have given the flower away. She gets into the same kind of trouble when she lets a snowball (containing a love letter) that Pacorus throws through her window fall out of her hands and roll to the fire, where Menelaus reads it. Pacorus' two aborted attempts to court Lucretia illustrate a further epistolary paradox, namely that a letter has both a dependent and an independent status. As *independent text* his letter is successful in conveying his intentions, which are all too clear to the accidental reader for whom the letter is not intended (i.e., Lucretia's husband). Yet as *dependent context* it is unsuccessful—Pacorus' words literally do not reach her because he has misinterpreted her action.[30]

The structurally significant midpoint of the text, the moment when Euryalus and Lucretia consummate their love, again refers explicitly to the relative distance separating words and deeds. At that moment, Euryalus, we are told, "remque verbis iungebat" (29) [matched his actions to his words (70)]. His discourse of desire is finally matched by physical fulfillment. Although Euryalus will enjoy Lucretia again, his amorous discourse will be juxtaposed to discourses of misogyny and cowardice. Here too, then, the gap separating word and deed is dramatized. As he hides under the bed to avoid discovery by Menelaus, we are told of his cowardly nature:

> His exterritus vocibus Euryalus, exsangvis fit, iamque Lucretiam odisse incipit, atque inter se: "Heu me fatuum!" inquit, "quis me huc venire compulit, nisi levitas mea? Nunc deprehensus sum; nunc infamis fio; nunc Cesaris gratiam perdo. Quid gratiam? utinam mihi vita supersit! . . . O me vanum et stultorum omnium stultissimum! . . . Hinc si me deorum quispiam traxerit: nusquam me rursus amor illaqueabit. . . . Non me amavit Lucretia, sed quasi cervum, in casses voluit deprehendere." (27)

> Terrified at this, Euryalus felt faint, and promptly began to hate Lucretia, saying to himself: "Dolt that I am! What brought me to this pass but my own folly? Now I am done for, now I'll be made a laughing-stock, and lose the Emperor's friendship. His friendship? I'll be lucky if I keep my life. . . . Oh emptiest and stupidest of all stupid mortals! . . . Oh, if some God were to get me out of this, never again would I be trapped by love. . . . Lucretia never loved me, but wished to catch me, like a stag, in her toils." (64–66)

The irony of these words is readily apparent in that Lucretia loved him all along, whereas it was he, in fact, who is guilty of having ensnared her. That he is exercising nothing more than male lust is reinforced by his rather unromantic equine analogy: "Tu meum equum ascendes Menelae, ego tuam uxorem equitabo" (43) [You will mount my horse, Menelaus, but I will mount your wife (112)].

As Euryalus, disguised as a laborer, leaves Lucretia after this tryst to return to his quarters, his thoughts are—rather surprisingly—again focused not on his amorous ecstasy, but on his job: " 'O! si nunc,' inquit, 'se obvium mihi daret Caesar, meque agnosceret, quam illi habitus hic suspicionem faceret, quam me rideret!' " (30) [If the Emperor were to meet me now and recognize me, what suspicions this dress would arouse in him, how he would laugh at me. I would be a fable for everyone and a laughing-stock for him (73)]. His fear of being discovered, as he speaks to Nisus, Achates, and Palinurus (three prominent figures from the *Aeneid*),[31] provokes him to misogyny:

> "Heu me stultum!" inquit, "feminae meum tradidi caput. Non sic me pater admonuit, dum me nullius feminae fidem sequi debere docebat? Ille feminam dicebat animal esse indomitum, infidum, mutabile, crudele, mille passionibus deditum. Ego, paternae immemor disciplinae, vitam meam mulierculae tradidi. Quid si me, oneratum frumento, aliquis agnovisset? Quod dedecus, quaenam infamia mihi et meis posteris evenisset! Alienum me Caesar fecisset,

tamquam levem et insanum punivisset; potuissem haec contemnere." (30–31)

"Alas," cried he, "fool that I am, I have put my fate into a woman's hands. This is not what my father advised, when he taught me never to put faith in any woman. He used to say, woman is an unmanageable animal, false, fickle, and cruel, the slave of a thousand passions. And now, forgetful of my father's precepts, I have given my life to a mere woman. What if someone had recognized me carrying corn? What disgrace, what infamy for me and my posterity! The Emperor would have dismissed me, and punished me for my levity and madness." (74–75)

This diatribe is especially incongruous given that Euryalus is no longer in any danger of being discovered, having returned safely to his house, put on his accustomed attire, and explained to his associates that he has triumphed over Lucretia.

The Virgilian subtext clearly serves to diminish his dignity still further by once again underscoring the word/deed dichotomy. Retrospective fear of ridicule felt by a lover disguised as a bumpkin is wholly undignified and unthinkable in the context of the *Aeneid*. The fact that Euryalus is uttering the discourse of a cowardly lover to Nisus, the person who contracted the notorious bawd to deliver the first love letter, is even more striking. For we recall the mortal self-sacrifice of these two warriors in the *Aeneid*, Book 9 as Nisus swears fidelity to Euryalus, saying: "nulla meis sine te quaeretur gloria rebus; / seu pacem seu bella geram, tibi maxima rerum / verborumque fides" (Fairclough, 9.278–80) [I shall seek no glory / in any thing without you; whether I/ find peace or war, always my final trust / for act and word shall be Euryalus (Mandlebaum, 9.370–73)]. The mortally wounded Nisus avenges his friend's death, being physically united with him as he expires: "super exanimum sese proiecit amicum / confossus placidaque ibi demum morte quievit" (9.444–45) [pierced, he cast himself upon his lifeless / friend; there, at last, he found his rest in death (9.590–91)].

Underscoring this incorruptible bond of friendship, the poet eulogizes them as follows: "Fortunati ambo! si quid mea carmina possunt, / nulla dies umquam memori vos eximet aevo, / dum domus Aeneae Capitoli immobile saxum / accolet imperiumque pater Romanus habebit. / Victores praeda Rutuli spoliisque potiti" (9.446–50) [Fortunate pair! If there be any power / within my poetry, no day shall ever / erase you from the memory of time; / nor while Aeneas' children live beside / the Capitol's unchanging rock nor while / a Roman father still holds sovereignty (9.592–97)]. Word and action were consubstantial for these two lovers, whereas for Lucretia and Euryalus they are not.

The unforgettable final image of the two Virgilian friends dying in each other's arms is recalled by Aeneas Sylvius during the third visit of Euryalus and Lucretia. When she faints "sive timore nimio, sive gaudio, exanimata" (Dévay, 45) [with too much fear or too much joy (Grierson, 116)], he is "exterritus" (45) [terrified (116)], and thinks of running away: " 'Si abeo,' inquit, 'mortis sum reus qui feminam in tanto discrimine deseruerim. Si maneo, interveniet Agamemnon, aut alius ex familia et ego peribo. . . . Heu! quam optabilius erat, in huius me potius gremio, quam istam in meo sinu defecisse!' " (45) ["If I go away now, I deserve to die, leaving a woman in such a plight. But if I stay, Agamemnon will turn up, or some other member of her household, and I'll be killed. . . . Alas, how much more gladly had I died on her breast, than have her die on mine!" (117)].

Despite these words, Euryalus actually has no intention of "dying on her breast," as the *Historia*'s denouement unambiguously demonstrates; his words and actions diverge markedly. Letter 10 consists of Euryalus' response to Lucretia's request that he carry her off as Paris did Menelaus's wife, Helen. Euryalus refuses to abduct this latter-day wife of Menelaus for several reasons (recalling the legalistically argued series of excuses advanced by Aeneas to Dido as he is about to depart): First, because it would reflect badly on her honor: "Quid de te diceretur? Quis rumor exiret in orbem! 'Ecce Lucretiam, quae Bruti coniuge castior, Penelopeque melior dicebatur: iam moechum sequitur, immemor domus, parentum et patriae. Non Lucretia, sed Hippia est, vel Iasonem secuta Medea!' " (49) [What will people say of you, what tale will be spread abroad? "See Lucretia, who they said was more pure than Brutus' wife, truer than Penelope; now she is off with her seducer, abandoning her home, her kinsmen, and her country. She is no Lucretia, but Hippia, or Medea with her Jason" (126)]. Secondly, he would be destroying his own honor (Dévay, 49). In addition, were he to cease being the Emperor's servant, he would be acting in a fiscally irresponsible manner: "Ego Caesari servio: is me virum fecit potentem, divitem; nec ab eo recedere possum, sine mei status ruina" (49) [I am the Emperor's servant, and he has made me powerful and rich. To leave him would be my ruin (127)]. Moreover, were Euryalus to abandon his lucrative employment, he would not have the money to support her; and, as a final argument, he says: "Si curiam sequerer, nulla quies esset. Omni die castra movemus" (49) [If I follow the court, you will have no peace. Here today, there tomorrow (127)]. Euryalus thus clearly puts his job prospects and quotidian considerations before his relationship. Consequently, he counsels Lucretia to adopt this same attitude: "Nec furori magis, quam tibi blandiaris" (49) [Do not indulge your passion more than you would yourself (128)].

Lucretia, however, does just that as she has all along; she keeps her word by acting accordingly. She is as faithful as the legendary Lucretia, wife of

Tarquinius Collatinus, who upon being raped took her own life. The *Historia*'s Lucretia, twice alluded to her Roman namesake (Dévay, 10, 49), is, on the one hand, an ironic inversion of her predecessor, since she commits adultery, yet maintains fidelity to her lover, and dies for him. However, the relationship of the Renaissance heroine to her ancient paradigm is not one of simple inversion, since they both altruistically died for what they believed. Thus, they both conform to the exemplary mode of mythic behavior that the latter-day Euryalus, Nisus, Menelaus, and Agamemnon are incapable of doing. The transcendence of the word, the consubstantiality of word and action that defines the epic world, is inoperative in its fifteenth-century transformation.

So that we do not miss the point of the phenomenological (and actantial) chasm separating Lucretia from Euryalus, Aeneas Sylvius ends his narrative by closing the letter to Marianus in an ironically contradictory manner. Whereas the beginning of the letter to Marianus claims that once Lucretia had died, Euryalus "vero posthac nunquam verae laetitiae particeps fuerit" (3) [from that time, never had any part in true happiness (xx–xxi)], the end abruptly informs us that he:

> nec consolationem admisit, nisi postquam Caesar, ex ducali sangvine, virginem sibi, tum formosam, tum castissimam, atque prudentem, matrimonio iunxit. Habes amoris exitum, Mariane mi amantissime, non ficti, neque, felicis; quem, qui legerint, periculum ex aliis faciant, quod sibi ex usu fiet; nec amatorium poculum bibere studeant, quod longe plus alöes habet, quam mellis. Vale. (52)

> would not be consoled, until the Emperor wedded him to a maiden of ducal rank, most beautiful, and chaste, and virtuous. And now, my dearest Marianus, you have heard the outcome of this love, a true story and an unhappy one. And may all who read it take a lesson from others that will be useful to themselves: let them beware to drink the cup of love, that holds far more of bitter than of sweet. Farewell. (135)

Since Euryalus fares very well after the unfortunate interlude with Lucretia, the cup of love does not seem bitter because he successfully compromised his words of undying fidelity in order to further his career. The only one for whom the experience of love may be construed as bitter is Lucretia, because of the integrity she demonstrated in remaining faithful to the ideal she had articulated at the beginning of their involvement. Thus, if any lesson at all is to be gleaned from the *Historia*, it appears to be that steadfastness to one's ideal leads to lamentable consequences—a cynical realization indeed.

If we return to the initial consideration of Lucretia in light of Fiammetta, we see that they are in fact worlds apart. For unlike Fiammetta's pathological vacillation, Lucretia possesses the resolve necessary to act in accord with her words, to function as mythic absolute. Lucretia's tragedy is that she anachronistically resides in a novelistic world. Fiammetta's problem, on the other hand, is that she is incapable of functioning either as a (romance) mythic absolute or as a novelistic individual. It is, significantly, the antagonistic tension of these two environments which generates the *novela sentimental*.

# PART TWO
## THE ALLEGORICAL PARADOX

# FIVE

## FAILED EROTICISM

## (*SIERVO LIBRE DE AMOR*)

THE HEROIDEAN letter structure in Juan Rodríguez's writing is
by no means confined to his *Bursario*. For his *Siervo libre de amor*
which initiates the *novela sentimental* genre also consists of a lover's
extended epistolary monologue.[1] Speaking of this formal affiliation, Olga
Impey aptly remarks: "In the huge 'novelesque' letter that is the *Siervo libre*,
those readers familiar with Ovid's *Heroides* will easily recognize various
Ovidian reminiscences and epistolary devices."[2] Beyond the retrospective
psychological narrative which the *Siervo libre* and *Heroides* have in common,
there is in both works a preponderance of epistolary monologue: "the entire romance can be viewed as Juan Rodríguez's epistolary monologue, a
monologue which in turn contains other shorter monologues, both spoken
and written down in letters."[3] At the same time there are, however, some
essential differences between the two texts.

The extended letter that forms the *Siervo libre* results from a *demanda*—
the request made by Gonçalo de Medina (a judge from Mondoñedo who
occupied the post of Rodríguez when the latter entered the Franciscan
order): "La muy agria relación del caso, los pasados tristes y alegres actos
y esquivas contemplaciones, e ynotos e varios pensamientos qu[e] el
tiempo no consentía poner en efecto por escripturas"[4] [The very difficult
narration of the relationship, the sad events, joyful actions, and hidden
thoughts that at the time you were not able to write down].

By this narrative configuration Rodríguez introduces a significant innovation in terms of the accustomed Ovidian speech situation. That is, unlike
the *Heroides*, this letter is addressed not to a lover but to a male confidant
and it narrates completed actions and emotions in the past. At the time of
writing it is not attempting to persuade a beloved or to elegiacally lament
the writer's fate. For, as we shall witness, the lover ultimately rejects the
accustomed discourse of desire entirely, and in so doing, Rodríguez offers
a radical remotivation of the speech situation initiated by the *Heroides*.

Literary historians accord the *Siervo libre* a privileged status—that of
being the first manifestation of the *novela sentimental*. Indicative of this
sentiment is César Hernández Alonso's judgment.[5]

Despite this consensus as to the *Siervo libre*'s originary nature, semantically it remains a very controversial subject. It is viewed by many as an

extended glorification of Rodríguez (both qua poet and qua protagonist) as a martyr of love on the model of Maçías.[6] Others understand it as a didactic *tratado* designed to illustrate the superiority of the intellect as against the fickleness of fortune (here synonymous with courtly love)—an interpretation that seems to be suggested by the work's full title: *The Servant Free[d] of Love*.[7] A third vein of interpretation finds the *Siervo libre* to be an ultimately ambiguous text (very likely unfinished), in which it is difficult, in the final analysis, to determine whether it is love or the intellect that is being valorized.[8]

With regard to the *Siervo libre*'s literary antecedents, there are those readers who see Boccaccio's *Elegia* as the obvious precursor, while others disagree entirely with this subtextual postulation.[9] It is only recently, with the important work of Gregory Andrachuk, that the strategic importance of Dante's *Commedia* for interpretation of the *Siervo libre* has begun to be recognized.[10]

The primary object of this chapter is to continue this promising line of inquiry by demonstrating the sustained presence and function of a Dantean subtext throughout the *Siervo libre*. More precisely, that this text makes extensive poetic use of certain thematic concerns and narrative configurations (particularly, that of poet/lover/beloved) established by Dante in the *Vita Nuova* and elaborated in the *Commedia*. For as we shall see, Rodríguez establishes Dante as his only vernacular *auctor* in order to redeploy him radically, to "unravel" Dante's literary tapestry, as it were, in order to illustrate not the potential of human love as emblematized by Beatrice, but rather the limitations of human love. Moreover, this unraveling is achieved by questioning the discourse of desire in an eminently heroidean manner—exposing its novelistic (polysemous) nature and its ultimate inefficacy.

Inscribed within this global epistle to Gonçalo de Medina is a first-person account of a lover who refers to himself with a considerable degree of verbal ambiguity as the "Siervo libre de amor" (Prieto, 65) [the Servant free(d) of love *or* the Free Servant of Love]. This Siervo travels through an elaborate allegorical landscape that is characterized most prominently by three paths, each with its corresponding mythological deity and arboreal emblem. The ample path of Venus (represented by the myrtle tree) signifies "el tiempo que bien amó y fue amado" (65) [the time when he loved well and was loved]. The path of Hercules (with its symbolic poplar tree), more narrow than the first path, indicates "el tiempo que bien amó y fue desamado" (66) [the time when he loved well but was unloved]. It points downward and represents despair. The third path—the most narrow of all—is that of Minerva (whose emblem is the olive tree), representing "el tiempo que no amó ni fue amado" (66) [the time when he did not love, nor was he loved]. These three paths and the affective states they represent correspond to the tripartite structure of the work.

Close reading of the *Siervo libre* reveals that a series of verbal reminiscences from Dante (strategically situated at the beginning of the text) are intended to serve as an "opening signal" for the Dantean subtext operative throughout the work to follow, which is essential to its interpretation.

Intertextual references to the *Commedia* found at the outset of the *Siervo libre* are in fact striking. In each case we have a *selva oscura* that is both a physical landscape and a metaphor for the protagonist's psychological quandary (his spiritual and emotional disorientation); each protagonist undertakes his journey in order to achieve domination over his passions; both journeys begin with a visit to the Elysian Fields in which the protagonist functions as a "new Aeneas" of sorts. Furthermore, both works involve a tripartite pilgrimage, a progression from Passion to Free Will to Intellect. At the same time, the *Siervo libre* and the *Commedia* are both literary autobiographies in which there exists a tension or oscillation between the time of writing and the time of the narrative—the narrative strategy first employed by St. Augustine in the *Confessions* for the purpose of recounting his conversion to Christianity. Significantly, both Dante and Rodríguez are writing about conversion. The density of such intertextual resonances becomes increasingly apparent as the works unfold; so does their particular import for Rodríguez del Padrón's creative *translatio* of Dante.

The explicit naming of Dante in the *Siervo libre*'s prologue serves to orient our reading and our understanding as to Rodriguéz's treatment of his literary progenitor. What is at issue in this passage is the function of pagan antiquity in the *Commedia*, specifically its Virgilian resonances. Dante the poet in the *Inferno* (Cantos 1 and 2) establishes a program of associations whereby Dante operates as a new (Christian) Aeneas,[11] in addition to valorizing throughout the poem the virtuous pagans (chief among them Virgil), and their potential as Christian analogues. Rodríguez boldly rejects this fundamental Dantean attitude by divesting pagan antiquity of the Christian context that Dante had bestowed upon it.

It is precisely the rejection or inversion of the Dantean construct that allows the second author to make poetic capital out of it. Indeed, Rodríguez is quite unequivocal in his devaluation of this antique subject matter, as witnessed by the remarks he makes to Gonçalo de Medina, to whom the *Siervo libre* is addressed:

como tu seas otro Virgilio e segundo Tulio Ciçero, príncipes de la eloquençia, non confiando del mi symple ingenio, seguiré el estilo, a ty agradable, de los antiguos Omero, Publio Maro, Perseo, Seneca, Ovidio, Platon, Lucano, Salustrio, Estaçio, Terençio, Juuenal, Oraçio, *Dante*, Marco Tulio Ciceryo, Valerio, Lucio, Eneo, Rycardo, Prinio, Quintiliano, trayendo fiçiones, según los gentiles nobles, de dioses dañados e deesas, *no porque yo sea honrrador de aquellos, mas pregonero del su grand error, y syeruo yndigno del alto Jhesús.*[12] (67)

given that you may be another Virgil, and a second Cicero [princes of elo-
quence], not trusting my simple wit, I will emulate the style of the ancients
which you find so pleasing: Homer, Publius Marus, Perseus, Seneca, Ovid,
Plato, Lucan, Sallust, Statius, Terrence, Juvenal, Horace, *Dante*, Marcus Tuy-
lius Cicero, Valerius, Lucilius, Ennius, Ricardus, Priscian, and Quintillian. I
will offer fictions in the manner of the noble pagans, of betrayed gods and
goddesses, *not because I wish to honor them, but rather as a proclaimer of their
great error, and as a humble servant of almighty God.*

Rodríguez's explicit attitude toward antiquity, we see, is quite unambiguous. In addition, his inclusion of Dante (the only vernacular poet
named in this catalogue of pagan authors) further underscores his definitive negation of Dante's extensive program of "virtuous pagans" in the
*Commedia.*[13]

Entendimiento, the protagonist's guide, explicitly refers to him as a "second Aeneas"—but one who functions as an inversion of Dante's "new
[Christian] Aeneas." In this context, the guide asks his charge the following rhetorical question:

Piensas asy entrar esentamente en la casa de Pluton, dios infernal, según hizo
Eneas, hyjo de la deesa, por cuyo mandado la sabia Sebilla le aconpañava, e
por más que le segurava, temiendo las penas e pauorosos monstruos que an-
dauan por las Astigias, no padesçió que la fuerte espada no tendiese, segun
dize Vergilio, *Eneydas*, contra las sombras infernales, que son la aborrida
muerte, que passan las ánimas de la presente a la otra vida? (78–79)

Are you intending to enter the house of Pluto, the infernal god, as Aeneas
did? He, the son of the goddess by whose decree the wise Sibyl accompanied
him, and despite her assurances, fearing the torments and horrifying monsters
who inhabit the Styx and carry souls from this life to the next, did not shrink
from using his sword, according to Virgil in the *Aeneid*, against the infernal
shades which represent hateful death?

This "new [Spanish] Aeneas" intends to journey to the Elysian Fields—
meaning death by suicide—for he sees it as the only way to deal with the
shattering experience of his unrequited love. Hence he acts as a profoundly
un-Christian Aeneas. Here, then, we see Rodríguez exploiting Dante for
a substantially different (indeed diametrically opposed) poetic purpose.
What was one of Dante's fundamental structuring principles (the redeployment of pagan matter in Christian terms) is undone, rewritten by the *Siervo
libre*.

Finally, the pilgrim is willfully abandoned by his guide, Entendimiento,
who refuses to accompany him on his journey to Hell:

no es mi voluntat de pasar, ni seguir tu dañada compañía; e solo más quiere prender la angosta vía, que demuestra la verde oliua, avnque muy áspera sea, que mal acompañado yr contygo a la perdiçión. (81)

it is not my will to proceed any further, or to continue in your misguided company. I prefer to follow the narrow path alone, the path of the green olive tree, although it is an arduous path, rather than going to perdition in your bad company.

It is difficult to imagine a guide more different from Dante's Virgil than this one.

If we place the *Siervo libre* next to the *Vita Nuova*, further important correspondences become visible. Reflecting on the relationship of the two male protagonists to their respective ladies—both of which resulted in the writing of the poetic texts under consideration—we see that they are fundamentally (and symetrically) opposed. Dante, as we learn in the *Vita Nuova* (chap. 37–38), was overtaken by love for a *donna gentile* whom he first noticed gazing at him from a window. As described in this work, his love for her prevailed for a time over his love for Beatrice. Hence he rejected the worthy woman for the unworthy. He moves from a state of false perception to that of true perception (a process redescribed most elaborately in the *Commedia*), in which he must (re)learn to love (properly) his worthy woman (Beatrice)—the emissary of God. Because of his psychological *selva oscura* the pilgrim must descend into Hell—the place inhabited by "those who have lost the good of intellect" (i.e., knowledge of God).[14]

In the *Siervo libre* the configuration, significantly, is reversed: the protagonist has been rejected by an *un*worthy *señora*. This false *señora* does not lead the protagonist to God—indeed, she is the path away from Him. Furthermore, Beatrice is one and the same *donna* who was initially perceived falsely and thereafter perceived rightly by the pilgrim. In contradistinction to this progression, Rodríguez contrasts two different women: a false *señora* (the anonymous earthly woman who has rejected the protagonist) and a true one, namely Synderesis—the allegorical representation of Wisdom, the only one who can lead the protagonist to God.[15]

A significant split in the Dantean configuration is thus effected by the *Siervo libre*. For while Dante is a (divine) love poet in whose discourse the pilgrim is inscribed or contained, Rodríguez (el Siervo) is a pilgrim in whose discourse a (human) love poet is inscribed—and ultimately rejected. Consequently, while Dante's configuration consists largely of poetic *fusion* (love for Beatrice which leads directly to love of God, i.e., religious truth arrived at through the mediation of poetry), Rodríguez's configuration represents an *unraveling* of it (and of the conflation of amatory and religious imagery operative in the conventional discourse of courtly love—the starting point for both poets).

The second part of the text, including the intercalated tale of the two lovers (occupying virtually half of the entire *Siervo libre*), illustrates both the love/religion conflation essential to the traditional courtly love idiom and Rodríguez's unraveling of it.[16] Having been rejected by his lady, we find the Siervo at the end of the first part, withdrawing to "[el] templo de la grand soledat, en compañía de la triste amargura, saçerdotissa de aquélla" (Prieto, 75) [the temple of great solitude, in the company of Bitter Sadness, the goddess of that temple]. Such a profoundly distressing sight is the Siervo, that he literally disorients the natural world. When he seeks the shade of the myrtle tree, representative of Venus, it immediately sheds its leaves, the songbirds replace their sweet melodies with screeching (*gritos*) and dirges (76). The effect of his suffering is so overpowering that it even turns the chestnut-colored horse black (77). So marked is his suffering that it even succeeds in silencing the birds, affecting even the purportedly insensitive plant world: "las mudas aves, criaturas, plantas non sentibles, en tal mudança de su proprio ser, por causa mía" (77) [the mute birds, other animals, insentient plants, altered from their natural state because of me]. This reaction, an extreme example of the "pathetic fallacy," depresses him even further, leading him to the downward path of despair, consecrated to Hercules. It is no accident that this doleful transformation of the natural world reenacts its response to the death of Orpheus (*Met.* 11.44–47):

> Te maestae volucres, Orpheu, te turba ferarum,
> te rigidi silices, te carmina saepe secutae
> fleverunt silvae, positis te frondibus arbor
> tonsa comas luxit.[17]

The mourning birds wept for thee, Orpheus, the throng of beasts, the flinty rocks, and the trees which had so often gathered to thy songs; yes, the trees shed their leaves as if so tearing their hair in grief for thee.

This extreme reaction by the flora and fauna is occasioned by the (physical) death of Orpheus which is precipitated by his (metaphorical) death as a lyric poet, at the death of Eurydice. He can no longer sing of love for women. In like fashion, the response of the natural world to the Siervo here prefigures his own metaphorical death as lyric poet. What must be stressed, however, is the object of the poets' songs after they shed their devotion to their respective ladies. While Orpheus's heterosexual love turns to homoeroticism, the Siervo's earthly love becomes religious devotion.

As he is contemplating suicide, the Siervo falls asleep, at which point he experiences a dream containing a love story—the *Estoria de dos amadores*—of the faithful Ardanlier and Lyessa. Ardanlier and Lyessa are in love, yet he becomes the object of Yrena's affections as well. The second woman swears eternal fidelity to Ardanlier, yet he remains faithful to Lyessa. The complication in the idealistic love of Ardanlier and Lyessa is not, as we might expect, a love triangle, but the young knight's father, King Croes. Since their parents fear the blossoming of the children's adolescent passion, the lovers flee to the woods, where they build "vn secreto palaçio, rrico y fuerte, bien obrado; y a la entrada, vn verde, fresco jardýn de muy olorosas yeruas, lyndos, frutíferos árbores" (Prieto, 88) [a secret palace, well made and strong; at the entrance (there was) a verdant garden full of fragrant grasses (and) graceful fruit trees].

This story is doubly significant, for in addition to advancing the pilgrim's own affective development, this intercalated novella relies heavily on the *Heroides*. As Impey has observed:

> Just as the lives of Hypermnestra and Lynceus are threatened by Danaos, so too are those of Lyessa and Ardanlier by Croes, the latter's father. In much the same way as Paris and Oenone before them, Ardanlier and Lyessa take refuge in the woods and live in happy solitude for many years; finally, the irate Croes locates Lyessa, who, according to him, should be put to death. Lyessa's plea for mercy, the reasons she advances why her life should be spared, as well as her death by the sword, are inspired either by the text of Dido's epistle or by its Alfonsine adaptation. Whereas in *Heroides* VII Dido tries to move Aeneas to pity and make him stay in Carthage by introducing the idea of a hypothetical son, in Alfonso's version the possibility of having a son becomes more than a probability, a solution adopted by Juan Rodríguez—witness Lyessa's words (89–90). Some of the most notable topoi occurring in the letter that Ardanlier sends to Yrena after Lyessa's death (the letter is stained with his blood, and, like Dido, [his] suicide by falling on a sword . . . are certainly Ovidian). The epitaph carved on the tomb of Lyessa and Ardanlier is probably inspired by the funerary inscriptions that conclude so many of Ovid's *Heroides*.[18]

The epitaph inscribed upon the tombs of the lovers reveals the (highly literary) dialectic tension generated by Rodríguez between the amorous and religious registers. More precisely, the sepulchral inscription reads as follows:

EXEMPLO Y PERPETUA MEMBRANÇA
CON GRAND DOLOR,
SEA A VOS, AMADORES
LA CRUEL MUERTE DE LOS MUY LEALES
ARDANLIER Y LYES[S]A,
FALLECIDOS POR BIEN AMAR.
VERSOS DE LAS SEPULTURAS

REYNANTE SATURNO EN LA MAYOR ESPERA,
MARES CON VENUS JUNTO EN LA SEGUNDA ZONA,
DECLINANTE ZODÝACO A LA PARTE HAUSTRAL;
COMBURO PASANDO EL PUNTO DE LIBRA;
EL SOL QUE TOCAVA LA VISA DEL POLO.
CUYOS ENTEROS CUERPOS EN TESTIMONIO DE LAS OBRAS
PERSEVERAMOS LAS DOS RYCAS TUMBAS, FASTA EL
PAUOROSO DÍA QUE A LOS GRANDES BRAMIDOS
DE LOS QUATRO ANIMALES DESPIERTEN
DEL GRAND SUEÑO, E SUS MUY PURIFICAS ANIMAS
POSEAN PERDURABLE FOLGANÇA (102)

May the cruel deaths of the faithful Ardanlier and Lyessa (who die because they loved well) serve as a perpetual example to you, O lovers. They died when Saturn was ruling in the major sphere, Mars and Venus were together in the second zone, as the zodiac was declining; the path of the celestial sphere being in Libra and the sun positioned toward the pole. We preserve their bodies in two richly ornamented tombs as a testimony to their deeds until the terrifying day when to the loud roaring of the four beasts they will awaken from the great sleep, and their purified souls will enjoy eternal rest.

What Rodríguez effects in this epitaph is a subversion of our "generic expectations." That is, we are led to expect a final (pagan) apotheosis of the lovers, yet our attention is abruptly shifted from such a glorification of human love to a concern with the (Christian) Day of Judgment instead: "EL PAUOROSO DÍA QUE A LOS GRANDES BRAMIDOS DE LOS QUATRO ANI-MALES DESPIERTEN DEL GRAND SUEÑO, E SUS MUY PURIFICAS ANIMAS PO-SEAN PERDURABLE FOLGANÇA." The four beasts in question are the four beasts of the Apocalypse, referred to in Rev. 4:4–6 and Ezek. 1:1–14. Christian salvation is the one fate that we do not expect the lovers either to seek or to attain; at no point have they, Yrena, or any other of the lovers involved in this intercalated tale shown any concern for (or even awareness of) religion.

The allusion here to the four apocalyptic beasts is quite unexpected. However, the reference is meant to be read as yet another strategically chosen Dantean resonance. For, we remember, it is precisely these beasts who accompany Beatrice when she appears in *Purgatory*.[19] By choosing to include this seminal detail, Rodríguez implicitly, yet boldly, juxtaposes for his readers the sterile, pagan love of Ardanlier and Lyessa with the Christian love of Beatrice. Indeed, the story of these two lovers, including the veneration of and pilgrimage to their tombs by other lovers, is presented as an overt, profane subversion of the cult of Santiago de Compostela.[20]

We are told that the secret dwelling place of Ardanlier and Lyessa is located in "la antyga çibdat Venera, que es en los fynes de la pequeña

Françia, oy llamada Gallizia . . . " (Prieto, 88) [the ancient city of Venera, which is located at the edge of little France, now known as Galicia . . . ]. As Antonio Prieto explains, "Cibdat Venera" clearly refers to Santiago de Compostela: "*Venera* es la concha de los peregrinos. Las alegorías sacroprofanas de las páginas siguientes parecen induzir a ello" (88) ["*Venera* is the pilgrims' shell. The mixture of sacred and profane allegories in the pages that follow the reference point to this meaning"]. Venera, of course, carries with it the added connotation of venereal—pertaining to the cult of Venus, as in the "leyes venéreas" (86). Indeed, the mausoleum of the two lovers takes on the aspect of the holy shrine, with all the mystique and ceremony that Santiago de Compostela implies. People (i.e., lovers) from all parts of the world come to venerate this lovers' "holy city":

> grandes prínçipes affricanos, de Asya y Europa, reyes, duques, condes, caualleros, marqueses y gentiles omnes, lyndas damas de leuante y poniente, meridion y setentryon, con saluo conduto del Rey d[e] España venían en prueva de aquesta aventura: los caualleros, deseando auer gloria de gentileza, fortaleza y de lealtat; las damas, de fé y lealtat, gentileza y grand fermosura, segúnd la conquista les otorgava. (103–4)

> great princes from Africa, Asia and Europe, kings, dukes, counts, marquis, gentlemen, beautiful ladies from east and west, south and north, all undertook this quest with safe passage guaranteed by the King of Spain: the knights wished to distinguish themselves by their courtliness, fortitude and loyalty, the ladies, by their faith and loyalty, courtliness, and great beauty, according to the outcome of their adventure.

Thus, what confronts us is clearly a pilgrimage of love—not religion—to Santiago.[21] The fact that the lovers' *escudo* is a leopard skin is equally revealing, since as Dante indicates in *Inferno* 1.32, it is the emblem of lust.

Further commingling of the sacred and profane occurs as we are told that this secular shrine is the "nuevo templo de la deesa Vesta, do reynava la Deesa de amores" (Prieto, 101) [new temple of the goddess Vesta, where the goddess of love reigned]. We expect the "nueva deesa" to be the Virgin Mary, as Prieto explains in his gloss on this passage: "Juan Rodríguez afirma que el templo de Vesta se edificó sobre el de Venus, quizá con una intención simbólica y probablemente sea una manifestación de la hipérbole sacroprofana fundiendo a Vesta con la Virgen María" (101) [Juan Rodríguez indicates that the temple of Vesta was built over Venus's temple, an affirmation that may carry a symbolic value; moreover, by conflating Vesta and the Virgin Mary, it is probably also an example of the hyperbolic commingling of sacred and profane elements]. For, the sepulchral inscription on the tombs of the two lovers follows directly after the reference to Vesta supplanting Venus. As a result, this epitaph may be seen as an emblematic separation of the amorous and religious registers that are consistently combined in the writing of courtly love lyric.

With the sepulchral inscription Rodríguez establishes an astral (pagan) point of reference for the death of the two lovers who died "POR BIEN AMAR"—a highly charged term in the Spanish Middle Ages. As Brian Dutton explains, *buen amor* was used to designate either "the love of God, and consequently, charity, brotherly love, and the courtly love of the poets" (i.e., *fin' amor*).[22] Thus, while recalling to the reader the mutual loyalty of the two lovers, *bien amar* simultaneously reminds us that they have had no regard for anyone or anything outside of their immediate relationship. In fact, it is this narcissistic self-absorption of the putatively "true love" that results in multiple deaths (those of Ardanlier, Lyessa, and Lamidoras) and great suffering (principally that of Ardanlier's father, but also of the emperor and countless others).

Moreover, this narcissism is strikingly reflected in the speech situation to which it gives rise; that is to say, the characters speak and/or write with a kind of heroidean solipsism whose communicative monologism can be represented as follows:

Croes's speech to Lyessa (89)
Lyessa's speech to Croes (89–90)
Croes's speech to Lamidoras (90)
Ardanlier's speech to Lamidoras (91)
Lamidoras's speech to Ardanlier (92–93)
Ardanlier's letter to Yrena (93–95)
Ardanlier's invocation to the deceased Lyessa (95)
The emperor's letter to Croes (99)

Each of these communications—with the exception of Lyessa's to Croes—is a "representative" rather than a "directive." Lyessa tries (and tragically fails) to convince Croes that he should not kill her, because she was obeying Ardanlier, but even more importantly, because she is pregnant with his son. This revelation has no effect on the monarch; her words are incapable of convincing him. And while his slaying of Lyessa is an unacceptably cruel act, he is driven to this barbarity as a result of the lovers' narcissism. Ardanlier is not merely his only son, but a world-renowned knight who has disappeared for a period of seven years, totally ignoring his responsibilities to the kingdom. Since Croes sees Lyessa as the source of his beloved son's grave misconduct, he not only kills her but, significantly, does not even bother to answer her. Similarly, he rails against Lamidoras, calling him a traitor and having no interest in discussion. Lamidoras offers no reply.

For his part, Ardanlier offers a paradoxically monologic discourse to Lamidoras when he returns. As he raises his sword to kill the old servant, whom he wrongly perceives to have been unfaithful and from whom he expects no reply, Lamidoras states the facts of Lyessa's tragic death. Although Lamidoras is resigned to die "los ojos puestos en tierra, e las manos plegadas colgadas del pecho" (Prieto, 92) [his eyes focused on the ground, his folded arms hanging from his chest], assuming that his words will fail to convince Ardanlier of his innocence, they do in fact. The reason for this communicative success is because Ardanlier and Lamidoras share respect and admiration for Lyessa. It is not the speaker/message that determines the illocutionary force of the words, but the degree of receptivity on the part of the addressee/context.

Ardanlier's letter to Yrena offers another unexpected addressee response. In this case it is an epistolary monologue in which he swears his fidelity, even in death, not to her but to Lyessa: "Piensa lo que creo pensarás sy tu fueras madama Lyessa, según que Yrena, e vieras a mi, requestado de nueva señora, amar, en desprecio y oluidança de ty; creo no lo ouieras en grado, mas con grand rrazón predicarías a mi desleal" (94) [Imagine what you would think if you were Lyessa instead of Yrena, and you would see me approached by a new lady, loving in disregard for you, forgetting you. I think you would not be pleased, but would instead with good reason call me disloyal]. This rejection clearly does not solicit a response. Yet it has as unanticipated effect as did Lamidoras's narrative of Lyessa's death; indeed, the effect of Ardanlier's letter is even more unexpected. For Yrena, rather than becoming irate or at least sullen at this epistolary rejection, interprets it in the opposite manner, as the incentive to change her life, devoting herself henceforth to the preservation of the memory of the true lovers—Ardanlier and Lyessa.

Ardanlier's brief invocation to the deceased Lyessa, before he kills himself, necessarily precludes a response. At the same time, however, its solipsism is diminished by the spiritual union it projects. Finally, the emperor's letter to King Croes similarly precludes a reply, stipulating in addition that "porque entre los enemigos ha de ser breue la fabla y luenga la enemistat, no te hazemos más larga epístola" (99) [because among enemies speech should be short and enmity long, we do not make this letter any more lengthy]. That the emperor has no wish to debate the king is all too apparent by his closing remark that the king's life "antes de muchos días fenesçerá a nuestras muy poderosas manos" (99) [before too many days have passed, will end as a result of our powerful hands]. Given that Ardanlier was the only son who could inherit his father's realm, the destruction of the kingdom is now assured. The tremendously destructive power of love's narcissistic disregard for anything but itself could not be more graphically depicted.

The lovers have consistently ignored their spiritual fate, having given themselves over to the pagan god of love instead of the Christian love of God. They are, as a result, doomed and not intended to enjoy "PERDURA-BLE FOLGANÇA" (102), but its opposite, according to Christian doctrine, when they awaken from the "GRAND SUEÑO" (102). Upon awakening from his own "graue sueño" (107) [deep sleep], the poet-protagonist has realized the error of the two lovers (as well as that of Maçías). As a result, the novella functions in fact as negative exemplum,[23] for when he regains consciousness the protagonist has completely altered his perception. Rather than being a lovesick victim of unrequited passion, he now seeks instead the path of reason very fervently:

> Complida la fabla [fabula—exemplum] que passado entre mí avía, con furia de amor endereçada a las cosas mudas, desperté como de vn graue sueño a grand priesa diziendo: "Buelta, buelta, mi esquyvo pensar, de la deçiente vía de perdiçión quel árbol pópulo, consagrado a Hércules, le demostrava al seguir de los tres caminos en el jardýn de la ventura: e prende la muy agra senda donde era la verde olyva, consagrada a Minerua, quel entendimiento nos enseñava quando partyó ayrado de mí." (107)

> When the exemplum that I had experienced was over, I awoke as if from a profound dream, addressing myself to my mute surroundings, saying adamantly: "Come back, come back, my misguided judgment, from the downward path of perdition which the poplar tree (representing Hercules) showed him when he followed the three paths in the garden of fortune. Take the arduous path of the green olive tree (representing Minerva), which understanding pointed out to us when she angrily abandoned me."

With this reaction by the protagonist, Rodríguez effects a definitive split in the love/religion binome of courtly love, which at the same time constitutes a split in the Dantean configuration of love for Beatrice leading directly to love of God.

Moreover, while Dante may be said to "remotivate" lyric in the *Vita Nuova* and romance in the *Commedia*, Rodríguez fuses a remotivation of both genres into the *Siervo libre*. By "generic remotivation" here I mean simply the exploitation of these two traditionally nondidactic genres for didactic—hence extratextual—purposes, the move from a traditionally representational mode of discourse to an illustrative one. In this case it is the illustration of religious allegory.

This subversion of the Dantean lyric self is further emphasized by a subversion of the medieval topos of birdsong as metaphor for the lyric poet.[24] As we have seen, the protagonist of the *Siervo libre* repeatedly has the effect of silencing the birds of the woods. This is quite an extraordinary situation given the medieval lyric convention of birdsong as metaphor for the poet's song. The *Siervo libre* thus involves an inversion of the stock presentation of the archetypal love poet. It is also important to note that this inversion of the lyric-poet-as-bird metaphor operates consistently throughout the work, since the only time that the birds do sing in the presence of the protagonist is subsequent to his awakening from the dream of Ardanlier and Lyessa. The moment of awakening is, of course, always highly significant in medieval literature: it indicates a new awareness of truth on the part of the character in question and hence may be seen as a metaphor for the moment of conversion.

At this juncture in the *Siervo libre* it is springtime (the canonical season of love) and the flock of birds, rather than singing of human love, sings of Divine love: "en son de alabança / dezía vn discor: / 'Servid al Señor /pobres de andança' " (Prieto, 110) [in the manner of praise a chorus sang: "Serve the Lord, misguided ones"]. It is important to note that the protagonist does not heed their advice, however: "yo por locura / canté por amores" (110) [I irresponsibly sang of human love]. The birds immediately fall silent at this resumption of his love lament and he, in order to attract them once again, decides to use the ploy of singing joyously: "por los más atraher / a me querer responder, / en señal de alegría / cantava con grande afán / la antygua canción mía" (110) [in order to attract them into responding, I sang my old song in a joyful tone].

The Siervo appears here to be distancing himself from the love-martyr Maçías now; having assumed a happier tone, he seems to be overcoming his sense of loss, stating that "Dios y mi ventura / m'atraydo a tal estado" (110).[25] This is, significantly, the protagonist's first mention of God in the entire text, and in the next quatrain he explicitly dissociates himself from Maçías—with whom he had formerly identified himself so intensely: "No se que postremería / ayan buena los mis días, / quando el gentil Maçías /priso muerte por tal vía" (110) [I do not know what pleasant end my life will have, given that Maçías died because of that path].

Although he continues to sing about his lady, he increasingly distances himself from his prior state of grief and lamentation, accomplishing this distancing in two highly literary ways. First, he creates a play of temporalities in the refrain to his last stanza: "*Ya*, señora, en quien fiança / catyvo de mi trystura" (111; italics added) [*Now*, my lady, in whom trust, victim of my sadness]. Although this is an admittedly elliptical refrain, the word *ya* definitively denotes a temporal play (then versus now), presumably the "then" of his lovesick self as opposed to the "now" of his superior (distanced) perspective.[26] This interpretation is further strengthened by the scene that immediately follows: "E asy errado por las malezas, mudado en las más altas árbores de mi escura maginança, por devisar algún poblado, falléme ribera del grand mar, en vista de una grand vrca de armada . . ." (111) [Thus wandering through the woods, transformed in the treetops of my dark imagination, in order to find an inhabited place, I found myself on the seashore, in view of a great warship . . . ]. The phrase *mudado en las más altas árbores de mi escura maginança* is very important here, for it echoes the poet-as-bird metaphor at the same time underscoring the fact that a fundamental change has taken place in the poet. *Mudado*, of course, means either "changed" or "moulted" (i.e., the shedding of a bird's feathers in springtime). Thus the poet is perched in the tallest trees, after shedding his old feathers—those inoperative feathers of the traditional love poet—having now acquired a superior perspective that allows him to have an unobstructed view of Synderesis (Wisdom personified), a greatly modified avatar of Dante's Beatrice. Moreover, this shedding of (love) feathers recalls the shedding of the Tree of Love's leaves: "el lindo arrayan, consagrado a la deesa Venus . . . en punto que sobre mí tendió las verdes ramas, fue despojado de su vestidura" (76) [the attractive myrtle, devoted to the goddess Venus . . . as soon as it spread its branches over me, shed its leaves]. By this detail we see that the *Siervo libre*'s fundamentally antilyric nature has thus been established virtually from the outset of the work.

Continuing the Dantean rewriting, the advent of Synderesis to the protagonist recalls in several significant ways the advent of Beatrice to Dante in *Purgatorio* 30. Gregory Andrachuk suggestively indicates this intertextual reference:

> As Dante will rise from his act of contrition in possession of his free will, so Rodríguez will be able to follow his chosen path ("después de libre, en compañía de la discreción"). As Dante was directed by Beatrice, the symbol of Divine Revelation and knowledge, so Rodríguez . . . has decided to follow the path of wisdom. Synderesis' coming in a ship, accompanied by the seven virtues, parallels the arrival of Beatrice, for just as the procession of the chariot represents the Church, the ship can be seen to symbolize the same thing. The presence of the seven virtues awaiting the repentance of the sinner is implicit in the medieval belief that the lover guilty of "loco amor" has lost all of these.[27]

I would add that the validity of this interpretation may be further strengthened by additional details such as the description of Synderesis as a "señora mastresa"—similar to the description of Beatrice in *Purgatorio* 30.58–60: "Quasi ammiraglio che in poppa e in prora / viene a veder la gente che ministra / per li altri legni, e ben far l'incora . . . " [Like an admiral who goes to stern and bow to see the men that are serving on the other ships, and encourages them to do well . . . ].

These fundamental similarities, however, serve to highlight a series of essential differences. On the one hand, what had been figurative language in Dante's depiction (the simile "like an admiral," as well as the ship) becomes literal in Rodríguez del Padrón's presentation of his reworked Beatrice figure. On the other, Synderesis qua character is "una dueña anciana" [an elderly lady] who is "vestida de negro" (111) [dressed in black]. She thus contrasts quite strikingly with Dante's portrayal of Beatrice (*Purg.* 30. 28–33):

> . . . dentro una nuvola di fiori
> che da le mani angeliche saliva
> e ricadeva in giù dentro e di fori,
> sovra candido vel cinta d'uliva
> donna m'apparve, sotto verde manto
> vestita di color di fiamma viva.

. . . within a cloud of flowers, which rose from the angelic hands and fell down again within and without, olive-crowned over a white veil a lady appeared to me, clad, under a green mantle, with hue of living flame.

Beatrice is dressed as a youthful maiden, and Dante, upon seeing her, recalls his former love for her (l. 39)—a human, earthly love: "d'antico amor sentì la gran potenza" [I felt old love's great power]. Because this phrase hearkens back to Dante's condition as a lyric lover in the *Vita Nuova*, Rodríguez makes his female figure of salvation the very antithesis of a young maiden evoking thoughts of love—i.e., an old woman dressed in black ("cubyerta de duelo," 111). Both women, nonetheless, are united by their association with the olive tree (Minerva's emblematic tree in the case of Synderesis and *Purg.* 31.31 for Beatrice). Moreover, Rodríguez's instance of rewriting is entirely consistent with his unraveling of the lyric component of Dante's poet/lover/beloved configuration described above. Synderesis is obviously an antilyric figure (both in her age and appearance), more reminiscent perhaps of Boethius' Lady Philosophy, and she could not be more alien in appearance from the figure of Beatrice, the earthly woman who led the pilgrim from human to Divine love.

It is Rodríguez's reworking of Dante's poet/lover/beloved configuration that makes visible the *Siervo libre*'s true semantic value. Despite the composition of exemplary love poetry and the intense courtly love for his lady, words fail to effect reciprocity. It is essential to note, moreover, that this novelistic perception of the constraints of human discourse will, in fact, pervade each of the *novelas sentimentales*. Indeed, more than any other distinctive feature, it is this attitude toward the constraints of language that unites these texts.

Beyond the thematic issue of love—whether it is the courtly or Christian variety that is valorized by the *Siervo libre*—the matter of closure is an equally debated issue. Yet, here too, I maintain, the rewriting of the Dantean subtext indicates that poetic closure has been achieved. Andrachuk reasons that: "the *Siervo libre* as we have it is not as Rodríguez intended it to be; that is, the third part of the work is entirely missing."[28] This attitude represents a widely held interpretation. If, however, we consider the textual function of the first appearance of Beatrice in the *Commedia*, we realize that Rodríguez has, in fact, set down his last sentence.

The arrival of Beatrice in her triumphal chariot drawn by the Griffon (half eagle, half lion, symbolic of Christ) constitutes a pageant of revelation. Her appearance coincides with the end of the pilgrim's purgation—with his intellection of his fall, leading (in the canto immediately following) to his full confession. As a result, it is not necessary for Rodríguez's protagonist to make explicit confession as Dante's did. If we have fully understood the Dantean subtext, we do not need a "tercera parte" to be elaborated for us by the poet.[29] It is entirely in keeping with the poetics of Rodríguez's creative reworking of Dante to diverge from him markedly, having first established a firm intertextual frame of reference. Because he has chosen to recall the explicit moment of conversion in Dante's poem, there is no need for an explicit confession in his own work—it would be redundant. His is an implicit yet unambiguous pageant of revelation, wholly original precisely because of the implicitness of its presentation.

Finally, we are told that Synderesis "vyno en demanda de mis aventuras; e yo esso mesmo en recuenta de aquéllas" (Prieto, 112) [came to inquire about my adventures; and I to recount them]. The text thus ends with her request that the protagonist confess. Also significant in this connection is the explicit use at this point of the word *aventura* (the archetypal episodic romance unit of narration), thereby emphasizing the definitive transformation of the protagonist's romance identity (as Christian pilgrim), in opposition to his former identity as venereal pilgrim. This recounting of the pilgrim's adventures also recalls the "rrecuentas de las aventuras" (101) [recounting of adventures] sought by Yrena in her capacity as counterfeit Synderesis figure. She, we recall, arrived at the shrine of love in El Padrón by ship, accompanied by a retinue of women, all dressed in somber clothing, "en rrecuenta de las aventuras [de amor]." As such, Yrena functions, in effect, as an oxymoronically misguided Synderesis.[30]

Synderesis' request constitutes the culmination of the unraveling of the Dantean configuration. It is the request of Synderesis that the protagonist recount his *aventuras* (the progression of his intellect) that is presented as the real motivation for writing the *Siervo libre*. Thus the text operates as a "closed system," for the poet-protagonist is necessarily writing from the perspective of one who has already met Synderesis. For this reason it is a finished work that, if the subtext and its function have been properly interpreted, leaves no ambiguity as to its conclusion.

From the perspective of the end, two additional observations can be made concerning the text's relationship to the *Heroides*. The first has to do with a temporal progression within the epistolary monologue structure. With the Ovidian collection, we glimpsed the private lives of (remote) mythological figures. Thereafter, with the *Elegia* we encountered the private life of a contemporary medieval woman trying to emulate those remote mythological beings. With the *Siervo libre* we now witness the private life of a contemporary author and the fictional figures of his own creation who are not only contemporary, but entirely Spanish as well. It is in this context that we can understand the significance of Rodríguez's rejection of Dante's notion of virtuous (pre-Christian) pagans and of the mythological past in general. He strategically rejects the portrayal of the past in order to represent his subjective state entirely by means of the present. This commitment to the present, needless to say, is a crucial step in the forging of the novel.[31]

Another observation arises from this reading of Rodríguez's text. Namely, how is it possible that this first *novela sentimental* represents a rejection of human love? Does this fact not seem to indicate that it is an anti–*novela sentimental* instead? This latter conclusion is the one I arrived at in an earlier treatment of the *Siervo libre*.[32] Upon further scrutiny of this novelistic corpus, however, I realize that despite its wholesale rejection of courtly love, the text projects an attitude toward language that derives from the *Heroides* and remains constant throughout the *novelas sentimentales* written after the *Siervo libre*. It is the discourse of alienated love, an awareness of the limits of discourse itself as a communicative mechanism that unites the texts within this corpus. The powerlessness of words to effect deeds (the Siervo's inability to attract his lady, despite his loyalty and exemplary verses; Lyessa's failure to convince Croes to spare her life; Yrena's totally unpredictable reaction to Ardanlier's letter) is thematized.

The way the protagonist resolves this problem of untranscendent language is by rejecting it, embracing instead the transcendence of Divine language. Within the texts written after the *Siervo libre*, escape from the failure of discourse will (like Fiammetta's madness and Lucretia's suicide) take the form of still other extreme measures. It is this perception of the existential constraints of amorous discourse—a discourse of impotence and solipsism—that Rodríguez has learned from the *Heroides*, and which his successors will problematize even further.

# SIX

## THE UNTRANSCENDENT VISION

### (*SATIRA DE FELICE E INFELICE VIDA*)

S EMIOTICS—as Umberto Eco reminds us—"is in principle the dis-
cipline studying everything which can be used to lie."[1] And allegory
is a case in point, a semiotic system that necessarily participates in
two fundamental forms of deception. It claims to offer direct access to the
axiology that is its subject matter. Yet this is not possible since the nature
of words is nominal rather than real. On the other hand, it does offer direct
access to the words that constitute its real subject. To admit this, however,
would expose its inherent deception. The separation of signifier from signified offered by allegory is presented as merely provisional and rhetorical, an
attempt to project what Derrida calls the "epoch of the logos"[2]—rather
than problematizing language and viewing this distance as definitive, as
more linguistically skeptical ages do.

Whether overtly or covertly, allegory posits and explores cognitive models, and it does so by rewriting canonical texts. Such is the case, for example, in the relationship of the New Testament to the Old Testament, of the
*Psychomachia* to the *Aeneid*, or of the *Ovide moralisé* to the *Metamorphoses*.
This decidedly recuperative dimension of allegory is acknowledged by Joel
Fineman when he observes that: "It is as though allegory were precisely
that mode that makes up for the distance, or heals the gap, between the
present and a disappearing past, which without interpretation would be
otherwise irretrievable and foreclosed."[3]

I would qualify Fineman's remark by saying that precisely because it is
such a powerful metalinguistic tool, allegory can function not only as recuperative polemic, but as an equally effective instrument of axiological subversion. For as Maureen Quilligan observes in speaking of Melville's *Confidence Man*, "the question basic to all allegory is do words lie, or do they
thrust at the truth?"[4] The *Satira de felice e infelice vida* written by Pedro de
Portugal between 1449 and 1453 is—I would argue—a text of which this
question should be asked, for it constitutes a subversion of the very amorous discourse that it purports to valorize. In addition, this text is the second of three, along with the *Siervo libre* and *Triste deleytaçion*, that will
result in failed allegory.

To a fifteenth-century Spanish audience, the generic designation *satira*
indicated a general moral function (praise of virtue and reprehension of

vice), based on the fourteenth-century definition offered by Benvenuto da Imola in his commentary on the *Divine Comedy*: "satyra . . . tractat enim de virtutibus et viciis"[5] [satire . . . treats of virtues and vices]. Hence a didactic framework is implied.[6] Obviously this definition diverges from the normative view of satire which assumes a particular diction as well. To quote Northrop Frye, "two things are essential to satire; one is wit or humor, the other is an object of attack."[7] The satirist was, even in antiquity, "the [one] who jokes about serious things."[8] Interpreters of the *Satira* are consistently meticulous about attributing Don Pedro's usage to Benvenuto rather than to the generally accepted one.

· Representative of the critical consensus, Julian Weiss observes that: "It is not hard to see how the term *satira*, with its polarity of praise and blame, should be thought to be a perfectly appropriate label for a work which simply conforms to the conventional situations of courtly love, where tradition demands the self-abasement of one partner and the exaltation of the other."[9]

Thus a serious instructive function (in this case an amatory one) is indicated by the critical tradition, as a result of which the *Satira* has been subtextually allied with the *Roman de la Rose* of Guillaume de Lorris, in Spain with Rodríguez's *Siervo libre de amor*, formally speaking, and the *Triunfo de las donas* in semantic terms.[10] To the contrary, however, these suggested analogies are instructive precisely because of the *Satira*'s marked divergence from them—highlighting its own boldly original metaliterary import. The clear polarity (abasement/exaltation) claimed by Weiss, although endemic to courtly love, is seriously called into question with this text. So is the narrow definition of *satira* that it borrows from Benvenuto.

A look at the dedicatory epistle that prefaces the work gives an early indication of the *Satira*'s self-conscious departure from the linguistic integrity demanded by allegory—for allegory will be persuasive only to the extent that it can guarantee the epistemological value of its words. Logically (given that the action takes place entirely within the lover's head) this is the only letter in the *Satira*. Despite this unique status, however, it provides the reader with a clear orientation as to the letter writer's concerns. The letter, addressed by Don Pedro to his sister Doña Isabel, opens with a revealing description of his waking vision (this is not a dream) as an "estudiosa e pequeña obra" [brief, erudite work], which constitutes "el primero fructo de (sus) estudios"[11] [the first fruit of (his) studies]. At this point the accustomed courtly hermeticism of the medieval vision and its attendant proemial forematter gives way, becoming radically resemanticized as Don Pedro situates it within the context of medieval encyclopedic learning. Rather than citing one of Ovid's familiar erotic treatises, he incongruously invokes Valerius Maximus in order to underscore the need to produce an edifying narrative:

Fabla Valerio, en el titulo octavo de su octavo libro, diziendo: "El Affricano mayor, fatigado, al orilla de la mar se yva, e coger alli pedrezuelas e veneras recuenta." Et si esta occupaçion ligera es loada, quanto mas lo sera exerçitar el ingenio, asayar el entendimiento, confirmar la memoria en cosas virtuosas, utiles e honestas? (4)

Valerius Maximus, in Book 8, chapter 8 of his book, remarks that: "Scipio Africanus Major, feeling tired, would go to the seashore to collect stones and count scallop shells." And if this trivial activity is praised, how much more worthy of praise would be the exercise of the mind, of understanding, the confirmation of virtuous things that are useful and meritorious?

This reference to Valerius Maximus is noteworthy for more than one reason. On the one hand, it is generically inappropriate within the erotic pseudoautobiography to find a concern for extratextual didacticism, particularly as in this case, where the didacticism is of a moral (rather than erotic) nature. By definition its concern is obsessively centered instead on the lover's psychological states of hope, despair, etc. On the other, the ostentatious citation of Book 8, chapter 8 of the *Factorum et Dictorum Memorabilium* is significant because it is a misattribution.[12] At first glance it might appear perhaps that this error is an unwilled oversight. Yet we soon discern that it forms part of an extended program of radical manipulation on the part of Don Pedro.

In fact the novelty of his interest in combining and/or juxtaposing the erudition of book learning with the discourse of love extends far beyond his reference to Valerius Maximus and his avowed concern for didacticism. For the *Satira* (which he calls his "pequeña obra") consists of a short love narrative that is dwarfed by no fewer than one hundred glosses[13] that alter the discursive status of the allegorical vision immeasurably. By their sheer size (and consequent obtrusiveness) these glosses seem very comparable to those that we encounter in Juan de Mena's *Coronación* (1438–49). Yet this analogy is quite imprecise. For not only is Mena's text different by virtue of its appending of prose gloss to verse text (while Don Pedro glosses prose with prose), but, more importantly, in the nature of the respective glosses.

The practice of writing a gloss on one's own text recalls Dante's *Vita Nuova* since he is the first poet to have actually commented on his own work in a systematic exegetical manner, as he proudly proclaims. Along similar lines, Christine de Pisan's *Epitre d'Othea* (c. 1402) combines lengthy prose interpretations of the short verses that begin each different section. Mena approximates both, as Inez Macdonald explains: "Juan de Mena's *Commentary* recalls both Dante and Christine, for he divides his verses into parts in the same way that Dante did, explaining each part, or each line, separately, and even giving some verses a threefold meaning where he thinks it necessary, while the uncertainty of the form he employs

and the fact that he gives much space to the legends and their common-
sense explanation recalls the manner of Christine de Pisan."[14]

Nonetheless, this exegetical procedure which is common to Dante,
Christine, and Mena is not that of the *Satira*. Don Pedro is equally interested in drawing our attention to his glosses: "Ffize glosas al testo, aunque
no sea acostumbrado por los antiguos auctores glosar sus obras" (Fonseca,
9) [I wrote glosses to the text, although the ancients were not in the habit
of glossing their own texts]. Yet, as a close reading of the text will illustrate,
the function of his glosses is descriptive rather than interpretive, which
further contributes to the uniqueness of *Satira*'s discursive structure.

An additional function is served by the prefatory letter by its idiosyncratic linguistic usage. That is, while first establishing the scrupulously didactic stance of Don Pedro's *Satira*, it simultaneously undercuts it. In order
to achieve this axiological complexity Don Pedro problematizes the meaning of the term *satira* itself. The word is first introduced according to its
accustomed association of moral valence:

> satira . . . quiere dezir *reprehension* con animo amigable de corregir; e aun este
> nombre satira viene de satura, que es *loor*, e yo a ella primero *loando*, el femineo
> linage propuse *loar*, a ella amonestando como siervo a señora, a mi *reprehen-
> diendo* de mi loca thema e desigual tristeza.[15] (5)

> "Satira" means a *reproach* made with the friendly corrective intention; the
> name *satira* derives from *satura*, which means *praise*, and because I wish to
> *praise* her, I decided to praise the female gender, admonishing her as a servant
> does his lady, while *reproaching* myself for my imprudent subject and inordi-
> nate sadness.

It is important to note, however, that *loor* and *reprehension* (whose
initial usage referred exclusively to the amorous relationship of the lady and
her lover) suddenly become transferred to the written artifact itself—its
potential merits and flaws—which his sister will determine according to
her refined editorial discernment:

> segund dixe, muchos deffectos cont[iene]. Sera muy neçessario que la suma
> prudencia vuestra emiende aquellos, e los yerros suyos con amigable correçion
> los reprehenda e, reprehendida e emendada, sea digna de algund loor, o a lo
> menos no digna de reprehension. (8)

> As I have indicated, it has many defects. It will be necessary for your great
> discernment to emend them, and reproach its errors in an amicable manner.
> Once corrected, may it be worthy of some praise or at least not be worthy of
> reproach.

Here then it is literary—not moral or amatory—exemplarity that is at
issue. Moreover, it is a kind of exemplarity that permits a calculated degree

of obscurity at certain junctures in the text, obscurity which will, paradoxically, shed interpretive light: "en algunos lugares [es] escura [la obra] porque la vuestra muy llena industria sabera de quales jardines salieron estas flores mias, e a la escuridat dara lumbre e claridat muy luziente" (8) [in some places the work is obscure because your discernment will know from which gardens these flowers came, and you will illuminate the darkness]. In a notable departure from allegorical procedure, this remark indicates that the allegory will remain unglossed. As Elena Gascón-Vera meaningfully remarks, "The allegory, therefore, is introduced from the beginning of the text and maintained throughout, without being subjected to any interpretation."[16]

There follows a third, appreciably different, usage of *loor* and *reprehension*. From the laudable impulse of objective literary merit, these terms now become associated with an evident lack of objectivity:

> por vos ser assentada en la cumbre de la honor mundana . . . con la rodilla fincada en suelo, suplico que de las caninas e venenosas lenguas, mas habiles a *reprehender* que a *loar*, la libre, deffienda e ampare, e le acresçiente titulo de honor e de auctoridat, dando lugar a los sçientes que la miren e castiguen con ojos amigables e amoroso açote, e atapando las bocas de los simples o ponçoñosos retractadores no osen de la morder e llagar de enerboladas llagas. (8)

> Because you are seated at the apex of worldly honor. . . I beg you on bended knee to protect it from the cur-like venomous tongues, which are more prone to reproach than to praise. Defend it and allow it to gain an honorable title and authority, giving the wise the opportunity to judge it in a positive light, keeping the malicious tongues of detractors away, so that they will not dare to bite and poison it.

In short, Don Pedro asks his sister to use her political influence to guarantee a favorable reception for his work. At this point he is ignoring the work's literary value and is only interested in receiving positive reviews. All detractors are, moreover, labeled *ignorantes*, while supporters are identified as *sçientes*. A blatant lack of objectivity, the wholly unexemplary impulse of self-aggrandisement therefore prevails here, with good readers offering *loor*, and bad voicing *reprehension*. This is, needless to say, a far cry from Benvenuto's postulation.

The fourth and final attribution of the *loor/reprehension* binome is as subjective and unexemplary as the last, this time basing itself on sibling coertion:

> por el amor inmutable que, segund dixe en comienço, siempre senti que la vuestra singular virtud me avia, do proçedera loor a mi obra, aunque no lo merezca. Ca, sy todas las cosas tienen dos entendimientos, uno de loor, e otro

de reprehension, no dubdo *yo* que en toda esta obra mia e en cada parte della sea dado por la señoria vuestra el mejor que atribuyrse le pueda, e lo otro desechado, como cosa indigna de parescer ante la magestad real. (8–9)

The immutable love that, as I said earlier, I felt you always had for me, will result in praise for my text, even if it does not deserve it. For, if all things are made of two natures, one praiseworthy and the other critical, I do not doubt that Your Mercy will speak of the whole work in its various parts in the highest terms, and what is rejected will be eliminated, as unworthy to appear before royalty majesty.

Don Pedro's words here amount to a *captatio benevolentiae* designed to elicit the most favorable reading possible. And by their polysemy, these four appreciably different usages of *loor* and *reprehension* serve as an unmistakable "opening signal," a warning to the reader concerning the narrator/protagonist's conflicting (deceptive) discourse.

Finally, the letter of hermeneutic orientation refers to a justification for the copious glosses. Within it Don Pedro affirms that they are essential— that lacking them the work would be "mas causadora de quistiones que no fenesçedora de aquellas" (10) [raising more questions than it answers], that without them "no fenesçerian jamas demandas a los ignorantes, e aun en algunas cosas a los sçientes seria forçado de rebolver las foias" (10) [the ignorant would incessantly ask questions, and even the informed readers would need to keep turning back the page]. This statement is of interest for two reasons. First, it restores *sçientes* and *ignorantes* to their normative identification of wise and ignorant, rather than indulgent and stern, critics. Consequently, his misuse of these terms in their previous, highly idiosyncratic, appearance is underscored. In addition, the narrator's unreliability is highlighted by the fact that his glosses are quite often remarkably unhelpful. Proof of the largely unnecessary nature of the glosses is echoed, for example, by Antonio Paz y Mélia in his edition, where he refuses to reproduce them in their entirety, explaining that "the author fills the margins with explanatory glosses, which I have chosen to suppress, both because of their great length and because they treat material which can be consulted in any mythological dictionary."[17]

Yet this modern editor misses the point. Instead of offering interpretation in his largely superfluous glosses, Don Pedro is using them narratively. And, as we shall see, he is juxtaposing the gloss and the text, two very different speech situations, in order to reveal the mechanisms underlying each one. Indeed, rather than ignoring the glosses, the reader should note the high degree of importance with which Don Pedro invests them.

In this context he chooses, somewhat surprisingly, to refer to his text in its entirety as "mi Argos" at the end of the dedicatory epistle, explaining that:

Asy como aquel çient ojos tenia, asy aquella çient glosas contyene, e asy como
el ojo corporeo al cuerpo alunbra e gia, asy la glosa al testo por senblante
manera faze, quitando dudas a los leyentes. (12)

Just as he has one hundred eyes, so too the text has one hundred glosses, and
just as the physical eye illuminates and guides the body, so the gloss acts upon
the text by eliminating doubts in the readers.

A moment's reflection reveals that Argus, the hundred-eyed sentinel
whose plight is recounted in *Metamorphoses* (1.624–723), is a curious
choice of emblem for the *Satira*. For one thing, he is a failed sentinel, as the
story makes clear. He is, we recall, instructed by Juno to keep her lustful
husband, Jupiter, away from Io. To this end he keeps watch over her since
for him, "era natural la perpetua vegilia, e el sempiterno acatamiento contra
el" (Fonseca, 11) [perpetual vigilance was his nature and eternal surveillance of him (Jupiter)]. Nonetheless, Jupiter overpowers Argus not by
physical force, but by a ruse, sending Mercury (disguised as a shepherd) to
distract him with the story of Pan and Syrinx. As Argus listens to this story
his eyes close one by one, causing him to fall asleep, thereby providing
Mercury with the opportunity to decapitate him. Juno is so moved by the
watchman's death that she decides to immortalize him, changing him (specifically his hundred eyes) into the tail of the peacock. And as a result,
Argus implicitly signifies both a failed sentinel and a metamorphosis. In
like fashion, I maintain, the *Satira* is a purposefully failed sentinel; it does
not seek to offer "ojos del entendimiento" but rather eyes (glosses) that are
transformed into something new, a new type of gloss which oxymoronically is not meant to function exegetically,[18] but narratively.

The newness of this enterprise can be understood by comparison with
the function of description in fifteenth-century Spain. Speaking of *descriptio*
during the time in which Don Pedro was writing, Macdonald explains its
characteristics as follows: "Description, in the fifteenth century, is still either completely practical, as in those accounts of events to be found in
chronicles, or didactic. . . . But when we come to Garcilaso, and later to a
Góngora, we find that description is there for its own sake; that instead of
teaching us something, it is used merely to give pleasure, like a picture. Its
object is to call up sets of ideas, to recall associations in our minds, and so
present us with a richly toned picture of the subject."[19]

In a dramatic reversal of the normative medieval procedure, Don
Pedro's gloss functions in a fundamentally narrative rather than interpretive manner that, in part, anticipates the Renaissance usage of *descriptio*
articulated by Macdonald. Indicative of this discursive practice is his conclusion to the gloss on Argus, where he appends not an interpretive remark, but additional narrative detail to Ovid's account. Explaining that
Argus was turned into the peacock's tail, the glossator concludes that the
tail has many eyes, some large, others small:

de lo qual es de presuponer el mençionado pastor [Argus] no yguales ojos, mas diversos e dispares obtener, e por ende el auctor ymitando a aquello por la senblante orden começo su camino e siguio su viaje. (13)

from which we must suppose that the aforementioned shepherd [Argus] had eyes of different sizes, and in like fashion the author [Don Pedro], imitating Argus's face, undertook his journey

This interest in narrative where we would expect interpretation points to Don Pedro's fascination with the two principal discursive modes of the Middle Ages, myth and allegory. Stated simply, myth corresponds to *histoire* as defined by Benveniste (third-person speech in the past without intervention of the speaker), and allegory to *discours* (speech in which the speaker tries to influence his audience). Harald Weinrich further explores this distinction for the Middle Ages, remarking that: "With its narrative aspect reduced and its key events immobilized in the form of tableaux, myth becomes comparable to the kind of allegory so dear to the Middle Ages. The allegorical figures, for example, of the *Roman de la Rose*— Hatred, Felony, Baseness, Avarice, Old Age, Hypocrisy—could easily be found painted on the walls of a garden: they do not contain any narrative or actantial element, they are totally static."[20]

To illustrate this fundamental distinction more concretely, let us synoptically trace the treatment of Argus in the texts of Ovid, Jean de Meun, the *Ovide moralisé*, and the *Satira*. In the *Metamorphoses* Argus is known for his exceptional eyesight and physical prowess. When he is beheaded we learn only that Juno, moved by compassion for his plight, transformed his eyes into the tail of the peacock. We as readers can choose to interpret the reason for Argus's falling asleep as boredom (because he has just heard the seemingly identical story of Diana),[21] but no such causal relationship is indicated by the Ovidian story itself. Pure narrative is at issue in this particular case, and in the *Metamorphoses* as a whole.

By contrast, Jean de Meun refers to Argus (vv. 14381–94) as failed vigilance. Yet he does so not because Argus was unable to guard Io, but for a substantially different reason, a hypothetical situation. As La Vieille observes:

> Nus ne peut metre en fame garde
> S'ele meïsmes ne se garde:
> Se c'iert Argus qui la gardast,
> E de ses cent eauz l'esgardast,
> Don l'une des meitiez veillait
> E l'autre meitié someillait,
> Quant Jupiter li fist trenchier
> Le chief, pour Yo revenchier,
> Qu'il avait en vache muee,

De fourme humaine desnuee;
(Mercurius le li trencha
Quant de Juno la revencha),
N'i vaudrait sa garde mais rien.
Fos est qui garde tel mairien.[22]

No man can keep watch over a woman if she does not watch over herself. If it were Argus who guarded her and looked at her with his hundred eyes, of which one half watched while the other half slept, his watchkeeping would be worth nothing. (To revenge Io, whom [he] had changed into a cow and stripped of her human form, Jupiter had his head cut off. Mercury cut it off and thus revenged her against Juno.) Argus's watch would be worth nothing in this case; the man who guards such an object is a fool.[23] (vv. 14381–94)

Since women are so wily, even the most vigilant of sentinels, Argus himself, would inevitably suffer defeat by their machinating minds. An extradiegetic, extratextual allegorical purpose is thus served by the mythological watchman in this case, a very different purpose from that which Ovid intended. Indeed, it constitutes a serious misreading of Ovid, whereby Io was portrayed as a hapless victim instead of a manipulative female.

Still more distant from its original discursive function is the portrayal of this episode in the *Ovide moralisé*. Weinrich refers to this influential thirteenth-century text in terms of its notable rewriting of Ovid as follows: "In this text (in its prose as well as its verse version) the narration, for example, of the myth of Narcissus, is followed by the moral of the story, that is, by the translation of the narrative into expository (or allegorical) terms. Linguistically speaking, the signs of the discourse have changed; it is above all the verb tenses that are affected by this. And since these signs are meant to indicate how the reader should react, the *Ovide moralisé* requires a different reading, or even a different reader, than an unmoralized Ovid."[24]

With the example of Argus, not only is the narrative motion of the initial myth transformed into a static allegory, but he is simultaneously redefined from his neutral status as the pawn of the gods into an admonitory emblem of human folly, resulting from his contamination with the narcissistic peacock:

Les ieus sont les mondains delis,
Dont li paons se glorefie.
Li paons home senefie,
Plains d'orgueil et d'outrecuidance.
Orgueilleus hom n'a sa baance
Qu'a fere pompe et mener moë:
C'est li paons, qui fet la roë
De sa coë et s'en outrecuide.

> Orgueilleus met tout son estuide
> En avoir les mondains delis
> De mes, de robes et de lis
> Et de richesces et d'onnour,
> D'estre apelez mestre et seignor,
> De soi polir et cointoier,
> Si veult les humbles mestroier
> Et les povres metre a martire.[25]

The eyes represent worldly pleasures, / in which the peacock revels. / The peacock signifies man, / who is full of pride and presumption. / The prideful man desires / only with pretention: / He is the peacock, who flaunts his tail /and prides himself on this. / Prideful, he centers all his attention / on worldly pleasures / food, clothes and bed / Wealth and honor, / being called master and lord, / displaying himself, / thus he wishes to dominate the humble / and martyrize the poor.

By contrast, Don Pedro daringly identifies Argus with Prudence, quite deceptively acknowledging his fidelity to Ovid: "por Argos la prudençia entender se puede" (Fonseca, 12) [Argus is synonymous with prudence]. It is important to note that in his capacity as glossator Don Pedro is being as self-consciously problematic here as he was in generating the unresolved polysemy of *loor* and *reprehension*. While indicating his fidelity to Ovid (thereby valorizing the *auctor*), Don Pedro simultaneously distorts him by interpreting Argus's vigilance in the Ovidian narrative as Prudence—a substantially different (cognitive) quality implying that the "ojos corporeos" of the Ovidian text are instead "ojos del entendimiento." Moreover, he explains that: "En cada parte de la ovidiana estoria son diversos integumentos poeticos non dignos aqui de proseguir, mas por Argus la prudençia entender se puede, por Mercurio los sentidos, por el canto e dulçura del instrumento siringa los falagueros deleytes induzientes el sueño de la perpetua muerte" (12) [In each part of the Ovidian narrative there exist various poetic integuments which are not worth repeating here, but Argus is to be understood as representing prudence, Mercury the five senses, by the song and sweetness of the instrument known as the syrinx, the enjoyable pleasures that lead to death]. Since "el sueño de la perpetua muerte" (which allegedly stems from the "falagueros deleytes") was Argus's fate, it is blatantly contradictory to call him "prudencia," for he represents instead "imprudencia" if any abstraction at all can be attributed to him. What we see in this gloss on Argus is the consciously generated antagonism of two contradictory interpretations. Its effect is to undercut any interpretive value since the contradictory terms cancel each other out, rendering it neutral. As such, I would argue that the interpretive neutrality of Argus makes him in fact an apt emblem for the unevaluative nature of the *Satira* as a whole.

That Don Pedro is actively trying to subvert interpretation in favor of unexegetical, descriptive narrative can be likewise substantiated by additional attributions of "prudençia" both to his lady (102) and to the allegorical figure of Prudence (50). The analysis that follows will make clear that each of these cases is as revealing (and difficult to justify) as the equation of Argus with Prudence personified. Rather than striving for clarity in the referentiality of *signans* and *signatum*, what confronts us is willed obfuscation.

Briefly stated, the diegetic thread of the *Satira* is the story of a lover (Don Pedro) tormented by unrequited love for his anonymous lady (a protracted, five-year affliction to be precise). As we might expect, because of this affective torment he has lost his free will, finding himself in "[una] muy tenebrosa cárçel" (15) [a very dark prison]. In this distraught state the lover curses Fortune, finding her cruelty to be greater than that of Nero or Hannibal, among others, and challenging her to defend herself: "Responde, o mesquina, fabla e di de que bien te puedes alabar!" (30) [Answer me, wretched one, say in what way you are worthy of praise!]. The introduction of history into the hermetic courtly system (effected here by the inclusion of Hannibal and Nero) is striking at this point, as it will be throughout the *Satira*.

Whereas the erotic pseudoautobiography traditionally confines itself to describing the lover's psyche in minute detail, Don Pedro consistently disrupts this self-contained courtly aesthetic, which by the fifteenth century had become an inoperative—semantically exhausted—form. And by consistently juxtaposing the subjective states of the individual with historicity, the tension of self and other (one's inability to control his objective environment), Don Pedro is replacing the anticipated lyric structure with novelistic discourse. That Don Pedro is being highly manipulative is obvious, for as Paul de Man explains, "more than ordinary modes of fiction, allegory is at the furthest possible remove from historiography."[26] While the writing of history concerns itself with unsystematic particularity, unfolding in temporal sequence, allegory is a closed system dealing with universals or absolutes that are atemporal. Moreover, while history recounts empirically verifiable data, allegory seeks to represent necessarily unverifiable phenomena, which by their very nature cannot be represented.

While the lover continues to rail against the injustices of Fortune, his Discreción appears and confronts him ("*mi* discreción": 34). She is the first of several subjective allegorical personifications we encounter in the *Satira*, and it is precisely this subjectivity evinced by Discreción that recalls the *Roman de la Rose*. As Hans-Robert Jauss explains: "With Guillaume de Lorris . . . the allegory of the rose succeeds, in spite of everything, in reflecting the individual, and thus detaches itself from the allegorical tradition of the Middle Ages: it no longer describes in objective terms the personifications of the conflicting forces in the lady's psyche; it presents them only from the point of view of the lover, as successive aspects of the love object."[27]

Discretion personified (advancing the kind of argument we would expect from Prudence) tells him that his pursuit of the lady defies all reason since she rejects him. Indicating that Piramus, Ardanlier, and Maçías died for ladies who reciprocated their love, she baldly asserts that:

> yo te veo mas inhumanamente que alguno de aquestos muerte padesçer, e sofrir; e mucho mas contra rason, porque, si los otros murieron, murieron por aquellas de quien eran amados e queridos, e tu moriras por aquella que de tu bien una sola hora non tiene memoria. (40–41)

> I see you dying and suffering more inhumanely than any of the rest, and very unreasonably, for if the others died, they did so for ladies who reciprocated their love, whereas you will die for a lady who cannot remember you even for an hour.

Having Discreción (a courtly fixture dedicated to the advancement of amorous liaisons by means of discreet behavior) tell him to abandon the enterprise entirely is virtually a contradiction in terms. What we soon learn, however, is that the anomalous discourse of Discreción by no means constitutes an isolated example in the *Satira*. For no sooner has Discreción departed than the Seven Virtues (three theological and four cardinal) appear, with Prudençia as their spokesperson. This configuration, coming as it does soon after the reference to Ardanlier and Maçías, gives us the impression that Don Pedro may be intending to pick up where the *Siervo libre* leaves off—at the moment when Synderesis, accompanied by the Seven Virtues (convinced that the Siervo has renounced earthly love), asks the lover to recount his perspective on the love affair ("la muy avisada Synderesis . . . vyno en demanda de mis aventuras; e yo esso mesmo en recuenta dellas": 111–12).[28]

The Prudençia whom we encounter in the *Satira* is quite distinct from the *Siervo libre*'s Synderesis, however. For rather than leading the lover away from the fallen pursuit of earthly love to the virtuous contemplation of divine love, she does just the opposite—articulating a discourse as strikingly alien to her nature as Discreción's respective discourse. Prudençia and her entourage come to praise Don Pedro's lady in the most hyperbolically inflated terms imaginable, claiming at the outset the shocking admission that the lady in question surpasses even the Virtues themselves:

> Aunque algunas valerosas mugeres o notables ombres algunas de nos posseyessen o possean, no ganaron corona de perfecçion. Mas sola esta inclita señora nuestra ovo de nos la exçellencia sola esta ovo de nos todo nuestro fructo. (55)

Although some valorous women or notable men possessed or possess some of [our virtues], they never achieved perfection. Only this outstanding lady contained all excellence, this one possessed all of our fruits.

The oxymoronic imprudence of Prudençia is quite unmistakable as she claims, for example:

Qual *Pitagoras*, qual *Diogenes*, qual *Platon*, qual *Aristotiles*, o qual otro *philosopho* o *paladio*, que en el universo floresçiesse, su sabiduria al saber, entendimiento e prudençia desta vuestra soberana señora se podera egualar? (68–69)

What Pythagoras, Diogenes, Plato, Aristotle or other philosopher who flourished in the world could equal the wisdom, understanding and prudence of your superior lady?

Moreover, the subversiveness of Prudençia's advice is evidenced not simply by the nature of her remarks, but by their extensiveness as well. She offers a seemingly endless gallery of illustrious analogies all of whom the lady is (unconvincingly) said to surpass. The distance separating word and deed is considerable. On the one hand, even in the unlikely event that the lady approximated the accomplishments of one of the paragons of wisdom invoked by Prudençia, she could obviously never equal (much less surpass) them all. On the other, all we know about her is that she spurns the lover. For this reason the hyperbole is unconvincing to say the least.

The validity of this discourse is undermined not only by its length, hyperbole, and uncharacteristic nature (e.g., having Prudençia praise the attractive way the lady walks [123]),[29] but also by the encyclopedic range of the analogies evoked—illustrious men and women, pagan and Christian, who had distinguished themselves by conquering virtually insurmountable odds (Esther, Lucretia, Portia, St. Catherine, to name only a few). What strikes us most about the examples offered by Prudençia is that they are not in the least analogous to the anonymous lady who has accomplished nothing more than to project profound indifference toward her suitor. Consequently, the lady is unavoidably deflated by the plethora of ill-suited analogies. In so doing, Don Pedro is juxtaposing the encyclopedic discourse of the late Middle Ages with courtly discourse in order to illustrate the virtually absolute hermeticism of the latter. Yet the generic contamination is reciprocal of course—serving simultaneously to diminish not simply the authority of the personification allegory but also of its gloss as a viable instructional mechanism. What remains intact, indeed what is valorized after this deconstruction of allegory and interpretive gloss is myth—i.e., the narrative per se.

The lover refutes the uniformly glowing assessment of the lady offered by Prudençia, forcing the Virtues to enlist the aid of Piedad (Compassion)

in their defense against the lady's calumniator. She too notably contradicts
her name by being very uncompassionate, telling the lover to blame himself
for his plight—not his unobliging lady: "Tu, mas constante que bien co-
nosçido, o tu, indigno juez, de quien judgas? Quexate contra la adversa
fortuna, quexate contra la triste costellaçion o planeta en que naçiste!"
(137) [You, whose love is unreciprocated, you, unworthy judge, whom are
you judging? Rail against your bad luck, your astrological sign or the
planet under which you were born!].

Victory is unequivocally accorded to the lover as he eloquently defeats
the Virtues by his admirably logical argumentation,[30] at which point the
vanquished ladies hastily disappear. In a self-proclaimed exemplary allegory the defeat of the Seven Virtues is just as inconceivable as the courtly
discourse that these ethical virtues have articulated. Moreover, the validity
of the allegorical debate structure—so influential in the Middle Ages—is
likewise definitively eroded. Yet even more shocking is the lover's admission that his triumph has no beneficial effect, that it has actually made
matters much worse for him:

> Aunque vençedor me viesse, por aver vençido, quede mas triste con muchos
> e mas varios pensamientos que sy vençido me viera, ca veya grand culpa pos-
> seer aquella cuya culpa a mi era pena mayor que mis innumerables penas, cuya
> culpa, por escusar mi muerte, en tal caso no querria. (153)

> Although I had won, by winning I was even sadder than if I had lost. For I
> realized the guilt of her whose fault is my greatest sorrow, a fault that, because
> it would explain my death, I did not want.

In other words, the lover lucidly realizes the self-defeating consequences
of yielding to despair for a woman who does not reciprocate his affection,
with whom he has had a love-hate relationship. This paradoxical defeat
despite victory is extremely important, for the problematized relationship
of word and deed established by the prefatory letter thus extends much
further, encompassing the very epistemological assumptions of personification allegory—that we are situated in the "epoch of the logos," as Derrida
defines it, where signifier and signified are coextensive. Or, as Carolyn Van
Dyke remarks, "As traditionally conceived [allegory] actually generates the
eventual discovery of genuine meaning and of congruence between signi-
fiers and signifieds."[31] This type of heuristic function, so essential to allegory, is conspicuously absent from the *Satira*.

Closer scrutiny of the explanatory glosses reveals that Don Pedro's subversive poetics operate throughout the putatively exegetical mechanism
as well. We have already noted the untenably hyperbolic praise accorded
by the narrator and personifications to his lady, the inappropriate nature

of the comparisons which they draw. Yet the full extent of the inappropriateness is only understood by a careful reading of the massive glosses, for by their sheer size they dwarf the lady, rendering her insignificant indeed.

Beyond such quantitative considerations, still other techniques of deflation are employed by Don Pedro in the glosses so that we will not mistake the true import of his metaliterary text. Broadly speaking, the exegetical gloss amounts, as Francisco Rico explains, to "the intellectual practice of attempting to 'complete' a text, to develop some implicit elements and to consider other explicit ones apart from their immediate context, to supply facts and consider the original as if it contained them. It is a procedure lucidly described by Marie de France: 'gloser la letter' and 'de leur sen le surplus mettre.' "[32]

Given that a gloss is designed to clarify interpretation, Don Pedro pointedly uses it as a vehicle of obfuscation, highlighting for example the discrepancy among various authorities regarding the true location of Cytherea, rather than attempting to clarify it:

> Çitarea—Esta fue Venus . . . e este nombre quieren algunos que le pertenesçe por ser nasçida en la ysla Çitarea, una de las yslas Ciclades, ante llamadas Porfires. Pero los mas çiertos auctores averiguan no ser asy, ante la ysla agora llamada Chipre posseer el nombre de Çitarea, por ay aver nasçido la deesa Çitarea, et este nombre disen obtener Venus por un alto monte a ella consagrado llamado Çithera. (57)

> Cytharea—This was Venus. . . and some attribute this name to the fact that she was born on the Island of Cytherea, one of the Cyclades which were formerly known as the Porphyry Islands. But the most respected authorities claim that it is not so, but that the island now known as Cyprus was previously called Cytherea because the goddess Cytharea was born there, and this name resulted from the fact that Venus had a mountain named Cytherea in her honor.

Instead of explaining why he disagrees with "the most respected authorities," he offers narrative where we would expect commentary, in the process casting doubt on his own competence or at least revealing himself to be arrogant—not to mention the fact that Cytherea was never identified as one of the Cyclades (being clearly separated from that chain by a considerable distance). For the same reason, Cyprus was not geographically confused with Cytherea. (Because of her personal association with each of the two islands, however, Venus herself was known either as Cytherea or the Cyprian. Don Pedro is confusing this onomastic association with geography.) Finally Porphyry is an alternate name for Cytherea (not the Cyclades).[33]

The fact that Don Pedro intentionally sets out to diminish his credibility as exegete, valorizing *histoire* where we would expect *discours*, is revealed by an additional feature of his authority. Namely, in the context of his most long-winded glosses he explicitly draws our attention to his verboseness. A three-page gloss, for example, is referred to as a "breviloquio" (91) [ brief speech]. Likewise, in the middle of a six-page note he interjects a concern for prolixity, which he wishes to avoid at all costs: "Otras grandes e infinitas cosas escrivieron de Minerva, lo qual agora no conviene desir, salvo dar fin a la presente grossa por evitar prolixidat" (61) [Additional important things were written of Minerva, which are not included here so as to avoid being prolix]. A full page later, still within the same gloss, he remarks: "per no traher fastidio con luenga fabla e incompuesta, do fyn a esta breve grosseta" (62) [in order to not be annoyingly prolix, I conclude this brief gloss]. Not surprisingly, it is during his moments of greatest prolixity that he voices such a fervent commitment to terseness. We can interpret this discrepancy between word and deed as comical because of its contradictory nature or at the very least, as imperceptive. In either case the authority of his words is seriously called into question.

Blatant contradiction is another feature in Don Pedro's program of exegetical subversion. In one breath love is definitively characterized as "loco e syn rason" (89) [mad and unreasonable], which "se llama llaga . . . porque assy como la llaga trahe dolor que quita el reposo corporeo" (89) [is called a wound . . . because like the wound it inflicts pain that makes repose impossible]. This traditional negative assessment is overturned on the next page of the gloss, however, where love is endowed with a highly beneficial effect:

> Son, e yo non negare averlos visto, algunos mançebos grosseros, peresosos, no despiertos para alguna gentilesa, virtud o noblesa. . . . El amor los reforma como de nuevo a contrarias condiçiones. E porque estas propriedades suso tocadas pertenesçen al no amador, e las sus contrarias al amador, devio ser la flecha que fiere para desamar de plomo, que es pesado, negro e de poco valor, e la que fiere para amar ser de oro, graçioso al viso, confortativo al animo, e de muy grand valor. (90)

> There are, and I do not deny having seen them, some uncouth and lazy youths who are oblivious to any refinement, virtue or nobility. . . . Love reforms them to the opposite condition. And because the aforementioned properties belong to the nonlover, the dart that causes one not to love should be made of lead since it is heavy, black, and of little value, and the one that causes love should be of gold, visually pleasing, spiritually uplifting and of great value.

Love's depiction here could not be more positive. Realizing that the mutually exclusive negative and positive accounts invalidate one another, the reader perceives that the glossator is clearly interested not in instruction, but in generating skepticism, forcing him into understanding that these glosses are qualitatively different. They are, in effect, a rejection of the instructional imperative that underlies the glossator's art.

The choice of decidedly problematic historical figures as illustrative examples is a further dimension of tampering that takes place. When, for instance, the narrator-protagonist rails against the cruelty of Fortune, calling her the "enemiga de toda virtud" (30), he offers as evidence Fortune's mistreatment of Lucius Cornelius Sulla, a notoriously objectionable figure. Rebuking Fortune personified, he indicts her by saying:

> Çiertamente tu amenguaste tanto su grandeza, tu embaraçaste tanto su magnifiçencia, que la muy puxante fortuna, con su sumo poder, pero le fizo magnifico e muy poderoso vencedor de las estrañas e civiles huestes, nombre de tirano cruel e malvado quitar ni apartar non le pudo. (32)

> Certainly you so diminished his reputation and his greatness that despite the fact that he was victorious in combating both foreign incursions and civil strife, he was never able to rid himself of the infamous reputation of cruel tyrant.

This is a bad example of Fortune's unfairness, to say the least, since Sulla was in fact a cruel tyrant. So as to ensure that his ill-suited historical example will not go unobserved, Don Pedro appends a very revealing (and lengthy) gloss the first part of which suffices to illustrate his very tongue-in-cheek procedure:

> *Luçio Sila*—O Luçio Sila, la mano tembla, el gesto se muda, el coraçon se afruenta, el seso se espanta, queriendo escrevir tus bestiales e innumerables cruesas. Ca por çierto aquellas te fisieron indigno del nombre de bienaventurado, el qual tus muchas e magnificas victorias te otorgaron. Retienenme aquellas, refrenan mi pluma que tus maldades no escriva. . . . Miedo me he que paresca en la presente obresilla mas amigo de Maurio que tuyo, pues callo tus victorias gloriosas e escrivo tus terribles inhumanidades. Assy que si la presente narraçion me no costriñiese a escrevir, visto el un estremo e el otro, no te loaria ni te vituperaria, mas tu me perdonaras, bevedor de la sangre de tu naturalesa, ca lo fago mas *como* cosa neçessaria que voluntaria. (30)

> *Luçio Sila*—O Lucius Sulla, my hand trembles, its gesture frozen, my heart affronted, my mind terrified, wishing to write of your bestiality and innumerable atrocities. For clearly such deeds made you unworthy of the good name to which your many magnificent victories entitle you. May your good accomplishments keep me from recounting your wickedness. . . . I am afraid that this little work of mine will show me to be more friendly toward Marius than

toward you, since I write of your crimes against humanity rather than your glorious victories. If the present text did not constrain me to write thusly, seeing the two extremes of your behavior I would neither praise nor denigrate you. But please forgive me, imbiber of human blood, for necessity constrains me to do so; it is not by choice.

By this gloss we see that Don Pedro himself is well aware that Sulla is hardly an apt example of a man unjustly treated by fortune, since he was at least as barbarous as he was a positive influence. Moreover, the inappropriateness of such an axiological dilemma in the context of exemplarity is definitively (and humorously) exposed as Don Pedro confesses his great fear at the possibility of incuring the wrath of the "bevedor de sangre."

Questioning the authority of the *auctores* is another transgression committed by Don Pedro. While relying heavily on Isidore of Seville at several junctures in his text, he also takes issue with him on occasion, for example concerning the etymological association of Vesta:

El arçobispo ispalense, *Libro Ethimologiarum*, la llama Proserpina e Juno, lo qual paresçe contradesir a la verdat, porquanto Proserpina, Juno e Vesta son tres deesas departidas. Pero a ello se podria dar la declaración e que semblasse evidente que se pudo desir verdaderamente lo que dixo el sabio varon. Mas porque paresçeria cosa superflua de declarar esta dubda e seria larga la escriptura, yo remitto los leyentes a lo que brevemente toque en la glosa de Diana; e si dello no fueren satisfechos, ayan por respuesta e sepan que yo no fise esta obreta para colegir ni declarar todas las cosas e dubdas del universo, ca no es quien lo pueda ni sepa faser en pequeña narraçion, mas aquellas que so breve tractado se podrian desir e que occurrian al proposito brevemente las declare. (112–13)

The Archbishop of Seville, in his *Liber Etymologiarum*, refers to her as Proserpina and Juno, which seems to contradict the truth since Proserpina, Juno, and Vesta are three different deities. However, it seems clear that the wise man was capable of having said just that. But because it would appear superfluous to voice skepticism over it and because it would require a lengthy explanation, I refer my readers to the brief section in the gloss on Diana. And if they are still not satisfied, let them know that I did not write this little text in order to declare all the doubts that exist in the universe, since no one can accomplish that in a brief narrative. But those doubts that can be set forth in a brief treatise (and that are relevant) I have noted briefly.

Thus not only does he question Isidore's judgment, but he also promises to explain why he does so—flatly asserting immediately thereafter that he will not give any explanation since it is not relevant to his argument. What follows is an even more irrelevant, contradictory, and long-winded reiteration of his commitment to relevance and brevity. The chasm separating what he says from what he does could hardly be greater; the calculated comicality of the disparity is obvious. In short, we see that the exegesis strays as far away from normative gloss procedure as does the allegory.

Obvious misinformation is another technique that provokes the reader to discount the authority of the exegetical apparatus. A notable example of this practice comes in a statement that distorts the *Heroides'* first epistle, that of Penelope to Ulysses:

> Assy lo dise Ovidio, libro de las "Ereydas," epistola prima: El amor es cosa llena de temor e de sospecha. E entre los amadores ha una qualidat de amantes que subito aman e subito desaman, contienden, reconçilianse, tienen quasi en un mismo tiempo desseos contrarios, lo qual non fasen los otros posseedores de algunas passiones: e por lo suso dicho devieron dar a Cupido alas, assy lo dise el mençionado arçobispo en el nombrado libro. (89)

> In the first epistle of the *Heroides* Ovid says: "Love is full of fear and suspicion." And lovers quickly fall in and out of love, they fight, become reconciled, virtually displaying contradictory emotions at the same time. This is a trait unique to them. And because of this, they should flee Cupid, as the aforementioned archbishop indicates in the aforementioned book.

Don Pedro's readers were doubtless aware of this critical distortion in his misrepresentation of the first heroid, written by the long-suffering Penelope, a universal emblem of uxorial steadfastness.

If further proof were required to demonstrate the manipulative, unedifying nature of the glosses, we find remarks such as the one that ends the gloss on Artemisia. Narrating how she honored her beloved deceased husband, the glossator explains that she not only constructed monuments in his memory but, in a supreme act of devotion, had him cremated, at which point she swallowed the ashes, entombed herself, and died. From this display of intense loyalty, the narrator abruptly and unjustifiably shifts gears, turning his discourse of praise for this laudable female into misandry:

> Qual marido se fallara jamas que tan piadosamente e con tanta sobra de amor honrrasse a su muger? Por çierto ninguno. Mas ayna se fallaran innumerables que aun sus mugeres no han bien dexado la presente vida e ellos ya tienen el segundo matrimonio conçertado. Que al se deve desir, salvo que el leal amor que las dueñas han a sus maridos es con virtud mantenido, mas no de rason devido. (124–25)

> Who could ever find a husband who would treat his wife so compassionately and with such love? No one, to be sure. More readily one finds innumerable husbands who do not even wait for their wives to die before they contract a

second marriage. What else is there to say except that the loyal love that women have for their husbands stems from virtue, for it runs counter to reason.

Useless repetition and cross-referencing is also interjected by the glossator, an example of which can be seen in his note on the "moço de las doradas alas" [the youth with the golden wings], an obvious periphrasis for Cupid:

Porque a Cupido moço e con alas pintavan, segund esto mas largo en la glosa de Cupido se manifiesta, le llamo aqui el auctor moço de las doradas alas. (155)

Because Cupid used to be depicted as young and winged, as is evident from the lengthy gloss on Cupid, the author here calls him the youth with golden wings.

At this point the exegete adds insult to injury, as it were, for not only is the reference obvious, but to remind us of his previous (highly protracted) gloss on the same topic is almost more than the reader can bear.

The final and perhaps most blatant means by which the glossator unravels the authority of his discourse occurs very near the end of the *Satira*. In the context of a long description in which the astronomical figure of the dragon is mentioned and heavily glossed, a highly significant pronominal shift occurs. Whereas Don Pedro has categorically stated in the prefatory letter that he is the author of the glosses as well as the allegory (carefully employing either the third-person "el auctor" or the first-person "yo" in a given gloss), he abruptly combines both in the same gloss (italics added):

Porque *el auctor* introduze cauda del dragon fue forçado a la *mi* diestra esplicar lo suso escripto, e de declarar que *el auctor* se movio a lo dezir por manifestar la causa e manera del eclipse del sol que, a la sazon quando el testo mençiona, en la cauda o cola del dragon se fazia. (173)

Because *the author* introduces the tail of the dragon, it is necessary for *me* [my right hand] to explain the above, and to indicate that *the author* was led to mention it in order to illustrate the nature of the solar eclipse which, when it is mentioned in the text, was in the shape of the dragon's tail.

Within this unnecessarily verbose astronomical description, the pronominal duality definitively deflates the narrator's authority.[34] Not only have the two interpretive modes of allegory and gloss been shown to be remarkably uninterpretive, he has, it would appear, lost control not only of his authority but of his identity as well. Or rather, with this final *léger de main* he is dramatically underscoring the highly manipulative persona from which he has generated his text.

By the end of our reading of the *Satira* what can be stated unambiguously is that the two interpretive mechanisms of allegory and gloss have failed completely in resolving the narrator-protagonist's *psychomachia*. The ending is totally unresolved:

> la desnuda e bicordante espada en la my diestra mirava, titubando, con dudoso pensamiento e demudada cara, sy era mejor prestamente morir o asperar la dubdosa respuesta me dar consuelo. La discriçion favoresçe e suplica la espera, la congoxosa voluntad la triste muerte reclama, el seso manda esperar la respuesta, el aquexado coraçon, gridando, acusa la postrimeria. (174)

> I stared at the naked, double-edged sword in my right hand, vacillating as to whether it was better to die quickly or hope that the unlikely response would relieve my pain. Discretion advises the latter, but my will advises suicide, reason suggests that I wait for the reply, my suffering heart inclines toward death.

The insoluble vacillation between the logic of empirical reality and the illogic of lyric, of Don Pedro's subjective state, thus prevails until the very end. The significance of this lack of closure is paramount, for it signifies that allegory's fundamentally heuristic function has failed. The recognition that it is unrealistic to expect that his beloved will capitulate suggests the appropriateness of suicide. Suicide, however, will definitively extinguish even the palest glimmer of hope. The circularity of such indecisiveness is, moreover, very reminiscent of Fiammetta's psychological quandary.

Beyond this lyric vacillation, however, Don Pedro achieves a distinctly and radically new kind of discourse by demonstrating the novelistic potential of allegory. He spectacularly defeats the Seven Virtues and sustains a love-hate relationship with his lady. Nonetheless, as we have seen, his logic fails to bring him consolation. At the same time, his encyclopedic wisdom—the overpowering erudition of the glosses—likewise fails him; objective erudition and subjective experience are shown to be alien discourses. In the end he is as helpless—indeed rather more so—than at the beginning. And as such, the *Satira* exhibits an attitude toward language analogous to that which Paul Zumthor finds operative in French literature of the time: "Narrative discourse, eroded by reasoning, by glossing, by the growing pressure of referential exegencies which weigh down upon it, collapses at the same time as the optimistic synthesis of the great philosophical *summae*, drawing along in their catastrophe the confidence, of which they had been testimony, in our possibilities of knowledge and understanding, and in our competence to make a coherent world exist by means of language."[35]

The exemplary mechanisms of allegory and gloss are shown to be ineffectual in combating the irrationality of love. The nominal rather than real coexistence of signifier and signified has been recognized, and as a result, the positivistic function of words is being denied. As such, the modes of allegory and exegesis are being used discursively in the same way that we have seen epistolarity function. Here too the potential distance separating word from deed is dramatized.[36] And for this reason the *Satira* is, in the last analysis, a novelistically untranscendent vision.

# SEVEN

## ETIOLOGICAL SUBVERSION

### (*TRISTE DELEYTAÇION*)

THE ONTOLOGY of language is currently the subject of intense literary investigation. Witness, for example, the impact of Searle, Austin, Foucault, Derrida, and Bakhtin. With the renewal of interest in historicism, Bakhtin—the "formalist heresiarch," a relentless critic of abstraction, devoted to questions of authority—emerges as one of the most timely theorists. As Caryl Emerson explains: "Bakhtin profoundly redefined the Word itself and attempted to infuse it with its original Greek sense of *logos* ('discourse'). For Bakhtin, words cannot be conceived apart from the voices who speak them; thus every word raises the question of authority."[1]

To implement this authority-based investigation, Bakhtin introduces the concept of the chronotope[2]—a spatiotemporal binome—"the set of distinctive features of time and space within each literary genre."[3] As Bakhtin himself explains: "In literature, the chronotope has an essential generic signification. It can be stated categorically that genre and generic species are precisely determined by the chronotope."[4] Moreover, "the represented universe can never be chronotopically identical with the real universe."[5]

In other words, a given genre is a (selective) simulacrum of reality or model of the world. In chronotopic terms, then, we can, for example, speak of the space of lyric as the mind's subjectivity, and of lyric time as the eternal present. Similarly, the temporal referent of hagiography is the past-present-and-future, which corresponds to the spatial domain of Earth and Heaven.

Each chronotopic mode of representation, moreover, projects a particular axiology. Identical elements can be used in radically different functions, as Jauss observes:

> Thus for example the different structures of the fairy tale and the novella cannot be grasped only through the oppositions of unreality and everyday-ness; naive morality and moral casuistry; the self-evident wonder of fairy tales and the "unheard-of-event," but rather may also be understood through the different signification of the same figures: "One puts a princess in a fairy tale next to a princess in a novella, and one notices the difference."[6]

It is this type of axiological divergence effected by two distinct chronotopic milieux (novella and romance) that the anonymous *Triste de-*

*leytaçion* explores. E. Michael Gerli and others situate this text somewhat tentatively within the *novela sentimental* corpus. In his words: "If it belongs to any literary genre, *Triste deleytaçion* belongs to that of the sentimental romance. . . . The action which it depicts is essentially psychological, relying upon allegory, symbolism, and a journey to the Other World to represent the workings of the emotions and the imagination."[7]

By contrast, in the only article to date written on this text, Martín de Riquer views it not as poetic fiction, but as nonfiction—an autobiographical novel, a *roman à clef*—as a result of which the author disguises his true identity behind the letters "F.A.D.C.": "If we assume that the novel is autobiographical, we can be sure of interpreting one of these initials correctly; since the author-protagonist is religious, it is probable that the first letter, 'F,' corresponds to Fra., which refers to members of military orders. From this hypothesis we can conjecture that the author of *Triste deleytaçion* may have been Fra. A. de C."[8]

In contradistinction to both of these positions, the aim of this chapter is to demonstrate that the text in fact constitutes a novelistic undermining of the familiar erotic pseudoautobiograpy. To repeat, the existence of a princess (or in this case, of courtly love intrigue) does not necessarily guarantee the existence of romance. Likewise anonymity does not necessarily designate nonfiction.

In a highly suggestive remark, María Rosa Lida asserts that the oxymoron of the work's title (*Triste deleytaçion*) was inspired by another such grammatical paradox—namely Rodríguez's *Siervo libre.*[9] This suggested filiation is quite convincing given the historical importance of the *Siervo libre* as the first manifestation of this novelistic subgenre in Spain, and also given Rodríguez's prominence in *Triste deleytaçion*—he being the most frequently named author.

To María Rosa Lida's observation I would add that the oxymoron of each title reflects the chronotopically dialogic structure (in axiological terms) at issue in each text.[10] As Julia Kristeva aptly explains, "for Bakhtin, dialogue can be monological, and what is called monologue can be dialogical. With him, such terms refer to a linguistic infrastructure that must be studied through a semiotics of literary texts. This semiotics cannot be based either on linguistic methods or logical givens, but rather, must be elaborated from the point where they leave off."[11] In the *Siervo libre* we find the courtly and Christian idioms in dialogic confrontation. In *Triste deleytaçion* it is the unreality of courtly romance and the cynical empiricism of novella discourse that are at issue. And, while Rodríguez is referred to explicitly by name more than any other author in *Triste deleytaçion*, it is Boccaccio in fact who provides the most extensively exploited subtext. A simple numerical calculation gives us an initial indication of F.A.D.C.'s potential for misrepresentation. Significantly, while the author of *Triste deleytaçion* explicitly mentions only one of Boccaccio's works by name (the *Elegia di madonna*

*Fiammetta*), he exploits twelve of the *novelle* of the *Decameron*—virtually all from Day 5—in which Fiammetta herself reigns.[12] No other work is so programmatically recalled as the *Decameron*, despite the implicitness of its presentation. Most of these subtextual references are made by Free Will in her debate against Reason. However, their presence in fact signals the introduction of a novella chronotope that will be deployed consistently throughout *Triste deleytaçion* from beginning to end.

The first indication of divergence from the overtly fictive chronotope of romance in favor of an adherence to that of the novella is the narrator-protagonist's insistence on maintaining strict verisimilitude—that he is recounting a historically true story which occurred in 1458. The prologue itself begins with this detail of temporal specificity:

> Venido a conocimiento mio, ahun que por via jndirecta, vn auto de amores de vna muy garrida e mas virtuosa donzella, y de hun gentil honbre, de mi como de si mismo amigo, en el tiempo de cinquenta y ocho, concorriendo en el auto mismo hotro gentil honbre y duenya madrastra de aquella, yo, consideradas las demasiadas penas y afanes que ellos hobedeçiendo, Amor procurado les auia, quise para siempre en scrito pareçiesen.[13]

> Having come to my attention (although indirectly) a love afffair between a virtuous maiden and a gentleman (who is my friend as well as hers), in 1458 (in which another gentleman and the lady's stepmother also participated), and, considering the pain and pleasure they had suffered, I decided to immortalize them in writing.

This claim to veracity is enhanced by the fact that the five principal characters are referred to by means of totally impersonal tags: El Enamorado, la Señora, El Amigo, La Madrastra, and La Madrina. The effect of such depersonalization is twofold. First, it (as well as the author's decision to designate himself simply as "F.A.D.C.") suggests that we may be reading an historical (and potentially compromising) account. Alternatively, it may be argued that these generic designations function in precisely the opposite way—not a change of names intended to protect the guilty, but (as in *Lazarillo de Tormes*, for example) as a way of designating universal human types.[14]

It is also important to note that the narrator-protagonist's scribal activity is not the product of pure altruism, but of self-interest, for as he admits, it is written to convince his own lady not to be ungrateful—to woo her back from a temporary separation:

> Que mi deseo traspostado en aq*ue*lla *senyora* q*ue* por más bien y hutil fue de mi syempre querida, sta jnuención como propio bien le quise narar en suma, por*que* aquel *be* guarneçido de tanta perfeçion por flaqueza de sperança, qu'es causa dar fin amor, viniese a perder aq*ue*lla voluntat q*ue* la yzo tanto mia,

siguiendo el entento del jnvestigado dezir mio, venga a cobrar por contrarias
obras aquell grado que hizo a ella e a mi tanto catiuos. (1–2)

To the Lady whom I have always loved I wished to narrate this fiction in the
hope that by reading it she would (by reading about contrary deeds) regain
that measure of love which took us both captive.

From this admission we see that the narrator-protagonist's overriding
concern with historical veracity (to "no aplicar fiçion": 1) is soon belied by
his calling it an "invención," and by the presence of allegorical figures. As
he is traveling to see his lady, he is confronted by Fortune, who informs
him of the events that will befall him, referring to him as "Verbino" ("que
quiere dezir dos vezes onbre: la vna significa ser mal aventurado, y la otra
ser bien aventurado; que el que sta e biue en desauentura no biue": 2)
[which means "twice born": the first refers to the unfortunate man, and the
other to the fortunate one; for he who lives unhappily does not live]. Falling asleep in an attempt to alleviate his love suffering, he witnesses a debate—the familiar medieval dispute between Reason and Free Will. As
with virtually everything else in the text, however, this familiar scene takes
an unexpected turn. In this case it is the combination of a predictable series
of arguments with some unanticipated ones that stem from the indecorous
comportment of these two figures, who behave more like the proverbial
haggling fishwives than as dignified abstractions. Reason offers just such an
argument, for example, when she claims (quite haughtily and unreason-
ably) to her opponent: "vos no sabeys que sin pasar por las potençias y
sentidos nuestros la libertat encadenar no se puede. . . . ¡sin mi ninguna
cosa se aze!" (12) [You don't know that without passing through (my
rational) powers and senses one's free will cannot become enslaved. . . .
Without me nothing happens!]. Given human nature, it should come as no
surprise that Free Will (despite her own equally churlish behavior) wins the
dispute.

At the conclusion of the debate the narrator's discourse concerning the
protagonist inexplicably turns from the first person to the third, referring
to himself now as "El Enamorado."[15] The conventional first-person erotic
pseudoautobiography is thus recast into the novelistic third-person without any explanatory transition at all. In this way the narrative in effect
moves outside of the private space of the protagonist's subjectivity into the
public arena, where he is objectified, observed interacting in society. The
corresponding chronotopic temporal frame is no longer the timelessness
of dreamlike unreality, but rather the un-oneiric obstacles posed by empirical reality. The significance of this distancing from first- to third-person is
paramount, for as Bakhtin explains, the questioning of a hero's discourse,
its efficacy, is fundamental to the novel, a gesture that radically distinguished it from epic (and, I would add, from romance as well).[16] The

chronotopic displacement of the lover from the initial romance setting to a novelistic one, furthermore, implies a shift from exemplary personal idealism (exotic and heroic) to unexemplary social realism (domestic and largely unheroic). This is precisely the incongruous milieu in which the lover finds himself. It is, significantly, this novelistic environment—not (as we would expect) his lady's disposition—that poses the consistent obstacle to his success.

Briefly stated, the protagonist falls in love and his initial advance (in the form of a love letter) is—as often happens—rejected. At this point, the predictable courtly intrigue takes on an unexpected novella-like turn when the Lover's Friend (El Amigo) immediately suggests what in the courtly idiom would be unthinkable—that he find another lady:

> Que con liberalidat
> fuyreys donde sta ella,
> porque no tengays querella
> de su jesto ny beldat;
> Seruireys a otra dama
> por amores,
> y trocadas las pasiones
> el pensamiento desama.
>
> (35–36)

You will freely leave the place where she is found, so that you will not quarrel either with her demeanor or with her beauty. You will serve another lady for love, and when one's passions are diverted, you will forget [the one who spurned you].

This advice, while expedient, is hardly appropriate within the dictates of *fin' amor*. Equally discordant to courtly behavior is the Lover's suggestion that the Friend seduce the Lady's Stepmother—for the sake of expediency, so that his own affair may proceed more smoothly (40). Although he has never seen, much less met, the Stepmother, the Friend accepts this suggestion and he succeeds. Meanwhile, the Lover goes off to war in order to prove his valor, and while en route, lost in amorous reverie, he falls off his horse: "el *enamorado*, con la presente fatigua y poca defensa de cosa que ayudar le pudiese, costrenydos los esperitos, amorteçido cayo del caualo" (42) [the lover, as a result of his fatigue and defenselessness since his spirit was subdued, fainted, falling off his horse]. This detail is clearly comical, but also realistically believable, serving an epistemological function. It is striking here because the chronotope of romance tends to exclude the intrusion of such empirically real phenomena as weakness caused by a lack of sleep. Novelistic discourse, on the other hand, deals precisely with such unheroic and universal quotidian necessities.[17]

The narrative turns next to a didactic sequence in which the Lady is instructed by her Godmother on the subject of men. Here, too, incongruity prevails as empirical reality overtakes courtly ideal. The Godmother discourses on men, offering very contradictory advice to her pupil. First she claims that a choleric man makes the best lover ("Que sea el enamorado tuyo colerico"), thereafter declaring that old men (not 25-year-olds) are in fact the best—because they are constant (62). Speaking of these older men, La Madrina explains:

> por el bien q*ue* las quieren no piensan sino en complazerlas en quanto pueden ni saben; y mas, q*ue* trabaian quanto pueden en alegar los bienes para la vegez; no son bariables en sus amores, mas firmes e costantes, y no curan de dar razon a otra senyora de la q*ue* tiene*n*. E los mançebos por el contrario . . . no les tienen lealdat en presençia, ni en absençia firmeza. (62)

> Because of their love, they think of nothing but pleasing [their ladies]. And, in addition, they do what they can to guarantee comfort in old age; they are not fickle in their love, being instead constant; and they do not think of showing interest in any other lady. Young men, by contrast . . . are faithful neither in the lady's presence, nor in her absence.

In like fashion, after claiming that the Lady must choose one lover to live with for her entire life, the teacher then asserts that men clearly prefer the "one-night stand" (43), following it with another contradiction: "¿no sabes tu q*ue* vno te a de amar, vno te a de seruir, vno te a de stimar y aquel te a de onrar, y te a [de] dar pasatiempo en la jouentut y reposo en la vegez, y no muchos?" (68) [Don't you realize that the same man will love, serve, and esteem you; and he will honor you and provide entertainment in your youth and comfort in your old age, rather than a series of men?]. The Lady is justifiably confused at the Godmother's ability to contradict herself. A discussion of the "double standard" by which men behave and by which they judge women follows—a further blatantly *un*romance subject. This is an alien discourse to be sure, something that we would expect in response to clerkly misogyny. Even more shocking than this cynically conceived misandrist diatribe, however, is the misogynistic discourse that the Godmother delivers. Speaking of the capacity of women to deceive men, she remarks that:

> ellas los enganyan en la mesa; los enganyan en la sala, los enganyan en la . . . cama, los enganyan en las danças, los enganyan en las justas, los enganyan en la yglesia, los enganyan en la lengua, y en el gesto y mirar. (65)

> They deceive them at table, in the drawing room, . . . in bed, at dances, jousts, in church; they deceive them by means of their speech, their gestures, and their glances.

It is important to note here that deception is valorized, indeed it is pointedly equated with salvation itself: "si la pasion de la ofensa que l'es ffecha la empare, fingelo desimulando el malo y demostrando el bueno, lo seruira y obedeçera como su vida, como ste sea el camino de la salbaçion" (88) [If the passion of the offense you do him emperils you, hide it, feigning the bad and displaying the good: thus he will serve you and will obey you as his life, as if this were the road to salvation]. Such misogyny in the mouth of a woman is striking in virtually any context. Yet, within the chronotope of romance it is anathema. The Godmother, in her lengthy discussion, ranges from idealistic *fin' amor* to an anatomy of novella deception that is very reminiscent of the *Decameron*. What confronts us here is a view of men and women that is far more complex than the romance world permits.

At the conclusion of this lengthy and unidealistic exposé of amorous deception, our attention is once more focused on the unfolding affairs of the Lady and Lover, and of the Friend and Stepmother. Their intrigues accord in several significant ways with the unheroic, deceptive behavior that has just been presented in abstract, theoretical terms, thus continuing the confrontation of novella and romance.

Indeed, *Triste deleytaçion* displays a consistent interest in concretizing abstractions, and it does so in two ways. The first is the initial articulation of amorous behavior in theoretical terms followed by a specific proof, as in the example just cited. The other, which E. Michael Gerli has observed, consists of the concretization of courtly metaphors:

> The image of the voyage is integrated into a fundamental pattern of style, metaphor and action in *Triste deleytaçion*. What is said metaphorically in one context, for example, is often dramatized in the next. In the debate between Reason and Will we encounter a clear instance of unity which our author derives from imagistic deployment. One of the predominant forms of comparison employed in the debate comes from navigation and seafaring. Speaking of the anxieties of falling in love, Will refers to the "mar de tempestuosa furia" which lovers must navigate. . . . Later, of course, the comparisons of Will and Reason are dramatized in the Lover's allegorical journey in the Other World, where he navigates the perilous shoals of love.[18]

The effect of the first type of concretization (from theory to practice) has the effect of proving the unheroic nature of the characters whom we encounter in action. The effect of the second, the literalization of metaphorical language is to trivialize it by exposing its artificiality.[19]

Architectural space confirms the chronotopic deviation from romance to novella. It is not the locus amoenus, castle, or "palaçio Aborintio" (21) in which the author situates *Triste deleytaçion*, but houses in an urban setting.

This space is replete with spies, meddlesome old ladies, and "vellacos"—figures that populate the novella world, not romance.[20]

Among the logical realities that romance tends not to treat are the consequences of adulterous love, focusing more on the pleasures of the love itself. Here, significantly, the focus is reversed: the author of *Triste deleytaçion* chooses to highlight precisely the conjugal domesticity and the perils that adultery implies. The Friend's advances to the Stepmother do not go unnoticed by a servant who informs the betrayed Husband, who in turn instructs the servant to kill the Friend. Here too, however, the author is intent on deflating the reader's chronotopic expectations. For rather than murdering him, the servant merely succeeds in slashing his ear (69): "vn dia, falleçiendole las fuerças del animo, por mas seguredat suya em presençia de su senyor con vn punyal por detras al *amigo* diere, y con el temor q*ue* traya salbo el cauo de la oreia cortara" (107) [one day, because he was scared (the would-be assassin), in the presence of his master, came upon the Friend from behind, but as a result of his fear, he managed only to cut a piece of (the lover's) ear]. The Friend and the Lover agree to wreak revenge on "aquel vellaco" (109) (as they refer to the offended Husband), once more signaling the axiological attributes of the novella world. The Stepmother reinforces this vengeful impulse by vowing to effect the revenge (108) in order to "repar[ar] vuestra honrra y [la] mía." As we see, it is brute expedience not decorum, much less a sense of honor, that is projected. Words are undermined by actions as blatantly here as they are in the other *novelas sentimentales*.

The betrayed Husband has the Stepmother (his wife) murdered, and here too we see the authority of novella discourse being affirmed. For, in effect, it overtakes the one remaining love affair, for when the Stepmother is killed the Lover and Friend exhibit a notable lack of dignity by fleeing to Barcelona to hide from the Husband. Having vowed to kill him, their flight can only be interpreted as cowardly expedience since they are concerned not with upholding their oath, but with evading his wrath. The abandoned Lady also hides (cloistered in her sister's house). The Lover's cowardice (also his inefficacy) is further reinforced as he disguises himself as a *romero* (a beggar or pilgrim) (140). Yet, very much unlike Tristan of the *Folie Tristan*, the Lover here is recognized and, therefore—without seeing his Lady—must flee once more. Since she does not hear from him, and motivated apparently by expedience rather than true religious vocation, she becomes a nun.

The realistic third-person prose narrative abruptly ends here. And, in a shift that is as unanticipated as the initial change discussed above from the first- to the third-person, we return now to the first person. The realistic prose we have witnessed until this moment inexplicably turns to unrealistic (indeed supernatural) verse in the form of an extraterrestrial (other-worldly) journey in the final quarter of the text. This new landscape is the familiar erotic Afterlife which one routinely finds in allegorical love litera-ture. As such, it signals a return to the chronotope of romance, but with a difference.

Like Dante's otherworldly journey, that of the Lover is presented not as a dream, but as literal truth. This extraterrestrial realm, basing itself struc-turally on Dante's spatial conception, is tripartite in nature—divided into Hell, Purgatory, and Heaven. Yet, as Michael Gerli notes: "While Dante deals with a wide, metaphysical conception of love in his *Commedia* . . . our author occupies himself exclusively with the courtly notion of it."[21] Also in accord with Dante, this otherworld includes historically real—and even contemporary—figures. The similarities end there, however, for we soon see that the Boccaccian axiology that characterized the prose narrative pre-vails in the verse as well. Indeed, the first people whom the Lover encoun-ters are, as Gerli notes,[22] strikingly reminiscent of the protagonists of *De-cameron* 5.8, where we find two hellish apparitions—a suicide and his scornful beloved (the cause of his death). Both are consigned to Hell, in which he is forced to pursue her, finally capturing her so that he can stab her, severing her back in order to tear out her cold heart and have it de-voured by the dogs. This hideous spectacle is repeated every Friday, as the suicidal lover explains. Moreover, the punishment is Dantean both in its cyclical nature, and because the punishment for prodigality (presented in *Inferno* 13 of the *Commedia*) is precisely that of being perpetually devoured by hounds. The fate of Lano of Siena and Giacomo of Padua, infamous spendthrifts of the thirteenth century, are described as follows:

> Di rietro a loro era la selva piena
> di nere cagne, bramose e correnti
> come veltri ch'uscisser di catena.
> In quel che s'appiattò miser li denti,
> e quel dilaceraro a brano a brano;
> poi sen portar quelle membra dolenti.

Behind them the wood was full of black bitches, eager and fleet, like grey-hounds loosed from the leash. On him who had squatted they set their teeth and tore him piecemeal, then carried off those woeful limbs.[23]

This Dantean punishment, however, is problematized in Boccaccio's text, for the prodigal narrator of the event (Nastagio degli Onesti, which translates literally as "Resurrection of the Honest") exploits this grizzly scene very dishonestly—to terrify his own lady into submission, that if she does not agree to marry him she will suffer the same dire consequences as the dismembered damsel in Hell. Nastagio's successful coercive techniques thus constitute an inversion of what his name implies. It is important to note that with this novella Fiammetta's command—that Day 5 be devoted to "di ciò che ad alcuno amante, dopo alcuni fieri o sventurati accidenti, felicemente avvenisse" (Segre, 320) [adventures of lovers who survived calamities or misfortunes and attained a state of happiness (McWilliam, 405)]—is severely strained.

F.A.D.C. modifies the Boccaccian subtext by focusing not on the lady, but the knight's prodigality in love. More precisely, Isabel, daughter of the French Dauphin, commits suicide because the man she loves, Mosén Castell, does not return her love. He, meanwhile loves Leonor of Mallorca who, by disdaining him, casts him into such a state of despair that he too takes his own life.

The outcome of this unfortunate triangle is that in Hell on a nightly basis the knight pursues Isabel, attacking her with his sword, mutilating her body by cleaving her in two. The violence does not stop there, however, for he rips out her heart with a pair of fiery tongs whereupon he throws it into the fire. For her part, Leonor is not spared either. Rather, she is accompanied by a grisly spirit who dismembers the knight: "aquel [spiritu inmundo] sin benignidat / el cauallero tomo, / en dos partes lo partio / con muy poca piadat" (Langbehn-Roland, 145) [that hideous spirit, without any kindness, seized the knight, mercilessly cleaving him in two].

By this rewriting, F.A.D.C. not only complicates the *Decameron* tale, he problematizes its signification by punishing the faithful lady (Isabel) as Boccaccio had punished the unresponsive, scornful lady who had, according to her lover, "per lo peccato della sua crudeltà e della letizia avuta de' miei tormenti" (Segre, 364) [sinned by her cruelty and by gloating over my sufferings (McWilliam, 459)]. This recasting calls into question the exemplarity of the punishments found in F.A.D.C.'s Hell—thereby also distancing his narrative from Dante's even further. This constitutes one of the text's most blatant expressions of etiological undermining.

What is being valorized in *Triste deleytaçion*, as it is in the *Decameron*, is sexual compromise through coercion. The Dantean system of Divine retribution is clearly inoperative here. Interestingly, right after the Lover enters Hell, where he sees Boccaccio, he himself is nearly devoured by a dog:

> Sin darme ningun spaçio,
> con stremo poderio,
> en vn muy fondo palaçio,
> do vi de llexos Bocaçio,
> me leuaron por un rio;
> ya qu'a la puerta llegado
> me soltaron vn alan
> que staua ali atado,

el qual me hubo tragado
lugo, sin mas ademan.

(Langbehn-Roland, 175)

Without giving me any room, / with great strength, / they took me by boat /to
a very expansive palace, / where I saw Boccaccio in the distance. / And there,
as I arrived at the door, / they turned a dog on me / who was tied there. / He
would have eaten me / without any trouble.

The Boccaccian subtext of Day 5 thus serves to suggest that the Lover
himself—like the dismembered damsel—also misuses the chronotope of
romance. His dedication to expedience above all—specifically his flight
and consequent abandonment of his Lady—certainly corroborates this
suggestion.

In addition, this Boccaccian subtext functions as an opening signal for
the very un-Dantean axiology of the journey in *Triste deleytaçion*—despite
the superficial chronotopic resemblance. The Lover's own fate corroborates the fact that no causal relationship exists between how one behaves
in life and his fate in the Afterlife—a blatant inversion of the Dantean
etiology.

Although the Lover is a self-proclaimed Orpheus (102), he, unlike Orpheus, did not consciously choose to undertake the perilous journey to the
otherworld. His repeated association with Hippolytus serves an analogous
function. For "Verbino" is a rendering into Spanish of "Virbius / Bis Vir,"
the "Twice Man." And it is a periphrasis for Hippolytus, as Marguerite
Chiarenza explains: "From Servius' commentary on the *Aeneid* (VII.761)
. . . the name 'Virbius' took on the etymology of 'bis vir,' 'twice a man.'
Servius' note is . . . the principal source for the etymology:

"Theseus mortua Hippolyte Phaedram, Minois et Pasiphaae filiam, super-
duxit Hippolyto. Qui cum illam de stupro interpellantem contempsisset, falso
delatus ad patrem est, quod ei vim voluisset inferre. Ille Aegeum patrem roga-
vit ut se ulcisceretur. Qui agitanti currus Hippolyto inmisit focam, qua equi
territi eum traxerunt. Tunc Diana eius castitate commota revocavit eum in
vitam per Aesculapium, filium Apollinis et Coronidis. . . . Diana Hippoly-
tum, revocatum ab inferis, in Aricia nymphae commendavit Egeriae et eum
*Virbium*, quasi *bis virum*, iussit vocari."[24]

After Hippolyta had died, Theseus imposed Phaedra, daughter of Minos and
Pasiphaë, on Hippolytus as stepmother. And because he despised that one
[Phaedra], who was making continual appeals to him to commit incest, he
was falsely denounced to his father, allegedly because he had wanted to use
violence on her. That one [Theseus] called upon [his] Aegean father [Nep-
tune] to avenge him. And, while Hippolytus was driving his chariot, he sent

a sea-monster against [him], because of which the horses, terrified, dragged
him off. Then, Diana, because she had been moved by his chastity, brought
him back to life through the agency of Aesculapius, son of Apollo and
Coronis. . . . After he had been recalled from the underworld, Diana en-
trusted Hippolytus to the nymph Egeria in Africa, and commanded that he be
called *Virbium,* as if to say *twice a man* [my translation].

It is this renaming, moreover, that led Hippolytus to be associated with
Christ. His "death and resurrection, or rather his rebirth under the new
name of 'Virbius' became the central point of interest to Christian
mythographers," as Chiarenza remarks.[25] The association that F.A.D.C.
makes between the Lover (who entered into Hell purely by accident) and
Christ underscores the former's unwilled journey all the more. The Lover's
arbitrary expulsion from Hell (Langbehn-Roland, 114) underscores still
further the etiological subversion operative in this unique journey to the
Afterlife.

Indeed, his notable lack of courage is emphasized even further when he
unceremoniously (and comically) climbs up a tree when pursued by wild
beasts. Once again, his actions are expedient but unacceptable in the romance idiom. This arboreal detail also recalls (contrastively) the protagonist of the *Siervo libre* at the moment of conversion, when he rejects earthly
love, embracing Synderesis: "mudado en las más altas árbores de mi escura
maginança (Prieto, 111) [altered in the tallest treetops of my dark imagin-
ing]. Rather than being a witness to the infernal torments of others, as the
Dantean pilgrim was, this *romero* is not a distanced observer, but an unwilling victim—ridiculed and abused by the inhabitants of Hell. Here, too,
novelistic verisimilitude prevails in that the malefactors continue to exercise their wickedness against each other and (as they behaved during their
lifetimes) against the innocent as well. In this way, the artificiality of the
good versus evil binome of romance is exposed. The Dantean system of
Divine retribution is similarly undermined.

The fact that the Lover is saved from Hell, passing through Purgatory to
Heaven itself, is—as we are explicitly told on several occasions by Fortune
and her emissaries—because she has decided that the God of Love will save
him.[26] Both in the form of prophesy and by the Lover's place in the Book
of Fate (Langbehn-Roland, 111, 118–19) this outcome is affirmed. The
wholly arbitrary nature of one's fate is corroborated, for example, by the
placement of Boccaccio in Hell (175) and the notorious misogynist Pedro
Torrellas in Heaven (193). The placement of Torellas in this privileged
locus is all the more shocking in light of the Madrina's unforgiving designation of him as "nuestro enemigo mortal, mosen Pero Torrellas [quien dixo]
contra la honra nuestra en aquellas abominables coplas 'Mujer es vn animal—qual dizen honbre jnperfeto—proqreado en el defeto—del buen

calor natural' " (83–84) [our mortal enemy, Mosén Pedro Torrellas (who spoke) against our honor those abominable verses: "Woman is an animal—which they call an imperfect man—procreated in the defect—of good natural heat"].

Equally unlikely as candidates for this amorous paradise are the figures of Virgil, Helen of Troy, Juana Scrivana (Jane Doe), Penthesilea, queen of the Amazons, and a multitude of merry clerics who reside there. With similar levity, F.A.D.C. places Rodríguez—whose biography as well as the *Siervo libre* testify to his wholesale rejection of courtly love—in this lovers' heaven.[27] Thus we see the traditional medieval allegory procedure (an initial dream followed by an interpretive, teleological gloss) is here reversed. The elaborate unrealistic vision is preceded by a gloss that has the effect of diminishing the authority of allegorical discourse per se—because it artificially oversimplifies the problematic, novelistic chronotope that has prevailed until virtually the end of the text.

Substantiation of F.A.D.C.'s departure from the normative portrayal of the erotic hell is also evident from Chandler Post's study, despite the fact that he was apparently not familiar with *Triste deleytaçion*. Speaking of the presentations of the erotic hell in medieval Spain, Post discerns two basic forms. The first depiction involves "a real abyss of retribution" whereas the second is only a metaphorical one, "a crystallization of the lover's woes in the actual world."[28] An additional distinctive feature is that in the first type, the author is a spectator, while in the second he actively participates in the suffering. Finally, there is a "conspicuous absence of contemporaries from the places of punishment in the former class and their abundance in the latter."[29] The author of *Triste deleytaçion* obviously departs from these two traditional depictions by himself participating in a "real" hell.

In this way the author of *Triste deleytaçion* effects a notable generic transformation—which, in its procedure, is analogous to Boccaccio's novelistic innovation. Of this transformational procedure Jauss observes that:

> An astonishing multiplicity of older narrative or didactic genres enter into Boccaccio's *Decameron*: medieval forms such as the exemplum, the fabliau, the legend, the miracle, the *lai*, the *vida*, the *nova*, love casuistry, Oriental narrative literature, Apuleius and Milanese love-stories, local Florentine histories and anecdotes. . . . Boccaccio transposed the given thematic and formal multiplicity into the unmistakable structure of a new genre through determinable transformation, the rules of which may be defined formally as placing the plot-schemata in a temporal dimension, thematically as the calling into question of moral norms.[30]

Both Boccaccio and the anonymous author of *Triste deleytaçion* in effect motivate a series of monologic structures by combining them into a dialogic (or polyglot) one. In so doing, both authors participate in the inevitable chronotopic shift from "high" to "low" genres, which Bakhtin defines by means of a scientific analogy, in terms of Ptolemy and Galileo: "High" genres preclude any depiction or valorization of contemporary reality; "events and heroes receive their value and grandeur precisely through . . . association with the past."[31] The discourse of "high" genres is authoritative, "official," since it aims at perpetuating hierarchical authority formulated in the past. The "low" genres, on the other hand— especially the novel—are "associated with the eternally living element of unofficial language and unofficial thought (holiday forms, familiar speech, profanation)."[32]

At a given point in time, the "high" genres, such as romance (which exhibit a kind of artificial, oversimplifying "Ptolemaic language consciousness") are confronted by the polysemous "Galilean language consciousness" that Bakhtin privileges as "novelistic." It is precisely this novelistic transition that is programmatically dramatized by *Triste deleytaçion*.

# PART THREE

## LINGUISTIC TRANSGRESSIONS

# EIGHT

## PANDERED WORDS

### (*ARNALTE Y LUCENDA*)

W E ROUTINELY speak of the "poetic economy" of a given text. The use of the economic metaphor in the sphere of literature is, in fact, an ancient practice originating with Aristotle's *Poetics*.[1] As Marc Shell explains, "literary works are composed of small tropic exchanges or metaphors, some of which can be analyzed in terms of signified economic content and all of which can be analyzed in terms of economic form."[2]

*Arnalte y Lucenda* offers a bold illustration of this principle by metaphoric exchanges involving words, clothing, money, and sex.[3] Since Menéndez Pelayo's unfortunate pronouncement in 1907 that *Arnalte* constitutes a "first draft" ("primer esbozo") of the *Cárcel de amor* (an opinion derived from his reading of *Arnalte* in a French translation), critics have sought to articulate a genetic progression between these two texts published one year apart, in 1491 and 1492 respectively.[4] The damage done by this rather impressionistic remark can be rectified, however, by a brief consideration of the texts' literary reception.

Three principal veins of criticism have emerged in this interpretive activity, namely, structural, stylistic, and narratological. In structural terms, as many readers have indicated, the two texts share an undeniable affinity by sharing five basic elements of plot: (1) Both male protagonists are rejected by the ladies whom they serve; (2) each lady, convinced by a third party that she should be more compassionate toward her suitor, first writes to and then meets with the lover; (3) a rival for each lady's affections interferes in each relationship, threatening its survival; (4) the lovers each kill their respective adversaries; (5) the lady in each text definitively rejects her suitor.[5]

Despite these structural parallels, however, there is an obvious increase in thematic complexity in the *Cárcel*, given the social tension operative within it. Whereas Arnalte and Lucenda concern themselves with affairs of the heart, Leriano and Laureola must additionally contend with affairs of state, since she is the king's daughter.

Armando Durán, for example, concurs with Bruce Wardropper's account for the added social conflict generated by the *Cárcel*, by reiterating his explanation, namely: "la tensión vivida por la aristocracia española como resultado de la desintegración de los códigos medievales de conducta."[6] Yet, of course, one would be hard put to find an extraliterary (sociohistorical) causal relationship that could account for the lack of social conflict in *Arnalte*. The difference, I would argue, lies not in San Pedro's desire to project social verisimilitude but rather, as we shall see, in his metalinguistic concerns.

Taking Durán's structural observations as her point of departure, Dorothy Severin offers a considerably more detailed structural model of the *Arnalte* which illustrates, in her words, San Pedro's "advance in his plotting and structural technique" in the *Cárcel* as compared with *Arnalte*.[7] The structure of the *Cárcel* does indeed reflect a greater degree of symmetry in its structure. But this fact does not necessarily constitute proof of progress or advancement. The *Prose Lancelot*, for example, is far less symmetrical in its structure than Chrétien's *Lancelot*, but no less advanced or sophisticated in its plotting.

Keith Whinnom uses a different approach, focusing on a comparative stylistic study in which he attributes the diminution of Latinate syntax and lexicon to humanistic concerns in the *Cárcel*:

> The ultimate explanation of this reform in San Pedro's art-prose is clearly to be sought, beyond the personal taste of Marina Manuel, in the changing intellectual climate of the period of the Reyes Católicos, and in particular in the advent of humanism. . . . The whole essence and intention of the humanist rhetorical reform may be summed up in the terms of Nebrija ("no de manera que sea la salsa más quel manjar") or Encina ("el guisado con mucha miel no es bueno") "More meat less sauce."[8]

While the results of Whinnom's stylistic analysis are irrefutable, I would question his attribution of the two appreciably different styles to two very different literary climates since the works were written roughly seven years apart (c. 1481 and c. 1488), but published within a year of one another (1491 and 1492).[9] Fourteen years later even Whinnom himself attempted to acknowledge that the matter is not so simply resolved if we consider, for example, the elevated diction employed throughout *Arnalte* for the narration of very mundane matters: "In making the style of *Arnalte y Lucenda* so consistently high-flown, San Pedro offended, not just against the tenets of the new rhetoric which came in with humanism, but against the precepts even of medieval rhetoric."[10] At the same time, the style of *Arnalte* is, as Whinnom notes, exemplary: "The characters speak to each other just as though they were writing letters. . . . San Pedro is following quite scrupulously the dictates of late classical and medieval rhetorical theory."[11] His decision to publish one year apart two works written in two radically different styles is, I would suggest, to be attributed more plausibly (both in chronological and aesthetic terms) to San Pedro's poetic design—

his innovative desire to juxtapose an archaizing style and courtly idiom with an entirely new usage.

Of the traditional amorous lexicon that we find in *Arnalte*, Dinko Cvitanovič remarks somewhat disparagingly that: "The lexicon is no more innovative than the plot, being quite predictable of the genre: desertion, loneliness, fear, and fatigue." But here too, I would maintain, it is precisely the use of such predictable, almost "semantically exhausted" words that is significant because of the new context in which San Pedro situates them for his own metalinguistic purposes.

That the usage itself is incongruous has in fact been commented upon by a number of critics. Regula Langbehn-Roland, for example, observes that this incongruity stems from the disparity between Arnalte's idealistic words and his unidealistic, aggressive behavior:

> Thus we have before us in Arnalte another type of lover than in Leriano. Leriano never deviates in practice from what he expresses in words; in Arnalte we have a lover who is in his words just as courtly as Leriano, yet who throws the courtly rules overboard in his deeds. Through these deeds he is much more realistically drawn than the protagonist of the *Cárcel de Amor*; the fable consists almost exclusively of actions that refer to the event itself of love, and this event is in its individual elements clearly rooted in a living courtly reality, not in an ideal.[13]

Pushing this observation one step further, she claims that the incongruity is intended to produce laughter on the part of the reader.[14] The purpose of this perceived comicality in her estimation is a socio-historical critique of such un-reality-oriented, untenably egotistical lovers as they existed in San Pedro's day:

> The book is thus a critique of the behavior of one—it could be any or every— lover at the time of Diego de San Pedro, a critique of the very figure of this lover and of his possible behaviors, all of which miscarry in the face of the demands and possibilities of society, because they cannot be realized rationally within the framework of society and yet have no transcendental goal.[15]

Although Langbehn-Roland is correct in seeing Arnalte as being decidedly different from the *cancionero*-type passive sufferer, her assertion of comicality is highly debatable in this instance since, as Whinnom rightly indicates, "queda por demostrar que San Pedro notase [tales disonancias], por lo menos en la época en que la escribió" [it has yet to be proven that San Pedro would have been aware of such discrepancies, at least when he wrote *Arnalte*].[16]

In point of fact, neither San Pedro nor his readers have given any indication that Arnalte is a comical figure. To the contrary, if we look at the text's reception as reflected in the titles of its European translations, we see that laughter was decidedly not at issue in the interpretation of Arnalte: e.g., *L'Amant mal traicte de sa mye* (1539); *Dall'amante maltratratto* (1654); *Arnaldo, or the Injur'd Lover* (1660).[17]

What has generated this charge of comicality on the part of Arnalte in his pursuit of Lucenda are such acts as his disguise as a woman in order to impose himself upon Lucenda at Christmas Eve mass; forcing her, by his insistence, to dance with him in public; thrusting a letter into Lucenda's pocket; instructing his page to root through the garbage to see whether Lucenda has thrown out his letter, etc. From such behavior we see that Arnalte knows what he wants, and goes after it. Whinnom makes the important additional point that Ovid himself would have approved of such behavior: "That Arnalte, having fallen in love with Lucenda, should resort to all the tricks and strategems he can think of in order to approach her and win her affections, would have seemed to Ovid perfectly natural and right."[18] It is, after all, just such advice that we find detailed in the *Ars amatoria*.

The perceived incongruity exists only if we judge Arnalte by the passive, idealistic ethos of Ovid's *Amores* or the Spanish *cancionero* poetry or perhaps San Pedro's somewhat tongue-in-cheek *Sermón*.[19] San Pedro's innovation consists precisely of his highly original shunting of the passive, *Amores*-like *cancionero* idiom into the active, realistic love ethos of the *Ars amatoria*. What results is a surprisingly novelistic treatment of love precisely because it does not conform to the anticipated *leyes de amor*. Indeed, *Arnalte* constitutes a tour de force in narratological terms.

Yet it would appear that, once again under the influence of Menéndez Pelayo's myopic assessment, critics have tended to label *Arnalte* as primitive by comparison with the *Cárcel*. This judgment hinges primarily on the fact that in the earlier text the inscribed author figure functions merely as scribe ("notorio"), while in the *Cárcel* he is both a diegetically active character who mediates the love relationship as *medianero*, and the omniscient narrator. Nonetheless, the opposite case can be argued, as Gustave Reynier astutely remarked over one hundred years ago (before Menéndez Pelayo's disparaging assessment) when he stated that by comparison with the *Cárcel*, *Arnalte* is "sensiblement plus moderne"[20]—an argument he advances for a number of reasons. *Arnalte*'s greater modernity is evidenced, for example, by the fact that "In *Arnalte* the plot is freed from those disparate elements that complicate and overburden the *Cárcel*. We find neither allegorical descriptions nor irrelevant digressions (like the Defense of Women); there is only one chivalric episode, and it is a short one: the combat at the tourney ground. The interest in *Arnalte* is focused on the affective drama."[21]

Though Leriano's lengthy defense of women is, as we shall have occasion to see, decidedly not a "digression inutile," Reynier is correct in signaling San Pedro's narratological discovery. The effect of these few undistracting events is to focus virtually all our attention on San Pedro's psychological probing of his characters as achieved through their discourse. In addition, because of this notable shift from action to words Reynier suggestively likens *Arnalte* to the *Elegia*: "ce qui'il y a de remarquable dans cette action, c'est qu'elle est extrêmement simple, (la plus simple peut-être qu'on êut encore vue, la *Fiammette* mise à part) et qu'elle est encore très affranchie des circonstances extérieures" [What is remarkable here is that the action is very simple (the simplest perhaps that one has seen so far, aside from the *Elegia*) and that it is still quite free of external circumstances].[22] Also a mark of *Arnalte*'s perceived modernity, according to Reynier, are Arnalte's realistic, unexemplary behavior and Lucenda's highly individualized, enigmatic nature.[23] It must be emphasized, moreover, that we are not reading about kings and queens in the medieval manner (as in the *Cárcel*), but rather about two bourgeois individuals.

Voicing a similar appreciation in the twentieth century, Rudolph Schevill sees in *Arnalte* "mingled elements of the aristocratic and the bourgeois novel,"[24] whereas the *Cárcel* constitutes, in his view, a return to the medieval feudal tradition. Arriving at an analogous conclusion, Charles Kany finds in *Arnalte* a "mixture of aristocratic and bourgeois elements," while the *Cárcel* represents a return to "the courtly romance of chivalry."[25] More recently, Alfonso Rey has contributed further to this critical perception, considering *Arnalte* to be of equal—indeed greater—importance to the history of modern narrative than the *Cárcel*.

What Rey posits as the real mark of *Arnalte*'s innovation is its proximity to the pseudoautobiographical model offered by *Lazarillo de Tormes*:

> In reading *Arnalte y Lucenda* one may be reminded of *Lazarillo de Tormes* in spite of the notable differences that separate sentimental and picaresque narrative. In each case the protagonist (1) justifies by structural means his transformation into a narrator, (2) explains the present by means of the past, (3) carefully maintains his point of view, and (4) uses first-person narrative as a means of affirming his individuality. If this use of the first person represents the core of the [*Lazarillo*] and of later narrative, it is not unreasonable to view its use in *Arnalte y Lucenda* as novelistic.

By contrast, for Rey the *Cárcel*'s narrator "responde a esquemas medievales" [responds to medieval norms].[27] Yet Rey fails to recognize that the narrator's role in *Arnalte* (as both inscribed character and omniscient author figure) has a number of medieval analogues. In the thirteenth century the *Roman de la Rose* initiated this particular narrative configuration and gave rise to its programmatic transformation throughout the thirteenth, fourteenth, and fifteenth centuries in France by such writers as Machaut, Froissart, and Pisan, as well as in the rest of Europe.[28]

The intent of this discussion of *Arnalte*'s critical reception is not to prove the superiority or greater modernity of either text, but rather to restore the balance, to accord the same degree of serious consideration to *Arnalte* that the *Cárcel* has received in recent years. For in terms of their respective discursive strategies the two works are equally innovative, each in its own right, offering two distinct yet at the same time complementary meditations on linguistic usage—its potentials and constraints.

A number of critics have remarked on the disjuncture between Arnalte's words and his actions. Yet, as this discursive analysis will demonstrate, a related disjuncture or incongruity exists entirely within the domain of his linguistic usage as well—between the way he uses his words per se. Moreover, it is important to note that this incongruous verbal communication is not confined to Arnalte alone, characterizing each of the four principal characters in fact: Arnalte, Lucenda, Belisa, and Yerso.

The incongruity projected by all of these characters, I maintain, illustrates the fundamental linguistic principle of "exchange" first articulated by Ferdinand de Saussure, the crucial distinction between "value" and "signification":

> We must clear up the relation of value and signification or risk reducing language to a simple naming process. . . . To resolve this issue, let us observe from the outset that even outside language all values are apparently governed by the same paradoxical principle. They are always composed: (1) of a *dissimilar* thing that can be *exchanged* for the thing of which the value is to be determined; and (2) of *similar* things that can be compared with the thing of which the value is to be determined. Both factors are necessary for the existence of a value. To determine what a five-franc piece is worth one must therefore know: (1) that it can be exchanged for a fixed quantity of a different thing, e.g., bread; and (2) that it can be compared with a similar value of the same system, e.g., a one-franc piece, or with coins of another system (a dollar, etc). *In the same way* [italics added] a word can be exchanged for something dissimilar, an idea; besides, it can be compared with something of the same nature, another word. Its value is therefore not fixed so long as one simply states that it can be "exchanged" for a given concept, i.e., that it has this or that signification: one must also compare it with similar values, with other words that stand in opposition to it. Its content is really fixed only by the concurrence of everything that exists outside it. Being part of a system, it is endowed not only with a signification but also and especially with a value, and this is something quite different.[29]

In the case of San Pedro's text, it is the words "love," "honor," and "friendship" whose values are repeatedly exchanged. More specifically, these words are euphemistically employed by each of the characters in an attempt to manipulate their interlocutors—to persuade them to act according to their wishes. Words lose their normative semantic field—their objective meaning—as a result of their function as reflections of each individual's subjective needs. The programmatic polysemy that results can be concretely demonstrated by an analysis of the coercive power plays in which the characters engage, each time masking their manipulative inclinations in euphemistic terms.

If we look, for example, at the euphemistic exchange effected by Arnalte (disguised as a woman, when he confronts Lucenda in church) we see how he effects a double manipulation. By changing from his accustomed male attire to female dress, he is exchanging clothing for conversation—a chance to speak to her privately. At the same time, he manipulates the word "honor" in terms of currency and exchange:

> Si dizes que para ti es grand graveza fablarme, tu honra te[m]iendo, no te engañes, que mayor invirtud será matarme que remediarme te será fealdad. No quieras nombre de matadora *cobrar*, ni quieras por *precio* tan poco *servicios* de fee tan grande perder. No sé, para hazer a mí *deudor* y a ti *pagadora*, qué pueda dezirte [italics added].[30]

> If you claim that it is dangerous to address me because you are mindful of your honor, you are mistaken. For it would be a greater dishonor for you to kill me than to help me. Do not wish to *gain* the name of murderess, nor wish for so small a *price* to lose such faithful *service*. I do not know what I must say in order to make me a *debtor* and you a *creditor*.

Two key aspects of Arnalte's linguistic usage are revealed to us in this speech. First, he misleadingly exchanges the idea of feminine personal honor (chastity, personal reputation) with the public, legal system of honor—according to which she would become notorious as a murderer. Secondly, he explicitly uses the vocabulary of finance ("cobrar," "precio," "servicios," "deudor," "pagadora"), which reflects his desire to gain Lucenda's affection by arguing that she has entered into a contractual obligation. That is to say, he has offered more than enough service to justifiably expect to receive Lucenda's affection in return, as payment. Blatant contradiction prevails at this point, as he claims that he will be satisfied in offering nothing more than *cancionero*-style love-service to his lady (1.107), while in fact demanding reciprocity from her.

In a similarly unanticipated assertion made in a soliloquy soon after rejection by Lucenda, he interprets her negative attitude as an affront to his honor: "la honra ofendida e la vida en peligro ahora tienes" (1.111) [Your honor is now offended and your life is in danger]. He is confusing here the two distinct codes of (personal) love and (public) honor in a way that is fundamentally alien to both codes. What he does is to exploit the lofty idea of honor in a deceptive, self-aggrandizing manner just as he had invoked love.

Friendship is a third ideal that Arnalte recontextualizes for the sake of his own argument. Incensed upon learning that Yerso has just married Lucenda, Arnalte writes him a letter claiming that by so doing Yerso has violated their friendship: "me dexiste, dándome fee, aunque tú la servías, de dexar de ser suyo porque ella mi señora fuese. . . . Y agora, de mí te encubriendo, por muger la receviste, *faziéndote del galardón de mis trabajos poseedor*" (1.144; italics added) [You vowed that although you served her, you would give her up so that she would become my lady. . . . And now, concealing yourself from me, you have married her, *reaping for yourself the reward of my efforts*].

This claim is understandable given the degree of Arnalte's personal frustration. It is patently absurd, however, to assume that Yerso usurped the "galardón de [sus] trabajos"; again, for his *trabajos* Arnalte expects *pago* in the form of Lucenda's commitment to him. Such an expectation does not conform to the *ley de amor*, whereby the lover selflessly considers himself duly rewarded by the service that he devotes to his lady. And Arnalte is aware of this, having claimed earlier to Lucenda that "no querría [yo] mayor bien que poder con tu voluntad [mi] señora llamarte" (1.107) [I wished for nothing more than your permission to call you my lady]. On the one hand, this gratification is remarkably unsatisfying when viewed not in the *cancionero* context of the lyric artifice, but of the affective states of experiential reality. Likewise, the belief that Yerso would cease courting Lucenda—even though he has sworn to do so because of his friendship for Arnalte—is equally unrealistic. Arnalte seems surprisingly gullible in accepting Yerso's claim at face value, rather than interpreting it as a convenient opportunity whereby Yerso can monitor his rival's progress. On the other hand, Arnalte's markedly oblivious reading of the situation is entirely in keeping with the rest of his comportment in his self-centered quest.[31] Consequently, Arnalte falls into the trap that Yerso has set, frequenting his alleged friend's house on a regular basis in order to catch a glimpse of the woman who had become his obsession: "desde allí adelante más que Elierso su posada continué, pensando desde allá a la fermosa Lucenda ver" (1.124) [from this moment onward I spent more time in Yerso's house than he did since I hoped from that place to catch a glimpse of the beautiful Lucenda].

While Arnalte speaks to Lucenda of the self-sufficiency of love-service, seeking reciprocity instead, Lucenda, with equal deviousness, invokes the concept of honor in order to mask her indifference toward him. Similarly, when Belisa implores her to show even "fingido plazer" (1.126) [feigned interest] in her brother, Lucenda remains firm, again exploiting the concept of exchange: "si por otro *precio*, que honra no fuese, pudiese fazerlo, tanto libre en el *dar* como él en el *rescevir* [yo] sería. Pero pues [que] su *ganancia*, sin que yo *pierda*, ser no puede, de su sufrimiento y mi voluntad debe valerse" (1.127; italics added) [If I were able to achieve it for a *price* other than honor, I would be as liberal in *giving* as in *receiving*. But, since your *gain* cannot be effected without my *loss*, you must accept your suffering and respect my will].

In this connection Anna Krause makes a relevant observation about San Pedro's style in *Arnalte*, specifically his extensive use of antithesis: "The contrast of antithetical words and concepts as well as the use of recurring pairs is particularly striking: service–gift, pain–glory, love–remedy, honor–dishonor, fame–infamy resemble arabesques in an oriental tapestry."[32] Yet what Krause fails to comprehend is the reason for this preferred form of conceptual structuring, namely, the linguistic theory of exchange that San Pedro discursively illustrates throughout this text.

Although Belisa attempts to pressure Lucenda, arguing that she owes her the favor of placating Arnalte (even if it is only a feigned interest), Lucenda replies by insisting that for exactly the same reason Belisa owes her support, since Belisa herself would never compromise her own honor in this way: "no quieras para mí lo que para ti negarías" (1.127) [Do not impose upon me what you would never accept for yourself]. This temporary stalemate, however, is ultimately overturned as Lucenda capitulates to Belisa's pressure: "tanto amor te tengo que quiero, porque *ganes* tú, *perder* yo" (1.131; italics added) [Because I love you so deeply, I am willing to *lose* so that you can *win*]. She forfeits her honor so that her friend, Belisa, will be satisfied. Here, too, we see a motivation for amorous involvement— Lucenda's *amistad* for Belisa which results in her *piedad* for Arnalte (1.131),[33] which constitutes a glaring transgression of the *leyes de amor* that are repeatedly invoked. The sole reason why Belisa manages to persuade Lucenda of her highly incongruous proposal (to exchange her *philos* for *eros* directed at a third party) results from the nature of their particular friendship. Lucenda wants above all to please Belisa, viewing the risk to their friendship as being greater than the risk to her honor. Consequently, she is willing—albeit with considerable reluctance—to make the exchange. Significantly, the degree to which this action constitutes an exchange, and not a mask for a concealed affection, is demonstrated by the fact that when she is widowed and has the opportunity to marry Arnalte honorably, she adamantly refuses to do so.[34]

For her part, Belisa, in addition to coercing Lucenda to pretend love for Arnalte out of a misguided sense of friendship, exploits the term "honor" manipulatively. She augments the severity of a claim made earlier by Arnalte (that indifference toward him will result in his murder, casting Lucenda in the role of *matadora*), by indicating that she will be accused of not one but two murders—namely hers as well as Arnalte's. When, during her first attempt, Belisa calls Lucenda Arnalte's *matadora* (1.125) and this claim does not produce the desired effect, she makes their friendship an issue, knowing that it will bring results: "de . . . mi muerte ser[ás] causa" (1.129–30) [You will be the cause of my death]. With an equal degree of incongruity in the context of the love code, Belisa implicates the death of her (and Arnalte's) parents with Lucenda's honor, once more attempting to bring about a commitment on the part of Lucenda: "tú sabes bien que la corruta pestilencia pasada de nuestros padres y parientes nos dexó solos. Pues si tú por pequeño inconveniente el linaje quieres acabar, más reprehendida que loada serás" (1.126) [You are well aware that the plague left us bereft of our parents. So that, if you wish to extinguish our lineage for such a small inconvenience, you will be condemned rather than praised].

Despite its poignancy, this argument has no effect on Lucenda since it has no bearing upon the only persuasive factor (i.e., the friendship of these two women). For a similar reason, it is significant that Belisa uses this same argument somewhat differently—in an equally unjustifiable manner—with her brother, as he decides to withdraw from society. In an attempt to persuade Arnalte not to leave, Belisa says that her honor will be ruined if he abandons her: "bien sabes tú que la muerte de nuestros padres y parientes me fizo sola" (1.166) [You know that the death of our parents and relatives has left me all alone]. If he leaves, she argues, Yerso's relatives will defame her. Once again we see an attempt to argue the case in terms of an exchange—his departure for her honor; an exchange which, in this case, she hopes to prevent from happening. Belisa is unsuccessful at this point for two reasons. First, since her mission as go-between has definitively failed, Arnalte does not have a compelling reason to accede to her wish. Second, given the thoroughly honorable and legalistically proper way in which he behaved in the duel with Yerso, the king's adjudication of this dispute, and the favored status of the siblings in the royal court (1.168–70), Belisa's claim is notably unconvincing.

Finally, Yerso likewise engages in a comparable degree of euphemistic semantic manipulation stemming from his subjective desires. The most notable and repeated example of exchange that he attempts to effect has to do with the concept of friendship which he invokes in order to disguise for Arnalte his keen pursuit of Lucenda:

> Dízesme que la hermosura de Lucenda tu vida destruye; tu cuidado y el mío una causa los causa; y si ella tu bien adolesce, mi salud atormenta. Mas porque diversidad en tu voluntad y en la mía no se conosca, desde hoy de tal cuidado me descuido, dándote seguridad, por servicio hazerte, de poner en paz mis guerras. (1.123)

You tell me that Lucenda's beauty is destroying your life. But in fact your concerns and mine are one and the same; if she is destroying your well-being, she is destroying my health. However, so that your wishes and mine do not conflict, from this day onward I will give up my pursuit [of her] in order to serve you.

Yerso tangentially indicates in passing that his courtship of Lucenda is not progressing very favorably, but he claims that he will in any case give up the enterprise entirely in order to preserve his friendship with Arnalte. This seems rather improbable and—as we soon learn—Yerso's claim offers yet another clever verbal maneuver, achieving surveillance of his rival under the guise of preserving their friendship.[35] An even more daring and incongruous semantic substitution is attempted by Yerso when he insists to Arnalte that he in fact married Lucenda in order to guarantee their friendship:

> más por remedio tuyo que por provecho mío a Lucenda por muger resciví, creyendo que su casamiento para en tus males atajo sería; y como yo en disposición de mucha pena y poco vevir te viese, de hazer lo que fize pensé, porque la desesperança tu salud restituirte pudiese. (1.145)

> I married Lucenda because I was more concerned with remedying your situation than for my own benefit; thinking that her marriage would assuage your sufferings. And since I saw you suffering and so close to death, I considered what I could do to cure you.

Obviously, Arnalte cannot accept this reasoning since all of his own linguistic obfuscation regarding honor, friendship, and love has been aimed at one and the same thing (i.e., obtaining an affective commitment from Lucenda). The friendship of these two men, therefore, by contrast with that of the two women, necessarily fails. San Pedro calls our attention to these two distinct kinds of friendship by carefully identifying both Belisa and Yerso as "estrechos amigos" of Lucenda and Arnalte respectively. Indeed, there is a proliferation of doubles in this text.[36]

In addition to the two friendships, Belisa and Lucenda are affectively associated with the same man, namely Arnalte. Yet, of course, the nature of one woman's love is radically different from the other's—Belisa's fervent sororal love for Arnalte boldly contrasting with the absence of love in Lucenda's relationship to him. Likewise, the two men are affectively linked to one and the same woman, Lucenda. This repeated doubling structure serves to underscore the polysemy generated by the various characters since love, honor, and friendship are never conceived of or talked about in the same way by the various doubles. As such, this structure reinforces San Pedro's illustration of the principle of linguistic exchange.

Epistolarity as exploited in *Arnalte* further valorizes this discursive interpretation. In fact, San Pedro chooses to characterize the text precisely by its
reliance upon the letter form. It is significant in this connection that the
*Desprecio de la Fortuna* refers to *Arnalte* not by its title, but rather as:
"aquellas cartas de amores / escritas de dos en dos" [that series of love
letters written in pairs].[37] By describing the text as he does, San Pedro
identifies *Arnalte* as an epistolary novel. Whinnom further buttresses this
interpretation by recalling San Pedro's somewhat cryptic prefatory remark
in *Arnalte* that: "Bien pensé por otro estilo [mis] razones seguir, pero aunque fuera más sotil fuera menos agradable, y desta causa la obra del pen-
samiento dexé" (1.88) [Actually, I had thought of presenting my story in
a different manner, but, although it would have been more subtle, it might
have been less pleasing, therefore I abandoned it].

By comparing this passage and the epistolary description of the *Desprecio*, Whinnom arrives at an interesting conclusion concerning the importance of the letter form:

> It is as though with the gift of hindsight Diego de San Pedro regretted his
> failure to follow up his idea of presenting his story in a more subtle way, and
> at the same time wished to claim that he had the idea and that, however
> imperfectly the result matched his initial conception, he had in some way
> actually created the epistolary novel by compiling an exchange of love let-
> ters.[38]

Yet, while San Pedro was keenly aware of the paramount importance of
the epistle in the discursive structure of his text, both Whinnom's analysis
as well as San Pedro's own description in the *Desprecio* are somewhat misleading. Whinnom identifies San Pedro's innovation as the creation of "the
epistolary novel by compiling *an exchange* of love letters," but there is in
fact a notable lack of epistolary exchange in *Arnalte*. Presumably Whinnom
speaks of an exchange because he is taking San Pedro's description at face
value. However, the claim that the letters are "written in pairs" (implying
that each sender of a missive is also a recipient) is patently false.[39] In fact,
the configuration exhibited by the letters in *Arnalte* is actually quite revealing, and totally consistent with the discursive theory advanced by the text
as a whole. Their disposition is as follows:

[*Panegyric to Queen Isabella—by the narrator*] (1.93–100)
1. Arnalte's Letter #1 to Lucenda (1.103–5)
    [*Love-song to Lucenda—by Arnalte*] (1.109)
2. Arnalte's Letter #2 to Lucenda (1.114–15)
3. Lucenda's Letter to Arnalte (1.132–33)
4. Arnalte's Letter #3 to Lucenda (1.134–36)
5. Arnalte's Letter to Yerso (1.143–44)

6. Yerso's Letter to Arnalte (1.144–45)
7. Arnalte's Letter #4 to Lucenda (1.147–48)
    [7. *"Angustias de la Virgen"—by Arnalte*]
(1.150–65)

What becomes apparent from this epistolary schema is that the letters were clearly not written in pairs—either diegetically by the characters, or extradiegetically in their composition by San Pedro—since they total seven in number. Furthermore, they are not paired in terms of senders and receivers, since none of Arnalte's letters to Lucenda are answered by her. The only time she does write to him in a brief communication she is motivated not by his letters, but by Belisa's powers of persuasion. Immediately following one of Belisa's speeches, Lucenda agrees to write to Arnalte under the following condition: "le quiero escrivir, a condición que mi carta de sus guerras despartidora sea; y si más entiende pedir, a *pe[r]d[e]r* lo *cobrado* se apreciaba" (1.131; italics added) [I will write to him on the condition that my letter will abate his suffering; if you intend to ask for more than this, what has been *gained* until now will be *lost*]. This is obviously not the declaration of reciprocity that Arnalte seeks so desperately. Even rubrication evidence points to the failure of Arnalte's epistolary attempts to elicit reciprocity since the most authoritative edition (that of 1491) precedes Lucenda's letter to Arnalte with the following descriptive rubric: "Sigue la carta *primera* de Lucenda a Arnalte" (1.132; italics added) [Here follows Lucenda's *first* letter to Arnalte], implying that there are more to follow.[40] Arnalte's four letters, by contrast, are never identified numerically in the rubrics. The effect of this omission, like the inclusion of a numerical identification for Lucenda's only letter, boldly underscores the lack of epistolary reciprocity. The fact that the letters were clearly not written and exchanged "de dos en dos" could not be more apparent.

As the diagram makes clear, the only letter that does receive an epistolary response in return is the one sent by Arnalte to Yerso. Why, we may ask, do the love letters fail so obviously in their illocutionary function, whereas the challenge letter succeeds? This unique example of reciprocity is no accident, rather it is very much in keeping with the discursive theory of exchange that is programmatically articulated by San Pedro throughout the text. That is to say, Arnalte and Yerso share the same ideas about what constitutes honor, unlike all the other examples of semantic manipulation (euphemistic substitution calculated to fulfill a subjective need). They are not trying to substitute any other value for their collective understanding of what constitutes honor.

*Arnalte* is suggestively compared by Whinnom to Piccolomini's *Historia* in terms of the male protagonist's comic potential.[41] Irrespective of that issue, however, and of more central importance to the present discussion is the fact that the two texts share a real affinity in terms of their principle of epistolary reciprocity. Although Lucretia repeatedly protested Euryalus' advances, systematically responding to his directives with representatives,[42] because both individuals share the same attitude toward love, they inevitably become amorously involved. Her tearing up of Euryalus' first letter is recalled by Lucenda's tearing up of Arnalte's first letter. But the similarity stops there. For while Lucretia pieces her letter back together, reading and kissing it more than a thousand times and thereafter preserving it as if it were a holy relic, Lucenda, we assume, simply discards her first letter after mutilating it.[43]

Though the actions of these two women are ostensibly opposite, they in fact function as two corollaries of the same discursive principle. Lucretia, we recall, even before the time of Euryalus' first missive, was in love with him. Lucenda, by contrast, never felt a corresponding love for Arnalte. Whereas Lucretia's first letter to Euryalus protested his epistolary advance, we remember that the mere fact of its existence—its physical form—despite its ostensibly nonamorous content, was a positive semiotic indicator of reciprocity which Euryalus interpreted as such.[44] For this reason, at the moment when both lovers have openly acknowledged the amorous reciprocity that has existed all along, Piccolomini ceases to rely upon letters, replacing them with clandestine encounters. By analogy, since Lucenda never shares Arnalte's idea of love, she never responds by letter. Thus San Pedro's use of letters conforms to Piccolomini's as an implicit—but entirely consistent—corollary. Word and deed become coterminous in the first text (at least provisionally, until Euryalus has effected his conquest of Lucretia), whereas in the second such a fusion is prohibited by the affective disparity which remains constant.[45]

In keeping with this same discursive principle, we see, moreover, that the two poems and one song that San Pedro includes in *Arnalte* serve an analogous function; they are not at all extraneous, as is frequently alleged. The first poem (1.93–100), a lengthy panegyric to the queen delivered by the narrator who transcribes Arnalte's story, illustrates early on that it is not the illocutionary act of the sender/text, but the nature and degree of receptivity in the receiver/context that determines both the extent of its persuasiveness and its potential for polysemy. Arnalte asks the narrator whether the king, "[un] hombre de manificencia tan grande, igual compañía que le perteneciese tenía" (1.93) [a man of such magnificence, had a female counterpart of equal stature]. Arnalte smiles at the end of the lengthy recitation (1.100), explaining to the narrator that he was in fact very familiar with the queen's admirable attributes, and that his question was motivated not by a desire to obtain information, but rather to test his interlocutor's poetic abilities:

quise por saber lo que sabes oírte, y porque en ella [te] señalases, en plática tan fuerte quise ponerte; y esto porque de mis pasiones qui[e]ro notorio hazerte; y quise primero saber [lo] que sabes [y] si el recevimiento que merescen les harías. (1.101)

I wanted to hear what you have to say about her, your description, because I would like to make you the scribe [notary] of my passions. And I wanted first of all to find out your abilities as a poet, to determine whether you would adequately represent them.

Each illocutionary act has several possible interpretations, as novelistic discourse persistently reveals, and as San Pedro carefully and explicitly confirms here and throughout his text. Arnalte's song (1.109) similarly functions as an exemplary composition that does not result in the desired softening of Lucenda's obdurate behavior. The third intercalated composition, the *Siete angustias*, also fails in its immediate diegetic motivation (i.e., to gain solace for the suffering lover).[46] Nonetheless, while failing on this diegetic level, the poem simultaneously succeeds in its extradiegetic discursive motivation, namely, to illustrate the inescapable potential for polysemy (as well, of course, as San Pedro's accomplishments as a poet).[47] It is important to note that each of these three intercalated compositions constitutes an exemplary sample of its genre, the panegyrics to the earthly and divine queens as well as the love song. As such, they contrast boldly with the notably unexemplary semantic substitutions consistently imposed by the four characters. Paradoxically, however, despite their status as exemplary utterances their effect is analogous to that of the unexemplary utterances—an implicit but fundamental indication of the need for a constant, shared semantic value.

The kind of semantic exchange in evidence throughout *Arnalte* appears, unfortunately, to be the rule rather than the exception. Indeed, San Pedro's concern with this linguistic principle is borne out not only implicitly by a discursive analysis of this text, but explicitly as well, in the pointed advice he offers in his *Sermón*. The opening words of this text are directed precisely at the need for an awareness of one's speech community:

Para que toda materia sea bien entendida y notada, conviene que el razonamiento del que dize sea conforme a la condición del que lo oye; de cuya verdad nos queda que si hoviéremos de hablar al cavallero, sea en los actos de la cavallería; e si al devoto, en los méritos de la Passión; e si al letrado, en la dulçura de la sciencia; e assí por el consiguiente en todos los otros estados. (1.173)

So that the material will be fully comprehended, the argument of the speaker must conform to the understanding of the listener. From which precept it follows that if we address a knight we should refer to chivalric deeds; in speaking to a cleric we should allude to the Passion; and, in speaking to a scholar, mention the joys of scholarliness. Do likewise for all the other professions.

Acknowledging this recurring metalinguistic preoccupation in a note to his edition, Whinnom insightfully remarks that: "estos sentimientos, repetidos por San Pedro en varias ocasiones, son algo más que un tópico y parecen reflejar la verdadera convicción del autor" (1.171) [these sentiments, repeated by San Pedro on various occasions, are something more than a *topos*; they seem to reflect the true conviction of the author].[48] And, as we shall see, the *Cárcel* is as profoundly concerned with this problem as is *Arnalte*—from a markedly different yet complementary perspective.

Finally, the role of the narrator—despite his avowedly scribal function—further substantiates San Pedro's metadiscursive interests in *Arnalte*. Diegetically, he can be described as the wholly unobtrusive and unevaluative transcriber of another's adventure. Consequently this characterological split of the authorial personality into two different individuals—scribe and protagonist—invalidates to a considerable degree Rey's analogy of this text with *Lazarillo de Tormes*. Technically, we do not have the protagonist at the time of writing simply justifying his current attitude of alienation from society by imposing an interpretation of his life upon the reader.[49] Like Lázaro, Arnalte too is oblivious to his unexemplary behavior whereby he wants to make a public example (in this case, of Lucenda's misconduct—e.g., 1.100, 168, 170). Yet strikingly unlike Lázaro, the extradiegetic narrator who speaks directly to the inscribed "virtuosas señoras" at the beginning and end of the narrative proper serves an additional, evaluative, function that works to undermine the validity of Arnalte's confession. The narrator's final words—and those of the text as a whole—read as follows:

> vuestras mercedes no a las razones mas a la intención mire[n], pues por vuestro servicio mi condenación quise, haviendo gana de algund pasatiempo darvos, y porque cuando cansadas de oír y fablar discretas razones estéis, a burlar de las mías vos retrayáis, y para que a mi costa los cavalleros mancebos de la corte vuestras mercedes festejen, a cuya virtud mis faltas remito. (1.170)

> Ladies, do not consider the arguments but rather the intentions. In order to serve you I have condemned myself by wishing to offer you a pastime so that when you tire of hearing and speaking prudent arguments, you can laugh at my [foolish] ones. Likewise, I offer you this text so that young knights can, at my expense, serve you.

What is clear from this closing statement is that the narrator both distances himself from and disagrees with Arnalte's interpretation of his unrequited love—he is not merely functioning as scribe. When the ladies grow tired of listening to "discretas razones" he hopes that they will "burlar de las [suyas]," by which he implies that the *razones* offered in *his text* are not "discretas." What he implies is that the narrative is intended by him as a *pasatiempo* which the ladies cannot construe seriously. Indeed, he tells them somewhat cryptically that they should not dwell on "las razones mas la intención." In other words, they should not consider the arguments (*razones*) offered by the four characters, but instead the illocutionary *intención* behind the arguments. Rather, what they should consider most seriously are the subjective motivations responsible for the repeated semantic distortion resulting from euphemistic exchange.[50]

# NINE

## IMPRISONED DISCOURSE

### (*CÁRCEL DE AMOR*)

THE PERFORMATIVE function of language is the domain of speech act theory.[1] As John Searle puts it, "speaking a language is engaging in a (highly complex) rule-governed form of behavior."[2] All language seeks to accomplish some form of communication, which varies according to context. If, for example, the question "Who do you think you are?" is posed by a psychiatrist to a patient, we can assume that an analytical attempt is being made to sort out certain identity problems. On the other hand, precisely the same question, if posed in response to some form of perceived impropriety, is not intended to elicit information (a directive), but to register disapproval (an expressive)—being more exclamatory than interrogatory in its intent.

Clearly, the difference in usage is contextual, a function of the speaker's relationship to the addressee. Speech act analysis focuses on language as performance (its communicative polysemy) by identifying the so-called "cooperative principle" of a given speech situation (i.e., the shared knowledge of and adherence by interlocutors to the appropriate contextual rules). Deviance from the norm constitutes a violation of the cooperative principle, resulting in the creation of a new type of speech situation.[3]

Similarly, literature is performative on two levels. First, it offers fictional characters who among themselves exploit language performatively—attempting to act upon one another to produce certain effects. On another level, the author uses language to manipulate his reader. These two levels may, of course, vary markedly as to their cooperative principles. If we consider the character Don Quijote, for instance, his cooperative principle is defined primarily by the constraints of the chivalric behavioral and discursive mode, whereas the cooperative principle revealed by Cervantes to his reader is more akin to the modern novel. Thus for a literary speech act to be adequately described, both the cooperative principle as defined by the fictional characters as well as the cooperative principle presupposed by the work's generic identity must be determined and analyzed comparatively. Because of its generic complexity and its notable cooperative principle deviance, San Pedro's *Cárcel de amor* is particularly susceptible to discourse analysis. Indeed, the methodology of discourse analysis can help provide a more coherent interpretation of this seminal work (published in 1492), which is consistently regarded as the epitome of the *novela sentimental* corpus.

Although this text has received considerable scholarly attention, it has been primarily from only two critical perspectives. The first is a taxonomic concern with the *Cárcel*'s undeniably anthological quality. As Bruce Wardropper acknowledges, "Critics have conventionally regarded the work as an assemblage of disparate parts: an allegorical introduction, an epistolary tale of love, a chivalric episode, and a treatise on the worth of women."[4] As a compendium of discourses the *Cárcel* is viewed as offering a superlative example of each.[5] Beyond the rhetorical value of its structure, the work is, on a thematic level, seen as an illustration of the insoluble existential conflict of courtly values (represented by the male protagonist, Leriano) and chivalric values (steadfastly upheld by the female protagonist, Laureola), mediated by the fictional author figure who serves as go-between.[6] This view, however, is an oversimplification, since Laureola herself subverts the chivalric ethos by refusing to accept the (favorable) verdict of Leriano's adjudicated duel on her behalf; likewise, Leriano subverts the courtly ethos by publicly rescuing her from imprisonment.

The *Cárcel* is considerably more nuanced than either, on the one hand, the "irreconcilable worlds of passionate love [Leriano] and of honor [Laureola] in their extreme forms,"[7] or, on the other, the rhetorical anthology per se—or even the two combined. It is rather at the level of the illocutionary act that San Pedro's blueprint for the *Cárcel* becomes visible. Indeed, both the work's avowed anthological and ontological disparities take on an organic unity only when perceived from the perspective of the explicit extradiegetic addressee—Don Diego Hernándes[8] (as well as the implicit one, namely us). It is at this level that San Pedro makes discernible a programmatic structure that consistently deviates from the discursive conventions normally associated with a number of different medieval genres. The inextricable relationship of genre to speech act is, moreover, self-evident. Genres are, after all, types of discourse, each with its own premises, i.e., speaker/audience assumptions: "genres and subgenres can to a great extent be defined as systems of appropriateness conditions."[9]

The four generic discourses identified by Wardropper (allegorical, epistolary, chivalric, and encomiastic) can be further detailed into the following narrative segments: (1) allegory of Leriano's imprisonment; (2) psychological analysis in letters and interviews; (3) chivalric intrigue and warfare; (4) renewed psychological analysis in letters and interviews; (5) misogynistic diatribe by Tefeo; (6) feminist diatribe by Leriano (involving thirty-five proofs of the virtues of women), culminating in the illusory "communion" with the beloved—shredding her letters and consuming them with water as he dies.

The first of these segments has been a source of considerable controversy, which is understandable since it constitutes a radical redeployment of a familiar literary speech situation. On his way home from the war, the inscribed narrator (El Autor) is confronted by "un cavallero assí feroz de presencia como espantoso de vista, cubierto todo de cabello a manera de salvaje"[10] [a knight fierce of bearing and frightful to behold, covered all in hair, like a wild man].[11] This is the conventional personification of Desire who has captured Leriano. El Autor spends an uneasy night tormented by fear and pity at this distressing spectacle when, at daybreak, he suddenly notices near him "en lo más alto de la sierra, una torre de altura tan grande que [le] parecía llegar al cielo" (2.84) [on the highest point of the mountain range, a tower so high that (he) thought it must reach to the heavens (6)]. The minutely described monumental edifice is the *cárcel* itself, whose foundation and pillars are actually comprised of Leriano's mental states— his *fe*, *entendimiento*, *razón*, *memoria*, and *voluntad* (2.89).[12]

This allegorical love prison, however, departs from its other myriad examples in the medieval tradition because it appears in the *Cárcel* simultaneously with the diegetic "reality" established by San Pedro. This striking departure from the cooperative principle of the love prison metaphor has led many readers to misread this episode, assuming that it takes place within a dream.[13] Yet such is not the case; it is not a dream but a tangible "reality" within the poetic economy of San Pedro's text: "La alegoría no se separa claramente de los acontecimientos 'reales,' el Autor ha visto, no ha soñado (como Berceo) la cárcel," as Whinnom explains (2.52).

San Pedro diverges from the literary commonplace in order to graphically establish the programmatic manipulation of discourse that characterizes his text. What is normally portrayed only in dream visions—since it boldly defies reality—is here portrayed as forming part of the empirical experience itself. His insistence in foregrounding this lack of verisimilitude is, moreover, reinforced by (historically verifiable) autobiographical detail. Concrete references in the initial and final sentences of the narrative accord with San Pedro's actual identity as a resident of Peñafiel, and as servant of Don Juan Téllez-Girón, whom he no doubt accompanied in at least one summer offensive against the Moors in Granada. The commingling of history and allegorical fiction that we find here, moreover, is never resolved, thus reciprocally problematizing both discourses. Whinnom rightly emphasizes this ambiguity, remarking that: "la imposibilidad de distinguir [la alegoría] netamente del mundo 'real' otorga a toda la narración algo de fantástico e irreal, y a la vez la realidad de los hechos de la historia confiere a la alegoría una inmediatez y una proximidad conturbadoras" (2.52).

This initial narrative segment serves as the first in a series, each of which violates the "appropriateness conditions" associated with a particular illocutionary act. In so doing, San Pedro seeks to expose the contextual presuppositions and expectations that define a given speech act, in order to undermine them thereafter by introducing a strikingly different (overtly conflicting) speech situation. Indeed, the *Cárcel*, like the other texts of the *novela sentimental* corpus, may be said to function in large measure as a *mise en abîme* of literary discourse.

In the case of the allegorical prison, it is not simply the author/reader cooperative principle that is seriously altered, but the fictional cooperative principle of the characters as well. While on the diegetic level such love prisons are traditionally discernible to lovers and nonlovers alike, the narrator indicates that this particular prison can only be properly deciphered by those who are currently in love (which is not presently the case for him):

> vistas las cosas desta tu cárcel, yo dubdava de mi salvación, creyendo ser hechas más por arte diabólica que por condición enamorada. . . . La moralidad de todas estas figuras me ha plazido saber; puesto que diversas vezes las vi, mas como no las pueda ver sino coraçón cativo, cuando le tenía tal conoscíalas, y agora que stava libre dubdávalas. (2.92)

> When I saw what was in this prison of yours, I did not expect to escape alive, for I believed that these things had been created by diabolic magic rather than by the transports of love. . . . To know the meaning of all these allegories is a pleasure. Although I have seen them before on divers occasions, nevertheless, since they are perceptible only to a captive heart, when my heart was held prisoner I recognized them, and now that it is free, they perplexed me. (11)

Finally, this admission has the additional effect of establishing the author's (ironic) lack of omniscience regarding the imaginary universe he has created. Thus while Leriano observes the Maxim of Manner (the avoidance of ambiguity), El Autor does not. The question of the narrator's omniscience (or lack of it) at various junctures in the text is an issue that has received substantial critical commentary. It has been viewed by some as an inherent flaw, by others as an artistic necessity. Most recently, James Mandrell has demonstrated that there exists a clearly discernible progression from a lack of omniscience to an omniscient perspective, which is reflected in his mode of narrative presentation "marking not only a movement, as others have noted, but a progression from ignorance to enlightenment, from ingenuousness to extreme dexterity."[14]

The second narrative segment—the lengthy epistolary exchange that is mediated by the narrator—offers further evidence of violated appropriateness conditions and the resultant interpretive disjuncture stemming from their absence in both sender and receiver. In his capacity as mediator, the narrator explains to Laureola her salvific potential for the afflicted Leriano: "Si la pena que le causas con el merecer le remedias con la piedad, serás entre las mugeres nacidas la más alabada de cuantas nacieron. . . . harás tú tanto en quitalle la muerte como Dios en darle la vida" (2.95) [If, moved by pity, you offer him relief from the pain which you have caused him by your excellence, you shall be praised most highly of all the women ever born. . . . You can do as much in saving him from death as God did in giving him life (14)]. This presentation of the beloved as the deliverer who liberates the slave of passion from his bondage is, of course, the normative courtly depiction. It is initially met by Laureola with an equally stock response—the dilemma of public honor versus private amorous fulfillment, the predictable argument that if a woman's reputation is defiled, her very life is extinguished: "Si pudiese remediar su mal sin amanzillar mi honrra, no con menos afición que tu lo pides yo lo haría; mas ya tú conosces cuánto las mugeres deven ser más obligadas a su fama que a su vida" (2.103) [If I could cure his malady without besmirching my honor, I should do so no less eagerly than you have requested it. But you well know how much more women are obliged to preserve their reputations than their lives (20–21)].

Just as we have seen Leriano conform to the paradoxical discourse of courtly love—that his life is death without Laureola's devotion—we anticipate the heroine's capitulation as well. (Less likely, but also possible is that she may categorically reject Leriano's advances, as happens occasionally—with the heroine of San Pedro's *Arnalte*, for example.) However, as with the allegorical *cárcel* which is at once both metaphorical and "real," here too San Pedro first raises our expectations for this proverbial speech situation, only to undermine them thereafter. Acquiescence to an amorous relationship ("platonic" or otherwise) that is motivated by pity is not a desirable prospect in any age. More importantly, however, it simply does not exist as an option within the courtly idiom. Nonetheless, Laureola is quite unambiguous in doing just that:

> quien viese lo que te escrivo pensaría que te amo, y creería que mis razones antes eran dichas por disimulación de la verdad que por la verdad. Lo cual es al revés, que por cierto más las digo, como ya he dicho, con intención piadosa que con voluntad enamorada. (2.110)

> Whoever were to see what I have written to you would surely believe that I love you, and would think that what I have said was intended to conceal the truth and not to reveal it. And the reverse is true, for assuredly what I have said was, as I have told you, inspired by compassion rather than any amorous intent. (28)

Laureola, moreover, remains adamant in interpreting Leriano's request as her death warrant: "sin mi condenación no podías tú ser asuelto" (2.109–10) [You could not be set free without my being condemned (28)]. With this expressive the cooperative principle of courtly discourse is violated in terms of the Maxim of Relation. She rejects the two permissible interpretations, introducing instead an irrelevant one in the context of the courtly speech situation. In short, we see San Pedro violating the appropriateness conditions of this literary discourse as violently (in fact, more violently) than he did with the love-prison topos.

A further notable instance of such short-circuited discourse occurs in the third major narrative segment, involving the deflation of chivalric discourse which is effected principally by Laureola's father, the king of Macedonia, and by Persio, his perfidious vassal. Because of his own amorous designs on Laureola, Persio slanders both her and Leriano by maintaining that they are not only in love, but in addition that: "se veían todas las noches después que [el rey] dormía" (2.114) [they met every night as (the king) lay sleeping (30)]. The ephemeral (psychological) "libertad" bestowed upon Leriano by Laureola's pity (2.113) results in her own (physical) "encarcelamiento" (2.114), since the king arbitrarily chooses to believe Persio's account. As is to be expected, Leriano refutes Persio's charge of treason for having dishonored Laureola, vowing to prove by combat: "no sólo que no entré en su cámara, mas que palabra de amores jamás le hablé" (2.116) [not only that I never entered her bed-chamber, but that I never spoke one word of love to her (33)]. And, although the terms of combat put forth by Persio specify death or Leriano's recanting of his claim ("te entiendo matar o echar del canpo, o lo que digo hazer confesar por tu boca" [2.115]) [(I) intend to slay you, or drive you from the field, or force you to confess by your own mouth the truth of what I say (32)], they too are violated by the king. At the point where Leriano is about to deal the deathblow to Persio, who finds himself "en estrecho de muerte" (2.117) [in such mortal straits (34)], the king intervenes in order to defy this verbal contract. The reason for his unlawful intervention is the result of the influence of Persio's relatives who "suplicaron al rey mandase echar el bastón, que ellos le fiavan para que dél hiziese justicia si claramente se hallase culpado; lo cual el rey assí les otorgó" (2.117) [begged the king to cast down his staff between them, and guaranteed that Persio should be executed if he should be clearly shown to be guilty. The king granted this request (34)]. Leriano is justifiably incredulous at this resolution, a glaringly dishonorable breach of protocol, by which "sacáronlos del canpo iguales en cerimonia aunque desiguales en fama" (2.118) [they were conducted from the lists with equal ceremony even though they were unequal in honor (34)].

Both in his arbitrary acceptance of Persio's allegations as truth and in his unconscionable interruption of the combat, the king has deviated from the cooperative principle of royal adjudication—the royal mandate to act nobly (impartially) in determining and upholding justice. Specifically, he errs by undervaluing the Maxim of Quantity, the responsibility to make his contribution as informative as possible.

It is not simply an internal (interpersonal) matter, as Leriano points out, but a violation of the law of the land which must not be tampered with: "cata que guardando las leyes se conservan los naturales" (2.120) [it is by adhering to the laws that a king holds the loyalty of his subjects (35)]. It is, moreover, a transgression against Divine justice since, as the cardinal unambiguously reminds the king, in the chivalric register "right equals might." God invariably determines the outcome in favor of the virtuous party: "¿por qué das más fe a la información dellos que al juizio de Dios, el cual en las armas de Persio y Leriano se mostró claramente?" (2.131) [How can you choose to believe their statements rather than the judgment of God, which was clearly revealed in the combat between Persio and Leriano? (45)]. Persio, of course, is equally guilty of cooperative principle transgression according to the Maxim of Quality, the responsibility to refrain from uttering falsehood.

Significantly, the king thereafter produces a lengthy argument in support of his actions, justifying his discourse by invoking a number of exemplary kingly qualities which he exhibits. And in this connection, Whinnom's global assertion that, not only the king, but all the characters, "at least in their major utterances, have no individuality, but are simply the representatives of two viewpoints which are here shown as not easily reconcilable"[15] is inaccurate. The characters in their major utterances offer a storehouse of generic speech situations each of which systematically clashes with the next. Leriano creates the appropriateness conditions suitable to the courtly register, yet Laureola refuses to partake of that cooperative principle. She meanwhile operates in the context of Christian compassion, not the speech community and behavioral code of courtly love. The king likewise offers what appears to be an admirably lucid rationale for his comportment:

> Perdonando a Laureola sería causa de otras mayores maldades que en esfuerço de mi perdón se harían; pues más quiero poner miedo por cruel que dar atrevimiento por piadoso. . . . Bien sabéis que establecen nuestras leyes que la muger que fuere acusada de tal pecado muera por ello; pues ya veis cuánto más me conviene ser llamado rey justo que perdonador culpado. (2.132–33)

> Pardoning Laureola would be the cause of other and worse evil acts, which would be committed by people confident that I should pardon them. I would, therefore, far rather sow fear by my cruelty than encourage shamelessness by my clemency. . . . As you well know, our laws ordain that a woman accused of such a sin must die for it; and you have already seen how much more it behoves me to be known as a just king than a blameworthy pardoner of misdeeds. (46–47)

This reasoning conforms to the demeanor of an exemplary monarch—except, of course, that he perilously violates the Maxim of Quantity.

In her defense of Laureola, the queen invokes a different standard of exemplarity—kingly and paternal compassion. Yet she rapidly becomes aware of the ineffectual cooperative principle of the chivalric code of nobility. Since the king is so bent on vengeance, she offers herself as sacrificial victim in place of Laureola. The queen holds Laureola up as an exemplary martyr, which she has clearly become: "de las gentes serás llorada en cuanto el mundo durare" (2.135) [for as long as the world endures you will be mourned by all (50)]. However, true to San Pedro's discursive strategy, the queen in her own right departs from the appropriateness conditions befitting the bereaved maternal figure by vowing personally to exact bloody vengeance upon Persio:

A todos eras agradable y a Persio fuist[e] odiosa; si algund tienpo bivo, él recebirá de sus obras galardón justo; y aunque no me queden fuerças para otra cosa sino para desear morir, para vengarme dél, tomallas [he] prestadas de la enemistad que le tengo, puesto que esto no me satisfaga, porque no podrá sanar el dolor de la manzilla la secución de la vengança. (2.135)

The whole world loved you, and to Persio you became hateful. If I live a little longer he shall receive due payment for what he has wrought; and though I have only sufficient strength left to wish for death, in order to take revenge on him I shall borrow strength from my hatred, even though no vengeance can ever satisfy me, for executing vengeance upon him will not assuage the pain of my grief. (50)

Other (equally disparate) speech situations are introduced in rapid succession by the queen: consideration for the Afterlife ("quiere el Señor que padezcas como mártir porque gozes como bienaventurada" [2.136]) [the Lord wants you to suffer as did the martyrs so that you may enjoy eternal bliss as do His blessed saints (50)] in one breath, and the governmental concern for royal progeny in the next ("dexará el padre culpado y la madre con dolor y la hija sin salud y el reino sin heredera!" [2.136]) [leaving to a father his guilt and to a mother her grief, and depriving a daughter of her life and a kingdom of its heir! (50–51)].

In this powerful succession of pronouncements delivered by the queen, San Pedro once again dramatizes the panoply of disparate speech situations (the bereaved, the paternal, the vengeful, the religious, the genealogical, etc.), each of which presupposes a different set of appropriateness conditions necessitating a different cooperative principle.

Laureola herself adopts the discourse of the martyrological mode, offering now an additional (previously unexpressed) concern with posterity: "tú serás llamado padre cruel y yo seré dicha hija innocente, que pues Dios es justo, él aclarará mi verdad" (2.139) [you will be called a pitiless father and I shall be spoken of as an innocent daughter, for since God is just He will make plain the truth and my innocence (53)]. The standard is thus no longer innocence in the eyes of public opinion, but innocence in the eyes of God.

Since the normal channels of justice have failed him, Leriano decides to storm the prison in order to liberate Laureola as she awaits her death helplessly. This chivalric assault on the prison escalates into a major military confrontation with a series of six battles involving more than fifty thousand men and lasting for more than three months. As a result of this protracted struggle, Persio is killed and Laureola is exonerated when one of the three slanderers whom Persio had bribed to corroborate his account reveals it to be entirely fabricated. This episode offers a further type of cooperative principle deviance as Leriano departs from the knightly norm of behavior, advocating torture: "fue preso en aquella buelta uno de los damnados que condenaron a Laureola; y puesto en poder de Leriano, mandó que todas las maneras de tormento fuesen obradas en él hasta que dixese por qué levantó el testimonio; el cual sin premia ninguna confesó todo el hecho como pasó" (2.148) [they captured in that skirmish one of the accursed men whose testimony had convicted Laureola. When he was brought back and placed in Leriano's power, Leriano ordered that he should be put to every kind of torture until he told why he had given false evidence. But he, without any pressing, confessed the whole plot, just as it had happened (60)]. Leriano's order constitutes a glaring usurpation of royal authority, for while the king possesses the legal prerogative to have suspects tortured, a knight does not. The confessed slanderer thus reinstates the Maxim of Quality (truthful speech) which both he and his coconspirators had violated. Likewise, the king restores the Maxim of Quantity which he has ignored until this point.

The king requests that Leriano leave the court long enough to allow both sides to recover their composure. Since Leriano cannot be reunited with his beloved, he substitutes for this martial aggression his previous state of amorous submission: "viéndose apartado della, dexadas las obras de guerra, bolvióse a las congoxas enamoradas" (2.148) [seeing himself kept apart from her, and his martial labours completed, he returned to his amorous anguish (61)].

Meanwhile, despite the fact that Laureola has been vindicated, that her honor has been reinstated, she now refuses any contact with Leriano, "haviendo por mejor la crueldad honesta que la piedad culpada" (2.153) [(believing) that honorable cruelty is to be preferred to culpable passion (64)]. This is Laureola's last communication to Leriano. Thus the final installment of the epistolary relationship ends on a resoundingly hopeless note in terms of a possible reconciliation.

It should come as no surprise at this point in the fourth narrative segment that Leriano's all-consuming devotion to Laureola does not diminish. Indeed, Leriano's unrequited love debilitates him to such a degree that he becomes confined to bed, ultimately dying because of it. For this reason, one of Leriano's friends named Tefeo wishes to ascertain the identity of the woman for whom Leriano sacrifices himself, and so "díxole infinitos males de las mugeres; y para favorecer su habla truxo todas las razones que en disfamia dellas pudo pensar, creyendo por allí restituille la vida" (2.155) [he spoke to him all manner of ill of woman-kind, and to strengthen his case he adduced every argument that he could think of to slander women, believing that in this way he could restore Leriano to life (66)]. Tefeo, by virtue of his vocation as a knight, defies the Maxim of Quality by defaming women, since his profession is dedicated in theory to their defense.

In response to this misogynistic diatribe Leriano, far from acting as Tefeo had hoped, produces instead an impressive catalogue of twenty reasons why men should honor and protect women, as well as an anno-tated list of illustrious heroines. This speech is striking in that it has virtually nothing to do with Leriano's predicament. Whinnom percep-tively notes that: "perhaps the most surprising and revealing thing about Leriano's statement is that it makes only the most cursory reference to his own suffering and that it takes us away from the claustrophobic world of the anguished lover to contemplate religion, history, literature, music, dancing, costume, heroic deeds, and, above all, marriage and the proposition that a good woman is beyond all price."[16]

From this unexpected speech situation Whinnom concludes: "Leria-no's death is an unfortunate accident; it is the penalty which occasion-ally must be paid; but it does nothing to demonstrate that Leriano was essentially wrong."[17] I would argue, however, that Leriano *was* "essen-tially wrong," not on the affective level, but in his ignorance of the ap-propriate cooperative principle and its attendant maxims if language is to be effectively performative.

As words fail him and his death is imminent, Leriano ends his life in a gesture that seeks to effect the cooperative principle he has sought all along. In a final act of devotion—overtly reminiscent of transubstantia-tion—"hizo traer una copa de agua, y hechas las cartas pedaços echólas en ella, y acabado esto, mandó que le sentasen en la cama, y sentado, bevióselas en el agua y assí quedó contenta su voluntad; y llegada ya la hora de su fin, puestos en mí los ojos, dixo: 'Acabados son mis males,' y assí quedó su muerte en testimonio de su fe" (2.176) [he called for a cup of water, tore the letters into pieces, and dropped them into the water, and when he had done this he ordered them to sit him up in his bed, and when he was sitting, he drank them in the water, and rested content. And as the moment of death was now upon him, he fixed his eyes upon me, and said: "My sufferings are ended." And so his death stood witness to his constancy (82)].

In a very real sense, Leriano's eating of the words serves as an emblem of a "dead-end" speech situation. Words are presented as sterile objects rather than communication. Laureola's words and their communicative function are reduced to the status of a metonym for Laureola herself—one that displaces and precludes communication—leading to death, that is, silenced words.[18]

The work, therefore, fails entirely on the diegetic level. What Jorge Rubió Balaguer misperceives as a flawed feature of the *Cárcel* (namely, that "los personajes viven en constante monólogo")[19] is, in fact, the measure of San Pedro's poetic innovation. Despite their exemplary discourses, Leriano and Laureola never succeed in establishing a viable cooperative principle; the narrator's mediation in an attempt to effect a relationship does not work either. At the same time, however, the work succeeds brilliantly on the extradiegetic level. Not Leriano, nor Laureola, nor San Pedro the inscribed narrator—only San Pedro the author figure—is left totally fulfilled in his exemplary metalinguistic act. Starting from the perspective of a negative generic *summa*, San Pedro paradoxically makes poetic capital from the very system of bankruptcy of discursive generic traditions of the Middle Ages.

Epistolarity confirms this metalinguistic reading of the text by illustrating the communicative principle we have seen operate in the other texts, namely that epistolarity is reciprocal only when two letter writers participate in the same cooperative principle. Indeed, the *Cárcel* provides a privileged example of this principle for Laureola and Leriano never dialogue directly with one another, their relationship being exclusively epistolary.[20]

The entire text is inscribed within a letter that in turn contains a total of ten letters whose disposition is as follows:

1. Leriano's Letter #1 to Laureola (2.99–100)
2. Leriano's Letter #2 to Laureola (2.107–8)
3. Laureola's Letter #1 to Leriano (2.109–10)
4. Persio's Letter to Leriano (2.114–15)
5. Leriano's Letter to Persio (2.115–16)
6. Leriano's Letter #3 to Laureola (2.124–26)
7. Laureola's Letter #2 to Leriano (2.127–28)
8. Laureola's Letter to the king (2.138–39)
9. Leriano's Letter #4 to Laureola (2.151–52)
10. Laureola's Letter #3 to Leriano (2.152–53)

Letters 1 and 2 consist of Leriano's request that Laureola save his life by responding to his letter, and her reply—which stipulates that she has agreed to write in order to save his life (motivated, however, by pity rather than love), for she is adamant in preserving her honor. Letters 4 and 5 likewise treat a common cooperative principle, that is, truth as determined by martial combat. Significantly, though, this too is a conflict over the relationship of honor and the preservation of life. In the second exchange by the protagonists (6 and 7) we see another instance of the same cooperative principle, this time having to do with saving Laureola's life and its relationship to the personal honor of both Leriano and herself, as she languishes in prison awaiting execution. The final pair of letters (9 and 10), also written by Leriano and Laureola, again revolves around concern for the relationship between *vida* and *honra*—this time, as with the initial exchange of letters, the issue is his life and her honor. By this configuration we see that it is only during the brief periods in which the characters participate in the same cooperative principle that epistolary reciprocity occurs. Indeed, in general terms, Laureola and Leriano may be said to use letters in opposite ways: she uses them in order to distance herself from Leriano, while he uses them in an attempt to get closer to her.

I would like to conclude by considering what is perhaps the most suggestive independent validation of my discursive interpretation of San Pedro's *Cárcel*: Nicolás Núñez's continuation, which first appeared attached to San Pedro's original in 1496,[21] a text that has been consistently denigrated by modern scholarship. The repeated criticism that emerges of the sequel is that Núñez did not understand the *Cárcel*, since he tampered with the uncompromisingly exemplary discourse of the protagonists, reducing it to a rather prosaic love story.[22] I maintain, however, that Núñez, on the contrary, clearly understood the fundamental discursive strategy—the linguistic preoccupation—of his predecessor's work.

Much more than thematic misappropriation is at issue, however. For Núñez pointedly addresses three of the most widely debated questions in scholarship devoted to the *Cárcel*, namely: (1) whether Laureola was in love with Leriano; (2) what Leriano ultimately wanted from Laureola; and (3) whether he was justified in committing suicide.[23] Whinnom indicates this interpretive coincidence in order to show the ways in which Núñez misunderstands his model. Yet an even stronger case can be made to demonstrate the opposite, namely, that he not only understood but programmatically rewrote the *Cárcel* in such a way as to underscore his own originality.

The type of continuation offered by Núñez conforms to Harold Bloom's description of *clinamen*, that is, he adopts the subtext until a certain point at which he rejects its trajectory.[24] Núñez specifies that upon Leriano's death, El Autor should not have returned directly to Castile, but "deviera venirse por la corte, (y) a dezir a Laureola de cierto como ya era muerto Leriano"[25] [ought instead to have gone to the Court to inform Laureola at first hand that Leriano had at last died].[26] Otherwise, she would be oblivious to this fatality she had caused. In the sequel El Autor explicitly considers Laureola's rejection of Leriano to be unjustifiable. For this reason, while San Pedro's lady never acknowledges any amorous inclination toward Leriano, in the sequel she does.

Inadvertent misreading on the part of Núñez is not the case. Rather, he is (implicitly but boldly) achieving something that San Pedro was unable to achieve. While El Autor in the original text succeeded in evolving from an unomniscient and unsophisticated go-between to an omniscient and highly accomplished writer, he failed, as we have seen, in his principal desire to effect an amorous liaison between the two protagonists.[27] Quite logically Núñez designs his text to succeed where his predecessor had failed. As a result, for the first time since they have known one another Laureola and Leriano both participate in the cooperative principle of courtly love. The earlier dilemma between her honor or his life no longer obtains.

In order to effect this breakthrough, El Autor experiences a dream-vision in which Leriano's ghost and Laureola engage in an extended dialogic confrontation—a speech situation they never achieved in San Pedro's text, owing to Laureola's negative attitude. Leriano, we learn, has paid for his suicide by being consigned to Hell, and for her part, Laureola has become truly remorseful: "Más para dezirte verdad que para pagar tu pena, te hago cierto que si tu muerte creyera, antes la mía tomara que la tuya consintiera, porque me parece que fuera consciencia sofrillo" (63) [To tell you the truth, and not in order to compensate you for your suffering, I assure you that had I believed that you would die, I should have killed myself sooner than let you kill yourself, because I think it would have been right to do so (94)]. Nonetheless, as a result of Laureola's declaration of love and repentance for her cruelty, he declares that he gladly suffered the torments: "Muy más rica fue mi muerte / que mi vida, / si della quedáys servida" (58) [My death was richer far, / than was my life, / if by it you are served (89)]. What becomes clear is that Leriano could never have married Laureola, as she explains: "Leriano, según mi estado y linaje, por muger no me merecía" (68) [Leriano was not, given my rank and lineage, worthy to be my husband (98)]. Yet as a result of her initiative, they would have had the opportunity to visit regularly: "trabajara con el rey mi señor su libertad . . . para que entrasse en la corte y oviera lugar de verme" (68) [I might more earnestly and more frequently entreat the king my father to grant Leriano some freedom . . . and allow him to come to the Court and have some opportunity of seeing me (97–98)].

The final point to be made concerning Núñez's insightful continuation has to do with the presentation of the lovers by means of *letras*—brief poetic epigrams attached, in this case, to various articles of clothing worn by them (twelve worn by him and nine by her). These epigrams are metaphors for their love, functioning as a kind of anatomy of the affect. Taking one example from each protagonist, we find Leriano introduced as follows: "Traya . . . un jubón de seda amarilla y colorada, con una letra que dezía:

Mi passión a mi alegría / satisfaze / en fazella quien la haze" (58) [He wore
. . . a silken doublet, yellow and red, with a device which read: My suffering to my joy / is matched, / since it is she who causes it (89)]. Similarly,
the newly repentant Laureola is described as wearing: "una camiza labrada
de seda blanca con unas cerraduras y con una letra que dezia: Cerró tu
muerte a mi vida / de tal suerte, / que no saldrá sin la muerte" (61) [a shift
woven of white silk, fastened by drawstrings, and with a device which read:
Your death has laced my life / so tightly, / that it cannot escape except by
death. (92)]. Whinnom finds these *letras* to be inappropriate in the continuation: "[Núñez's] ingenuity is remarkable, and in a different context one
would not complain of these witty courtly exercises, but following upon
San Pedro's work they again have the effect of trivializing the protagonists'
emotions."[28]

To the contrary, however, the *letras* underscore Núñez's poetic innovation—offering a concrete testimony of his ability to transform the conflicting cooperative principles of honor versus life into the reciprocal cooperative principle of courtly love. The eaten letters that conclude San
Pedro's text are emblematic of Leriano's failed attempt to achieve a contiguity of desire—an extension of Laureola—and are replaced by the eloquent *letras* emblematizing the new relationship of similarity and reciprocity that the two lovers share, despite Leriano's death. In this way,
Núñez has ingeniously redefined the relationship in a metalinguistically
significant manner, thus replacing San Pedro's (failed) metonomy with his
own (successful) metaphor[29]—these being, in Roman Jakobson's classic
formulation, the two polar extremes of figurative language.[30]

# TEN

## THE BOOK AS GALEOTTO

## (*GRIMALTE Y GRADISSA*)

T HE INSTABILITY of the word—the configuration of signified and symbolized phenomena that Boccaccio explores in Fiammetta's *Elegia*—is corroborated in reverse by Juan de Flores in Spain in his explicit continuation of the *Elegia*, known as *Grimalte y Gradissa* (dating from the mid-1480s).[1] For as we shall see, Flores distinguishes his text from Boccaccio's by inverting the focus—i.e, by focusing on the implications of action (rather as is the case with the *Elegia*, on speech) in the enunciation/action binome. Indeed, Flores offers his readers *as* programmatic a rewriting of the *Elegia*'s metaliterary concerns as Boccaccio does of the *Heroides*.[2]

Not one but two couples are at issue in the Spanish text: Boccaccio's Fiammetta and Panfilo *and* Grimalte and Gradissa—all avid readers of the *Elegia*. In fact the text thematizes the act of reading and its effects to such a degree that it is often compared to Cervantes' concerns in *Don Quijote*. Joseph Gillet, for example, sees *Grimalte* as a prefiguration of the relationship of the *Quijote*'s second part to its first: "Boccaccio's characters have stepped outside their novel and outside the control of their author to continue their life in a story by another writer, in fact in another century, and the reader is left with a confusing impression of a timeless world inhabited by age-defying, almost permanent characters."[3]

Carrying the Cervantine analogy a bit further, however, I would advise that we remember the sage words of the trickster Sansón Carrasco at the beginning of Part 2 of *Don Quijote*—that "nunca segundas partes fueron buenas"[4] [second parts are never any good]—a laconic, ironic (consummately Cervantine) way of alerting the reader to the fact that the imaginary universe constructed by a sequel may differ radically from the text it continues.

More recently, Barbara Weissberger sees *Grimalte* as "a clear case—the earliest in Spanish literature—of *incitación* by means of the written word,"[5] a term coined by Américo Castro to indicate the overpowering effects of chivalric romances on Alonso Quijano. For Weissberger, the description Castro offers for the effects of reading as evidenced in *Don Quijote* may be applied to *Grimalte* with equal accuracy: "Books appear here, not as coldly objectified realities, with certain ideas or tales to present, but as being read, as a personal experiencing of values in which a person reveals his individuality while incarnating the living substance of the book into his own life. . . . Books are, therefore, what each reader makes of them by living through them. Literature becomes personalized and individual living reveals its latent poetic dimension."[6]

Weissberger is justified in indicating Flores' focus on the power of the word; however, the interplay of words (be they written or oral) and deeds is, as we have seen repeatedly, a distinctive feature inherent in all of the *novelas sentimentales*. Advocating a further degree of caution with the Cervantine analogy, Patricia Grieve makes a different, equally salient distinction between Flores' creations and their quixotic counterparts, namely, "however we choose to view Flores and judge the cleverness of his playing with fiction and reality . . . for the characters within *Grimalte y Gradissa* there is no doubt that those people who are subjects of written texts really existed, because they later show up as contemporary characters in the work."[7] Cervantes obviously blurs this distinction, as he does with so many others, in his text.

A third note of caution can be voiced concerning the analogic connection offered by Weissberger. Actually, it is not surprising in fact that Flores' overt continuation of the *Elegia* would be concerned specifically with the effects of reading since it is this "quixotic" tension *avant la lettre* between life and literature that defines Fiammetta herself. It is precisely this epistemological innovation that has led so many critics to regard Boccaccio's enterprise as the first modern European novel.

The practice of identifying origins—the first instance of any phenomenon—is admittedly a perilous procedure. Indeed, as noted above, the *Elegia* vies with the *Vita Nuova*, the *Jehan de Saintré*, and *Don Quijote* (among others) as the first modern novel. But if we are looking for texts that expose the power of reading, we need not confine ourselves to speaking of *Don Quijote* or even the *Elegia*. It is, rather, the *Divina Commedia* that offers an eloquent, "living," and much earlier proof of the dangers of reading, in the figures of Paolo and Francesca.

In *Inferno* 5 Francesca explains that she and her lover are being eternally punished for lust, which was prompted by their reading of a book. The book in question is the story of two other legendary lovers, namely Lancelot and Guinevere, whom Galahad brought together. It is at the moment when Lancelot kisses Guinevere for the first time, that Paolo and Francesca can not resist their own passion any longer, thereby capitulating to adultery. Francesca, in explaining to Dante the pilgrim how and why she and her lover have been consigned to Hell, explains the book and its effect by saying: "Galeotto fu' libro e chi lo scrisse" (*Inf.* 5.137) [Galahad was both the book and its author].[8] Since the time of Dante's depiction of these tormented lovers, the name of Galeotto has been associated with literary pandering and its dangers.

As with so many aspects of the *Commedia*, Boccaccio exploits the notion of the book as panderer, and even the name Galeotto itself, for his own devices. The *Elegia*, we recall, presents itself as anti-Galeotto (intended to warn unsuspecting women of the deceitful nature of men). Fiammetta is quite pointed in indicating this cautionary function of her diary. In an obvious sense, however, her text is a Galeotto, since it is her reading of the *Heroides* and *Metamorphoses* that has incited her passion—leading her away from her husband and toward adultery with Panfilo. The danger of just such a reader response (particularly in the case of women readers reading romances) is a perennial concern among ethical writers of virtually any age. Witness the codification of the term "quixotism" and the later coining of "Bovarism" (as a result of Flaubert's depiction of Madame Bovary as a reader of romance).

Boccaccio continues to exploit the Dantean notion of Galeotto in the *Decameron*, and he does so by inverting the configuration offered in the *Elegia*. Whereas the earlier text explicitly presents itself as anti-Galeotto but is a Galeotto in reality since it chronicles Fiammetta's alternately praised and despised capitulation precipitated by books, the *Decameron* officially bears the title of Galeotto (*Comincia il libro chiamato Decameron, cognominato Prencipe Galeotto*), yet it is not one. In his author's epilogue Boccaccio makes this point most emphatically when he asserts that the book is incapable of precipitating the reader's downfall: "Le quali [novelle], chenti che elle si sieno, e nuocere e giovar possono, sí come possono tutte l'altre cose, avendo riguardo allo ascoltatore" (674) [Like all other things in this world, stories, whatever their nature, may be harmful or useful, depending upon the listener (830)].[9] In order to underscore the relativity of reader response (which simultaneously functions as a witty denial of the causality posited by Dante), Boccaccio adds:

> Niuna corrotta mente intese mai sanamente parola: e cosí come le oneste a quella non giovano, cosí quelle, che tanto oneste non sono, la ben disposta non posson contaminare, se non come il loto i solari raggi o le terrene brutture le bellezze del cielo. (674)

> No word, however pure, was ever wholesomely construed by a mind that was corrupt. And just as seemly language leaves no mark upon a mind that is corrupt, language that is less than seemly cannot sully a mind that is well ordered, any more than mud will contaminate the rays of the sun, or earthly filth the beauties of the heavens. (830)

Bearing in mind these commentaries on the power of reading, Flores problematizes the Dantean and Boccaccian Galeotto constructs even further—in a way that dramatizes the unpredictability of reader response (i.e., the subjectivity of language).

The book, in this case the *Elegia*, is intended by Grimalte as a Galeotto by which to win the favors of Gradissa. He assumes that she will, by reading it, come to identify Fiammetta's unrequited love with his own. This identification of Grimalte with Fiammetta is in turn supposed to motivate Gradissa to reciprocate his love, thereby serving also as a correction of Fiammetta's plight. By his interpretation, we see here that Grimalte is a sentimental reader, and that he assumes Gradissa will be too.

Understanding Grimalte's identification with Fiammetta and his desire to have the *Elegia* function as Galeotto, Gradissa promises to return his love if he himself agrees to serve as Galeotto to reunite Fiammetta and Panfilo. With no intention of acting according to her discourse, she instructs her suitor to reunite the estranged Italian couple both in prose and in verse:

> hit a ganar la victoria aquella, con que ganays la mia. Y porque lo metrificado mas dulcemente atrahe a los sentidos a recibir la memoria, alende de lo informado, por esta mi cancion lo quiero mas refirmar assi:
>
> > Si quereys este bien mio,
> > Cobrarlo como quereys,
> > Hit alla do vos enbio,
> > Y fazet quanto podreys.
> >
> > Fazet alla que se vea
> > La que sus males me scrive
> > Con tal descanso que prive
> > La muerte que se dessea.
> >
> > De lo cual mucho confio
> > Segun amor me teneys,
> > Llegado do vos enbio,
> > Que buen remedio porneys.[10]

(6)

Go and win that victory, which will in turn guarantee my surrender to you. And because verse more gently persuades, I would like to reaffirm what I have just claimed by the following poem: If you want to receive my favors, / as you do, go there where I instruct you, / and do whatever you can. / Seek out the one / who writes her misfortunes to me, / and convince her not to yield / to suicide. / I have faith in your abilities, / since you love me. / If you accomplish what I ask, / you will be richly rewarded.

Gradissa's challenge is actually even more ambitious, for Grimalte must effect a lasting reunion and also send back a written account of it. Our attention is repeatedly called to his role as procurer—first by Gradissa, who refers to him as a *tercero* (5), then by Grimalte, who describes himself as a *tercero* to Panfilo (26), and finally, by Grimalte, calling himself a *medianero* (31) in the brief reunion of the Italian pair:

> despues que asi un poco stuvo en mirarlo suspensa, con tales senyales de gran-
> des mudamientos a mi bien ligeros de conocer y a quien su lazo no sabe
> ocultos, tomolo por la mano y a su secreta camara, retrahidos de los suyos, se
> apartaron, tomando a mi entre ellos por medianero. Y ellos assi retrahidos,
> ¿quien podria dezir las graziosas maneras que en este recebimiento passaron?
> Las quales, ahun que el iuyzio las siente, mi mano specificar no sabe, en special
> porque el caso consiste mas en actos que en palabras. Pero algo de lo visto no
> puedo callar; que no creo dos enamorados iamas mayores hoviesse, ni con tan
> lindos modos meior entenderse. Y sin duda, quanto mas yo los mirava, tanto
> de mayores gracias en mis oios eran representados, porque me parecia que el
> mismo dios de amores les ensenyava, para los quales cient mil secretos tenia
> reservados. (31)

> After spending a while staring at him in astonishment, with such altered signs
> that are familiar to those in love, and undetected by those who are not, she
> took him by the hand to her secret chamber. They withdrew from their ser-
> vants, taking me with them as their procurer. Thus withdrawn, who could
> recount accurately their pleasant reunion? Although the mind can conceive of
> it, my hand cannot do it justice, particularly because it consisted more of
> actions than words. But since I cannot remain silent about something which
> I have seen and, because two lovers never had a greater reunion, words are
> inadequate to describe it. And, no doubt, the more I gazed at them the more
> I saw of their graceful manner, because it seemed to me that the God of Love
> himself instructed them, for whom he had reserved 100,000 secrets.

Here too we see that Grimalte's sentimentality causes him to misread the scene, to read things into it that simply are not there. Even more revealing of Grimalte's intense sentimentality is the fact that he has accepted to undertake the mission of reconciliation outlined for him by Gradissa, although he realizes that it is a pretext devised by her to get rid of him. He has no illusions about Gradissa's motives, saying to her of the arduous and perilous mission: "lo fazeys con sperança de yo nunqua bolver" (7) [you demand it in the hope that I will never return]. With even greater lucidity he remarks, "quanto yo mas de piadat lamentava, tanto mas a crueldat la convertia, porque de passion de Fiometa queria tomar la vengança de su Pamphilo en mi" (12) [the more I begged for mercy, the more she resorted to cruelty, because she wanted to take revenge on Panfilo for Fiammetta's suffering through me]. He clearly understands the semantic relativism of her words—that she says one thing but means quite another. Yet he irrationally carries out the quest both because he loves Gradissa and because he identifies personally with Fiammetta's sufferings as well.

To demonstrate that one reader may have several different affective responses to a text, Flores endows Gradissa with an additional kind of response. Although her own situation bears no resemblance to Fiammetta's (indeed it is the opposite predicament in which the suitor is faithful much to her dislike), she too identifies with her. Consequently, she reads the *Elegia* not simply as a ruse by which she can rid herself of her all-too-loving suitor, Grimalte, but simultaneously (thus somewhat irrationally) as a cautionary tale warning women of the faithlessness of all men. In this connection, Barbara Matulka—more than fifty years ago—advanced the view of Gradissa as a "cruel beauty" and feminist who is intent on "inciting women to rebellion against masculine supremacy and faithlessness."[11] In point of fact, however, it is never made clear whether Gradissa really identifies with Fiammetta or whether her claim is nothing more than a convenient pretext. Waley places Gradissa's verbal ambiguity into the larger context of the work as a whole: "It is never explicitly stated that Gradissa is anything but sincere . . . but both the character of Grimalte and the malice of some other of her remarks make it likely that Grimalte's understanding of the situation is justified—that she wants to be rid of him and has found a convenient pretext to do so. Thus the reader is at several points induced to doubt whether the characters say what they mean or use expressed motives to mask true ones."[12] Besides her rather blunt and unamorous remarks such as "en tomar este trabaio por mi es el precio con que me haveys de comprar" (5) [taking on this job for me is the price you have to pay to buy me], Gradissa gives a rather lame excuse for not going after Fiammetta herself. She claims that she would "si el freno de la verguença no me templara" (5) [if the rein of respectability did not constrain me]. She could have emulated Fiammetta's own disguise as a religious pilgrim, yet she chose not to. Noting that in both of Flores' novels "what people say and do does not necessarily coincide with what they think and intend," Waley sees in these two texts "a sophistication of characterization akin to that of *La Celestina*."[13] I would add that the sophistication of characterization is a result of the global sophistication of language theory at issue in Flores' texts as well as all the other *novelas sentimentales*, of which the *Celestina* is a masterful late example.

For her part, Fiammetta (who is disguised as a religious pilgrim to mask her amorous pilgrimage) remains the deluded reader evidenced in her diary, still seeking to imitate the legendary heroines, still unaware that she lacks both their heroic uniqueness and resolve. Not only is she still committed to her marriage (at least publicly), but her case is simply that of the woman who attempts to endow a one-night stand with mythic proportions.

The fourth kind of reader, Panfilo, is an analytical reader, discerning the literary origins of the lady's delusion and trying to use that knowledge to keep her from dying of sadness. Invoking Roman antiquity and Lucretia (whom Fiammetta herself had invoked analogically in the *Elegia*), he explains:

> Mira exemplo en los antigos romanos que menospreciavan la vida por el famoso morir. Pues si aquella muerte que muy apareiada te veo te viniesse, no te daria tal lohor como aquella de Lucrecia, que para siempre quedara su memoria, y el fin della es loor y exemplo de los que bien viven. Pues aquello devemos guardar que mas loados nos haze. (34)

> Consider the example of the ancient Romans, who belittled life in place of a famous death. If you were to die now, you would not be praised as Lucretia was, she who will enjoy eternal memory, and whose death is praiseworthy and exemplary to those living. We must sustain that which affords us the greatest praise.

Panfilo tries to impress upon her the fact that their relationship does not merit her death, that it is not of the stature of the legendary females whom she invokes. He understands her unrealistic obsession with myth, and tries to speak to her on her own terms. Yet, of course, denying that she is of the same stature as the heroines of her deluded brain is devastating for her.

Like other authors of *novelas sentimentales*, Flores identifies himself with the fictional narrator-protagonist of his text: "Comiença un breve tractado compuesto por Johan de Flores, el cual por la siguiente obra mudo su nombre en Grimalte, la invencion del qual es sobre la Fiometa" (3) [Here begins the short treatise written on the (*Elegia*) by Juan de Flores who, for this purpose changed his name to Grimalte]. At the same time, this constitutes an innovation for as Weissberger remarks, "By pointing out to the reader that the name Grimalte is merely a pseudonym, Flores makes explicit what in previous romances of the sentimental genre was implicit: that very process of fictionalization whereby the 'yo' of the real author becomes the 'yo' of a character."[14] The rubrics "Dize Grimalte como auctor" (23) [Grimalte speaks in his capacity as author], and "El auctor" (57), preceded directly by "Grimalte dize la forma de la sepultura" (54) [Grimalte describes the tomb], which is followed immediately by the "Desafio de Grimalte a Pamfilo" (57) [Grimalte's challenge to Panfilo], expose Flores' self-consciousness with even greater clarity.

By replacing the *Elegia*'s first-person subjective structure with a second-person dialogic structure, *Grimalte* thus allows for a simultaneous multiplicity of interpretations of Fiammetta's love affair. As a result, not only she but Gradissa, Grimalte, and Panfilo will have occasion to discuss it both directly and at length. It is important to note, moreover, that the interest in reader response does not stop here, for Grimalte reports the reactions of additional readers whom he meets during the course of his quest to reconcile Fiammetta and Panfilo. While on his journey, as he inquires whether anyone has seen Fiammetta, we learn that many women tease him by claiming to be Fiammetta herself: "muchas Fiometas en quada villa falle, porque quien se quería fingir ser ella bien se passava sus tiempos scarnesciendose de mi" (13) [I found many Fiammettas in every village, for many pretended to be her, spending their time ridiculing me]. Textual autonomy (as well as the *Elegia*'s popularity) is further corroborated as we learn that old men are furious at Panfilo: "entre las gentes no hay otro razonar sino de vos. Y ahun los viegos con sperança de resucitar nuevos amores, si algun disfavor reciben de auqellas a quien requestan, no crehen que defectos suyos les priven de ser amados, mas antes piensan que vuestras culpas los enbaraçan" (27) [People talk of nothing but you. And even old men who hope to embark on love affairs, if they meet with any resistance, never blame any of their personal defects; rather, they think that you have spoiled their chances (by your deceitful behavior)]. Such perspectival pluralism is, as Weissberger suggests[15] eminently Cervantine. We must hasten to add, however, that it is a distinctive feature of every *novela sentimental*. Turning a private lyric experience public, showing how perspectivism leads to failed lyric is the recurring basic structure. With *Grimalte* it is a question of degree, not of kind.

Realizing that Boccaccio's Fiammetta had only two options—perpetual madness or suicide—Flores offers a different course by following a suggestion that Fiammetta offered and then rejected—namely, that she disguise herself as a religious pilgrim (a socially acceptable excuse for her true identity as a pilgrim of love). In spatial terms, there is a movement out of the solipsistic, paralyzing secrecy of Fiammetta's chamber to the public arena of the world at large (extending all the way from Iberia to Asia). The pathological, paralytic inaction of Boccaccio's text is replaced by a profusion of activity in the Spanish continuation. Also by way of distinguishing his work from that of his predecessor, we see a notable absence of mythological discourse in the Spanish continuation, and Fiammetta's obsessive claims to uniqueness are systematically countered by the other characters, who in turn assure her that her situation is, in fact, quite prosaically commonplace.[16]

For her part, Gradissa speaks from personal experience: "por ciertas speriencias tengo conocimiento de vosotros ser muy dulces en los principios de amor, y en los fines amarguos" (4) [I know from experience that you men are sweet in the beginning of a love affair, and bitter in the end]. Invoking the topos of "familiarity breeds contempt," Panfilo tries in vain to convince Grimalte that Fiammetta's experience is not in the least unusual: "es cosa comuna, que quan presto desseamos, tan presto avorrecemos; y aquello que todos hazeys, quereys que a mi solo culpe, siendo la pena vulgar" (28–29) [it is well known, that as soon as we fall in love we lose interest, and that that of which you are all guilty, you try to blame on me alone]. Far from feeling that he must try to make amends for his behavior, Panfilo adds that "yo a ninguno mas lealmente amarla no le conozco memoria" (29) [I know of no one who loved her more faithfully than I]. Not the duration of his love-service, but the quality of it is the important factor as far as Panfilo is concerned. In his futile attempt to prevent Fiammetta from dying of despair, Grimalte tries repeatedly to impress upon her the fact that her predicament is anything but unique (48, 50). While she is, of course, unwilling to accept the claim that her suffering caused by infidelity is *tan comun*, she uses the same locution to excuse her own infidelity when he tries to convince her to return to her husband:

> el peligro de mi marido, con que tantos temores me pones, yo stava dudosa, porque no todas las que peccan padecen luego la pena. Mayormente, que yo por mi adulterio mas penitencia que muerte me busco. Y la Fortuna y los diozes usarian mas de crueldad que de iusticia si otro verdugo buscassen sino a ti para satisfazer a hun yerro que tan comun a las mujeres conteçe. (38)

> Fear of my husband, which you are trying to elicit from me, will not work, since not all those who sin in this way suffer for it. Rather, I, in my adultery, seek to do penitence rather than to die. And Fortune and the gods would be more cruel than just if they sought any executioner other than you to carry out the punishment in a flaw which is so common among women.

By this last claim to commonness, Flores reiterates the duplicity that Fiammetta had admitted in her *Elegia,* a duplicity of which she is unaware. Even more is achieved by these multiple claims to being common, however. First, Flores recalls the *Elegia,* in which the nurse kept warning the distraught protagonist that such disillusionment is the rule in human relationships. He thereby offers an extended *amplificatio* of the theme. Yet at the same time, Flores departs markedly from the Boccaccian model by emphasizing two of the most basic concerns of the novel, namely, universality (not mythic uniqueness) and contemporaneity (not antique paradigms) are foregrounded by Flores' treatment. As Bakhtin explains in broad, theoretical terms:

> The formally constitutive feature of the epic as a genre is rather the transferral of a represented world in the past and the appurtenance of this world to the past. . . . To portray an event on the same temporal and axiological plane as oneself and one's contemporaries (and, therefore, from personal experience and invention) is to accomplish a radical transformation, and to step out of the world of the epic into the world of the novel.[17]

Despite the fact that Grimalte points out to Fiammetta that her condition is not in the slightest uncommon, that it is not a question of *nuevas leyes* (of infidelity) being instituted by Panfilo, it is revealing that when he speaks to Panfilo in person, he claims just that: "pues pareçe que nuevas leyes usays en amor" (Waley, 58) [it appears that you are using new rules for love]. This legal analogy is quite instructive. It continues yet another aspect of the Boccaccian subtext where, we recall, Fiammetta kept trying to excuse her failure by saying that Panfilo had rewritten the time-honored rules of love.[18] In addition, in metadiscursive terms, it reveals the relativity of discourse as such.

Whereas Boccaccio's Panfilo had simply disappeared, leaving Fiammetta and us to wonder whether he had left her to pursue another lady, Flores' Panfilo explains his actions and their motivation with considerable precision. As it turns out, Panfilo explicitly spurns Fiammetta for several different reasons. The first is because of her extreme egotism—her persistent and annoying claim to uniqueness: "tu siempre quisiste en todas cosas so-brarme, y mostrar mayor amor, y dezir mayores tus quexas" (20) [you always wanted to outdo me, to show that your love was greater and that your suffering was more intense]. The second cause for Panfilo's departure is that she has lost her honor and is, therefore, unworthy of love: "conozco de tu desseo mas que de tu cordura te dexastes vençer. . . . Si tu con el amor demasiado te plaze perder honor, los otros no lo quieren. Pero que bien es que seas liberal en aquello que a ti solamente te toca, mas que tu hagas mercedes de la honor de muchos es grande agravio, por cierto. Piensa que quadauno de la perdida tuya le alcança parte" (21) [I know that you chose to follow your passion rather than your reason. . . . If you choose to lose your honor because you love too much, others do not wish it. It is well to be liberal with that which affects only you, but that you jeopardize the honor of others is a great wrong, to be sure. Know that everyone else is affected by your loss of honor]. Finally, Panfilo explains that he does not want to tarnish her social reputation, advising her, therefore, to return to her husband (35)—which is a contradiction of his second argument, in which the loss of honor and reputation is viewed as a *fait accompli*.

To Grimalte he adds still other justifications for his behavior: (1) that no woman can keep the attention of a man indefinitely (28); (2) that he left in order to prevent Fiammetta from dishonor (29), and (3) that (in etymological fidelity to his name) a pleasing man should "spread the wealth," as it were: "el hombre que gracioso y dispuesto se conoce, razon es que reparta sus gracias por muchas, que no es iusto que sola una le goze" (29) [it stands to reason that the man who is well endowed and amenable should dispense his wealth among many women; it is an injustice to let only one woman enjoy it].

Fiammetta responds to this unconditional rejection by expiring, we assume—since the precise cause of death is never clarified (52). Grimalte buries her with great dignity and ceremony and, in order to avenge her death, he challenges Panfilo to a duel. Panfilo, however, seeing the (for him wholly unanticipated) effects of his words on Fiammetta, chooses instead to condemn himself to a life of penance in the desert. Thereupon Grimalte returns to Spain, where he writes to Gradissa explaining Fiammetta's death and Panfilo's vow of eternal penance. Gradissa is so aggrieved by this news that she swears never to love Grimalte "como Pamphilo pudo despedir aquella sin verguença, menos enpacho devo yo tener en despediros" (63) [since Panfilo was so shameless in dismissing her, I should feel even less in dismissing you]. She mistrusts men more than ever and interprets Panfilo's penitential oath as nothing more than a ruse to conceal his cowardice.

Realizing that Gradissa will never love him, Grimalte decides to join Panfilo to share his life as a recluse. This is easier said than done, however. For it is only after a twenty-seven-year search that Grimalte finally locates Panfilo in a remote part of Asia. (In the context of this journey it is interesting to note that Grimalte incongruously likens himself to Jason on his quest for the Golden Fleece: "no menos crimen era a los de aquell buscadores, que en el vieio y muy antigo tiempo la demanda a los del vellecino d'oro. Pero yo, menospreciando el peligro de mi vida, ahun que no armado de las armas, me fuy a tal victoria ganar" (65–66) [it was no greater challenge than the quest for the Golden Fleece in olden times. But, not intimidated by the risk to my life, although I had no weapons, went determined to be victorious]. This mythological attribution is no accident, being rather a (sub)conscious analogue to Fiammetta's equally incongruous identification of herself with Medea throughout the *Elegia*).[19]

When Grimalte finally finds Panfilo, the latter is barely recognizable (walking on all fours and naked, his skin blackened by the sun): "por su andar y pareçer diverso, en todas sus senyales a hun fiero animal pareçia" (Waley, 67) [by his mode of walking and his strange appearance, he looked like a wild animal]. It is only by virtue of the fact that Grimalte's hunting dogs drag him out of the cave in which he dwells (wherein he carries out his *penitencia*), that Panfilo reveals himself. Even more strange is Panfilo's reaction to the dogs, who pursue him, tearing at his flesh: "los canes mios muy agramente lo persiguian, mas ell ninguna cosa quexava ni dezia, antes en sus offiensas mostrava plazer. Y yo, vyendo quanto aspramente lo aquexavan que quasi me pareçia que lo despedaçavan, haviendo dell compassion, llame los canes y diles a comer" (67) [my dogs pursued him savagely, yet he did not complain or utter any words at all; rather he was pleased at their mistreatment of him. And I, seeing that they abused so brutally that they seemed to tear him apart, feeling compassion for him, called off the dogs and fed them].

Grimalte learns that he has, in addition to his troglodyte penitence, taken a vow of perpetual silence in deference to the memory of Fiammetta. And, although Grimalte tries to engage him in speech, it is to no avail. In desperation and as a last resort, Grimalte even sets his dogs on Panfilo: "yo enoiado de su callar, por ver si el dolor algo le haria dezir, por fuerça solte los perros, dandoles mas favor y sforçandolos fuerte contra ell, como si fuera animal salvaje" (67) [annoyed at his silence, and to see whether pain would provoke him to speak, (I) let loose the dogs, encouraging them to attack him as if he were a wild beast]. Yet violence, as he learns, is not the answer. Panfilo refuses to speak even after Grimalte explains that he has come to emulate him; that he too is a forlorn lover who has come to live out his life in the desert.

With a considerable degree of perplexity, critics have noted the incongruity of Grimalte's claim to resemble Panfilo, since the two are—in the obvious sense—opposites: Panfilo rejected his lady, whereas it was Grimalte's lady who rejected him. Waley goes so far as to view Panfilo's altered condition as an appendix, not central to the narrative. Speaking of Panfilo in an attempt to account for him, she claims: "When [Fiammetta] is dead, he undergoes a change of heart—and perhaps even achieves a degree of mental instability—becoming a repentant recluse; but this is rather an appendix to the main theme."[20] Flores, however, is focusing here not on superficial narrative detail, but on his—and Boccaccio's—fundamental theme, namely, linguistic usage.

It is highly significant to the language theory that Flores develops in this text that Panfilo refuses to respond until the moment when Grimalte literally gets on all fours and walks like Panfilo: "fuyme a lo mas spesso de aquell boscaie . . . y las manos puestas por el suelo en la manera que aquell andava, siguiendo sus pizadas, tom[e]lo por maestro de mi nuevo officio" (69) [I entered into the deepest part of the woods . . . and, placing my hands on the ground in emulation of the way in which he walked, following in his tracks, I chose him as the teacher of my new vocation]. It is only once Grimalte has guaranteed the truth-status of his words by his action that Panfilo breaks his silence, accepting him at that point as a fellow penitent. The cause of Panfilo's linguistic alienation is thus dramatically reversed. It constitutes, moreover, a striking departure from all the other instances of linguistic alienation—e.g., Lucretia's and Leriano's deaths, Fiammetta's madness, and Arnalte's self-imposed exile as a solitary anchorite.

Independent confirmation of this linguistic integrity is offered (contrastively) by the spectacle Grimalte and Panfilo witness three nights a week. On those occasions they are both subjected to an infernal vision of Fiammetta being tortured by ghastly demons who light up the sky by the flames that shoot forth from their eyes and from the two linguistically essential sensory organs—their ears and tongues: "Sallian de sus bocas unas encendidas llamas tan grandes y con tal gana resuffladas que sino lo que lo vehia, no lo puede consentir a verdad. . . . De los infernales fuegos que de sus oios y oreias sallian la escuradad de la noche en grande claridad tornaron" (71) [Burning flames of such size and intensity shot forth from their mouths that if one did not behold them for himself, he would never have believed it. . . . The infernal flames that spewed out of their eyes and ears lit up the nocturnal darkness]. After Fiammetta has spent the greater part of the night tormented by the devils, she is carried off by them in a cart. Grimalte once more swears eternal devotion to Gradissa, at which point he dies and the work ends there.

No interpretive consensus exists concerning this hellish apparition of Fiammetta. It has been viewed alternatively as punishment for her lust, adultery or, perhaps, suicide, yet none of these ethical concerns figure centrally in the text. Even more disconcerting is the fact that, as Waley remarks, "In literature, women shown suffering supernatural torments are usually being punished for cruelty towards their lovers."[21] Surely Fiammetta cannot be placed in this category.

I would argue, however, that the incongruity is only an apparent one—consistent in fact with the rest of the work in terms of the action/enunciation dichotomy that has defined Fiammetta since the opening pages of her *Elegia*: for in her infernal existence Fiammetta is—significantly—the victim of an assault on the *ears* and *tongue*, whereby she is denied the power of speech, as Grimalte explains: "ella començo a llamar mi nombre con proposito de algo dezirme, sino por el grande estorvo de aquellos que la seguian [no se oía]" (71) [she would call out my name with the intention of telling me (or Panfilo) something, but the demons who followed her would drown out her words]. Instead of allowing her to speak, they force her to suffer in actions the words of malediction she had so deceptively articulated in the *Elegia* (Book 5), for example, against Panfilo: "anzi tra li morti spiriti seguitandoti, con quelle ingiurie che di là s'adoperano m'-ingegnerò di noiarti . . . vegghiando, orribile mi vedrai, e ne' sonni spaventevole sovente ti desterò nelle tacite notti" (Segre, 1,041) [pursuing thee amongst the dead ghosts and fiends of Hell . . . I will continually plague and eternally punish thy damned soul for thy condemned and hateful deed. . . . Thou shalt see me in a most horrible shape, and in thy fearful sleep oftentimes will I awake and affright thee in the uncomfortable silence of the dark night (Hutton, 248–49)].[22] As we know, however, Fiammetta, as in her Italian existence, is too cowardly to threaten her comfortable domestic situation, much less to pursue Panfilo into Hell amid its ghastly apparitions. We see her—finally—being forced to act in accord with her speech, something she was incapable of doing in "real life." It is, moreover, a logical extension of the "quadrupedic alliance" of Panfilo and Grimalte—underscoring the need for action to guarantee the truth-status of speech, for symbolized event and signified utterance to accord.

Critics rarely miss an opportunity to remark on Grimalte's ineffectual nature, which borders on the comical. From the very beginning (when his gift of the *Elegia* to Gradissa backfires), to his incongruous mixture of chivalric and sentimental features, to the way he is treated by others, Grimalte's fragile self-image seems quite justified. Summing up the impression he creates, Waley writes: "in general he is a pathetic rather than a heroic figure, both as a result of his own actions and words and from the reaction of the other characters to him."[23] Paradoxically, however, this portrayal is also intended by Flores as a further commentary on his theory of language. Grimalte's comical failure is designed to highlight a much more important success. For while he obviously fails as lover of Gradissa and also as go-between for Fiammetta and Panfilo, he succeeds in one essential matter, namely he—as character—restores integrity to language by understanding at last (as Panfilo has understood) the need for word and deed to be mutually defining. The fact that this community of restored linguistic integrity is composed of only two members (who, moreover, are totally cut off from society) seems to indicate Flores' serious skepticism about the viability of this purified linguistic model for society at large. For in the last analysis, language is irreducibly (and dangerously) subjective. Enunciation and action rarely coincide.

This text, like the *Cárcel*, devotes only about one-third of itself to narrative, the rest being given over to dialogue and letters—and in the case of *Grimalte*, to an abundance of *cancionero*-style poetry (forty-two intercalated verses in fact).[24] Flores includes a total of seven letters, only four of which are exchanged. And they conform to the law of epistolary reciprocity we observed in San Pedro's work. The first pair is sent by Fiammetta and Panfilo (Waley, 19, 20). Her letter criticizes his behavior, eliciting an immediate response because he wishes to counter all of her criticisms, and to keep from having a personal interview. Although he does not have his way, the fact that they share a common interest—justification of their relationship—leads the first letter to get an immediate response. The other pair of letters (57, 59) involves Grimalte's challenge of Panfilo to a duel to exact expiation for his treatment of Fiammetta. Panfilo, meanwhile, responds because he is eager to suffer for his misbehavior—even though he chooses the unchivalric penitence of a hermit. Three additional letters are written (all addressed by Grimalte to Gradissa—62, 65, 73), yet they receive no reply because she feels they no longer have anything in common, since he has failed according to her stipulation of a duel with Panfilo.

The verses serve a similar metadiscursive purpose. More often than not, characters tend to reiterate in verse something they have just communicated in prose because, as they explicitly claim, they are convinced that verse is more persuasive. Time and again, however, the poetry is as unsuccessful in persuading the interlocutor or addressee as the prose. It is not a question of the particular literary genre the enunciator or writer chooses, but of the recipient's subjective state that determines his or her persuasion or lack of it.[25]

The irreducibly narcissistic nature of language is crystallized by Flores in the repeated image of the mirror. Gradissa claims to Grimalte that for her Fiammetta is a "speio de doctrina" [mirror of honor] concerning the deceptive nature of men (5). For Grimalte she is a "speio de beldat" (13) [mirror of beauty], while Panfilo tells her to look at herself with the "speio de honor" (41) [mirror of honor], in an attempt to save her reputation, and have her leave him alone. Of this specular configuration Grieve aptly remarks that "Fiammetta uses no mirror and admits no reality but that which she infers from her own emotions and desires."[26] Two additional observations should accompany her reading. Namely, that Fiammetta's own "speio," while not a physical looking-glass, is her consummately narcissistic diary, the *Elegia* itself, which she has never ceased gazing into. And also, that the "speios" of the other three characters (as well as the rural female impersonators of Fiammetta and the lusty old men who blame Panfilo for their amorous failures) are all operating on the same basis of their subjective epistemological and linguistic standards.

Finally, Flores effects closure in his narrative in a way that language theory is corroborated by spatial configuration. We have moved from the *Elegia*'s (inoperative) Heavenly realm of the mythological deities down to Earth, as it were, with the quadrupedic moment of communication, ultimately—and very appropriately—to the pit of Hell. In so doing, Flores continues and completes Boccaccio's metalinguistic act by definitively punishing the linguistic transgression of the counterfeit muse.

# ELEVEN

## LANGUAGE AND INCEST

### (*GRISEL Y MIRABELLA*)

D ISCOURSE"—as Michel Foucault observes—"was not originally a product, a thing, a kind of goods; it was essentially an act—an act placed in the bipolar field of the sacred and the profane, the licit and the illicit, the religious and the blasphemous. Historically, it was a gesture fraught with risks before becoming goods caught up in a circuit of ownership."[1] The liminal period referred to as the late Middle Ages explores the tension between these two types of discourse—the (potentially dangerous) social act and the literary commodity—in a variety of contexts.

In fifteenth-century Spain *Grisel y Mirabella* offers an illuminating case in point. This text by Juan de Flores continues his exploration of legal discourse begun in *Grimalte y Gradissa*. While *Grimalte* explores law in the (private, individual) amorous register, *Grisel* further problematizes the discourse of desire by placing it in the (public, universal) context of society. For in essence, *Grisel* examines the relationship between natural law and judicial law as they pertain to the discursive authority of their guarantor— the king.

As with *Grimalte*, here too a Boccaccian subtext tends to be posited but minimized—recognized but deemed unessential to an understanding of *Grisel*. Those who discount the orientation established by the first tale in Day 4 of the *Decameron* locate Flores' concern either in a formal consideration—the preponderance of debate[2]—or a semantic concern with fifteenth-century feminism.[3] Both issues, however, stem from Boccaccio's discursive postulation of nominalism. *Grisel*, like its subtext, is about language, about naming, about the legitimacy of discourse per se.

In Day 4 of the *Decameron* we find that Boccaccio orients our reading by devoting his prologue to the topic of natural law—the indomitable power of desire. Being criticized not only for portraying so much sex but for himself being totally obsessed by it in his advanced age, the author reminds his audience that "perché il porro abbia il capo bianco, che la coda sia verde" (258)[4] [although the leek's head is white, it has a green tail (329)]. The inevitability of human desire is reinforced in the prologue with the example of Fillipo Balducci, the widower. Deeply distressed by the death of his beloved wife, Fillipo decides to withdraw from the world by entering the service of God, taking his infant son with him. They live in a cave and the father "si guardava di non ragionare, là dove egli fosse, d'alcuna temporal cosa né di lasciarnegli alcuna vedere, acciò che esse da cosí fatto servigio nol traessero" (256) [took very great care not to let (his son) see any worldly things, or even mention their existence, lest they should distract him from his devotions (327)]. As a consequence of this recast Platonic cave, the boy grows into manhood without ever having seen a woman and entirely ignorant of the second sex. At the age of eighteen, however, he sees women for the first time and is predictably awestruck. Asking the name of these wonderful creatures, Fillipo deceptively identifies them as "gosslings," indicating also that they are evil. Despite these words of caution, the son exclaims that: "Elle son piú belle che gli agnoli dipinti che voi m'avete piú volte mostrati. Deh! se vi cal di me, fate che noi ce ne meniamo una colà su di queste papere, e io le darò beccare" (257) [They are more beautiful than the painted angels (of the church) that you have taken me to see so often. O alas! If you have any concern for my welfare, do make it possible for us to take one of these gosslings back with us, and I will pop things into its bill (328)].[5] The moral of this story is obvious, yet Boccaccio leaves nothing to chance, saying to his inscribed female readers that:

altra cosa dir non potrà alcun con ragione, se non che gli altri e io, che vi amiamo, naturalmente operiamo; alle cui leggi, cioè della natura, voler contastare, troppe gran forze bisognano, e spesse volte non solamente invano, ma con grandissimo danno del faticante s'adoperano. (260)

no reasonable person will deny that I and other men who love you are simply doing what is natural. And in order to oppose the laws of nature, one has to possess exceptional powers, which often turn out to have been used, not only in vain, but to the serious harm of those who employ them. (331)

The dangers of denying one's offspring their sexuality—the pursuit of natural law—is also the focus of *Decameron* 4.1. Tancredi, prince of Salerno, "signore assai umano e di benigno ingegno" (261) [a most benevolent ruler, and kindly of disposition (332)], was—we are told—"as passionately fond of [Ghismonda], his daughter, as any father who has ever lived" (332). After waiting until she was several years past the marriageable age, Tancredi finally permits her to marry, yet shortly thereafter she is left a widow. Ghismonda returns to her father's house, where, once again (as a result of his lustful inclinations) "poca cura si dava di piú maritarla" (261) [he was in no hurry to make her a second marriage (332)]. The father's repeated reluctance in letting his daughter go is the first sign of his incestuous desire. Realizing Tancredi's unwillingness to let her remarry, the beautiful daughter chooses a lover, a young valet in the service of her father named Guiscardo—"uom di nazione assai umile ma per virtú e per costumi nobile" (261) [a man of exceedingly humble birth but noble in character and bearing (333)]. To make her intentions known to Guiscardo, Ghismonda composes a letter, concealing it in a (phallically suggestive) reed which she hands him, saying: "Fara'ne questa sera un soffione alla tua servente, col quale ella raccenda il fuoco" (262) [Turn it into a bellows-pipe for your serving-wench, so that she can use it to kindle the fire this evening (333)]. (This is the first in a series of images that function not only on a literal level, but on a metaphorical level as well—one that refers to her sexuality.) Ghismonda's message is a phallic gesture not simply because she initiates the seduction, which comes in the form of a reed, but also because she has assumed the traditionally male role as writer (creator) who acts upon the passive female object of creation. The pen/phallus equivalence is a standard Western literary topos going back at least as far as Augustine. Derrida further elaborates this association when he explains that "the hymen is the always folded . . . space in which the pen writes its dissemination."[6] In essence, Ghismonda must take on this phallic role in order to counteract the tyranny of her own father's phallus.[7]

The metaphoric intent of this missive is obvious, once again illustrating Boccaccio's metalinguistic interest in this tale. Metaphor implies transference but—at the same time—usurpation of linguistic identity. For Ghismonda it is the rhetorical weapon by which she can counteract Tancredi's sexual usurpation—just as it serves his own transgressive desire. Guiscardo's correct deciphering of the message leads to a series of blissful trysts in Ghismonda's cave (it being an emblem of her female sexuality as well as the architectural space of her bedchamber) until, quite by accident, the discreet lovers are discovered by Tancredi. (Here, too, it is significant that the father's discovery stems from his incestuous inclinations, as suggested by a descriptive detail that the narrator mentions but does not elaborate—namely, that "appoggiato il capo al letto e tirata sopra sé la cortina, quasi come se studiosamente si fosse nascoso" (263) [the concealed Tancredi rested his head against the side of (Ghismonda's) bed and drew the curtain round his body as though to conceal himself there on purpose (335)], as he often did while awaiting her return.) At this point he falls asleep, concealed from the lovers' sight, awakening to the sounds of their amorous ecstasy.

Substantiation of Boccaccio's interest in sexual metaphor abounds, as Guido Almansi suggests. In the brief space of one paragraph, for example, we find the following concentration of suggestive details: The cave had been used "at some remote time in the past" (i.e., during Ghismonda's first marriage). This concealed space was virtually forgotten until "Love reminded the enamoured lady of its existence" (the sexual awakening after the bereavement of her widowhood). The passage into the cave is "a secret staircase . . . but the way was barred by a massive door." In a futile gesture, Ghismonda resists this barrier "for several days" (in an attempt to forestall an illicit liaison). Within the side of the mountain there exists a *spiraglio* ("shaft") which had been "almost entirely covered by weeds and brambles." It is through this narrow passageway that Guiscardo penetrates the cave, by means of a rope which he hitches to "a stout bush that had taken root at the mouth of the opening." He wears "a suit of leather to protect himself from the brambles."[8]

Having discovered the lovers, Tancredi feels totally betrayed by his daughter and his trusted valet. Guiscardo is abruptly seized and taken prisoner, remarking only that: "Amor può troppo più che né voi né io possiamo" (Segre, 264) [Neither you nor I can resist the power of Love (McWilliam, 335)]—recalling in a serious register the lesson of Fillipo Balducci.[9] (These words take on even greater significance since they are the only words uttered by Guiscardo that are recorded in the entire novella.) Tancredi is devastated and speaks of the "appalling dilemma" into which his daughter has cast him, oblivious to the fact that the dilemma itself stems from his own unnatural denial of her natural urge: "di te sallo Iddio che io non so che farmi. Dall'una parte mi trae l'amore, il quale io t'ho sempre più portato che alcun padre portasse a figliuola, e d'altra mi trae giustissimo sdegno preso per la tua gran follia" (264) [God knows what I am to do with you. I am drawn in one direction by the love I have always borne you, deeper by far than that of any other father for a daughter; but on the other hand I seethe with all the indignation that the folly of your actions demands (336)].

Although Tancredi condemns Ghismonda's actions, she pointedly asserts that her behavior stems directly from his unnaturally covetous behavior:

a questo non mi indusse tanto la mia feminile fragilità, quanto la tua poca sollecitudine del maritarmi e la virtú di lui. Esser ti dovea, Tancredi, manifesto, essendo tu di carne, aver generata figliuola di carne e non di pietra o di ferro. (265)

I was prompted to act as I did, not so much by my womanly frailty as by your lack of concern to marry me, together with his own outstanding worth. You are made of flesh and blood, Tancredi, and it should have been obvious to you that the daughter you fathered was also made of flesh and blood, and not of stone or iron. (337)

Her action—referred to as a "natural peccato" (265) [natural sin (337)]—is thus a natural response to his misguided *action* and also to his *words* of high praise for Guiscardo: "Chi il commendò mai tanto, quanto tu 'l commendavi in tutte quelle cose laudevoli che valoroso uomo dee essere commendato?" (266) [For was it not you yourself who sang his praises more loudly than any, claiming for him all the qualities by which one measures a man's excellence? (338)]. In his oblivious state, Tancredi never dreamed that his words would be interpreted by Ghismonda as they in fact were—as the direct cause of her falling in love with Guiscardo. He is unaware of the power of words; more precisely, of the distinction between word and context.

As Bakhtin explains, a unit of language is neutral, an utterance (a semantic context) is not. He observes that "words in the realm of language belong to no one, for they have only *significance*, a typical sense, whereas real *meaning*, which is what words acquire in the realm of utterance, involves particular people in actual social and historical situations. We not only know what 'joy' signifies, but we can also understand the meaning of locutions such as 'Any joy is now a bitterness to me.' Moreover, we can also understand further dimensions of the word 'joy' as they come up in actual utterances (such as this sentence)."[10] Thus Tancredi's words of praise for Guiscardo (as a worthy valet) are understandably construed by Ghismonda as praise for a worthy lover—literally the last interpretation her father would wish to endorse.

The eloquent speech that Ghismonda delivers to her father is notable for several reasons. First, despite her distressed state at realizing her father's vengeful inclination (and assuming that Guiscardo has already been killed), she maintains her composure and delivers an admirably conceived speech. This speech takes the form of a "verdictive"—it is a statement of fact (not a "directive," designed to persuade Tancredi to be lenient): " 'né a negare né a pregare son disposta, per ciò che né l'un mi varrebbe né l'altro voglio che mi vaglia; e oltre a ciò in niuno atto intendo di rendermi benivola la tua mansuetudine e 'l tuo amore" (Segre, 265) [I am resolved neither to contradict you nor to implore your forgiveness, because denial would be pointless and I want none of your clemency. Nor do I have the slightest intention of appealing either to your better nature or to your affection (McWilliam, 337)].

The substance of Ghismonda's speech offers proof that she acts in accord with her words, whereas Tancredi does not. On the one hand, the father claims that her welfare was more dear to him than anything else; on the other, he denied her the right to amorous fulfillment—even within the chaste bonds of matrimony. This action—imprisoning her in his house while claiming in his speech that he is a benevolent and just ruler—is clearly a violation of his self-perceived benevolence. Along similar lines, Ghismonda takes issue with the fact that Tancredi reproaches her "quasi turbato esser non ti dovessi se io nobile uomo avessi a questo eletto, che io con uom di bassa condizione mi son posta" (266) [more bitterly not for committing the crime of loving a man, but for consorting with a person of lowly rank (338)]. Boccaccio once more offers a meditation on metaphoric usage, as Ghismonda responds to this charge by differentiating between "titular" and "natural" nobility, according to which standards Guiscardo is a patrician (as Tancredi's earlier praise corroborates), the others being plebians in fact (nobility in name only). Thus Ghismonda repeatedly illustrates that Tancredi's *actions* do not conform to his *words*: "piú mirabilmente che le tue parole non potevano esprimere, non vedessi; e se pure in ciò alcuno inganno ricevuto avessi, da te sarei stata ingannata" (266) [I have seen him practise the very virtues for which you commended him, in a manner more wonderful than your words could express. So that if I was deceived in my estimate of Guiscardo, it was you alone who deceived me (338–39)].

Ghismonda's own case is precisely the opposite—her words unfailingly bear out her actions. In keeping with the linguistic behavior he has exhibited thus far, not only do Tancredi's words contradict his actions, but at the same time he disbelieves that his daughter's actions will bear out her words, that she will actually kill herself: "Conobbe il prenze la grandezza dell'animo della sua figliuola, ma non credette per ciò in tutto lei sí fortemente disposta a quello che le parole sue sonavano" (267) [Although Tancredi knew that his daughter had a will of iron, he doubted her resolve to translate her words into action (339)].

Feeling that his daughter deserves to be punished, but that she will recover from her sadness in due time, Tancredi devises what he perceives to be an exemplary punishment. And with a vindictiveness we might expect from a betrayed lover (rather than a father), he instructs a servant to present Ghismonda with a golden chalice containing the dead lover's heart.[11] Undaunted, Ghismonda kisses the heart repeatedly, praising it both metaphorically and metonymically: "Io son certa che ella è ancor quicentro e riguarda i luoghi de' suoi diletti e de' miei; e come colei che ancor son certa che m'ama, aspetta la mia, dalla quale sommamente è amata" (268) [I feel certain that his soul still lingers here within you, waiting for mine and surveying the scenes of our mutual happiness, and that our love for one another is as deep and enduring as ever (340)]. Despite this eloquence (and unlike us, the readers), her ladies-in-waiting "che volesson dire le parole di lei non intendevano" (268) [(were unable) to make any sense of her words (341)] since they are entirely ignorant of the secret affair. When Ghismonda has eulogized the heart at length, clutching it to her breast, she pours a poison into the chalice and imbibes it, saying, "Rimanete con Dio ché io mi parto" (269) [God be with you all, for I now take my leave of you (342)]. With this venereal reenactment of holy communion, she becomes one in body as well as in spirit with Guiscardo—thereby effecting the ultimate conjoining of her words and deeds.

Never having imagined that she would be faithful to her words, Tancredi is dismayed by her action. Too late he recognizes the validity of Ghismonda's claim to natural law—and his own linguistic transgression—by acceding to her desire to be buried next to Guiscardo (thus also making the affair public knowledge). The text ends in a scene of collective pathos, which Boccaccio describes as follows: "Tancredi dopo molto pianto, e tardi pentuto della sua crudeltà, con general dolore di tutti i salernetani, onorevolmente amenduni in un medesimo sepolcro gli fe' seppellire" (269) [As for Tancredi, after shedding countless tears and making tardy repentence for his cruelty, he saw that they were honorably interred together in a single grave, amid the general mourning of all the people of Salerno (342)]. Thus the prince belatedly recognizes that the unfortunate affair was in fact his doing, stemming from his abuse of (natural) law. While the sacrifice of Guiscardo conforms to a societal norm of judicial law, Tancredi, as the agent of justice, is invalidated by his perversion of natural law—which is at the root of his linguistic perversion.[12]

From this outcome we see that much more than the configuration of the cave—the locus of Balducci's linguistic deprivation and Ghismonda's sexual deprivation—unites the two narratives. Each father figure, an old widower with a single child, misuses words in order to control his child's desire—each is blind to the natural impulse toward sexuality. At the same time, however, these two texts appear to be thematic opposites, as Giuseppe Mazzotta remarks in his important study of the *Decameron*: "At first glance, the two readings in terms of naturalism and incest are contradictory, for if one upholds the rights of nature, the other is a sharp refutation of the very assumptions of a naturalist ideology."[13] Yet Mazzotta argues that this paradox is only an apparent one, that both texts are intended instead as an indictment of omniscient discourse: "In the world of Fortune's randomness, everyone's vision is impaired by blind spots. Claims of omniscient perspective by critics, lovers, prince or author are thus deflated by Boccaccio's text."[14] Accordingly, he sees Ghismonda as deteriorating into "madness and violence"[15] analogous to that of Tancredi. I would maintain, however, that the common (discursive) thematic that unites these two narratives involves *not* the existential misperception of omnipotence, but the linguistic perception of referentiality. For Ghismonda is—in an important (discursive) sense—the opposite of her father (and of Balducci). While their words consistently contradict their deeds, hers never do. Their counterfeiting of language contrasts boldly with her linguistic integrity whereby words and actions are mutually defining. Thus the distinction is neither between naturalism and incest nor the vicissitudes of Fortune. Rather, what is at issue is nominalism—the arbitrariness of signs, of which Ghismonda and Tancredi are two extremes.[16]

Finally, the fact that it is Fiammetta who narrates this novella is significant, further valorizing a metadiscursive reading of it by means of a typically Boccaccian irony—namely, as a narrative that punishes Tancredi's linguistic transgression (a flaw Fiammetta herself is guilty of, as her eponymous *Elegia* makes manifest). The thematic coincidence is not at all fortuitous.

Written in the 1480s (more than one hundred years after the *Decameron*), Flores' *Grisel y Mirabella* discursively complicates Boccaccio's basic structure significantly. Although this work departs from the usual first-person structure of the *novela sentimental* by offering instead a third-person account heavily laden with second-person debate, the work is in fact oriented by and inscribed within a letter. Consequently, the text is dominated from beginning to end by a first-person voice that—while implicit—is quite powerful.

The prefatory letter that precedes the text (labeled "Tratado compuesto por Johan de Flores a su amiga" [A Treatise Composed (by Juan de Flores) for his Lady])[17] tends to be ignored by critics although it is of seminal importance to interpretation here. Perhaps it is the atypical nature of this letter that results in its dismissal. For in it Flores reveals himself to be quite neurotically insecure about his writing. He speaks for example of the "falta de [su] flaco juizio" (333) [poorness of (his) judgment], claiming to his lady that "sin esfuerço de vuestra ayuda no podiera hazer cosa que razonable fuesse" (333) [without your help I would never dare to undertake this difficult task]. He explicitly claims, moreover, that he is nothing more than a scribe in this enterprise ("yo desto solamente soy scriuano") and that he has had the courage to write down this text because it serves to glorify womankind: "por la comunicacion de vuestra causa" (333) [to further your cause].

Yet he derives his strength not from the subject matter (the glorification of the lady he serves), nor from her (passive) acceptance of his labors—the normative male/female configuration. Instead, it is the promise of her active editorial participation that empowers him to write:

> Si vuestro fauor en ello no me ayudara: diera grande occasion ala riza y malicia delos hoyentes. y por esto lo enbio a vos senyora: como persona que lo malo encobrira: y lo comunal sera por mas de bueno touido. y si del todo fuesse inutil: que le dariades la pena que mereçen mis simples trebaios. porque non mas de a vos fuessen publicos mis defectos. pues es razon: que asi como haueys seydo causa de me dar soberbia: que seays reparo para la culpa dello. (333)

> If you were to deny me your assistance, there would be cause for laughter and derision on the part of the listeners. For this reason, I am sending [my text] to you, my lady, since you will eliminate its weaknesses, and improve it. And, if you decide that it is without merit, destroy it, so that my defects will not be made public. It makes sense that since you have been the inspiration for my text, you should also be the remedy for its shortcomings.

We see that Flores offers much more than the obligatory, reverential *captatio benevolentiae* required by the courtly idiom. This apology is quantitatively longer and qualitatively different as well. In place of the anticipated claim that his lady is beautiful, Flores praises her literary sensibilities. Such editorial complicity is striking within the *novela sentimental* corpus. Within the particular context of *Grisel*, I maintain, it is equally significant. By casting the anonymous *amiga* not simply as a muse figure (a passively inspirational woman) but as an active intellect, Flores adds a new virtue to the profeminist cause, which in turn leads us to expect *Grisel* to be an extended narrative encomium of female attributes. The fact that the text does not bear out the unproblematic, wholly laudatory orientation established in the prefatory letter is all the more striking. The letter establishes a generic expectation in the reader that will be calculatedly undermined during the course of the narrative itself. Flores' prefatory words claim one thing (unqualified profeminist adulation), but his extended discursive deed effects quite another—that is, the subordination of both pro- and antifeminist discourse to the nature and function of discourse itself.

In keeping with Boccaccio's essential argument, Flores also portrays a victimized princess and daughter (Mirabella) who has a secret affair (with Grisel) because her father (the king of Scotland) denies her right to natural law—to amorous fulfillment—even within the context of lawful matrimony. The father's perversion of natural law will, in this case, result in the deaths not only of the two lovers, but of many other subjects as well. This causal relationship is established at the outset of the narrative proper:

> el Rey su padre por no tener hijos: y por el grande merecimiento que ella tenia: era dell tanto amada: que a ninguno delos ya dichos la queria dar. y asi mismo en su tierra non hauia tan grande senyor a quien la diesse: saluo a grande mengua suya. de manera que el grande amor suyo era aella mucho enemigo. y como ya muchas vezes acaheçe quando hay dilacion en el casamiento delas mujeres: ser causa de caher en verguenças y yerros: assi a esta despues acahecio. (334)

> The king her [Mirabella's] father, since he had no sons, and because she was so virtuous, greatly loved his daughter. Because he did not wish to give her to any of the knights who pursued her, and since there was in fact no knight in his kingdom who deserved her, but rather a great lack of such a worthy person, the king's intense love for his daughter was to her a great enemy. And as often happens when a woman delays in marrying, she falls into error, as happened with her.

Because the king's incestuous desire prevents him from giving Mirabella in marriage, many knights vie for her hand, losing their lives in the process. It is a consequence of military not familial considerations (these multiple deaths), that the king decides to remove his daughter from public view by locking her up in a tower. (Flores chooses this architectural symbol of male sexuality—as opposed to Ghismonda's cave—advisedly, for it anticipates Grisel's more dominant role in the narrative by comparison with Boccaccio's Guiscardo. At the same time it is an emblem of Mirabella's imprisonment by her father's architectural, metaphorical phallus—a transparent, but logical substitution for Ghismonda's cave.)

It is as a direct result of Mirabella's imprisonment that she ultimately becomes involved with Grisel. Had her father not kept her from getting married by exhibiting the "grande amor . . . aella mucho enemigo" [great love . . . which was a great enemy to her], the tragic sequence of events would never have occurred. What becomes apparent from the opening paragraph, therefore, is that Flores models the causality of his text after *Decameron* 4.1—not after the *Chastelain de Coucy* (where a betrayed husband imprisons his adulterous wife, forcing her to eat her lover's heart) or other narratives involving a *coeur mangé*.[18] Like Prince Tancredi, the king of Scotland is reputed as "de todas virtudes amigo. y principalmente en ser iusticiero. y era tanto iusto: como la misma iusticia" (334) [the friend of all virtues, especially justice, he being justice personified]. Yet also like Tancredi, his impeccable commitment to judicial law is marred by his transgression of natural law—which irreparably deforms his authority, both verbal and actantial.

Further discursive complication of Boccaccio's novella results from the narrator's evaluative remarks, such as his ironic remark that: "en su tierra non hauia tan grande senyor a quien la diesse" (334) [there was (in fact) *no* knight in the kingdom who deserved (Mirabella)]—a value judgment the text will boldly disprove. Beyond this type of metadiscursive device, and much more extensive, is Flores' reliance upon the structure of debate. Not one but four debates in fact occur in the text: (1) between Grisel and the unnamed Other Knight; (2) between Grisel and Mirabella; (3) between Torrellas and Braçayda; and (4) between the queen and king. Each debate has serious implications for the language theory posited by Flores.

The theme of the two friends—a traditional motif whereby each is willing to sacrifice his life for the other—is evoked as soon as we learn that the king has incarcerated his daughter. Grisel and the Unnamed Knight—the two guards who have been assigned to protect Mirabella from potential suitors—are repeatedly described as "close friends." Both men alternately guard Mirabella and in addition are captivated by her. One night Grisel discerns a male figure descending an iron ladder leading to Mirabella's chamber, an intruder whom he confronts:

> firieron se el vno al otro muy fieramente. y los mantos enbraçados y las spadas sacadas conbatieron se hasta que en las aquexadas y secretas vozes se conocieron. y acordando se de su amistat strecha: y ahun por no ser dela casa cono-

cidos: stuuieron quedos. retrayendo se en vn lugar apartado donde el uno al
otro tales razones se dizen. (335)

Both attacked savagely, and hidden by their capes with their swords raised,
they fought until by their complaints they recognized one another's voice and
stopped fighting. Remembering their bond of friendship, and also not wanting to arouse the inhabitants of the house, they fell silent. Withdrawing to a
safe distance they began to debate.

The significance of the ensuing debate is that words fail to resolve the
dispute, to determine which man has the greater love for Mirabella. The
Unnamed Knight says that since they are friends they should not argue the
point. Instead he suggests the drawing of lots to determine the outcome.
Grisel replies that this suggestion of lots is demonstration enough that his
interlocutor does not love Mirabella, for if he did he would never jeopardize his love in such a fashion. In his own defense the Unnamed Knight
claims that he had suggested lots because he knew he had right on his side,
that God would guarantee his victory. To this conviction he adds that the
suggestion was made in order to spare his friend from a tragic outcome in
a duel. Grisel claims that this attitude is itself a further indication of his
rival's lack of love, since for a true lover suffering is unavoidable. The Unnamed Knight therefore proposes a duel to determine the outcome, for
God will surely resolve the dispute most equitably.

Surprisingly, the Unnamed Knight (who claims that God is on his side)
loses the duel. This constitutes a notable departure from convention for
the judicial duel is meant to be an index of Divine law, and those who
invoke such adjudication tend to win since "right equals might."[19] The
reference here to a transcendent order—a misreading of it—is, moreover,
the first in a series of allusions to a Christian axiology. Likewise the claim
made later on, that Grisel's death is a "miracle" (Matulka, 362) because it
demonstrates that he is more guilty than Mirabella, represents a similar
misappropriation of religious authority by society, whereas in fact Grisel
commits suicide because of his altruistic passion. The attribution of the
Apocalyptic darkening of the sun and sky (355) as a reflection of the
queen's attitude toward the death sentence for Mirabella functions in a
related (although opposite) manner. Namely, whereas we would expect
this meteorological phenomenon to be attributed to Divine authority, it is
explained instead as an instance of the "pathetic fallacy," whereby nature
mirrors the human affect. These are three in a number of examples of what
might be termed negative religious evocation, designed to undermine not
it, but its human misinterpreters. This form of religious misrepresentation
points to the global linguistic misappropriation exposed most visibly on
the level of plot.

Mirabella accepts Grisel's love and the couple engages in "la mas plaziente que peligrosa batalla" (337) [that battle which is more pleasurable than dangerous], until the king is informed of the affair, at which point the lovers are seized and incarcerated. In accord with the law of the land—the so-called Law of Scotland[20]—the initiator of the affair must be burned at the stake and the accomplice exiled for life, and it is this crucial degree of guilt that the king seeks to determine. (This ambiguity Flores generates is a pointed rewriting of the clear causality of Ghismonda's letter-laden reed and also—as we shall see—a way of turning the conflict of a particular father and daughter into a dramatization of linguistic usage in general.) True to his reputation for being impeccably just, the king proceeds in an orderly manner by appointing judges. These men in turn mount an investigation, yet they fail to discover anything since the affair was conducted with extreme discretion. Adopting a different strategy thereafter, they decide upon a debate, in which the lovers will dispute their relative guilt. The judges interrogate both lovers, resorting even to torture—as the medieval judicial system allowed. However, since the lovers know that the perceived more guilty party will die, they each claim total responsibility in order that the other's life be spared. In this debate, as in the first between Grisel and the Unnamed Knight, words do not serve a heuristic function, failing to determine the appropriate action to be taken. Because of this judicial impasse, the judges decide that the issue of relative guilt can only be determined by means of a third debate, this time between one man and one woman who will argue in general terms as to whether man or woman is more at fault in initiating seduction. The representatives chosen to debate this matter are forensic experts with universal reputations. They are Torrellas, the notorious archmisogynist poet of fifteenth-century Spain, and Braçayda, the notable female apologist from the Trojan war, who has been resuscitated for this occasion. To adjudicate this dialogic confrontation twelve judges are selected: "los quales fueron elegidos por personas de mucha consciencia y sin suspecha: con solennes iuramentos que fizieron de iuzgar segun fuesse su mas claro pareçer" (343) [chosen as people of great conscience and impeccable reputation. With a solemn oath they vowed to judge impartially].

Debate is the form of verbal violence *par excellence*. Debates were a tradition in medieval Europe in general, and in fifteenth-century Spain in particular. Nonetheless, the debate in question constitutes a departure from the norm and as such it is important to interpretation of *Grisel*. First of all, the issues debated by these two contestants have literally nothing to do with the attitudes projected by Grisel and Mirabella.[21] On the contrary, their self-sacrificing, idealistic bond of love could not be more alien to the thoughts, words (and ultimately deeds) of the cynical Torrellas and Braçayda.

From its inception, this debate is semantically "overdetermined." That is, neither opponent can speak objectively. Torrellas is an avowed misogynist and Braçayda a misandrist who pretends to represent victimized females while having gained notoriety for precisely opposite reasons—as victimizer of men and as an archetype of womanly infidelity.

Each contestant offers an arsenal of stock arguments to prove the greater guilt of the opposite sex. Torrellas, for example, says that since women are the daughters of Eve, they are obviously guiltier than men, at which point Braçayda reminds him that woman was created from Adam's rib, thus proving that men are more to blame.

Both participants are calculatedly unobjective. For this reason they function as a cynical inversion of the king's unconscious lack of objectivity. Yet at the same time they are—in a fundamental sense—discursively analogous. Just as the king's discourse of regal impartiality is invalidated by its context, so is their totally biased, sexist discourse. Again the epistemological fissure separating *signans* from *signatum* is exposed. Flores emphasizes this point by introducing a significant addition to the traditional compendium of predictable sexist argumentation; namely, in addition to their denigration of the opposite sex, both Braçayda and Torrellas programmatically accuse each other (and the sex they represent) of linguistic counterfeit—saying one thing while doing another. In this way they make explicit what has, until now, been presented implicitly (i.e., the dangers of the word/deed dichotomy we first encountered in the case of Tancredi).

Of equal significance is the explicit admission by each debater that they believe the legal system to be just. Braçayda expresses confidence that she will win since "en tierra tan iusta stamos" (Matulka, 345) [we live in such a just land]. This opinion is shared by Torrellas, who is confident of his own victory for the same reason—by virtue of the fact that this just land is inhabited by "tan magnifico Rey y Reyna y notables caualleros y damas" (351) [such a magnificent king and queen and notable knights and ladies]. In this way, Flores entirely dissociates the debate from the causality of the king's incestuous inclinations—of which the kingdom is ignorant. As such, Braçayda and Torrellas provide independent verification (and an extreme example) of the inescapably biased nature of any speech situation.

Torrellas wins the debate as we are told simply that the judges "fundaron por muchas razones ser ella en mayor culpa que Grisel" (355) [concluded, for many reasons, that Mirabella was guiltier than Grisel]. (The fact that no concrete reasons are given suggests that the decision of the jury—like the very premise of this judicial debate—is questionable to say the least. This too leaves us with the impression that unbiased, objective discourse is virtually unobtainable.)

After the sentence has been passed whereby Mirabella is consigned to death by immolation, Braçayda invokes God as the ultimate authority ("suberano iuez delos hombres" [355])—hoping that justice will prevail over what she considers to be (in retrospect) a prejudiced court. Having Mirabella die because a jury believes that women are the instigators of illicit love is incongruous, and we feel sympathy with Braçayda. Soon after this desperate divine invocation, however, she betrays our sympathies by advocating genocide. Because men are our enemies, she reasons, we should not further their cause:

> O malditas mujeres porque con tantos affanes de partos y fatigas quereys aquellos que en muertes y menguas vos dan el gualardon. o si conseio tomassedes en el nacimiento del hijo: dariades fin asus dias. porque non quedasen soietas asus enemigos. y alegre vida viuiessen. (355–56)

> O cursed women, who with so many toils of childbirth and suffering you love those who reward you with death and strife. Oh, if only you would agree to kill your male children at birth, so that you would not be subject to your enemies, you would live happily ever after.

In total frustration, Braçayda advocates that women cease dealing with men to any degree: "de aqui adelante ahun que los veamos morir: demos asus passiones disfauores por gualardon" (356) [henceforth, even if we see them dying: let us reward their passion with disfavor]. The implications of this charge are, of course, quite horrifying. For were women to follow this advice, the human race would literally perish.

The final and briefest of the four debates occurs between the queen and king. It is significant that here too words fail to convince and the ensuing action does not result from rational discourse. The queen pleads for Mirabella's life, yet the king refuses to spare her despite the queen's valid assertion that "en virtud y nobleza consiste: perdonar a quien yerra: ante que dar pena a quien no la mereçe" (357) [Virtue and nobility consist of pardoning transgressors, rather than condemning one who does not deserve it]. In desperation the queen offers to sacrifice her own life so that Mirabella may live. And, like the debate between Torellas and Braçayda, here too we find an incongruous proposal. While maternal love can account for some of the queen's motivation, it is aberrant—in terms of judicial logic—that she should sacrifice herself for an illicit love committed by another woman. The king is moved by his wife's offer to spare their child by sacrificing herself, yet he is unwilling to accept the substitution because it would be unjust. He argues that "si en mi alguna virtud hay: de aquella me precio. Ansi que pues sola iusticia es mi victoria: y lo mas loable en mi stado: no quiero perder aquello: que con tan grande studio y trabaio he ganado" (358) [If there is in me some virtue to be found, I value it. Thus justice alone is my victory, and the most praiseworthy attribute for a king. I do not wish to lose that which I have attained by such long study and hard work].

Nonetheless, the king belies this discourse of regal impartiality, contradicting both his words and actions—being himself so distraught that he offers to sacrifice his own life in place of his daughter's as did his wife: "mi muerte si la quieres: yo la atorgo. mas biuo que ella biua es impossible" (358) [If you wish my death, I grant it. But as long as I am alive, she cannot live]. These words not only fail to satisfy the queen, they cause her to break violently with the king: "el primero dia que te conoci fue la mi muerte . . . plaze me que tu crueza pueda tanto: que en hun dia sin fijos y mujer quedes solo" (359) [the first day I met you was death for me. . . . It pleases me that your cruelty is so great that in one day you are left without children or wife—alone]. Her aggressivity toward the king is quite unexpected because it departs from the norm of queenly decorum. Yet, of course, it is motivated by his own indecorous kingly comportment—his discursive counterfeit.

As Mirabella is being carried off to her horrible death (which fifteen thousand mourning virgins have assembled to witness), the lovers exchange their final words of love. To Mirabella's oath of eternal devotion Grisel says that were he to outlive her "seria hombre perdido sforçado el que sin vos beuir quiziesse que alli podria bien dezir Braçayda. quexando se dela poca fe delos hombres" (361) [would be reprehensible indeed if he still desired life after Mirabella's death—an example that would prove the validity of Braçayda's lament concerning the faithlessness of men]. Grisel's evocation of Braçayda's discourse on the faithlessness of men is one more unanticipated moment in the text. For Grisel is a paragon of faithfulness and amorous self-sacrifice. Having uttered these words, he demonstrates their integrity through his action—by leaping into the fire intended for Mirabella, so that her life might be spared. Mirabella lunges toward the fire to join her lover, but she is restrained by Braçayda and the other women who "delas llamas del fuego afuerça la quitaron" (362) [forcibly removed her from the flames]. It is no accident that those who prevent Mirabella from joining Grisel are women incapable of understanding the power of love. For, surely, it would be a much crueler fate for Mirabella to outlive Grisel, just as he had perceived the impossibility of a meaningful existence without her.

The bond of Mirabella and Grisel serves as an idealistic paradigm that none of the people around them can comprehend—let alone imitate. Evidence of this fact is offered immediately thereafter, as the spectators claim to have witnessed a miracle: "del cielo vino por marauilloso milagro dar muerte a quien la merecia: que contra la voluntad de Dios no diesse pena a quien no la mereçe" (362) [a miracle came from Heaven in order to kill the one who deserved it. For no one is ever killed by the will of God except he who deserves to be killed]. Except for Mirabella, no one understands Grisel's motivation, yet they are eager to designate him as the sacrificial victim (the obviously guiltier party deserving immolation) so that she may be spared. Similarly, the judges who had originally sentenced her to death are easily persuaded to revoke the sentence since Grisel has died.

Just as Grisel's words to Mirabella were not understood by any of the spectators, they likewise do not assume that Mirabella will kill herself—although she has explicitly indicated that she will do so (360). (This incredulity is reminiscent of Tancredi's disbelief of Ghismonda's potential for suicide.) Not only does Mirabella choose to end her own life, but the manner of her death is as violent as Grisel's, since she hurls herself into a den of lions where she is torn to shreds—*spedaçada* (363). The lion is not indigenous to Scotland, but there as elsewhere it is the emblem of regal authority. For this reason, it is very appropriate that she is destroyed by her father's identity. It is, moreover, significant that these lions are anthropomorphically endowed with erotic sensibilities—described as "delas delicadas carnes cada uno contento el apetito" (363) [each one sated his appetite with her delicate flesh]. She kills herself because life without Grisel has no meaning for her. And, although Mirabella has explained this fact *alta voce* to the assembled multitudes, they do not anticipate that she will in fact guarantee the truth of her words by her actions. It is equally revealing that rather than serving an exemplary function of amorous and linguistic fidelity (as the deaths of Ghismonda and Guiscardo did for the city of Salerno), the deaths of Grisel and Mirabella elicit a decidedly *un*exemplary reaction in the Scottish kingdom—resulting in even greater violence.

The escalation of violence is precipitated by Torrellas' unexpected infatuation with Braçayda following the death of Mirabella. By means of a letter he declares his love to Braçayda, at the same time indicating that he realizes he is unworthy and desirous of doing penance (365). The understandably incredulous lady shows the letter to the queen who sees Torrellas' affective change as an excellent opportunity for revenge against the man responsible for her daughter's death. She thus instructs Braçayda to reply by feigning a reciprocal interest in him—a pretext designed to lure the unsuspecting poet to a grisly death.

For his part, Torrellas' passionate declaration appears motivated by lust rather than love since he boasts to his friends that Braçayda will be an easy conquest. Upon arrival at Braçayda's chamber he is seized by the incensed and bloodthirsty females, bound with rope, fastened to a pillar and gagged so that he can not utter any words. The verbal violence of the debate is now replaced by physical violence as he is tortured by "mil maneras de tormentos" (369) [a thousand different torments]. As some women burn him with tongs, others flirt with cannibalism, tearing him to shreds with their nails and teeth (369). After he has been so brutally abused that he seems on the point of death, the women stop tormenting him in order to partake of a sumptuous dinner. The banquet takes place in close proximity to the mutilated Torrellas so that he can witness their enjoyment, and so that they can abuse him verbally before returning to their physical abuse. As the supper is concluded the women resume the torture of Torrellas, described now in terms of food: "despues que fueron alçadas todas las mesas fueron iuntas a dar amarga cena a Torrellas. y tanto fue de todas seruido con potages y aues . . . que non se como scriuir las differencias delas iniurias y offienças que le hazian" (369) [after the tables were cleared, the women went to give Torellas a bitter supper. He was served such soups and birds . . . that I am incapable of describing all the injuries and offenses which they caused him].

Two religious images are recalled by the treatment of Torrellas here, and they accord with the subverted religious motifs mentioned earlier. Namely, martyrdom and the Last Supper are each being enacted here in a perverted form.[22] In addition this supper constitutes a subversion of romance celebration. Rather than ending the text with the normative banquet in honor of the couple (in commemoration of order restored), we find instead a graphically lurid destruction of that ideal as represented by the physical destruction of Torrellas' body. The manner of his death—the poet's gory dismemberment at the hands of outraged females—recalls the dismemberment of another infamously misogynistic poet, that of Orpheus in Book 11 of the *Metamorphoses*. He likewise dies the victim of women (whom he has spurned since the time of Eurydice's death—favoring the love of young boys instead). It is from this affective switch that Orpheus derived his fame in the Middle Ages as the father of homosexuality. By this subtextual reminiscence, Flores suggests that Torrellas' view of women was anything but objective. Two further observations should be made in this context. The physical dismemberment—a metaphor of Torrellas' dismembered discourse—is an inversion of the amorous eucharist that ultimately united the lives of Ghismonda and Guiscardo. Ghismonda's metonymic act of contiguity—her physical incorporation of Guiscardo's heart (as well as the common casket they share)—likewise contrasts sharply with Mirabella's (paradoxical) metaphoric act of substitution—her physical dismemberment as metaphor of spiritual union.

Torrellas is a love-martyr *in malo* (the opposite of Grisel and Mirabella), which is why the women burn his ashes and carry them in pendants around their necks—rather than the traditional wearing of a locket containing a lover's portrait. Torrellas' martyrdom thus reflects as badly on him as it does on the bloodthirsty women who effect it.[23] Given the violent dissolution of the three relationships portrayed in the text (those of Grisel and Mirabella, the king and queen, and Torrellas and Braçayda), it is tempting to read the text as an illustration of René Girard's axiom that desire inevitably breeds disaster (rather than romance).

According to the Girardian view, the fault lies with the lovers who succumb to their passion, thus causing a chain reaction of multiple deaths and savage brutality that threatens the very fabric of society. It is because desire threatens society that the couple must be ritualistically eliminated. Ritual, as Girard explains, is nothing more than the exercise of "good violence."[24] The importance of ritual sacrifice is paramount, its absence, catacylsmic: "Mimetic desire is simply a term more comprehensive than *violence* for religious pollution. As the catalyst for the sacrificial crisis, it would eventually destroy the entire community if the surrogate victim were not at hand to halt the process and the ritualized mimesis were not at hand to keep the conflictual mimesis from beginning afresh."[25] Such ritual sacrifice serves as a form of catharsis, as an affirmation of the rules upon which a given community is predicated—that is the reason why societies create laws to punish transgressors. It is not that the crime will be undone by the act of punishing the guilty individual, it will serve instead as an example of behavior that society will not tolerate.

What we see graphically depicted in *Grisel* is precisely the opposite. After the twelve judges (clutching their bloodstained swords) pronounce the death sentence for Mirabella (Matulka, 355), rather than reverting to the peaceful status quo of orderly behavior, Scottish society breaks down before our very eyes. (This disintegration contrasts boldly with Boccaccio's more optimistic depiction of the city of Salerno—whose collective pathos serves to unify it.) The only legitimate successor to the throne (Mirabella) kills herself; the queen not only becomes estranged from the king, she takes the law into her own hands with the help of many other equally disaffected females. Braçayda's unnatural call for genocide—initially perceived as the passing rage of a provoked female—by the end seems to be within the realm of the possible. For his part, the king is incapable of stopping the murderous females, much less of bringing them to justice.

Given that this is the case, that with the sacrifice of Grisel and Mirabella the violence does not end, society not restored, it appears that it is not the lovers' desire that is at fault.[26] If it were, their deaths would have ended the chain of destruction, as Girard's phenomenology of sacrifice makes clear. One is tempted to conclude, therefore, that it is the law or, more precisely, the king as law-bearer, who is flawed. That, had he allowed his daughter to marry rather than preventing her from doing so out of his own incestuous desire, none of the tragedies would have occurred. In this connection, the fact that this incestuously inclined king is not eliminated (as happens in the Arthurian world, for example) indicates that we are not reading a romance. (If we were, the virtuous Mirabella would have inherited the kingdom from an equally virtuous father. Alternatively, they both would have perished as a result of their sexually transgressive behavior.) But Flores is suggesting something different.

Like her Italian predecessor, Mirabella dies not—as we would expect— of infanticide (the anticipated resolution of an incestuous union), but as a result of her own linguistic preference. Given the suggestion of incest that pervades the narrative, it is surprising—indeed shocking—that the father's incestuous urge does not achieve physical intimacy—the focus is not physical but verbal transgression. Unlike earlier medieval incest narratives, physical defilement is unnecessary. In fact, its elimination here is very revealing. For, what is at issue is nothing less than a new attitude toward language. The text is a negative, nominalist recasting of the early medieval discursive principle whereby the continuity of language guarantees genealogical succession—as Isidore of Seville had posited.[27] Juxtaposing the new attitude operative in the later Middle Ages with the earlier attitude, Bloch writes: "this [new] body of grammatical thought [the work of the speculative grammarians] is organized around synchronic categories; more committed to logical distinctions than to chronological sequence, continuity and origins; less oriented toward the 'verticality' of the single word—etymology or definition—than toward 'horizontal' problems of syntax and consignification."[28] A metaphoric attitude toward language thus replaces a metonymic one. This accords, moreover, with Jakobson's observation of "the [diachronically] alternative predominance of one or the other of these two processes."[29] The absence of physical violation in *Grisel* discursively illustrates these two antithetical modes of signification (the etymological and the syntactic), foregrounding the ubiquitous threat of linguistic violation and its dangerous implications—irrespective of lineage. The extent of Flores' interest in rejecting the traditional teleology of lineage is also visible in that no words exchanged by the father and daughter are recorded in the text—a striking contrast to Ghismonda and Tancredi. Likewise this explains why so much of the Spanish text is devoted to the debates of other discursive pairs. The result is an illustration of the universality of linguistic transgression. Indeed, a new kind of incest text is revealed—namely, the inescapable fact of linguistic incest. Language is "deprived of its hallowed function as support of the law, in order to become the cause of a permanent trial of [every individual] speaking subject."[30] For Kristeva, poetic discourse is incestuous in that it routinely transgresses codified forms of signification and social hierarchies of decorum.[31] In his text, Flores dramatizes the realization that not only poetic discourse—but *all discourse*, as it were— is inherently incestuous.

A further (and related) displacement of our generic expectations occurs in that the romance paradigm (on the model of Tristan) involves illicit love which shuns marriage. Here the situation is reversed. Mirabella and Grisel become furtively involved precisely because she is prevented by the king from marrying a vassal of his own choosing.[32] This reversal likewise signals Flores' very *un*-romance axiology.

The text ends with the words "Ansi que la grande malicia de Torrellas dio alas damas victoria: y ell pago de su merecido" (Matulka, 370) [Thus the ladies triumphed over Torrellas' wickedness, and he received just payment]. Given the behavior not only of Torrellas, but of his female torturers as well, the claim of "justice" is problematic indeed. It has even led some readers to argue that the negative portrayal of the women may have been inadvertent—unintentional. Yet both the savage and protracted quality of this portrayal make it difficult to imagine that Flores was unaware of what he was doing. We recall, moreover, that his text has been necessarily scrutinized and approved by his own lady by virtue of the fact that she did not destroy it as she was instructed to do if she found its portrayal of women objectionable.

As a result, I maintain that the text is neither misandrist nor misogynistic—or rather it is both. What is wistfully celebrated in the text is the couple of idealistic lovers whose words guarantee their deeds—in other words, the determinacy of signs. This successful private relationship bears no connection to the public and its laws. The admirable love and death of Grisel and Mirabella does not function exemplarily for the godless society of Scots; their amorously motivated words and actions do not convince others to emulate them. They are, as it were, two displaced romance characters (adhering to a kind of paradoxically prelapsarian language model) lost in a novelistic world. What is denigrated is not the (putatively destructive) desire of Grisel and Mirabella, but the linguistic perversion of society itself—its lamentable ability to generate verbal ambiguity and distortion.

It is significant that the only exception to the linguistic perversion that pervades the Scottish kingdom is an extradiegetic one—namely, the couple constituted by Flores and his lady. They perpetuate the philosophy of language projected by Grisel and Mirabella in an enduring verbal artifact—the eponymous text on which they collaborate. The discourse of dismemberment generated by the verbally incestuous Italian prince and Scottish king is finally ended—replaced by a linguistic integrity that exposes its devastating implications. In this way Flores and his lady respond to the Foucaultian distinction with which this chapter began. They offer a corrective to the potentially destructive social act by their own creative literary act. Does this also suggest that the creation of such linguistic integrity is largely a fictional pursuit? Perhaps.

What can be said with certainty, however, is that the text is much more than an illustration of the perennial conflict between law and desire, or misogyny and misandry. It is a parable of language.

# EPILOGUE
## PHYSICAL AND VERBAL VIOLENCE

I F WE CONSIDER the corpus of fifteenth-century *novelas sentimen-tales* as a whole, we find a surprising configuration. Rather than culmi-nating in melancholic courtly sentiment expressed by lovers who ex-pire passively, there exists instead a surprising preponderance of violence. Grimalte, Panfilo, and Arnalte literally become wild men as a result of their total alienation from society and its language;[1] Lyessa is brutally murdered by King Croes as is Torrellas by the incensed females who first mutilate and perhaps even cannibalize his body. Grisel, Mirabella, Leriano, and Ardan-lier all graphically commit suicide. Only Fiammetta appears to die in a rather nonviolent manner, although her perpetual infernal torment more than compensates for the manner of her mortal expiration. Most impor-tant, however, they are all, without exception, victims of linguistic aliena-tion. The Siervo escapes such a fate because, as we have seen, he rejects earthly love entirely. The lover of the parodic *Triste deleytaçion* spares him-self through his successful cynicism, while his counterpart in the *Satira* lingers perilously close to ending his life. The inability of all these lovers to live according to the discourse of desire is patent, resulting from the fact that the discourse itself is such a nominalistically problematic medium of exchange.

It is important to note, moreover, that the authors of these texts are interested in underscoring the problem of language rather than societal taboo by consistently rejecting the adulterous examples of Boccaccio's Fiammetta and Piccolomini's Lucretia. Despite the keen interest in adul-tery exhibited by the discourse of courtly love, the protagonists of the *novela sentimental* are not adulterous. They are pure in this sense, and yet they still fail in their pursuits, for their failure is predicated instead on the impure, transgressive nature of language itself.

This extreme physical alienation expressed through violence is, more-over, reinforced by a recurring chronotopic configuration of the *novela sen-timental*. Geographic remoteness prevails, as, for example, the *Siervo libre* moves from the allegorical *selva oscura* to the sylvan hideaway that permits Ardanlier and Lyessa to live free from the constraints of society (especially from King Croes), ultimately to the distant region of Galicia, where the lovers' shrine is visited by Africans and Asians as well as Europeans. The *Satira* takes place in the undifferentiated dreamscape of the lover's mind, populated by a host of alienating allegorical personifications of a courtly and ethical nature. *Arnalte*, meanwhile, involves a protagonist who is a native of Thebes and who finds himself quite estranged in his travels through Castile. *Grisel* unfolds in the kingdom of Scotland, while *Grimalte* entails a twenty-seven-year quest begun in Spain and concluded in a desolate part of Asia. Time references are, with few exceptions, similarly remote: either wholly fantastic (allegorically atemporal) or putatively "realistic," yet lacking in historical specificity.

The threat posed by this forbidding landscape further magnifies the existential alienation from language of the characters who inhabit it.[2] Moreover, the physical violence done to them mirrors the verbal violence manifested in generic terms by the consistent subversion of allegory, the failure of epistolarity, and the shattering of the *cancionero* lyric identity. Indeed, the letter, like the dream allegory and *cancionero* verse, is a profoundly lyric form. All three genres exploited by the *novela sentimental* exhibit the essential lyric conflict between personal and societal space and time[3]—the inability of the individual to control his environment through language. It is, as we have seen, this unrelentingly nominalistic perception that constitutes the radical innovation of the *novela sentimental*, the attitude that generates its novelistic discourse.

In light of this observation concerning language theory, I would like to conclude my study by indicating that the *novela sentimental* establishes the discursive originality that literary historians have traditionally accorded to *La Celestina*, first published in 1499. By way of articulating the revolutionary achievement of Rojas, Stephen Gilman boldly affirms that: "It is impossible to overestimate the unconventionality of his art. . . . He who would deal with Fernando de Rojas and *La Celestina* is confronted with discontinuity, the unprecedented greatness of a sudden and unexpected leap into a new world. . . giving life to lives of a sort which had never lived before in literature."[4] I would point out, however, that neither literature in general nor *La Celestina* in particular is created in the *ex nihilo* manner that Gilman claims. As Foucault observes, "if we are accustomed to presenting the author as a genius, as a perpetual surging of invention, it is because, in reality, we make him function in exactly the opposite fashion. One can say the author is an ideological product, since we represent him as the opposite of his historically real function."[5]

To be sure, Rojas complicated the basic discursive framework of the *novela sentimental*, but his achievement stems from a quantitative rather than a qualitative inspiration. As discursive analysis of the preceding texts bears out, his is not an originary discourse. Rather, he exploits several fundamental paradigms of *novela sentimental* composition, pushing each of them to further limits. Obviously, to do justice to this topic would entail the writing of another book. My aim here is simply to suggest some of the basic features of this intertextual relationship.

One of the most essential points of contact is a structural analogy shared by *La Celestina* and the *Cárcel*. In both texts, the lover is immediately and violently overcome with love, but is strongly rejected by the lady in question. As a result, he enlists the aid of a go-between. This messenger in each case elicits "piedad" in the beloved by elaborating the life-threatening "enfermedad" of the lover. The twenty-year-old lover expires in the *Cárcel*, lamented by his sixty-year-old mother, while in *La Celestina* it is the twenty-year-old beloved who is mourned by her sixty-year-old father.[6] In addition to this striking coincidence in their structure, several critics have identified speeches in *La Celestina* that are taken verbatim from the *Cárcel*.[7] However, beyond the immediate and undeniable subtextual reliance of *La Celestina* on the *Cárcel*, it exhibits compositional and discursive features that are firmly rooted in the *novela sentimental* corpus in general.

There is, for example, a chronotopic consideration. Rather than locating his imaginary universe in an atemporal frame and a remote geographical realm, Rojas establishes a contemporary, urban Spanish setting for his text. Thus he extends the potential for linguistic and societal alienation noted throughout the *novelas sentimentales* by equating his immediate environment with alienation. Not the kingdom of Scotland or Macedonia, but contemporary Spain itself is revealed to be alien. Its identity as "literature of immediacy"[8] is constantly invoked as a mark of *La Celestina*'s modernity, that it has, for the first time, left behind the outmoded fictional discourses of the Middle Ages for the "reality" depicted in Renaissance literature. This is a debatable assertion, however. For, on the one hand, the contemporary urban Spanish setting constitutes a departure from most (but not all) of the Spanish texts that preceded *La Celestina*,[9] yet, on the other, it signals a return to the chronotopic environment of their subtexts, Boccaccio's *Elegia* and Piccolomini's *Historia*. It is also significant in this context that Rojas was very likely the translator of the Latin *Historia* into its Spanish version, the *Historia de dos amantes, Eurialo y Lucrecia*.[10]

More important even than these attitudes toward space and time—the perception of immediacy as alienation—however, is a different compositional feature, namely linguistic alienation, which both the *Elegia* and *Historia* dramatize, as do each of the *novelas sentimentales* that were modeled on them, all of them based on the discursive relativism learned from the *Heroides*.

The potential chasm separating word and deed in each of these texts— Latin, Italian, and Spanish—is thematized repeatedly. Euryalus and Panfilo, for example, disguise their lust behind the refined diction of courtly love. Yet this is precisely what Calisto and Melibea are credited as having achieved. Not simply one of the lovers (or would-be lovers) is using words in an ambivalent or polyvalent manner, but both. Melibea as well as Calisto uses words in this way. Indeed, the basic linguistic principle and its effects are precisely the same as in the earlier texts. *Gozo*, for example, designates three appreciably different forms of love: "divine *gloria*, human *deleyte*, and animal *placer*."[11] *Triste deleytaçion* exhibits the same three senses of love, adding a fourth sense—namely, monetary remuneration, *pago*.[12]

The other characters in *La Celestina* exhibit this same type of linguistic relativism, including Pleberio—who is perhaps the most shocking in that he seems initially to be a pillar of linguistic as well as Stoic philosophical integrity. The gap separating his discourse of *ataraxia* from his ultimate ontological despair is irreconcilable. This outcome is all the more powerful given that we had come to expect Pleberio's eloquent wisdom based on experience to serve as the corrective to the destructive madness of the lovers' lust.[13]

Finally, Rojas intensifies the linguistic perception set forth in the *novela sentimental* by introducing a proliferation of discourses—the amorous, the Stoic, the paternal, the filial, the picaresque, etc., each one—like Pleberio's—undermining its own integrity. Referring to Petrarchan discourse, but equally applicable to any of the discourses Rojas generates, Gilman explains that: "Rojas causes his speakers to cite Petrarch in order that they may betray the gap between exemplary commonplaces . . . and the particular purposes and situations to which they are attached."[14] The same destruction of referentiality exists in the amorous discourse of the lovers and even in the picaresque discourse of the servants. Rojas' mastery of such nominalistic depiction is indisputable and he clearly complicates this attitude toward language further than his predecessors had done by increasing the number of discourses contained within his text. Yet, the *Cárcel*, we recall, offered a similar encyclopedia of discourses which undermined themselves. Here too, then, the discursive distinction between *La Celestina* and the *novela sentimental* is one of degree, not of kind. Linguistic solipsism is as inescapable in *La Celestina* as it was in its model texts.

The linguistic theory of Rojas' text, which Gilman perceives as unique, is exemplified by his reference to the solipsistic moment before Melibea leaps to her death: "The tower and Melibea's confession together express Rojas' acute realization that to be conscious is to be isolated—cut apart by space and cut off by time . . . even from those who are closest to us."[15] This lyric solitude, this severing of the word from its referent based on the inability of language to represent experience is the discourse of the *novela sentimental*.

Nonetheless, the nominalistic skepticism reflected by this literary form would soon give way to a new attitude toward language viewed as a performatively unproblematic communicative system.[16] This change came about with the dramatic renewal of interest in romance composition,[17] where the inherent power of words—their transparency—is never questioned, only the protagonist's personal fortitude in terms of such stable verbal and ideological systems. Of course, one might argue that this belief in linguistic integrity exists only within the confines of literary escapism and fantasy.

# NOTES

## PROLOGUE

1. See R. Bursill-Hall, *Speculative Grammars of the Middle Ages* (Paris: Mouton, 1971) for a detailed discussion of the *modistae* and their impact on the canonical notions of language theory that preceded them.

2. Marcelino Menéndez Pelayo, *Orígenes de la novela* (Madrid: Bally-Ballière, 1905), 1:299: "Simultáneamente con los libros de caballerías floreció, desde mediados del siglo XV, otro género de novelas, que en parte se deriva de él y conserva muchos de sus rasgos característicos, pero en parte acaso mayor fue inspirado por otros modelos y responde a un concepto de la vida muy diverso. Tal es la novela erótico-sentimental, en que se da mucha más importancia al amor que al esfuerzo, sin que por eso falten en ella lances de armas, bizarrías y gentilezas caballerescas, subordinadas a aquella pasión que es alma y vida de la obra, complaciéndose los autores en seguir su desarrollo ideal y hacer descripción y anatomía de los afectos de sus personajes. Es, pues, una tentativa de novela íntima y no meramente exterior como casi todas las que hasta entonces se habían compuesto, y aunque no produjo, ni podía producir, obras maestras, porque no habían llegado todavía los tiempos del análisis psicológico, dejó algunas curiosas muestras de retórica apasionada y trajo a nuestra prosa un nuevo e importante elemento" [At the same time that romances of chivalry flourished, beginning in the mid-fifteenth century, so did another novelistic genre, which is derived in part from the chivalric form. It should be stressed, however, that it was perhaps influenced even more by other literary models and responds to a very different view of life. The genre in question is the erotic sentimental romance, which emphasizes love rather than deeds, despite the fact that lances, pageantry and chivalric behavior are often found within it. These elements are subordinated to a central passion that is the focus of the work, and the authors of such fiction offer a detailed anatomy of the affect of their characters. The sentimental romance is, thus, an attempt at a novel of interiority rather than exteriority—which characterized virtually all preceding forms. And although it was not able to produce any masterpieces (because of the rudimentary form of psychological analysis it offers), this group of texts yielded some interesting examples of passionate rhetoric and brought to our prose a new and important element].

3. Ibid., p. 304: "mezcla de caballeresco y erótico, combinación del *Amadís* y de la *Elegia di madonna Fiammetta*." The group of texts identified as *novelas sentimentales* has fluctuated considerably since the time of its initial identification. As Deyermond observes: "Aunque Menéndez Pelayo, a principios del siglo XX, hizo un estudio de la ficción sentimental que incluye trece obras (más tres tardías que no se aceptan hoy como pertenecientes al género), la crítica posterior tendía a reducir el número, de modo que dos estudios recientes, los de Armando Durán y Dinko Cvitanovic, tratan sólo seite y nueve obras respectivamente. Para los no especialistas, el género abarcaba nada más de cinco obras: el *Siervo libre de amor*, dos de Diego de San Pedro (*Arnalte y Lucenda* y *Cárcel de amor*), y dos de Juan de Flores (*Grisel*

*y Mirabella y Grimalte y Gradissa)*" [Although Menéndez Pelayo, at the beginning of the twentieth century, identified thirteen works of sentimental fiction (in addition to three later texts that are no longer considered as part of the genre), later criticism has tended to reduce the number of texts. Two recent studies, for example, those of Armando Durán and Dinko Cvitanovič, treat only seven and nine works respectively. For the nonspecialist, the genre included only five works: *Siervo libre de amor*, two by Diego de San Pedro (*Arnalte y Lucenda* and *Cárcel de amor*), and two by Juan de Flores (*Grisel y Mirabella* and *Grimalte y Gradissa*)]. (A. D. Deyermond, "Las relaciones genéricas de la ficción sentimental española," in *Symposium in honorem Prof. Martín de Riquer*, ed. A. D. Deyermond, Antoni M. Badia i Margarit [Barcelona: Universidad de Barcelona, 1986], p. 75.)

To this group of five texts traditionally viewed as forming the "canonical" corpus I would add *Triste deleytaçion* and the *Satira de felice e infelice vida* since these two additional fifteenth-century works both adhere, as I hope to demonstrate, to the compositional criteria of the five so-called classic texts. Moreover, this group of fifteenth-century texts exhibits a kind of homogeneity not shared by the sixteenth-century texts occasionally associated with the *novela sentimental*.

4. Hans-Robert Jauss, *Toward an Aesthetic of Reception*, trans. Timothy Bahti (Minneapolis: University of Minnesota Press, 1982), p. 82.

5. In terms of the semantic ambiguity of the term *novela* and its consequences for medieval Spanish literature and modern literary historiography, see A. D. Deyermond, "The Lost Genre of Medieval Spanish Literature," *Hispanic Review* 48 (1975): 231–59.

6. As Northrop Frye explains, "Romance avoids the ambiguities of ordinary life, where everything is a mixture of good and bad, and where it is difficult to take sides or believe that people are consistent patterns of virtue or vice." *The Secular Scripture: A Study of the Structure of Romance* (Cambridge: Harvard University Press, 1976), p. 50.

Frye develops the notion of romance as the "epic of the creature" in a very interesting way, by interpreting one of Borges' stories from the collection entitled *El informe de Brodie*: "Borges says, in a little story called 'The Gospel According to Mark': 'generations of men, throughout recorded time, have always told and retold two stories—that of a lost ship which searches the Mediterranean seas for a dearly loved island, and that of a god who is crucified on Golgotha.' The Crucifixion is an episode in the biblical epic: Borges is clearly suggesting that romance, as a whole, provides a parallel epic in which the themes of a shipwreck, pirates, enchanted islands, magic, recognition, the loss and regaining of identity, occur constantly" (p. 15).

7. Tzvetan Todorov, *Mikhail Bakhtin: The Dialogical Principle*, trans. Wlad Godzich (Minneapolis: University of Minnesota Press, 1984), p. 66.

8. Bakhtin casts this tension in terms of the difference between "official" and "unofficial" discourse, in the Middle Ages for example, as follows: "It can be said, with some restrictions to be sure, that medieval man in a way led *two lives*: one *official*, monolithically serious and somber; beholden to strict hierarchical order; filled with fear, dogmatism, devotion, and piety; the other, of *carnival* and the *public place*, free; full of ambivalent laughter, sacrileges, profanations of all things

sacred, disparagement and unseemly behavior, familiar contact with everybody and everything" (Todorov, *Mikhail Bakhtin*, p. 78).

9. Walter L. Reed, *An Exemplary History of the Novel: The Quixotic versus the Picaresque* (Chicago: University of Chicago Press, 1981), pp. 4–5. For a broad overview of current theories of novelistic discourse, see Wallace Martin, *Recent Theories of Narrative* (Ithaca: Cornell University Press, 1986).

10. Mikhail Bakhtin, *The Dialogic Imagination*, ed. Michael Holquist (Austin: University of Texas Press, 1981), p. 89.

11. Charles Kany, in his study *The Beginnings of the Epistolary Novel in France, Italy, and Spain* (Berkeley: University of California Press, 1937), was the first critic to indicate the extensiveness of letter fiction to the *novela sentimental*.

12. In claiming the innovative nature of epistolarity as it appears in the *novela sentimental* the fictional nature of these letters must be stressed. For clearly, there existed a long and illustrious tradition of nonfictional letter writing in Europe. See, in this regard, Giles Constable, *The Letters of Peter the Venerable* (Cambridge: Harvard University Press, 1967), introduction to vol. 2 (on "Medieval Letter Collections"). The particular case of Spain is treated by Charles Faulhaber in his book, *Latin Rhetorical Theory in Thirteenth and Fourteenth Century Castile*, University of California Publications in Modern Philology, 103 (Berkeley: University of California Press, 1972).

The other point to be made in this regard is that Abelard and Heloise appear not to have been known in the Spanish Middle Ages. Of their potential reception in Spain, Deyermond writes: "no conozco ninguna alusión a la obra de Abelardo y Eloísa en la España medieval, ni hay, según creo, pruebas de la presencia de un manuscrito de la obra en una biblioteca española durante la Edad Media" ("Las relaciones genéricas de la novela sentimental," pp. 84–85). Nonetheless, Deyermond argues for a potential indirect influence of the correspondence exchanged by Abelard and Heloise (p. 84).

13. For the importance of the *Heroides* to the *novela sentimental*, see Olga T. Impey, "Ovid, Alfonso X, and Juan Rodríguez del Padrón: Two Castilian Translations of the *Heroides* and the Beginnings of Spanish Sentimental Prose," *Bulletin of Hispanic Studies* 57 (1980): 283–97, and "The Literary Emancipation of Juan Rodríguez del Padrón: From the Fictional *Cartas* to the *Siervo libre de amor*," *Speculum* 55 (1980): 305–16.

Explaining Boccaccio's achievement in the *Elegia*, which he terms an "Ovidian tale," Rudolph Schevill writes: "he created one work which pointed the direction toward a new kind of bourgeois love story, filled with illicit passion, and betraying in many places influence of the precepts of Ovid's *Grammar of Love*" (*Ovid and the Renascence in Spain*, University of California Publications in Modern Philology, 4 [Berkeley: University of California Press, 1913], p. 103).

An important and original recent addition to the study of the erotic dimension of these texts is Patricia E. Grieve's book, *Desire and Death in the Spanish Sentimental Romance (1440–1550)* (Newark, Del.: Juan de la Cuesta, 1987). In this work Grieve divides the *novela sentimental* corpus into two categories, "romances of frustrated love" and "romances of violent love," each of which she explores through the critical perspective of Girardian analysis.

14. Julia Kristeva, *Desire in Language*, trans. Thomas Gora, Alice Jardine, and Leon S. Roudiez (New York: Columbia University Press, 1980), p. 83.

15. See in this connection Chandler R. Post, *Medieval Spanish Allegory*, Harvard Studies in Comparative Literature, 4 (Cambridge: Harvard University Press, 1915).

16. "La novela sentimental o cortés española nace en el *Siervo libre* como fusión de una poesia de cancionero y una narración caballeresca. Esos dos mundos, conciliados, dan la sentimental, que es un producto nuevo y no una de sus partes integrantes. Y es un producto de enorme vitalidad formal que irá aprehendiendo distintos elementos estructurales de la novela griega, de la función epistolar, etc., en continua permeabilidad" (César Hernández Alonso, ed., "*Siervo libre de amor*" [Ph.D. diss., Universidad de Valladolid, 1970], 16).

17. Jacqueline Cerquiglini, "Typology of Lyric Manuscripts of the Fourteenth and Fifteenth Centuries with Emphasis on Machaut" (Paper delivered at the 1986 NEH Medieval Workshop at Mount Holyoke College, South Hadley, Mass.), 78.

18. Pamela Waley, "Fiammetta and Panfilo Continued," *Italian Studies* 24 (1969): 31.

19. Vincenzo Crescini, *Contributo agli studi sul Boccaccio con documenti inediti* (Torino: E. Loescher, 1887), p. 156.

20 Michel Foucault, "What Is an Author?" in *Textual Strategies: Perspectives in Post-Structuralist Criticism*, ed. Josué Harari (Ithaca: Cornell University Press, 1979), p. 155.

## ONE
### VICTIM AS ARTIST—*EPISTULAE HERODIUM*

1. Northrop Frye, *The Secular Scripture: A Study of the Structure of Romance* (Cambridge: Harvard University Press, 1976), p. 12.

2. Florence Verducci, *Ovid's Toyshop of the Heart: "Epistulae Herodium"* (Princeton: Princeton University Press, 1985), p. 294.

3. *Ars Amatoria*, trans. J. H. Mosley (Cambridge: Harvard University Press, 1929), bk. 3, v. 346. Also of interest in this connection is the catalogue of heroidean lovers offered in *Amores*, bk. 2, chap. 18.

4. William S. Anderson, "The *Heroides*," in *Ovid*, ed. J. W. Binnis (London: Routledge and Kegan Paul, 1973), p. 64.

5. Fredric Jameson, *The Political Unconscious: Narrative as a Socially Symbolic Act* (Ithaca: Cornell University Press, 1981), p. 107.

6. Anderson, "The *Heroides*," p. 65.

7. Howard Jacobson, *Ovid's "Heroides"* (Princeton: Princeton University Press, 1974), p. 354.

8. I disagree with the gender distinction perceived by some recent critics, e.g., Linda S. Kauffman, who writes: "In the *Heroides* Ovid is faced with the problem of inventing a female persona whose desire differs from the customary male construction of desire, and in Sappho he found clues to alternative models. The letters from

men to women that he added later highlight the contrast: where the men view love as penetration and domination, in Sappho's lyrics love is a forgetfulness of self, a delight in mutuality, in mirroring, and in giving pleasure to the beloved" (*Discourses of Desire: Gender, Genre, and Epistolary Fictions* [Ithaca: Cornell University Press, 1986], p. 55).

Kauffman's suggestion that the men represent action, domination, and the women passive acquiescence is not borne out by the text. I feel that Anderson comes closer to articulating the difference between the single and the paired letters (16–17, 18–19, and 20–21) when he explains that, "the poet has subordinated the man's letter to the woman's. Neither Paris nor Leander nor Acontius finds himself in a complex situation, and consequently none of them utters very complicated or penetrating feelings. The main purpose of the man's letter is to propel the woman into a dynamic situation where her feelings must be complex, where, at least in the case of Helen and Cydippe, she must struggle towards a difficult decision in her reply. . . . In some respects, then, Ovid has taken Helen and Cydippe and placed them now in the dominating position of the unresponsive men, addressed in letters 1–15. They are making a crucial decision for love, not desperately trying to recapture a love that has long escaped them. Inevitably, then, as Ovid correctly planned it, our interest focuses on the complex way in which the women respond to new and exciting pressures" (Anderson, "The *Heroides*," p. 71). It is , thus, not a gender distinction, but a discursive one.

9. Jacobson, *Ovid's "Heroides,"* p. 354.

10. Richard Lanham, *The Motives of Eloquence: Literary Rhetoric in the Renaissance* (New Haven: Yale University Press, 1986), p. 59.

11. Ibid., pp. 49–50.

12. Roland Barthes, *A Lover's Discourse*, trans. Richard Howard (New York: Hill and Wang, 1978), p. 3.

13. Tzvetan Todorov, "Reading as Construction," in *The Reader in the Text*, ed. Susan R. Suleiman and Inge Crossman (Princeton: Princeton University Press, 1980), pp. 74–75.

14. See Gérard Genette, "Frequency," chap. 3 of his *Narrative Discourse: An Essay in Method*, trans. Jane E. Lewin (Ithaca: Cornell University Press, 1980), pp. 113–60.

15. Todorov, "Reading as Construction," p. 73.

16. Verducci, *Ovid's Toyshop*, p. 16.

17. Janet Gurkin Altman, *Epistolarity: Approaches to a Form* (Columbus: Ohio State University Press, 1983), p. 13.

18. Todorov, "Reading as Construction," p. 73.

19. Jacobson, *Ovid's "Heroides,"* pp. 354–55.

20. L. P. Wilkinson, *Ovid Surveyed* (Cambridge: Cambridge University Press, 1962), p. 42.

21. For further elaboration of Bakhtin's views, see above, p. 4.

22. Tzvetan Todorov, *Mikhail Bakhtin: The Dialogical Principle*, trans. Wlad Godzich (Minneapolis: University of Minnesota Press, 1984), p. 58.

23. Lanham, *The Motives of Eloquence*, p. 63.

24. Jacobson, *Ovid's "Heroides,"* p. 90 n. 26.

25. Todorov, *Mikhail Bakhtin*, p. 58.

26. Altman, *Epistolarity*, pp. 117–18ff.

27. Ovid, *"Heroides" and "Amores,"* trans. Grant Showerman (Cambridge: Harvard University Press, 1977), vv. 3–6. All quotations from the *Heroides* refer to this edition.

28. Anderson, "The *Heroides*," p. 53.

29. "[*Histoire*] characterizes the narration of past events . . . events that . . . are presented without any intervention of the speaker in the narration. . . . [*Discours*] must be understood in its widest sense: every utterance assuming a speaker and a hearer, and in the speaker, the intention of influencing the other in some way" (Emile Benveniste, *Problems in General Linguistics,* trans. Mary Elizabeth Meek [Coral Gables: University of Miami Press, 1971], pp. 206–9).

30. Of closure and its paradoxical quality in the *Heroides*, Kauffman insightfully remarks: "In many of the epistles, the heroine considers ending her life, but she avoids every sort of closure and dedicates herself to nurturing her illusions: of his presence, of his eventual return, of her own identity as his beloved, of their mutual passion. Yet her strategy is simultaneously subversive, for she contests the fate to which her lover has abandoned her. Her epistle is simultaneously a love letter and a legal challenge, a revolt staged in writing" (*Discourses of Desire*, pp. 17–18).

31. Barthes, *A Lover's Discourse*, p. 3.

32. Moreover, as Kauffman aptly remarks: "Throughout amorous discourse, the heroine glorifies her tears, her heart, her tongue, her body as authentic registers of her emotions. Yet she disrupts the conventional impulse to think in terms of dichotomies, for she does not always glorify these elements at the expense of their opposites, as one might expect. Frequently, in fact, she subverts the traditional dichotomies of heart versus mind, speech versus writing, tongue versus pen, for 'to write' becomes synonymous with 'to live.' Writing comes to signify her life's blood, illustrating her identification of her body with the text" (*Discourses of Desire*, p. 37).

33. Kauffman, *Discourses of Desire*, pp. 32–33.

34. Mikhail Bakhtin, *The Dialogic Imagination*, ed. Michael Holquist (Austin: University of Texas Press, 1981), pp. 394–95.

35. Kauffman, *Discourses of Desire*, p. 45.

36. Bakhtin, *The Dialogic Imagination*, p. 394.

37. Verducci, *Ovid's Toyshop*, p. 71.

38. Jacobson, *Ovid's "Heroides,"* p. 6.

39. Ibid., p. 349.

40. Verducci, *Ovid's Toyshop*, p. 301.

41. Ibid., p. 303.

42. Ibid., p. 32.

43. Ibid., p. 304.

44. Todorov, *Mikhail Bakhtin*, p. 55.

45. Bakhtin, *The Dialogic Imagination*, p. 388.

46. Verducci, *Ovid's Toyshop*, p. 23.

## TWO
### EXEMPLARY COUNTERFEIT—*BURSARIO*

1. Quoted in Fausto Ghisalberti, "Medieval Biographies of Ovid," *Journal of the Warburg and Courtauld Institutes* 9 (1946): 44.

2. A. J. Minnis, *Medieval Theory of Authorship* (London: Scholar Press, 1984), p. 55. For additional perspectives on the medieval *accessus* see A. Quain, "The Medieval *Accessus ad Auctores*," *Traditio* 3 (1945): 215–64; and F. Quadlbauer, *Die antike Theorie der "Genera Dicendi" im lateinischen Mittelalter* (Vienna: Böhlaus, 1962).

3. The *Bursario* dates from the mid-fifteenth century and, as such, it constitutes a real innovation in vernacular literature by offering a complete translation of all of the *Heroides*. H. Dörrie acknowledges this text's importance as follows: "Unter den Randformen zieht der einzige spanische Beleg besonders Interesse auf sich. An und für sich waren Aragon, Kastilien und Portugal ebensogut für ein Auflühen der heroischen Briefdichtung vorbereitet wie Frankreich; Übersetzungen der *epistulae Herodium* erfolgten auf der iberischen Halbinsel vermutlich sogar früher als in Frankreich" [Among the peripheral forms, the single Spanish example is of particular interest. Aragon, Castille, and Portugal were actually just as well prepared as France for a blossoming of heroic epistolary literature; translation of the *epistulae Herodium* probably occurred on the Iberian peninsula even earlier than in France] (*Der heroische Brief* [Berlin: Walter de Gruyter, 1968], p. 156).

By contrast, "The first French edition of the *Heroides* in Latin was printed in Paris in 1499. . . [and] translations of some of the *Heroides* first appear in a collection of model love letters in the Fleurs du bien dire of 1598," according to Ann Moss in *Ovid in Renaissance France: A Survey of the Latin Editions of Ovid and Commentaries Printed in France before 1600* (London: The Warburg Institute, 1982), pp. 8, 17. See also Jacques Monfrin, "Humanisme et traduction au moyen âge," in *L'Humanisme médiévale dans les littératures romanes du XIIe au XIVe siècles*, ed. Anthime Fourrier (Paris: Klincksieck, 1964), pp. 217–46.

4. María Rosa Lida de Malkiel, "La *General estoria*: Notas literarias y filológicas (II)," *Romance Philology* 13 (1959): 1.

5. Olga T. Impey, "Ovid, Alfonso X, and Juan Rodríguez del Padrón," *Bulletin of Hispanic Studies* 57 (1980): 286.

6. Martin S. Gilderman, *Juan Rodríguez de la Cámara* (Boston: Twayne, 1977), pp. 119–20.

7. See in this connection Heinrich Sedlmayer, *Prolegomena critica ad "Heroides"* (Vienna: Gerold, 1878).

8. With the exception of the seventh heroid, which appears in Part 3 of the *Primera crónica general*, the ten remaining *Heroides* translations are contained in Parts 2 and 3 of the *General estoria*.

9. Olga T. Impey, "The Literary Emancipation of Juan Rodríguez del Padrón," *Speculum* 55 (1980): 315.

10. Impey, "Ovid, Alfonso X, and Juan Rodriguez del Padrón," p. 288.

11. Ibid., p. 287.

12. Moss notes that "The Sappho epistle (*Heroides* XV) . . . had been redis-covered in the fifteenth century [but] was often attributed to Statius" (*Ovid in Renaissance France*, p. 8). J. R. Ashton's information corroborates Moss's assertion, attributing Alfonso's omission of this letter to the fact that "Epistle XV, *Sappho Phaoni,* was beyond doubt missing from the Latin codex used by the Spanish trans-lator, missing as it is from all manuscripts of an earlier date than the fifteenth cen-tury and as it was from the one read by Planudes in the 13th" ("Ovid's 'Heroides' as Translated by Alphonso the Wise" [Ph.D. diss., University of Wisconsin, 1944], vi).

Elizabeth Harvey further specifies that "The manuscript history of the Sapphic epistle was separate from that of the *Heroides*; besides excerpts from it in the 12th-century *Florilegium Gallicum,* the letter appears in only one medieval source in conjunction with the other fourteen Ovidian epistles, and the evidence suggests that it was copied from a different source. From 1420 onwards, it is to be found in some two hundred manuscripts, all derived from a common source. Daniel Hein-sius established its order in the *Heroides* by placing it in the fifteenth position in his edition of 1629" ("Veuntriloquizing Sappho: Ovid, Donne, and the Erotics of the Feminine Voice," *Criticism* 31 [1989]: 135).

For a detailed history of the letter's transmission, see *Texts and Transmissions: A Survey of the Latin Classics,* ed. L. D. Reynolds et al. (Oxford: Clarendon Press, 1983), pp. 268–72.

13. See p. 27ff.

14. Florence Verducci, *Ovid's Toyshop of the Heart: "Epistulae Herodium"* (Princeton: Princeton University Press, 1985), p. 32. For a fascinating discussion of the wide range of methods by which medieval authors used previous texts to endow their own work with authority, see Brian Stock, *The Implications of Literacy* (Princeton: Princeton University Press, 1983).

15. As Michèle Perret observes: "la forme prose—réservée aux traductions et aux chroniques, était encore sentie comme liée à l'expression de la vérité historique et scientifique" [prose as a medium—restricted to translation and chronicles—was still perceived as linked to the expression of historical and scientific truth] ("De l'espace romanesque à la matérialité du livre," *Poétique* 50 (1982): 173.

Along similar lines, in speaking of the effacement of the author figure which occurs in prose, Bernard Cerquiglini explains that: "De même qu'il ne saurait y avoir en prose . . . deux locuteurs au sein du même discours, le texte comme lo-cuteur, élément définitionnel, constant, dont l'émergence a été notée à plusieurs reprises entre en conflit avec un autre locuteur: l'auteur. On ne s'étonnera donc pas de voir ce dernier progressivement éliminé, l'écriture-prose tentant par cette élimi-nation de répondre à la question: 'Qui écrit?'

"Le texte en vers présente ce qu'on nomme traditionnellement des interventions de l'auteur. Si la mise en prose était une simple translation, un dérimage, on pour-rait s'attendre à ce que ces interventions soient comme mécaniquement conservées" (*La parole médiévale* [Paris: Minuit, 1981], p. 111).

[Just as there cannot be—in prose—two speakers at the origin of the same dis-course, so the text as speaker—the constitutive, permanent element whose emer-gence has been repeatedly noted—enters into conflict with another speaker: the author. It is not, therefore, surprising to see the latter progressively eliminated, as prose attempts through this elimination to answer the question: "Who is writing?"

The text in verse contains what are traditionally called authorial interventions. If prosification were a simple act of translation—a derhyming—one would expect a quasi-automatic presentation of these interventions.]

16. José Ortega y Gasset, "Miseria y esplendor de la traducción," in *Obras completas* (Madrid: Espasa-Calpe, 1951), vol. 5, 2a. ed., pp. 448–49. Concerning Alfonso's translation practices see Fernando Lázaro Carreter, "Sobre el 'modus interpretandi' Alfonsí," *Ibérida* 6 (1961): 57–114.

17. *General estoria*, Segunda Parte 1–2, ed. Antonio G. Solalinde, Lloyd A. Kasten, and Victor R. B. Oelschläger (Madrid: Consejo Superior de Investigaciones Científicas, 1957–1961). This particular citation is taken from pt. 2, bk. 2, chap. 20. English translations are mine.

18. This observation is made by Impey, "Ovid, Alfonso X, and Juan Rodríguez del Padrón," p. 288.

19. All quotations in this paragraph are from Sedlmayer, *Prolegomena critica*, p. 98.

20. Juan Rodríguez del Padrón, *El Bursario*, in *Obras*, ed. Antonio Paz y Mélia (Madrid: Sociedad de Bibliófilos Españoles, 1884), p. 198. Unless otherwise noted, all subsequent quotations in the text are from this edition. English translations are mine.

21. *El Bursario*, ed. Paz y Mélia, p. 197 (italics added).

22. In an illuminating article, John Dagenais observes that "both the title of the *Bursario* and the glossatory prologues are direct translations of medieval Ovid commentaries dating probably from the early 13th century" and that "the word *bursarius*, it turns out, refers not to glosses on Ovid, but rather to the difficult lines within the text of Ovid itself. A 'versus bursarius' is one which is ambiguous or whose meaning is particularly obscure: 'Bursarius est versus in quo diverse possunt continuationes vel sententie reperiri' " ("Juan Rodríguez del Padrón's Translation of the Latin *Bursarii*: New Light on the Meaning of 'Tra(c)tado,' " *Journal of Hispanic Philology* 10 [1986]: 120, 122). Thus *bursario* is synonymous with polysemy. Of related interest is Hughes-V. Shooner, "Les *Bursarii Ovidianorum* de Guillaume d'Orléans," *Mediaeval Studies* 43 (1981): 405–24.

For two recent editors of the *Bursario*, Rodríguez's interest lies in telling a compelling story. They view his exemplary rubrics either as formulaic or as a *captatio benevolentiae*: "la tendencia moralizadora de los comentarios debe ser considerada, de una parte, como una fórmula de escuela aceptada por tradición y no muy sentida, de otra, como el deseo inconsciente de defenderse a sí mismos y a los lectores del instintivo gusto por aquel mundo fascinante de amores prohibidos" [the moralizing tendency of the commentaries should be viewed, on the one hand, as a literary topos and, on the other, as the unconscious self-defense mechanism by authors who want to protect themselves and their readers from the instinctive attraction toward the fascinating world of forbidden love] (*Bursario*, ed. Pilar Saquero Suárez-Somonte and Tomás González Rolán [Madrid: Universidad Complutense, 1984], p. 33). See also L. M. Lasperas, "La traduction et ses théories en Espagne au XVe et XVIe siècles," *Revue des langues romanes* 84 (1980): 81–92.

23. Charles Kany, *The Beginnings of the Epistolary Novel in France, Italy, and Spain* (Berkeley: University of California Press, 1937).

24. In this connection see Judson Boyce Allen, *The Ethical Poetic of the Later Middle Ages* (Toronto: University of Toronto Press, 1982).

25. Gérard Genette, *Palimpsestes* (Paris: Seuil, 1982), p. 297.

26. Verducci, *Ovid's Toyshop*, p. 117.

27. Ibid., p. 103.

28. In this context see H. R. Lang, "The So-called *Cancionero de Pero Guillén de Segovia*," *Revue Hispanique* 10 (1908): 51–81; and J. G. Cummins, "Pero Guillén de Segovia y el ms. 4144," *Hispanic Review* 41 (1973): 6–32.

29. "Por este Gisto podemos entender qualquier omne virtuoso sin engaño, que a buena parte, sin malicia, ayunta sus hijos, conuiene saber, sus dichos y obras, con sus sobrinas, que entendemos por las obras de Danao o de qualquier mal hombre, que por sucçesion de nuestro padre Adan puede ser su hermano. Esto dize bien Boeçio enel metro sesto del tercero libro de *Consolacion*: 'Omne hominum genus in terris simili surgit ab ortu.' " (*Bur.* 287).

30. Impey, "The Literary Emancipation of Juan Rodríguez del Padrón."

31. Ibid., p. 313.

32. Ibid., p. 309.

33. "Historically, the discourse of absence is carried on by the woman: Woman is sedentary, Man hunts, journeys; Woman is faithful (she waits), Man is fickle (he sails away, he cruises)" (Roland Barthes, *A Lover's Discourse*, trans. Richard Howard [New York: Hill and Wang, 1978], pp. 13–14).

34. Impey, "The Literary Emancipation of Juan Rodríguez del Padrón," pp. 314–15.

35. Ibid.

## THREE
### VOYEURISTIC BETRAYAL—*ELEGIA*

1. "Cada escritor crea a sus precursores" ("Kafka y sus precursores," in *Otras inquisiones* [Buenos Aires: Sur, 1963], p. 128).

2. Vincenzo Crescini, *Contributo agli studi sul Boccaccio con documenti inediti* (Torino: E. Loescher, 1887), p. 156.

3. Angel Valbuena Prat in his *Historia de la literatura española* (Barcelona: Gili, 1950), vol. 2, p. 278, is so convinced of the *Elegia's* influence on the *novela sentimental* that he begins the chapter entitled "La novela sentimental y otras formas en prosa" with a section called "Las derivaciones de la *Fiammetta* del Boccaccio." The *Siervo libre de amor* is the first *novela sentimental* and is also the first work considered by Valbuena Prat as a direct successor of the *Elegia*.

4. Vittore Branca, *Boccaccio: The Man and His Works*, trans. Richard Monges (New York: New York University Press, 1976), pp. 29ff., discusses the myth of Fiammetta. Her obvious fictionality is attested to, for example, by the fact that her date of birth is given as being 1310 in the *Filocolo*, 1313 in the *Comedia*, and after 1321 in the *Decameron*.

5. Thomas Bergin, *Boccaccio* (New York: Viking Press, 1981), p. 168.

6. Contrary to this critical perspective, Janet Smarr asserts that "although the *Elegia* resembles a seventeenth- or eighteenth-century novel of psychological analysis, such as for example the *Princesse de Clèves*, or even later novels, Boccaccio is not interested in psychology per se. He does not want us to empathize with Fiammetta; he wants us to see in her steadily worsening condition a demonstration of the effects of sin" (*Boccaccio and Fiammetta: The Narrator as Lover* [Urbana: University of Illinois, 1986], p. 132). Yet as discursive analysis demonstrates, *caritas* and *cupiditas* are not what Boccaccio seeks to illustrate in the *Elegia*.

7. *De vulgare eloquentia*, ed. Pier Vincenzo Mengaldo (Padova: Ed. Antenore, 1968), p. 39.

8. Robert Hollander, *Boccaccio's Two Venuses* (New York: Columbia University Press, 1977), p. 49.

9. For example, Bergin, *Boccaccio*, pp. 169, 179.

10. *Elegia di madonna Fiammetta*, in *Opere di Giovanni Boccaccio*, ed. Cesare Segre (Milan: Mursia, 1966), p. 947. All citations of the *Elegia* refer to this edition. The English translation is from *Amorous Fiammetta*, trans. Edward Hutton (Westport, Conn.: Greenwood Press, 1970), pp. xlix–li. All English references are to the Hutton translation.

Antonio Prieto (*Morfología de la novela* [Barcelona: Ed. Planeta, 1975], p. 273) is representative of much *Fiammetta* criticism that accepts Boccaccio's statement at face value: "'Voi leggendo non troverete favole greche ornate di molte bugie, né troiane battaglie. . . .' Es decir, no acomodará algo ajeno a un presente (como *Amadís* podrá estar acomodado en la historia de Ardanlier), sino que escribirá del presente, *será* presente en el que ir formándose (e informándonos) hasta en particularidades como su nostalgia de Nápoles ('lieta, pacifica, magnífica . . . '), donde intensamente vivió. No se recoge en Fiammetta como pasado sino que exclama desde ella su deseo de vivir, castigando en Fiammetta lo que pueda detener ese deseo de camino" ["You shall not, in reading of it, find any Grecian fables depainted and set forth with plausible lies, nor Trojan wars foul and loathsome by deadly gore" (Hutton, xlix–li) . . . . That is, he will not accommodate an alien time frame into the present (the way that *Amadís* can be incorported into the story of Ardanlier). Rather, he will write about the present, he will be present in the narrative, for example, in his nostalgic evocation of Naples ("merry, peaceful, magnificent"), where he lived very intensely. He does not see his past through Fiammetta, instead he proclaims, through her, his desire to live, criticizing in Fiammetta whatever might hinder that desire].

Cesare Segre, on the other hand, is one of the few modern critics who wisely attempt to consider the poetic potential of Boccaccio's extensive use of myth. See the essay, "Structures and Registers in the Fiammetta," in his *Structures and Time*, trans. John Meddemmen (Chicago: University of Chicago Press, 1979), pp. 66–92.

11. Boccaccio, *Decameron*, ed. Cesare Segre (Milan: Mursia, 1966), p. 29. All Italian citations refer to this edition.

12. Boccaccio, *The Decameron*, trans. G. H. McWilliam (Hammondsworth: Penguin, 1972), p. 49. All English translations are taken from this text.

13. Janet Altman, *Epistolarity: Approaches to a Form* (Columbus: Ohio State University Press, 1982), p. 84.

14. Gerald Prince, "The Diary-Novel: Notes for the Definition of a Sub-genre," *Neophilologus* 59 (1975): 478–79.

15. Sharon Cameron, *Lyric Time: Dickinson and the Limits of Genre* (Baltimore: Johns Hopkins University Press, 1979), p. 206.

16. See Eugenio Donato, " 'Per selve e boscherecci laberinti': Desire and Narrative Structure in Ariosto's *Orlando Furioso*," *Barroco* 4 (1972): 31. In Girard's words: "We believe that 'novelistic' genius is won by a great struggle against [the] attitudes we have lumped together under the name 'romantic' because they all appear to us intended to maintain the illusion of spontaneous desire and of a subjectivity almost divine in its autonomy" (René Girard, *Deceit, Desire, and the Novel*, trans. Yvonne Freccero [Baltimore: Johns Hopkins University Press, 1965], pp. 28–29).

17. Prince, "The Diary-Novel," p. 479.

18. *Tristia: Ex Ponto*, trans. Arthur Leslie Wheeler (Cambridge: Harvard University Press, 1965), vv. 1–14.

19. Smarr takes Boccaccio's claim that she writes both for other women and for Panfilo at face value: "Thus there are two different audiences each addressed by one of her roles. Panfilo she hopes to seduce; other women she hopes to warn away from enslavement to passion. . . . The double audience replaces the double author as a means of pointing out two quite diverse intentions or meanings of the text. Scholars who view Fiammetta in this work as a noble victim are responding the way she hopes Panfilo will. But other readers are intended to be horrified and repelled by what she has made of herself" (*Boccaccio and Fiammetta*, p. 131). While this double audience is imagined by Fiammetta, it must be stressed that it remains entirely imaginary.

20. Fiammetta's inability to act is all the more striking given her insistent citation of Senecan texts. See in this connection Segre, *Structures and Time*, pp. 254ff.

## FOUR
### MEDIATED DISCOURSE—*HISTORIA*

1. Jacques Derrida, as cited in Janet Altman, *Epistolarity: Approaches to a Form* (Columbus: Ohio State University Press, 1982), p. 212.

2. For example: Marcelino Menéndez Pelayo, *Orígenes de la novela* (Madrid: Bally–Ballière, 1905), 1: 303ff.; Rudolph Schevill, *Ovid and the Renascence in Spain*, University of California Publications in Modern Philology, 4 (Berkeley: University of California Press, 1913), pp. 101ff.; Gustave Reynier, *Le roman sentimentale avant 'L'Astrée'* (Paris: Colin, 1908), pp. 28–54.

3. Armando Durán offers a more detailed series of analogies (*Estructura y técnicas de la novela sentimental y caballeresca* [Madrid: Gredos, 1973], pp. 15–16).

4. Ibid., p. 18.

5. Keith Whinnom, "The *Historia de duobus amantibus* of Aeneas Sylvius Piccolomini (Pope Pius II) and the Development of Spanish Golden-Age Fiction,"

in *Essays on Narrative Fiction of the Iberian Peninsula in Honor of Frank Pierce*, ed. R. B. Tate (Oxford: Dolphin, 1982), p. 248.

6. Antonio Prieto, *Morfología de la novela* (Barcelona: Ed. Planeta, 1975), p. 275.

7. Ibid., p. 277. In the context of Prieto's claim, however, it is dangerous to equate the *tratado* with exemplarity, as Keith Whinnom convincingly argues in "*Autor* and *Tratado* in the Fifteenth Century: Semantic Latinism or Etymological Trap?" *Bulletin of Hispanic Studies* 59 (1982): 211–18.

8. Piccolomini, *De duobus amantibus historia*, ed. Josephus Dévay (Budapest: Heislerus, 1903), p. 2. All Latin references are to this edition.

9. Piccolomini, *The Tale of Two Lovers*, trans. Flora Grierson (London: Constable, 1929), p. xvii. All English references are taken from this translation.

10. "Uritur infelix Dido totaque vagatur / urbe furens, qualis coniecta cerva sagitta" (Virgil, *The Aeneid*, ed. H. R. Fairclough [Cambridge: Harvard University Press, 1974), 4.68–69). [Unhappy Dido burns. Across the city she wanders in her frenzy—even as a heedless hind hit by an arrow] (*The Aeneid*, trans. Allen Mandlebaum [New York: Bantam, 1971], 4.90–92). All references are to these editions.

11. Piccolomini himself acknowledged this unexemplary dimension of his work in his often quoted phrase: "Aeneam respuite [*or* rejicite], Pium respicite." However, as Whinnom remarks, "The motto is misleading, for it suggests a sort of Pauline or August[inian] palinode, a change of heart marked by his ordination (March 1446), elevation to the bishoprics of Trieste (1447) and Sienna (1450), appointment as cardinal (1456), and election as Pope (1458). . . . Although he repudiated *De duobus amantibus*, he could never bring himself to condemn his beloved Roman writers, who inspired it" (Whinnom, "The *Historia*," pp. 246–47).

12. "Non troverete favole greche ornate di molte bugie, né troiane battaglie," (Segre, p. 947).

13. Livy, *Titi Livi ab urbe condita*, ed. R. M. Ogilvie (Oxford: Clarendon, 1974), 1. lvi.

14. Charles Kany, *The Beginnings of the Epistolary Novel in France, Italy, and Spain* (Berkeley: University of California Press, 1937), p.39.

15. Ibid., p. 39.

16. Ibid.

17. Robert Day, *Told in Letters* (Ann Arbor: University of Michigan Press, 1966), p. 16.

18. Janet Altman's distinction between the memoir (e.g., the *Elegia*) and epistolary form (e.g., the *Historia*) is useful in this regard: "In the memoir novel, no matter how complex and a-chronological the treatment of time may be, we sense it primarily along a single continuum. . . . In the epistolary novel, however, our perception of time is more fragmented" ("The 'Triple Register': Introduction to Temporal Complexity in the Letter-Novel," *L'Esprit Créateur* 17 [1977]: 304). Space is likewise fragmented in the epistolary form. Both kinds of fragmentation present in the epistolary form clearly provide greater oppportunity for metaliterary structuring.

19. Ronald Rosbottom, "Motifs in Epistolary Fiction: Analysis of a Narrative Sub-genre," *L'Esprit Créateur* 17 (1977): 291 (italics added).

20. Altman, *Epistolarity*, p. 212.

21. Rosbottom discusses the first three types of readers ("Motifs in Epistolary Fiction," pp. 298ff.).

22. Cervantes exploits the same paradoxical configuration in *Don Quijote* (2.19): "El uno de los estudiantes traía, como en portamanteo, en un lienzo de bocací verde envuelto, al parecer, un poco de grana blanca y dos pares de medias de cordellate" (*Don Quijote de la Mancha*, ed. Martín de Riquer [Barcelona: Juventud, 1968], p. 670). All references are to this edition.

23. In reply to Don Quijote's question as to whether Ginés's autobiographical novel is finished, he receives the following reply: "Cómo puede estar acabado— respondió él—si aún no está acabada mi vida?" (1.22.209) ["How can it be"—he replied—"if my life isn't finished yet?" (my translation)].

24. Altman, *Epistolarity*, p. 126.

25. Mary Louise Pratt, *Toward a Speech Act Theory of Literary Discourse* (Bloomington: Indiana University Press, 1977), pp. 80–81.

26. Ibid., p. 80.

27. Ibid., p. 81.

28. *Pace* Day's claim that the letters constitute "expressives" as opposed to the "comparatively unemotional dialogue" (*Told in Letters*, p. 16).

29. That is, "diverted," "put far off," from the Old French *por* (forward) and *loing* (at a distance). The additional connotation of "wrongful attribution" and "stealing" is of secondary importance here but also quite relevant.

30. For an important exploration of epistolary displacement see Jacques Lacan, "La lettre volée," *La Psychanalyse* 2 (1956): 1–44.

31. Nisus (Trojan companion of Aeneas and friend of Euryalus), Palinurus (pilot of Aeneas's fleet), and Achates (Aeneas's faithful companion).

## FIVE
### FAILED EROTICISM—*SIERVO LIBRE*

1. I thank *Poetics Today* for permission to reprint portions of my article, "The Generic Status of the *Siervo libre de amor*: Rodríguez del Padrón's Reworking of Dante," *Poetics Today* 5 (1984): 629–43.

2. Olga T. Impey, "Ovid, Alfonso X, and Juan Rodríguez del Padrón," *Bulletin of Hispanic Studies* 57 (1980): 291.

3. Ibid.

4. Rodríguez del Padrón, *Siervo libre de amor*, ed. Antonio Prieto (Madrid: Castalia, 1976), p. 67. All Spanish citations are taken from this edition. The English translations are mine.

5. "La novela sentimental o cortés española nace con el *Siervo libre* como fusión de una poesia de cancionero y una narración caballeresca. Esos dos mundos, conciliados, dan la sentimental, que es un producto nuevo y no una de sus partes integrantes" [The Spanish sentimental or courtly novel originates with the *Siervo libre* as the fusion of *cancionero* lyric and chivalric narrative. This sentimental environment results from the commingling of these two worlds; it is a new form, entirely different from either one of its constituent parts.]. César

Hernández Alonso, *Siervo libre de amor* (Valladolid: Universidad de Valladolid, 1970), p. 16.

6. Carlos Martínez Barbieto, *Maçías el enamorado y Juan Rodríguez del Padrón: estudio y antología* (Santiago de Compostela: Sociedad de Bibliófilos Gallegos, 1951).

7. D. L. Bastianutti, "La función de la fortuna en la primera novela sentimental española," *Romance Notes* 14 (1972): 394–402.

8. Gregory Peter Andrachuk, "A Further Look at the Italian Influence in the *Siervo libre de amor*," *Journal of Hispanic Philology* 6 (1981–82): 51.

On the other hand, Edward Dudley, "Structure and Meaning in the Novel of Juan Rodríguez: *Siervo libre de amor*" (Ph.D. diss., University of Minnesota, 1963), and Alonso (n. 4 above) see the work, quite rightly in my opinion, as complete.

9. María Rosa Lida, "Juan Rodríguez del Padrón: Influencia," *Nueva Revista de Filología Hispánica* 8 (1954): 322–23, finds no correspondence between the two texts. Antonio Prieto, in the introduction to his edition of the *Siervo libre*, posits a vague relationship between the *Elegia* and the *Siervo libre* essentially on the basis of Rodríguez's exploitation of Boccaccio in his other works. Most recently, Barbara Weissberger, " 'Habla el Auctor': *L'Elegia di madonna Fiammetta* as a Source for the *Siervo libre de amor*," *Journal of Hispanic Philology* 4 (1980): 203–36, discerns a clear interrelationship between the two texts.

10. Andrachuk, "A Further Look at Italian Influence in the *Siervo libre de amor*."

11. See Robert Hollander, "Dante's Use of *Aeneid* in *Inferno* I and II," *Comparative Literature* 20 (1968): 142–56.

12. Italics added.

13. We seem to have here a situation not unlike that of Petrarch's attitude toward Dante in theory and practice: on the one hand, a stern denial of Dante's literary artistry, on the other, an extensive exploitation of Dantean subtexts. In this context see Thomas M. Greene, "Petrarch and the Humanist Hermeneutic," in *Italian Literature: Roots and Branches*, ed. G. Rimanelli and K. J. Atichity (New Haven: Yale University Press, 1976), pp. 201–24; Robert Durling, " 'Giovene donna sotto un verde lauro,' " *Modern Language Notes* 86 (1971): 1–20; and Nancy J. Vickers, "Re-membering Dante: Petrarch's 'Chiare, fresche et dolci acque,' " *Modern Language Notes* 96 (1981): 1–11.

14. Dante Alighieri, *Inferno* 3.18. All references and translations from the *Commedia* are taken from the text of *The Divine Comedy*, ed. and trans. Charles S. Singleton, 3 vols. (Princeton: Princeton University Press, 1970–1975).

15. Interestingly, both Dante's Virgil and his Beatrice exist exclusively as personification figures in Rodríguez's text—further evidence of his creative transformation of Dante.

16. For a discussion of this pan-European phenomenon see Johan Huizinga, *The Waning of the Middle Ages*, trans. F. Hopman (London: E. Arnold, 1927), and for its Spanish manifestation see María Rosa Lida, "La hipérbole sagrada en la poesía castellana del siglo xv," *Revista de Filología Hispánica* 8 (1946): 121–30.

17. Ovid, *Metamorphoses*, trans. Frank Justus Miller (Cambridge: Harvard University Press, 1977).

18. Impey, "Ovid, Alfonso X, and Juan Rodríguez del Padrón," p. 291.

19. *Purgatorio* 29.92–108:

> vennero appresso lor quattro animali,
> coronati ciascun di verde fronda.
> Ognuno era pennuto di sei ali;
>   le penne piene d'occhi; e li occhi d'Argo,
>   se fosser vivi, sarebber cotali.
> A descriver lor forme più non spargo
>   rime, lettor; ch'altra spesa mi stringe
>   tanto ch'a questa non posso esser largo;
> ma leggi Ezechïel, che la dipigne
>   come li vide da la fredda parte
>   venir con vento e con nube e con igne;
> e quali i troverai ne le sue carte,
>   tali eran quivi, salvo ch'a le penne
>   Giovanni è meco e da lui si diparte.
> Lo spazio dentro a lor quattro contenne
>   un carro, in su due rote, trïunfale,
>   ch'al collo d'un grifon tirato venne.

20. Javier Herrero offers a very different reading of this intercalated love story: "Yrena's purified love for Ardanlier is the Christian self-sacrificing charity which moves her to dedicate her life to Vesta (a figure here for the Virgin Mary), to live in chastity, to profess in a religious order and to offer a life of penance for the salvation of a sinner's soul" ("The Allegorical Structure of the *Siervo libre de amor*," *Speculum* 55 [1980]: 762).

21. For a discussion of the pilgrimage motif in the *Siervo libre*, see Edward Dudley, "Court and Country: The Fusion of Two Images of Love in Juan Rodríguez's *El siervo libre de amor*," *Proceedings of the Modern Language Association* 82 (1967): 117–20.

22. Brian Dutton, " 'Buen amor': Its Meaning and Uses in Some Medieval Texts," in *"Libro de buen amor" Studies*, ed. G. B. Gybbon-Monypenny (London: Tamesis, 1970), p. 111.

23. As Bastianutti, "La función de la fortuna," p. 398, observes, "La *Historia de los dos amadores*, Ardanlier y Liesa, que también acabaron sus amores con la muerte . . . sirve para ayudarle a escoger el camino que el Entendimiento le consejaba" ["The *Historia de los dos amadores*, Ardanlier and Lyessa, who likewise ended their love in death . . . serves to help him choose the path advocated by Entendimiento"].

24. This is a commonplace of lyric poetry, both *troubadour* and *trouvère*. The topos is poeticized at the structurally significant midpoint of the conjoined *Roman de la Rose*, where Jean de Meun's God of Love describes him literally as a bird, feathers and all: "je l'afublerai de mes eles . . ." (*Le Roman de la Rose*, ed. Ernest Langlois [Paris: Société des Ançiens Textes Français, 1922], v. 10,637). See also Peter F. Dembowski, "Vocabulary of Old French Courtly Lyrics—Difficulties and Hidden Difficulties," *Critical Inquiry* 2 (1976); and Paul Zumthor, *Essai de poétique médiévale* (Paris: Seuil, 1972). For the metaphorical association of the lyric poet

with birds and birdsong in Spanish poetry, see Eugenio Asensio, *Poética y realidad en el cancionero peninsular de la edad media* (Madrid: Gredos, 1957), esp. pp. 247–51.

25. The phrase "Dios y mi ventura" is, of course, a commonplace in Spanish literature, found in texts as disparate as the *romances antiguos* and the *Lazarillo*. Within the context of the *Siervo libre*, however, the force of this first mention of God is not diminished by Rodríguez's use of a formulaic expression.

26. This temporal distancing seems to be echoed by the "*antygua* canción" (vs. the "nueva," which he sings joyously). In this connection, see Olga Impey, "La poesía y la prosa del *Siervo libre de amor*," in *Medieval, Renaissance and Folklore Studies in Honor of John Esten Keller*, ed. Joseph R. Jones (Newark, Del.: Juan de la Cuesta, 1980), pp. 171–87. Andrachuk, on the other hand, sees no such distancing: "El poema termina sin que el poeta comprenda perfectamente el mensaje de las aves" [The poem ends before the poet has fully understood the message of the birds]: "Prosa y poesía en el *Siervo libre de amor*," in *Actas del sexto congreso internacional de hispanistas*, ed. Alan M. Gordon and Evelyn Rugg (Toronto: Asociación Internacional de Hispanistas), p. 62.

27. Gregory Peter Andrachuk, "On the Missing Third Part of the *Siervo libre de amor*," *Hispanic Review* 45 (1977): 178.

28. Ibid., p. 179.

29. In fact, the *Paradiso*, considered in its entirety as a third stage in the learning process of the protagonist, is implicit in the appearance of Synderesis. This is also because Dante's apprenticeship with Beatrice (lasting from *Purgatorio* 30 to *Paradiso* 30.90) is an apprenticeship of the intellect.

Robert Hollander, *Studies in Dante* (Ravenna: Longo, 1980), p. 34, elaborates the progression of the pilgrim's learning as follows:

| Dante's Development | Locus | Guide |
|---|---|---|
| I. Correction of the will | *Inf.* 1–34 | Virgil |
| II. Perfection of the will | *Purg.* 1–29 | Virgil |
| III. Correction of the intellect | *Purg.* 30–*Par.* 30.90 | Beatrice |
| IV. Perfection of the intellect | *Par.* 30.90–33.145 | St. Bernard |

30. Colbert I. Nepaulsingh makes this point when he writes: "Yrena, of course, is mistaken in thinking that Ardanlier and Lyessa have 'puríficas ánimas' that will be rewarded with 'perdurable forgança'; what she and other pilgrims of love, like the narrator, believe to be paradise is, actually, hell, as the narrator's Entendimiento tried earlier to tell him ('offreçiéndote a las penas que allá sufren los amadores, avnque tu piensas que biuen en gloria,' p. 79). Thus, the vision of the shrine and tombs of Ardanlier and Lyessa that the narrator has is a hellish vision of false glory, its counterpart is the true vision of Synderesis and her companions with which the narrative ends" (*Towards a History of Literary Composition in Medieval Spain* [Toronto: University of Toronto Press, 1986], pp. 163–64).

31. As Bakhtin explains, "To portray an event on the same temporal and axiological plane as oneself and one's contemporaries (and, therefore, from personal experience and invention) is to accomplish a radical transformation, and to step out

of the world of the epic into the world of the novel" (Tzvetan Todorov, *Mikhail Bakhtin*, trans. Wlad Godzich [Minneapolis: University of Minnesota Press, 1984], p. 89).

32. Brownlee, "The Generic Status of the *Siervo libre de amor*," pp. 641–42.

## SIX
## THE UNTRANSCENDENT VISION—*SATIRA DE FELICE E INFELICE VIDA*

1. Umberto Eco, *A Theory of Semiotics* (Bloomington: Indiana University Press, 1976), p. 6.

2. Jacques Derrida, *Of Grammatology*, trans. Gayatri Spivak (Baltimore: Johns Hopkins University Press, 1976), pp. 10ff.

3. Joel Fineman, "The Structure of Allegorical Desire," in *Allegory and Representation*, ed. Stephen J. Greenblatt (Baltimore: Johns Hopkins University Press, 1981), p. 29.

4. Maureen Quilligan, *The Language of Allegory: Defining the Genre* (Ithaca: Cornell University Press, 1979), p. 90.

5. Benvenuto da Imola, *Comentum super Dantis Aldigherij "Comoediam*," ed. J. P. Lacaita (Florence: G. Barbera, 1887), 1.18. For the seminal importance of Benvenuto's commentary in Spain see Louis M. La Favia, "Il primo comento alla *Divina Commedia* in Spagna," *Hispano-Italic Studies* 1 (1976): 1–8.

6. Earlier in his prologue La Favia equates every text with praise and criticism: "omne poema et omnis oratio poetica aut est laudatio, aut vituperatio; omnis enim actio et omnis mos non versatur nisi circa virtutem et vicium" (ibid., p. 8).

7. Northrop Frye, "The Nature of Satire," *University of Toronto Quarterly* 14 (1944): 5.

8. Gilbert Highet, *The Anatomy of Satire* (Princeton: Princeton University Press, 1962), p. 233.

9. Julian Weiss, "Juan de Mena's *Coronación*: Satire or *Sátira*?" *Journal of Hispanic Philology* 6 (1981–82): 123.

10. Because of its use of personification figures who represent the lover's subjective states, the *Satira*'s debt to the *Roman de la Rose* is always mentioned by critics.

Elena Gascón-Vera acknowledges the importance of an additional subtext: "Seguramente don Pedro se inspiró para los personajes femininos que nombra en la *Satira* en la adaptación que don Alvaro de Luna hizo de la obra de Boccaccio, *De claris mulieribus*, en el *Libro de las virtuosas mujeres* (1446) . Casi todos los personajes que don Pedro incluye en sus glosas y en el texto se encuentran en la obra de don Alvaro" [For the feminine characters mentioned in the *Satira* Don Pedro was definitely inspired by Alvaro de Luna's adaptation of Boccaccio's *De claris mulieribus* in the *Libro de las virtuosas mujeres* (1446). Nearly all of the characters included by Don Pedro in his glosses and in the text as well can be found in Don Alvaro's work] ("*La Satira de felice e infelice vida*," in *Don Pedro, Condestable de Portugal* [Madrid: Fundación Universitaria Española, 1979], p. 108).

Most recently, E. Michael Gerli asserts that: "The *Satira* derives its overall allegorical structure, thematic strain of sentimental complaint, and autobiographical analysis of the emotions from [the *Siervo libre*] . . . [but its] debt to Rodríguez del Padrón's *Triunfo de las donas* is considerably greater. . . . The *Triunfo* is a general defense of all women, the *Satira* a vindication of the virtue and goodness of one woman—the narrator's alternately loved and despised lady" ("Toward a Revaluation of the Constable of Portugal's *Satira de felice e infelice vida*," in *Hispanic Studies in Honor of Alan Deyermond*, ed. John S. Miletich [Madison: Hispanic Seminary of Medieval Studies, 1986], pp. 112–13).

11. *Satira de felice e infelice vida* in *Obras completas do condestável dom Pedro*, ed. Luis Adão da Fonseca (Lisbon: Fundação Calouste Gulbenkian, 1975), p. 3. All subsequent citations refer to this edition.

12. Fonseca indicates (ibid., xxx) such discrepancies ("a inclusão de letras ou palavras não presentes nas fontes é indicada por [ . . . ]"), but he does not try to account for them in any way.

13. There are in fact 102 glosses.

14. Inez Macdonald, "The *Coronación* of Juan de Mena: Poem and Commentary," *Hispanic Review* 7 (1939): 128.

15. Italics added. *Satura*, as defined by Isidore, however, has nothing to do with *loor* and *reprehension*, being associated instead with *abundantia*, which refers either to writing or alimentation: (1) "Satura vero lex est quae de pluribus simil rebus eloquitur, dicta a copia rerum et quasi a saturitate," (2) "satura . . . est vario alimentorum adparatu conpositum" (*Etimologías*, ed. José Oroz Reto, 2 vols. [Madrid: Biblioteca de Autores Cristianos, 1983], 1.516 and 2.494, respectively).

16. "La alegoría, por tanto, está introducida desde el principio del texto y se mantiene a lo largo de toda la obra, sin que haya intención de interpretarla." Gascón-Vera, *Don Pedro*, pp. 94–95.

17. "El autor llena las márgenes de glosas explicativas, que suprimo, así por su gran extensión, como por ser materia conocidísima de todo el mundo y que en cualquier diccionario de mitología puede leerse." Paz y Mélia, on the *Satira de felice e infelice vida*, in Vol. 29 of *Opúsculas literaries de los Siglos XIV a XVI*, ed. Antonio Paz y Mélia (Madrid: Sociedad de Bibliofilos Españoles, 1892), p. xxii.

18. Contrary to this view, Gerli asserts that: "The voluminous explanations of the examples from antiquity which the author provides are wisely presented as glosses and do no more than underline his prodigious learning at an early age as well as attest to the humanistic inclinations of his spirit. Each mythological example is relevant to the narrator's context" ("Toward a Revaluation," pp. 114–15).

19. Macdonald, "The *Coronación* of Juan de Mena," p. 143.

20. "Le mythe réduit dans son caractère narratif et immobilisé dans son caractère événementiel sous forme de tableau, est par là devenu comparable à l'allégorie si chère au Moyen Age. Les allégories, par exemple, du *Roman de la Rose*—Haine, Felonie, Vilanie, Avarice, Vieillesse, Papelardie—pourraient fort bien se trouver peintes sur les murs d'un jardin: elles ne comportent aucun élément narratif ou événementiel, elles sont absolument statiques." Harald Weinrich, "Structures narratives du mythe," *Poétique* 1 (1970): 31.

21. As G. Karl Galinsky explains: "The repetitiousness of many metamorphosis stories posed a serious problem to Ovid's undertaking and, since he overcame it so brilliantly, he can afford to call attention to it with ironic playfulness. He does so at the earliest possible opportunity in Book One (1.689ff.). The only love stories we

have heard up to that point are those of Daphne and Io, which are sufficiently different from one another, not in the least because of their different metamorphoses. The third such story, that of Syrinx (1.689–712), completely repeats the pattern of the first. Daphne worships Diana; so does Syrinx. Both times a god is the suitor of an unwilling girl, and both times a river god effects the metamorphosis. In both stories a transformation takes place into a plant, which becomes the emblem of the god. Even minute details reinforce the repetitious effect, such as the mention of the golden arrow-point of Cupid (1.470) and the golden bow of Diana (1.697). The result of it all is that even Argus, who has ninety-eight more eyes than the reader, falls sound asleep after less than twelve lines of the story (1.700)" (*Ovid's "Metamorphoses": An Introduction* [Berkeley: University of California Press, 1975], p. 174).

22. Guillaume de Lorris and Jean de Meun, *Le Roman de la Rose*, ed. Ernest Langlois, 5 vols. (Paris: Société des Ançiens Textes Français, 1922), vv. 14381–94.

23. *The Romance of the Rose*, trans. Charles Dahlberg (Princeton: Princeton University Press, 1971).

24. "Dans ce text (et dans sa version en vers aussi bien que dans sa version en prose), la narration, par exemple, du mythe de Narcisse est suivie de la morale de l'histoire, c'est a dire de la traduction du récit en style argumentatif [allégorique]. Linguistiquement parlant, les signaux du discours ont changé; ce sont surtout les temps verbaux qui s'en trouve affectés. Et puisque ces signaux doivent indiquer au lecteur le comportement approprié, l'*Ovide moralisé* requiert une autre lecture, voire un autre lecteur, qu'un Ovide non moralisé." Weinrich, "Structures narratives du mythe," p. 30.

25. Cornelis de Boer, ed., *L'Ovide moralisé* (Amsterdam: Müller, 1915–38), 1.4116–31.

26. Paul de Man, "Pascal's Allegory of Persuasion," in *Allegory and Representation*, ed. Stephen J. Greenblatt (Baltimore: Johns Hopkins University Press, 1981), p. 1.

27. "Chez Guillaume de Lorris . . . l'allégorie de la rose parvient malgré tout à donner un reflet du singulier et s'écarte ainsi de la tradition allégorique du Moyen-âge: il ne décrit plus objectivement les personnifications des penchants en conflit dans le coeur de la dame; il ne les présent plus que du point de vue de l'amant, comme des aspects succesifs de l'être aimé." Hans-Robert Jauss, *Genèse de la poésie allégorique française au moyen-âge* (Heidelberg: Carl Winter, 1962), p. 23.

In this connection see also, Hans-Robert Jauss, "Form und Auffassung der Allegorie in der Tradition der *Psychomachia* (von Prudentius zum ersten *Romanz de la Rose*)," in *Medium Aevum Vivum: Festschrift für Walter Bulst*, ed. Hans-Robert Jauss and Dieter Schaller (Heidelberg: Carl Winter, 1960), pp. 179–206.

28. Strikingly unlike the protagonist of the *Siervo libre*, however, the *Satira's* protagonist does not renounce earthly love by the end of the text. His *psychomachia* (based not on religious considerations, but on his love-hate relationship with the lady) remains unresolved at the work's conclusion. Hence, I disagree with Gerli when he says that the *Satira's* "overall allegorical structure, thematic strain of sentimental complaint, and autobiographical analysis of emotions [derives from the

*Siervo libre]*" ("Toward a Revaluation," p. 111). Don Pedro sets up a similar configuration (the authoritative female personification accompanied by the Seven Virtues) in order to diverge from it boldly.

Likewise I disagree with Gerli's opinion concerning the relationship of the *Satira* to the *Triunfo de las donas*: "The *Satira*'s debt to Rodríguez del Padrón's *Triunfo de las donas* is considerably greater than to the *Siervo libre*. . . . The *Triunfo* is a general defense of all women, the *Satira* a vindication of the virtue and goodness of one woman—the narrator's alternately loved and despised lady" (ibid., p. 112). It is precisely the fact that she is an "alternately loved and despised lady" that illustrates the marked divergence of these two texts.

29.  What makes the inflated hyperbole even more apparent is the author's occasional shift to the discourse of moderation. As Gascón-Vera observes, "paradó jicamente, el prototipo de los atributos físicos del ideal de mujer expuesto por el Condestable es una mezcla de hipérbole exagerada por una parte y de absoluta moderación por la otra. A la vez que compara su belleza e inteligencia a la de las diosas paganas, pone como valor preponderante los atributos espirituales de su discreción, su gracia y su moderación en el vestir, en el mirar, en el hablar" [paradoxically, the attributes of feminine beauty developed by Don Pedro are a mixture of extreme hyperbole on the one hand, and absolute moderation on the other. At the same time that he compares her beauty and intelligence to the pagan goddesses, he emphasizes as essential the spiritual attributes of her discretion, her gracefulness and moderation in the way she dresses, the way she looks at people and the way she talks to them] (*Don Pedro*, p. 90).

30.  As follows: (1) It is the obligation of "[el] gentil, alto e virtuoso coraçon . . . aver merçed, dolor e sentimiento de los tristes infortunados" (Fonseca, 141) [the kind, lofty, and virtuous heart . . . to have mercy and compassion for those who are sad and unfortunate]; (2) the lady's cruelty blinds her, "judgando el bien por mal, la virtud por viçio, e la verdat por mentira o falsedat. Et sola esta çeguedat fasia al rey egipçio passar los mandamientos del nuestro buen Dios" (142) [leading her to mistake good for evil, virtue for vice, and truth for falsehood. It was this same blindness that led the king of Egypt to pass laws against our Lord]; (3) realizing that his quest is a lost cause, the lover concludes that "antes que nasçido me [fue] ordenado, ni creo que la bienaventurada gloria, ni las Furias infernales me fisiessen olvidarlo ni un solo punto o momento" (150) [it was so ordained before I was born, and I believe that neither eternal salvation nor the Furies of hell would be able to make me forget it or any of its details].

31.  Carolyn Van Dyke, *The Fiction of Truth* (Ithaca: Cornell University Press, 1985), p. 28.

32.  ". . . el habito intelectual de enfrentarse con un texto en disposición de completarlo, de desarrollar unos elementos que se suponen implícitos en él y aislar otros explícitos para considerarlos independientemente del contexto, de suplir datos y dar cuenta del original como si los contuviera. Es una operación lúcidamente descrita por Marie de France: 'gloser la lettre' y 'de lur sen le surplus mettre.' " Francisco Rico, *Alfonso el sabio y la "General estoria"* (Barcelona: Ariel, 1984), p. 168.

33.  That these geographical distinctions were operative in Don Pedro's day is corroborated by maps 11 and 19 of A. E. Nordenskiöld's *Facsimile Atlas to the Early*

*History of Cartography*, trans. Johan Adolf Ekelöl and Clements R. Markham (Stockholm: P. A. Norstedt, 1889).

34. The conclusion of this lengthy explanation rather humorously and laconically reads: "Pero esto se pudo dezir e aclarar en tan obscura e no usada a los indoctos materia por del todo a aquellos no quedar dubdosa e obfuscada" (174) [But this could be clarified in such an obscure way for the sake of uneducated readers so that they would not find it ambiguous].

35. Paul Zumthor, "Narrative and Anti-Narrative: *Le Roman de la Rose*," *Yale French Studies* 51 (1974): 204.

36. Focusing on the etymology of the term "allegory," Angus Fletcher reminds us: "In the simplest terms, allegory says one thing and means another. . . . Allegory would turn [something] into something other (*allos*) than what the open and direct statement tells the reader. Pushed to an extreme, this ironic usage would subvert language itself, turning everything into an Orwellian newspeak" (*Allegory: The Theory of a Symbolic Mode* [Ithaca: Cornell University Press, 1982], p. 2). Don Pedro's originality lies precisely in his bold illustration of "saying one thing and meaning another."

## SEVEN
## ETIOLOGICAL SUBVERSION—*TRISTE DELEYTAÇION*

1. Caryl Emerson, "The Outer Word and Inner Speech: Bakhtin, Vygorsky and the Internalization of Language," *Critical Inquiry* 10 (1983): 248.

2. Introducing the notion of *chronotope*, a spatiotemporal complex characteristic of every novelistic subgenre, Bakhtin makes a curious terminological remark: "The term *chronotope* is used in mathematical biology where it was introduced and adapted on the basis of [Einstein's] theory of relativity. The specific meaning it has come to have there is of little interest to us; we will introduce it here, into literary studies, somewhat like a metaphor (somewhat, but not quite)" (Tzvetan Todorov, *Mikhail Bakhtin*, trans. Wlad Godzich [Minneapolis: University of Minnesota Press, 1984], p. 14).

For further discussion of the chronotope, see also Cesare Segre, "Cronòtopo," in *Logos semantikos: Studia linguistica in Honorem Eugenio Coseriu*, ed. Horst Geckeler, Brigitte Schlieben-Lange, Jürgen Trabant, and Harald Weydt (Madrid: Gredos, 1891), vol. 1, pp. 157–64; and Segre's "What Bakhtin Left Unsaid," in *Romance: Generic Transformation from Chrétien de Troyes to Cervantes*, ed. Kevin Brownlee and Marina Scordilis Brownlee (Hanover, N.H.: University Press of New England, 1985), pp. 23–46.

3. Todorov, *Mikhail Bakhtin*, p. 83.

4. In addition, it is important to note that Bakhtin uses the term chronotope in somewhat different ways at different times. Todorov, *Mikhail Bakhtin*, p. 83, expresses this variation as follows: "Bakhtin does not use the notion of chronotope in restricted fashion, and does not limit it simply to the organization of time and space, but extends it to the organization of the world (which can be legitimately named 'chronotope' insofar as time and space are fundamental categories of every imaginable universe)."

5. Ibid., p. 52.

6. Hans-Robert Jauss, *Toward an Aesthetic of Reception*, trans. Timothy Bahti (Minneapolis: University of Minnesota Press, 1982), p. 82.

7. E. Michael Gerli, ed., *Triste deleytaçion: An Anonymous Fifteenth Century Castilian Romance* (Washington, D.C.: Georgetown University Press, 1982), pp. viii–x.

8. "Si aceptamos que la novela es autobiográfica, casi podemos tener la seguridad de interpretar una de estas iniciales, pues ya el protagonista-autor escribe siendo religioso, es muy probable que la primera letra, la .F., corresponda a *Fra*, propia de los caballeros de las órdenes militares. Avanzando en esta hipótesis podemos conjeturar que el autor de la *Triste deleytaçion* pudo ser Fra. A. de C." Martín de Riquer, "*Triste deleytaçión*, novela castellana del siglo xv," *Revista de Filología Española* 40 (1956): 56.

9. María Rosa Lida de Malkiel notes that *Triste deleytaçion*: "enumera entre los enamorados célebres a los héroes del *Siervo libre de amor*. Es probable que el oximoron de este último título haya sugerido el de *Triste deleytaçion*" (*Estudios sobre la literatura del siglo XV* [Madrid: Porrúa, 1977], p. 143).

10. All three texts (I include here the *Satira*) exhibit an interest in exposing the impossibility of romantic love. For this purpose the *Siervo libre* juxtaposes courtly and Christian values, ultimately negating the former and embracing the latter. The *Satira* similarly juxtaposes courtly and Christian values. Yet it judges both to be inadequate for the lover who both defeats the Seven Virtues and is left with a hopelessly unreciprocated love. *Triste deleytaçion* offers a different juxtaposition of discourses by contrasting the courtly ethos with the markedly different ethos of the novella world.

11. Julia Kristeva, *Desire in Language*, trans. Thomas Gora, Alice Jardine, and Leon S. Roudiez (New York: Columbia University Press, 1980), p. 67.

12. In his notes (*Triste deleytaçion*, pp. 125, 129) Gerli ennumerates the twelve stories involving amorous pairs:

6:1.  Ghismonda and Guiscardo
5:1.  Cymon and Iphigenia
5:2.  Gostanza and Martuccio
5:3.  Agnolella and Boccamazza
5:4.  Ricciardo and Caterina
5:5.  Minghino and Agnesa
5:6.  Gian di Procida and Restituta
5:8.  Nastagio degli Onesti and the daughter of Paolo Traversari
5:9.  Giovanna and Federigo degli Alberighi
7:7.  Beatrice and Anichino
7:8.  Sismonda and Ruberto
10:10.  Griselda and Gualtieri

13. Regula Langbehn-Roland, ed., *Triste deleytaçion* (Morón: Universidad de Morón, 1983). All subsequent Spanish citations are taken from this edition. All English translations are mine.

14. The blind man, priest, squire, etc., because of the impersonal, "generic"

quality of their identifications, come to represent all members of their respective classes.

15. The narrative begins in the first-person, whereby the lover recounts his misfortunes "por yo ser el mas mal tractado / de Amor y el mas leal" (2). This autobiographical account continues until page 27, where it abruptly and without explanation shifts to a third-person account of the lover: "Fforçado el enamorado de Amor, no pudo registir que el querer suyo con la presente carta a su amada senyora comunicase, y ahun dezir de Amor quanto es el poder suyo, y lo que consigo traya para que ninguno no se podia con gran trabajo d'el defender."

16. Mikhail Bakhtin, *The Dialogic Imagination*, ed. Michael Holquist (Austin: University of Texas Press, 1981), p. 388.

17. Gerli draws an analogy (*Triste deleytaçion*, p. xv) between the Lover's falling off his horse and Euryalus' falling off of his own mount in the *Historia de duobus amantibus*. However, the two are not, in fact, analogous: Euryalus' action is the stylized manifestation of being lovestruck, whereas the Lover falls off of his steed because of sheer fatigue. F.A.D.C. thus continues to exhibit his interest in contrasting the literary conventions of courtly literature with empirical reality.

18. Ibid., p. xxi.

19. The literalization of metaphorical language is a very important factor not only in *Triste deleytaçion*, but in the *novela sentimental* in general; lovers literally going mad as a result of unrequited love, commiting suicide, etc. This concretization of the metaphor is, likewise, a fundamental compositional technique of Fernando de Rojas's *La Celestina*. See in this context Stephen Gilman, "The Fall of Fortune: From Allegory to Fiction," *Filologia Romanza* 16 (1957): 337–57, and his *The Art of "La Celestina"* (Madison: University of Wisconsin Press, 1956), pp. 125ff. Another important study of this technique is Theodore L. Kassier, "*Cancionero* Poetry and the *Celestina*: From Metaphor to Reality," *Hispanófila* 56 (1976): 1–28.

20. Also in keeping with the unidealizing world of the novella is the repeated equation of the act of love not with *gloria* or some other such accustomed exalted euphemism, but with monetary remuneration. (Langbehn-Roland, *Triste deleytaçion*, pp. 19, 41, 67, 114, and 116 offer examples of this equation.)

21. Gerli, *Triste deleytaçion*, p. xvii.

22. Ibid., p. 129.

23. Dante, *Inferno* 13.124–29, ed. and trans. Charles S. Singleton (Princeton: Princeton University Press, 1970).

24. Marguerite Mills Chiarenza, "Hippolytus's Exile: Paradiso XVII, vv. 46–48," *Dante Studies* 84 (1966): 65–66.

25. Ibid., p. 66.

26. The effect of this detail is to reinforce the etiological subversion at issue throughout *Triste deleytaçion*.

27. Besides his taking of religious orders late in his life and the outcome of the *Siervo libre*, Rodríguez's rejection of courtly love is evidenced in his *canción* entitled "Fuego del divino rayo" and in the "Dezir que fizo Juan Rodríguez del Padrón contra el amor del mundo."

28. Chandler R. Post, *Medieval Spanish Allegory*, Harvard Studies in Comparative Literature, 4 (Cambridge: Harvard University Press, 1915), p. 75.

29. Ibid., p. 76.

30. Jauss, *Toward an Aesthetic of Reception*, p. 92.

31. Bakhtin, *The Dialogic Imagination*, p. 18.

33. Ibid., p. 20.

## EIGHT
### PANDERED WORDS—*ARNALTE Y LUCENDA*

1. "A tragedy, then, to be perfect according to the rules of art, should be of this construction [i.e., ending in misfortune, etc.]. Hence they are in error who censure Euripides just because he follows this principle in his plays, many of which end unhappily. It is, as we have said, the right ending. The best proof is that on the stage and in dramatic competitions, such plays, if well worked out, are the most tragic in effect; and Euripides, faulty though he may be in the *economy [oikonomia]*, is felt to be the most tragic of poets." Aristotle *Poetics* 1453a22ff, in *Aristotle's Theory of Poetry and Fine Art*, ed. S. H. Butcher (New York: Dover, 1951).

2. Marc Shell, *The Economy of Literature* (Baltimore: Johns Hopkins University Press, 1978), p. 7.

3. Shell notes the recurring exchangeability of words for money, clothing, and sex (ibid., pp. 3, 15).

4. Menéndez-Pelayo admits to only having read it in translation: "Este librito es de tan extraordinaria rareza que nunca he podido leerle en castellano" (*Orígenes de la novela* [Madrid: Bally-Ballière, 1907], 2.317).

5. This summary conforms to the one in Armando Durán, *Estructura y técnicas de la novela sentimental y caballeresca* (Madrid: Gredos, 1973), p. 25.

6. Bruce W. Wardropper, "El mundo sentimental de la *Cárcel de amor*," *Revista de Filología Española* 37 (1953): 168–69.

7. Dorothy Sherman Severin, "Structure and Thematic Repetitions in Diego de San Pedro's *Cárcel de amor* and *Arnalte y Lucenda*," *Hispanic Review* 45 (1977): 169.

8. Keith Whinnom, "Diego de San Pedro's Stylistic Reform," *Bulletin of Hispanic Studies* 37 (1960): 14.

9. I rely on the dating offered by Keith Whinnom in *Diego de San Pedro* (Boston: Twayne, 1974), p. 13.

10. Ibid., p. 86.

11. Ibid., p. 67.

12. "El léxico mismo no indica mayores variantes [que la trama] y responde a una terminología que se hace ya común en el género: desierto, soledad, temor, fatiga." Dinko Cvitanovic, *La novela sentimental española* (Madrid: Prensa Española, 1973), pp. 129–30.

13. "Somit haben wir in Arnalte einen anderen Typ des Liebhabers vor uns als in Leriano. Leriano geht in der Praxis nie von dem ab, was er in Worten ausdrückt, bei Arnalte haben wir einen Liebhaber vor uns, der in seinen Worten ganz so

höfisch ist wie er, doch in seinen Taten die höfischen Regeln über Bord wirft. Er ist durch diese Taten viel realistischer gezeichnet als der Protagonist der *Cárcel de Amor*; die Fabel besteht fast ausschliesslich aus Handlungen, die sich auf das Liebesgeschehen als solches beziehen, und dieses ist in seinen einzelnen Elementen deutlich aus einer lebendingen höfischen Realität, nicht aus einem Ideal erwachsen." Regula Langbehn-Roland, *Zur Interpretation der Romane des Diego de San Pedro* (Heidelberg: Carl Winter, 1970), p. 127.

14. "Seine Handlungen sind so gewählt, dass sie recht eigentlich in eine Komödie gehören sollten: die Verkleidungsszene, die Heimlichkeiten, der nach dem Brief suchende Page sind in sich drastische Motive, welche nach Gelächter verlangen. Doch kommt es nirgends in dem Buch zu einer wirchlich komischen Stelle, weil der elegische Ton, in welchem erzählt wird, dies alles ganz ernst erscheinen lässt, denn die Diskrepanz zwischen Rede und Handlung kommt dem Helden, der ja auch der Erzähler ist, nicht zum Bewusstsein" (ibid., 128) [His actions are so chosen that they should actually belong in a comedy: the masquerade scene, the deceptions, the page searching for the letter are in themselves drastic motifs that demand laughter. Yet it never comes in this book to a truly comic point, because the elegiac tone in which the story is told makes all of this seem quite serious; the hero, who is also the narrator, is not aware of the discrepancy between speech and action].

15. "Das buch ist, wie sich hieraus ergibt, eine Kritik an dem Verhalten eines— irgendeines, jedes—Liebhabers der Zeit Diego de San Pedros, an der Figur dieses Liebhabers selbst und seiner möglichen Verhaltensweisen, die alle an den Forderungen und Möglichkeiten der Gesellschaft scheitern, weil sie nicht rational innerhalb derselben verwirklicht werden können und doch kein tranzendentales Ziel haben" (ibid., p. 142).

16. Diego de San Pedro, *Obras completas*, vol. 1, ed. Keith Whinnom (Madrid: Castalia, 1973): 1.59.

17. In like fashion, *L'Amant resuscité de la mort* (1555) offers an additional (and highly serious) Virgilian analogy: "sera il possible que vous nous puissiez faire une Dido plus amante qu'estoit Arnalte? Sera il possible que vous nous descriviez un Eneas plus cruel et rigoreux, plus mal traittant s'amye Dido, que Lucenda a esté envers Arnalte?" [Will it be possible for you to give us a Dido who is a better lover than Arnalte? Will it be possible for you to describe to us an Aeneas who is more cruel and harsh, who treats his beloved Dido worse than Lucenda treats Arnalte?]. Gustave Reynier, *Le Roman sentimentale avant "L'Astrée"* (Paris: Colin, 1908), p. 73.

18. Whinnom, *Diego de San Pedro*, p. 81.

19. See ibid., pp. 88–95.

20. Reynier, *Le Roman sentimentale*, p. 66.

21. "Dans *Arnalte* l'intrique est dégagée de ces éléments disparates qui compliquent et alourdissent la *Prison d'Amour*. Ici ni tableau allégorique, ni digression inutile (comme la Défense des Dames); un seul épisode chevaleresque, et très court: le combat en champ clos. L'intérêt est concentré sur l'action sentimentale" (ibid., 71).

22. Ibid.

23. "Sa résolution dernière est tout à fait inexpliquée. A-t-elle aimé Yerso, le jour où il est devenu son mari? Comme Lauréole a-t-elle été offensée dans son orgueil si suceptible par le scandale d'un combat public dont elle a eu l'air d'être l'enjeu?" (ibid., 72) [Its final resolution is totally unexplained. Did she start loving Yerso the day he became her husband? Like Laureola, was her hypersensitive pride offended by the scandal of a public combat in which she seemed to be the prize?].

24. Rudolph Schevill, *Ovid and the Renascence in Spain* (Berkeley: University of California Press, 1913), p. 118.

25. Charles Kany, *The Beginnings of the Epistolary Novel in France, Italy and Spain* (Berkeley: University of California Press, 1937), p. 41.

26. "Leyendo *Arnalte y Lucenda* se puede recordar *Lazarillo de Tormes* pese a la falta de vinculación entre los géneros sentimental y picaresco. En ambos casos el protagonista (1) justifica estructuralmente su conversión en narrador, (2) explica el presente remontándose al pasado, (3) mantiene cuidadosamente su punto de vista y (4) utiliza la narración primopersonal como medio de afirmación individual. Si ese uso de la primera persona constituye la médula de la novela anónima y de una parte de la narrativa posterior, no es descabellado calificar como novelesco su empleo en *Arnalte y Lucenda*." Alfonso Rey, "La primera persona narrativa en Diego de San Pedro," *Bulletin of Hispanic Studies* 58 (1981): 98.

27. Ibid., p. 99.

28. See, in this connection, Pierre-Yves Badel, *"Le Roman de la Rose" au XIVe siècle: Etude de la réception de l'oeuvre* (Geneva: Droz, 1980), and Kevin S. Brownlee, *Poetic Identity in Guillaume de Machaut* (Wisconsin: University of Wisconsin Press, 1984).

29. Ferdinand de Saussure, *Course in General Linguistics*, trans. W. Baskin (New York: The Philosophical Library, 1959), p. 115. This concept is explored further by Jacques Derrida in his essay "La mythologie blanche," *Poétique* 5 (1971): 1–52; by R. A. Shoaf, *Dante, Chaucer, and the Currency of the Word* (Norman, Okla.: Pilgrim Books, 1983); and by Shell, *The Economy of Literature*, p. 7.

30. This and all subsequent Spanish references are to the Whinnom edition, *Obras completas*: 1.107. The English translations are mine.

31. Only for a fleeting moment does Arnalte feel jealousy toward Yerso (ibid., 1.124).

32. "Es especialmente frecuente la antítesis de palabras y de conceptos y las parejas recurrentes: servicio–galardón, pena–gloria, amores–remedio, honra–deshonra, fama–infamada, semejan arabescos en una tapicería oriental." Anna Krause, "El 'tratado' novelístico de Diego de San Pedro," *Bulletin Hispanique* 54 (1952): 273.

33. Along these same lines Lucenda says: "le quiero escrevir, a condicion que mi carta de sus guerras departidora sea; y si más entiende pedir, a pe[r]d[e]r lo cobrado se apreciba" (1.131) ["I want to write to him provided that my letter definitively end his supplications; and if he dares to ask for more, he should be prepared to lose everything"].

34. Whinnom makes an important observation in his introduction to the *Obras completas* in this regard: "la oferta—y su aceptación—del asesino del marido está en el *Yvain* francés y en una forma modificada (asesino del padre) en las *Mocedades de*

*Rodrigo*" (1.58) [the offer—and acceptance (of marriage)—to the husband's murderer exists in the French *Yvain* and, in a modified form (the father's murderer), in *Mocedades de Rodrigo*].

35. Yerso even offers Arnalte his house as a vantage point from which to hopefully catch a glimpse of Lucenda: "desde allí adelante más que Elierso su posada continué, pensando desde alla a la fermosa Lucenda ver" (1.124) ["from that time onward I visited not Elierso so much as his house, thinking that there I would have an opportunity to see the beautiful Lucenda"].

36. Patricia Grieve offers a useful discussion of the word *soledad*—its notable polysemy—which is relevant in this context: *Desire and Death in the Spanish Sentimental Romance (1440–1550)* (Newark, Del.: Juan de la Cuesta, 1987), pp. 32–38.

37. Diego de San Pedro, *Obras completas*, vol. 3, ed. Dorothy Sherman Severin and Keith Whinnom (Madrid: Castalia, 1979): 3.276. All subsequent Spanish citations refer to this edition. The English translations are mine.

38. Whinnom, *Diego de San Pedro*, p. 72.

39. Does this discrepancy perhaps imply that the assessment of the *Cárcel* and *Sermón* (Diego de San Pedro, *Obras completas*, vols. 2 and 3) as given in the *Desprecio* are similarly unreliable—a manifestation of the old-poet-recanting topos? It seems probable given the reductively critical terms in which San Pedro speaks:

> Aquella *Cárcel de Amor*
> que assí me plugo ordenar,
> ¡qué propia para amador,
> qué dulce para sabor,
> qué salsa para pecar!
> Y como la obra tal
> no tuvo en leerse calma,
> he sentido por mi mal
> cuán enemiga mortal
> fue la lengua para el alma.
>
> Y los yerros que ponía
> en un *Sermón* que escreví,
> como fue el amor la guía
> la ceguedad que tenía
> me hizo que no los vi.
> Y aquellas cartas de amores
> escriptas de dos en dos,
> ¿qué serán, dezí, señores,
> sino mis acusadores
> para delante de Dios? (3.11–30)

40. The 1491 edition, as Whinnom explains, "nos ofrece el texto más completo" (*Obras completas*, 1.79).

41. See *Obras completas*, 1.57–60.

42. See pp. 78–79.

43. Clearly this is Arnalte's assumption as well since he instructs his page to root through the garbage in search of it.

44. Cf. p. 80.

45. This analysis thus offers evidence to corroborate Whinnom's belief that San Pedro had read Piccolomini, but on totally different grounds. The filiation (which he claims "is virtually impossible to demonstrate"—"The *Historia de duobus amantibus* of Aeneas Sylvius Piccolomini (Pope Pius II) and the Development of Spanish Golden-Age Fiction," in *Essays on Narrative Fiction in the Iberian Peninsula in Honor of Frank Pierce*, ed. R. B. Tate (Oxford: Dolphin, 1982), p. 252—since he finds verbal reminiscences attributable to a common source) exists instead on the level of epistolary discourse per se.

46. "Pues como las angustias así acabase, por el desmerescer mío no merescí de Nuestra Señora ser oído; y como viese que en Dios ni en ella ni en las gentes remedio non fallava, de verme donde gentes ver no me pudiesen determiné" (1.166) ["I finished the poem and, since my unworthiness prevented me from being heard by the Virgin Mary, and realizing, furthermore, that I would not be aided either by God or by my lady or by other people, I decided to go where no one would be able to find me"].

47. The independent publication of these poems in *cancioneros* further attests to this fact.

48. On San Pedro's inscribed audience in general, see Langbehn-Roland, *Zur Interpretation der Romane*, esp. pp. 24–28.

49. Curiously, Rey himself ("La primera persona narrativa," p. 101, n. 3) makes the distinction between the "I-protagonist" and the "I-witness" configurations, but seems to conflate them in his text as he compares *Arnalte* to *Lazarillo*, saying: "en ambos casos el protagonista justifica estructuralmente su conversión en narrador" (p. 98).

50. By this distancing from Arnalte's story the narrator, if anything, is closer to the anonymous author of the *Lazarillo* who, in his prologue, undermines the values that Lázaro has chosen. In this connection see Stephen Gilman, "The Death of Lazarillo de Tormes," *Proceedings of the Modern Language Association* 81 (1966): 149–66.

## NINE
## IMPRISONED DISCOURSE—*CÁRCEL DE AMOR*

1. I thank the *Romanic Review* for permission to reprint substantial portions of my article entitled "Imprisoned Discourse in the *Cárcel de amor*," *Romanic Review* 78 (1987): 188–201.

2. John Searle, *Speech Acts: An Essay on the Philosophy of Language* (Cambridge: Cambridge University Press, 1969), p. 12.

3. Searle identifies five principal types of illocutionary acts (performative functions): representatives, directives, commissives, expressives, and declaratives. To these functions, H. P. Grice applies four sets of "conversational maxims" that are observed in acquiescing to the cooperative principle: (1) the Maxim of Quantity

("Make your contribution as informative as possible"); (2) the Maxim of Quality ("Make your contribution one that is true"); (3) the Maxim of Relation ("Be relevant"); and (4) the Maxim of Manner ("Avoid obscurity of expression"). See in this context, Mary Louise Pratt, *Toward a Speech Act Theory of Literary Discourse* (Bloomington: Indiana University Press, 1977), esp. 79ff., 125ff.

4. Bruce Wardropper, "Allegory and the Role of 'El Autor' in the *Cárcel de amor*," *Philological Quarterly* 31 (1952): 41. Also important in this connection is Dorothy Sherman Severin, "Structure and Thematic Repetitions in Diego de San Pedro's *Cárcel de amor* and *Arnalte y Lucenda*," *Hispanic Review* 45 (1977): 165–69.

5. See the introduction by Keith Whinnom in Diego de San Pedro, *Obras completas*, vol. 2, ed. Keith Whinnom (Madrid: Castalia, 1972): 2.44ff.; Joseph F. Chorpenning, "Rhetoric and Feminism in the *Cárcel de amor*," *Bulletin of Hispanic Studies* 54 (1977): 1–8; and Ivy A. Corfis, "The *Dispositio* of Diego de San Pedro's *Cárcel de amor*," *Iberomania* 21 (1985): 32–47.

6. Peter Dunn discusses this configuration of the text in his very suggestive article, "Narrator as Character in the *Cárcel de amor*," *Modern Language Notes* 94 (1979): 187–99.

7. Ibid., p. 196.

8. The entire text in fact is inscribed within a letter written to Don Diego.

9. In this regard see Elizabeth C. Traugott, "Generative Semantics and the Concept of Literary Discourse," *Journal of Literary Semantics* 2 (1973): 10ff.

10. San Pedro, *Obras completas*, 2.81. All subsequent Spanish citations from the *Cárcel* refer to this Whinnom edition (see note 5, above).

11. Nicholás Núñez, *Prison of Love (1492) Together with the Continuation by Nicolás Núñez (1496)*, trans. Keith Whinnom (Edinburgh: Edinburgh University Press, 1979). All subsequent English translations from the *Cárcel* refer to this edition.

12. On antecedents of the archetectural allegory in this text see Barbara E. Kurtz, "Diego de San Pedro's *Cárcel de amor* and the Tradition of the Allegorical Edifice," *Journal of Hispanic Philology* 8 (1984): 123–38.

13. For example, Wardropper, "Allegory and the Role of 'El Autor,'" p. 42.

14. James Mandrell, "Author and Authority in *Cárcel de amor*: The Role of 'El Autor,'" *Journal of Hispanic Philology* 8 (1984): 99–122. (This is also a further argument against the erroneous biographical identification of El Autor with San Pedro himself.) Regula Langbehn-Roland offers a useful discussion of the autobiographical discourse in her book, *Zur Interpretation der Romane des Diego de San Pedro* (Heidelberg: Carl Winter, 1970), esp. 189ff.

15. Whinnom, in his introduction to Núñez's *Prison of Love*, p. xxiv.

16. Ibid., p. xviii.

17. Ibid.

18. As such this scene recalls (contrastively) Ghismonda's metonymic consumption of Guiscardo's heart in *Decameron* 4.1 (which functions as an emblematic affirmation of amorous fulfillment).

E. Michael Gerli gives an interesting reading of this passage in terms of the *ars moriendi* tradition, as well as suggesting the Boccaccian subtext in "Leriano's Libation: Notes on the *Cancionero* Lyric, *Ars moriendi* and the Probable Debt to Boccaccio," *Modern Language Notes* 96 (1981): 414–20.

19. Diego de San Pedro, *Cárcel de amor*, ed. Jorge Rubió Balaguer (Barcelona: Gili, 1941), p. 8

20. The only possible exception to this is the brief encounter in which Leriano kisses Laureola's hand, which gives rise to Persio's slanderous accusations. In any case, however, no dialogue is recorded.

21. Moreover, it continued to be appended to San Pedro's text. As Whinnom acknowledges in his introduction, "no Spanish printer ever saw fit to discard Núñez's sequel when republishing the ever-popular *Prison of Love*, and one must seriously wonder whether the adulteration of San Pedro's message did not in some way contribute to the acceptability of their joint work" (*Prison of Love*, p. xxxii).

22. For example, Marcelino Menéndez Pelayo, *Orígenes de la novela* (Madrid: Bally-Ballière, 1905), 1.323: "aunque este suplemento fue incluído en casi todas las ediciones de la *Cárcel de amor*, nunca tuvo gran crédito, ni en realidad lo merecía, siendo cosa de todo punto pegadiza e inútil para la acción de la novela."

23. Keith Whinnom observes this parallelism in "Nicolás Núñez's Continuation of the *Cárcel de amor*," in *Studies in Spanish Literature of the Golden Age Presented to Edward M. Wilson*, ed. R. O. Jones (London: Tamesis, 1973), p. 361.

24. "*Clinamen*, which is poetic misreading or misprision proper; I take the word from Lucretius, where it means a 'swerve' of the atoms so as to make change possible in the universe. A poet swerves away from his precursor, by so reading his precursor's poem so as to execute a *clinamen* in relation to it. This appears as a corrective movement in his own poem, which implies that the precursor poem went accurately up to a certain point, but then should have swerved, precisely in the direction that the new poem moves" (Harold Bloom, *The Anxiety of Influence: A Theory of Poetry* [Oxford: Oxford University Press, 1973], p. 14).

25. Nicolás Núñez, *Cárcel de amor*, in *Dos opúsculos isabelinos*, ed. Keith Whinnom (Exeter: University of Exeter Press, 1979), p. 51. Subsequent Spanish citations refer to this edition.

26. Nicolás Núñez, *Prison of Love*, p. 83. All subsequent English translations refer to this edition (see note 11, above).

27. The progression is a definitive one, although Mandrell problematizes the trajectory from ignorance to omniscience on the basis of a detail that occurs in the final sentence—namely, that El Autor speaks of his obligation to "vuestra merced" whereas, according to the prologue, it is San Pedro who owes such fealty. As a result, Mandrell perceives "an ambivalence that works against attributing the final sentence of the work either to the narrator, El Autor, or to the author, San Pedro" ("Author and Authority," p. 119). Similarly, he observes that "El Autor, in an uncanny anticipation of Lázaro, implicates San Pedro's patron in a fictional process by ending his fiction, the story of the *cárcel*, with a reference to something that was presented as real in the Dedication and Prologue, 'vuestra merced' " (ibid., p. 119). Yet the implication is not uncanny, for all autobiographical narrative is necessarily a fictive structure (a creative re-presentation of the past that is unavoidably contaminated by the present teleological perspective of the time of writing). It is simply

this fact that San Pedro underscores in his authorial bildungsroman. For a recent and insightful treatment of the inherently fictive quality of autobiographical discourse see Paul John Eakin, *Fictions in Autobiography: Studies in the Art of Self-Invention* (Princeton: Princeton University Press, 1985).

28. Whinnom, in his introduction to *Prison of Love*, p. xxxii.

29. Proof of this "success" lies in the relationship's ability to surmount death itself.

30. See Roman Jakobson, "The Metaphoric and Metonymic Poles," in *Fundamentals of Language*, ed. Roman Jakobson and Morris Halle (Paris: Mouton, 1971), pp. 90–96.

TEN
THE BOOK AS GALEOTTO—*GRIMALTE Y GRADISSA*

1. On questions of dating, Boccaccio as subtext, and matters of technique and style, see Juan de Flores, *Grimalte y Gradissa*, ed. Pamela Waley (London: Tamesis, 1971), as well as Waley's article, "Fiammetta and Panfilo Continued," *Italian Studies* 24 (1969): 15–31. Also useful, primarily for information on sources and antecedents is Barbara Matulka, *The Novels of Juan de Flores and their European Diffusion: A Study in Comparative Literature* (New York: Institute of French Studies, 1931).

Another critic who gives lengthy consideration to the question of the *Elegia* in relation to *Grimalte* is Dinko Cvitanovič, *La novela sentimental española* (Madrid: Prensa Española, 1973). I obviously do not share his view that the importance of the Boccaccian subtext is minimal: "La historia de Fiometa . . . es apenas una parte muy exigua de la obra de Flores, a tal extremo que es su punto de partida o su continuación" (p. 274).

Known perhaps more widely in Europe as a result of its translation by Maurice Scève, *La deplourable fin de Flamete* (1535) also figures, in a fragmented way, in his lyric cycle, *Délie*. In this context, see Matulka, *The Novels of Juan de Flores*, pp. 305ff., as well as Enzo Giudici, *Maurice Scève traduttore e narratore: note su "La Deplourable fin de Flamete"* (Cassino: Garigliano, 1978).

2. Indeed, there exists in *Grimalte* considerable "verbal borrowing" from the *Elegia*, as Waley observes ("Fiammetta and Panfilo Continued," p. 24).

3. Joseph E. Gillet, "The Autonomous Character in Spanish and European Literature," *Hispanic Review* 24 (1956): 181.

4. Cervantes, *Don Quijote de la Mancha*, ed. Martin de Riquer (Barcelona: Ed. Juventud, 1968), p. 567. English translation is mine.

5. For an interesting discussion of the book-within-a-book structure of the *Grimalte*, see Barbara F. Weissberger, "Authors, Characters and Readers in *Grimalte y Gradissa*," in *Creation and Re-creation: Experiments in Literary Form in Early Modern Spain. Studies in Honor of Stephen Gilman*, ed. Ronald E. Surtz and Nora Weinerth (Newark, Del.: Juan de la Cuesta, 1983), pp. 61–76.

6. Américo Castro, "Incarnation in *Don Quijote*," in *Cervantes Across the Centuries*, ed. Mair J. Benardete and Angel Flores (New York: Dryden Press, 1947), p. 159.

7. Patricia Grieve, *Desire and Death in the Spanish Sentimental Romance, 1440–1550* (Newark, Del.: Juan de la Cuesta, 1987), p. 79.

8. All citations from Dante are taken from *Divina Commedia*, 3 vols., ed. and trans. Charles S. Singleton (Princeton: Princeton University Press, 1970–1975).

9. Italian citations from the *Decameron* are from the edition edited by Cesare Segre (Milan: Mursia, 1966); English translations are from the edition translated by G. H. McWilliam (Hammondsworth: Penguin, 1972).

10. All Spanish citations from *Grimalte y Gradissa* are taken from the edition edited by Pamela Waley (see note 1, above). The English translations are mine.

11. Matulka, *The Novels of Juan de Flores*, p. 259.

12. Waley, *Grimalte y Gradissa*, p. 1.

13. Ibid., p. 51.

14. Weissberger, "Authors, Characters and Readers," pp. 67–68.

15. Ibid., pp. 66ff.

16. Allusions to Fiammetta's situation as commonplace are found, for example, in Waley on pp. 3, 4, 17, 28, 29, 38, 48, 50, and 51.

17. Tzvetan Todorov, *Mikhail Bakhtin*, trans. Wlad Godzich (Minneapolis: University of Minnesota Press, 1984), p. 89.

18. See pp. 62–63.

19. For example, pp. 67, 249, 258, 261, 342, 343, and 344 in *Elegia di madonna Fiammetta* in *Opere di Giovanni Boccaccio*, ed. Cesare Segre (Milan: Mursia, 1966).

20. Waley, "Fiammetta and Panfilo Continued," pp. 18–19. Likewise, Weissberger speaks of this episode as a "curious epilogue" ("Authors, Characters and Readers," p. 74).

21. Waley, *Grimalte y Gradissa*, p. xxxvii. The infernal punishment of women who have abused their lovers is studied by William Allen Nielson in "The Purgatory of Cruel Beauties," *Romania* 29 (1900): 85–93.

22. English translation from *Amorous Fiammetta*, trans. Edward Hutton (Westport, Conn.: Greenwood Press, 1970).

23. Waley, *Grimalte y Gradissa*, p. lii.

24. For a discussion of this poetry see Waley, *Grimalte y Gradissa*, lv–lvii, and Grieve, *Desire and Death*, pp. 79–93.

25. The last words of the text constitute a surprising admission by Flores, namely, that the poetry contained throughout his text was composed not by him but by Alonso de Córdoba: "La sepultura de Fiometa, con las coplas y canciones quantas son en este tractado, hizo Alonso de Cordova. Y acaba la obra. Deo gratias" (Waley, *Grimalte y Gradissa*, p. 74).

Waley finds the poems to be quite irrelevant to the discursive structure of Flores' text: "They add nothing to the narrative or the subject matter and have little poetic merit, and the fact that they were written not by Flores but by Alonso de Córdoba, of whom no other writings are known, would seem to make them alien to the conception of the novel were it not that each verse or set of verses is introduced in the course of the prose text" (ibid., p. lvi).

I disagree with her interpretation of the poetry. This information is entirely consistent with Flores' basic discursive belief that it is neither the choice of genre nor the particular words that determine the receptivity of the addressee. The same words can be uttered in a variety of contexts to different effect. Here we have thought all along that Grimalte/Flores was reciting words of his own invention (reflections of his own affect), whereas in fact they had been composed previously by another poet, for a completely different context. (The final poem, for example, "Los pensamientos de amor . . . ," is taken from *Tristán de Leonís*, a poem of lament uttered by the knight Melianes who is in love with Queen Ginebra.)

26. Grieve, *Desire and Death*, p. 92.

## ELEVEN
## LANGUAGE AND INCEST—*GRISEL Y MIRABELLA*

1. Michel Foucault, "What Is an Author?" in *Textual Strategies: Perspectives in Post-Structural Criticism*, ed. Josué Harari (Ithaca: Cornell University Press, 1979), p. 148.

I thank the *Romanic Review* for permission to reprint here my article "Language and Incest in *Grisel y Mirabella*," *Romanic Review* 79 (1988): 107–28.

2. Echoing Marcelino Menéndez Pelayo's comment, Carmelo Samonà characterizes *Grisel* as an "esile cornice narrativa che racchiude il nucleo dottrinale del *debate*" (*Studi sul romanzo sentimentale e cortese nella letteratura spagnola del quattrocento* [Rome: Carucci, 1960], p. 109). Samonà is justified in underscoring the prominence of dialogue in this text since no less than three-fourths of it is taken up by debate. This dialogic structure is suggestively viewed by Samonà as having an undeniable impact on *La Celestina* (ibid., p. 113).

3. Barbara Matulka sees *Grisel* as she saw *Grimalte*, namely, as a stridently pro-feminist text. Thus Torrellas' death at the hands of outraged females is interpreted as exemplary: "In describing so minutely the cruel torture and death of Torrellas [Flores] seems to have adapted the punishment which the other famous misogynist, the Archpriest of Talavera, had suggested as a suitable vengeance of the irate ladies against whom he had thundered his violent abuse" (*The Novels of Juan de Flores and their European Diffusion: A Study in Comparative Literature* [New York: Institute of French Studies, 1931], p. 116). Indeed, Matulka further asserts that Torrellas' minutely (i.e., realistically) described death was not only accepted as just, but in addition that "it was taken as a historical fact and set up as an example of the cruel fate that awaited the enemies of women" (ibid., p. 166).

4. Italian citations from the *Decameron* are from the edition edited by Cesar Segre (Milan: Mursia, 1966); English translations are from the edition translated by G. H. McWilliam (Hammondsworth: Penguin, 1972).

5. Balducci's words of caution not only fail to convince his son, but his metaphoric attempt at deception gets him into further trouble: "'Io non voglio; tu non sai donde elle s'imbeccano!'—e sentí incontanente piú aver di forza la natura che il suo ingegno" (Segre, 257) ["Certainly not," said his father. "Their bills are not where you think, and require a special sort of diet." But no sooner had he spoken than he realized that his wits were no match for Nature (McWilliam, 328)].

6. Jacques Derrida, *Of Grammatology*, trans. Gayatri Spivak (Baltimore: Johns Hopkins University Press, 1976), pp. lxv–lxvi.

7. Milicent Marcus, in her book *An Allegory of Form* (Palo Alto: Anma Libri, 1979), pp. 52ff., offers an illuminating series of examples of the reversed sex roles exhibited by Ghismonda's "virile" composure and Tancredi's "feminine" lachrimosity. I would add that this inversion is meant not simply to highlight Tancredi's unnatural love for his daughter, but also to emphasize the greater authority of her discourse since she comports herself with the controlled, regal demeanor that the distraught prince himself lacks.

8. Guido Almansi, *The Writer as Liar: Narrative Technique in the "Decameron"* (London: Routledge and Kegan Paul, 1975), pp. 141–42.

9. Several critics have commented on the fact that Guiscardo's words echo those of Francesca da Rimini in *Inferno* 5 of the *Divine Comedy*. Luigi Russo, for example, distinguishes Ghismonda from Francesca saying that the latter exhibited an interest in spiritualized love, the former a carnal attraction (*Letture critiche del "Decameron"* [Rome: Laterza, 1986], p. 159). By contrast, Marcus recalls that "Francesca makes the body the exclusive subject of her lament" (*An Allegory of Form*, p. 48).

Yet it is important to note that Ghismonda is in fact morally superior for two reasons. First, because she chose Guiscardo as a result of her ethical concern for spiritual (as opposed to titular) nobility. Second, she initiated the relationship only because her father would not allow her to remarry. Francesca's motivation is quite another matter. She was married at the time, thus yielding to lust by her involvement with a married man (Paolo Malatesta), her husband's younger brother.

10. Michael Holquist, "Answering as Authoring: Mikhail Bakhtin's Trans-Linguistics," *Critical Inquiry* 10 (1983): 312.

11. Guido Almansi, *The Writer as Liar*, p. 150.

12. Marcus speaks of Tancredi's "triumph": at the time of their deaths he "gains ascendancy over the couple in his capacity as father and king" (*An Allegory of Form*, p. 60). However, if he may be said to gain ascendancy, it is only after he has undergone a painful process of linguistic education, a kind of purgation whereby he finally must admit the referentiality of language, the all-important relationship of word to deed, by acknowledging his fault and publicly burying the lovers together.

13. Giuseppe Mazzotta, *The World at Play in Boccaccio's "Decameron"* (Princeton: Princeton University Press, 1986), p. 134.

14. Ibid., p. 158.

15. Ibid., p. 151.

16. Marcus focuses her interesting analysis of *Decameron* 4.1 on the significance of metaphor in this tale. Indicating that this figure of language characterizes Ghismonda's affair from its inception (*An Allegory of Form*, p. 59), Marcus sees its function here (as in Balducci's tale) as serving to illustrate reality rather than masking it (ibid., p. 51). I would argue, however, that it is not metaphor that conceals or reveals "truth," but the perspective of the enunciator and interlocutor that is the issue. Although, for example, Balducci himself exploits metaphor to mask the truth, his son does not perceive it as such; for him it does serve to illuminate the situation, in this case that the attractive creatures are called "gosslings."

In this connection, Marcus's claim that Tancredi violates "the terms of metaphor itself by presenting Guiscardo's heart to 'gli occhi della fronte' " (ibid., p. 60) is relevant, for it illustrates, I would argue, that metonymy is as much an issue in this novella as is the concretization of metaphor. Indeed, Tancredi's fundamental problem results from his metonymic misperception of his daughter, that she is not autonomous but an inseparable part of his identity. The "correction" of this misperception occurs only at the tale's end, when the metonymic identification of Guiscardo and Ghismonda is definitively (and publicly) acknowledged by him. Not only does Ghismonda clutch Guiscardo's heart to hers, but they are fixed in a perpetual metonymically contiguous posture by sharing the same casket. It is thus the referentiality both of his metaphoric and metonymic usage that Tancredi finally learns to correct at the expense of his daughter's life.

17. *Grisel y Mirabella*, in *The Novels of Juan de Flores* (see note 3, above). All Spanish citations refer to Matulka's edition. The English translations are mine.

18. Although she analyzes *Grisel* in regard to *Decameron* 4.1, Matulka does not perceive the relationship of the Scottish king's linguistic transgression to that of his Italian predecessor.

19. As R. Howard Bloch explains, "the judicial duel belongs to the series of ordeals common to any primitive sense of justice in which legal process remains indistinguishable from divine law" (*Medieval French Literature and Law* [Berkeley: University of California Press, 1977], p. 18).

20. "In the [twelfth-century] lives of St. Kentigern we find very clearly explained an ancient 'Law of Scotland,' according to which the king carries out, against his own daughter, the penalty of death for illicit love while unmarried" (Matulka, *Grisel y Mirabella*, p. 162).

21. That this debate is not just extraneous, but novel as well, is reflected in the title of an English adaptation of *Grisel: A Paire of Turtle Doves: or, the Tragicall end of Agamio, wherein (besides other matters pleasing to the reader) by way of dispute between a knight and a lady is described this never before debated question, to wit: Whether man to woman, or woman to man offer the greatest temptations and allurements unto unbrideled lust, and consequently whether man or w[o]man in that unlawful act, be the greater offender*. (See Everett Ward Olmstead, "The Story of *Grisel and Mirabella*" in *Homenaje ofrecido a Menéndez Pidal: Miscelánea de estudios lingüísticos, literarios e históricos*, 2 vols. [Madrid: Hernando, 1925], 2.371–72.)

22. A. D. Deyermond notes this inversion in his book entitled *A Literary History of Spain* (London: Ernest Benn, 1971), p. 165.

23. Patricia Grieve observes that Torrellas' death constitutes a recapitulation of all the other deaths: "At least one aspect of each of the other deaths can be found in the spectacular torture-murder of Torrellas. The knights die somehow because of an entrapment of Mirabella's beauty. Otro Caballero [the Other Knight], like Torrellas, was slain during the night by a friend. His words were the cause of his death, since Grisel found offensive the suggestions made by Otro Caballero. Because of Torrellas' verbal debasement of women, resulting, ultimately, in Mirabella's suicide, the Queen sought his death. Grisel's suicide was a leap into the flames (like the flames of love), while Torrellas was tortured by 'fieras llagas.' After Mirabella's leap during the night into the courtyard, hungry lions devoured every inch of her flesh, leaving only her bones. Her mother and ladies-in-waiting metamorphosed by rage into lion-like creatures, clawed the flesh from Torrellas' bones until none remained"

(*Desire and Death in the Spanish Sentimental Romance, 1440–1550* [Newark, Del.: Juan de la Cuesta, 1987], p. 67).

I would add that these reminiscences force us to compare each of the deaths in relation to that of the calculating, professional misuser of language, Torrellas, and, ultimately, to linguistic usage itself. In so doing, what becomes apparent is that these multiple deaths reflect a number of different attitudes toward language.

24. René Girard, *Violence and the Sacred*, trans. Patrick Gregory (Baltimore: Johns Hopkins University Press, 1977), p. 37.

25. Ibid., p. 148.

26. For an alternate reading see Grieve (*Desire and Death*, pp. 70–73), who views the text as an illustration of Girard's principle, as a "demythification" of love and its destructive effects.

27. "Ex linguis gentes, non ex gentibus linguae exortae sunt" (San Isidro, *Etimologías*, 2 vols., ed. José Oroz Reto [Madrid: Biblioteca de Autores Cristianos, 1983], vol. 1: 9.1.14.

28. R. Howard Bloch, *Etymologies and Genealogies* (Chicago: University of Chicago Press, 1983), p. 160.

29. Roman Jakobson, "The Metaphoric and Metonymic Poles," in *Fundamentals of Language*, ed. Roman Jakobson and Morris Halle (Paris: Mouton, 1971), p. 92.

30. Julia Kristeva, *Desire in Language*, trans. Thomas Gora, Alice Jardine, and Leon S. Roudiez (New York: Columbia University Press, 1980), p. 137.

31. Kristeva's interest here is for "the intrinsic connection between literature and breaking up social concord: Because it utters incest, poetic language is linked with 'evil'; 'literature and evil' (I refer to a title by Georges Bataille) [and] should be understood, beyond the resonances of Christian ethics, as the social body's self-defense against the discourse of incest as destroyer and generator of any language and sociality. This applies all the more as 'great literature,' which has mobilized unconsciousness for centuries, has nothing to do with the hypostasis of incest (a petty game of fetishists at the end of an era, priesthood of a would-be enigma—the forbidden mother); on the contrary, this incestuous relation, exploding in language, embracing it from top to bottom in such a *singular* fashion . . . defies *generalizations* [yet] still has this common feature in all outstanding cases: it presents itself as demystified" (ibid., p. 137).

32. For a discussion of romance and the social threat it poses, especially in terms of the Tristan myth, see Denis de Rougement, *Love in the Western World*, trans. Montgomery Belgion (Princeton: Princeton University Press, 1983).

## EPILOGUE

1. In this context, see A. D. Deyermond, "El hombre salvaje en la novela sentimental." *Filología* 10 (1964): 97–111.

2. In his book *Wild Men in the Middle Ages* (Cambridge: Harvard University Press, 1952) Richard Bernheimer describes the generalized portrait of the medieval wildman as follows: "The picture drawn by medieval authors of the appearance and

life of the wild man is . . . very largely a negative one, dominated by the loss or absence of faculties which make human beings what they are. The wild man may be without the faculty of human speech, the power to recognize or conceive of the Divinity, or the usual meaningful processes of the mind. What remains after losses of this kind of magnitude, is a creature human only in overall physical appearance, but so degenerate that to call him a beast were more than an empty metaphor" (p. 9). It is important to note that Arnalte, Grimalte, and Panfilo do not conform to this portrait. They have chosen a life of speechless solitude, which results not from bestial madness but their sense of alienation from language, its performative inefficacy and lack of referentiality .

The other familiar association of the wild man is with lust. We find this portrayal in the figure of Deseo personified at the beginning of the *Cárcel* (Whinnom, 2.81ff.).

3. See Sharon Cameron, *Lyric Time: Dickinson and the Limits of Genre* (Baltimore: Johns Hopkins University Press, 1979), pp. 201–73.

4. Stephen Gilman, *The Spain of Fernando de Rojas: The Intellectual and Social Landscape of "La Celestina"* (Princeton: Princeton University Press, 1972), p. 357.

5. Michel Foucault, "What Is an Author?" in *Textual Strategies: Perspectives in Post-Structural Criticism*, ed. Josué Harari (Ithaca: Cornell University Press, 1979), p. 159.

6. This structural similarity is noted by Peter G. Earle in "Love Concepts in *La Cárcel de amor* and *La Celestina*," *Hispania* 39 (1956), p. 92

7. See, for example, Florentino Castro Guisasola, *Observaciones sobre las fuentes literarias de "La Celestina"* (1924; reprint, Madrid: Consejo Superior de Investigaciones Científicas, 1973), and María Rosa Lida, *La originalidad artística de "La Celestina"* (Buenos Aires: Editorial Universitaria de Buenos Aires, 1962).

8. For a different aspect of the role of "literature as immediacy" in Spain, see Harry Sieber, "The Romance of Chivalry in Spain: From Rodríguez de Montalvo to Cervantes," in *Romance: Generic Transformation from Chrétien de Troyes to Cervantes*, ed. Kevin Brownlee and Marina Scordilis Brownlee (Hanover, N.H.: University Press of New England, 1985), pp. 203–19.

9. *Triste deleytaçion*, for example, projects such an urban, "realistic" contemporary Spanish milieu (the year 1458) despite the occasional appearance of certain allegorical figures and revivified historical characters. To a considerable extent, *Arnalte* also exhibits an interest in this type of chronotopic milieu.

10. See Miguel Marciales, *Sobre problemas riojanos y celestinescos [Carta al Dr. Stephen Gilman a propósito del libre "The Spain of Fernando de Rojas"]*. Mérida: Universidad de los Andes, 1983.

11. Gilman, *The Spain of Fernando de Rojas*, p. 388.

12. See p. 171, note 16. *Arnalte* effects a similar equation of *amor* and *pago*; see pp. 150ff.

13. An additional feature presented as a radical innovation of *La Celestina* is the abundance of dialogue. Here, too, it is anticipated by the *novela sentimental*. The preponderance of debate in *Grisel* is interpreted by Carmelo Samonà as an undeniable influence on the technique of *La Celestina* (*Studi sul romanzo sentimentale e cortese nella letteratura spagnola del quattrocento* [Rome: Carruci, 1960], p. 113).

On an even more basic level, the letter is essentially "an exchange of written dialogue," as Patrizia Violi observes in her analysis, "Letters," in *Discourse and Literature*, ed. Teun van Dijk (Amsterdam: J. Benjamins, 1985), p. 149. The oral communication found in Rojas' text owes much to the written dialogic communication which is one of the hallmarks of the *novela sentimental*.

14. Gilman, *The Spain of Fernando de Rojas*, p. 372. Speaking of Rojas' distortion of exemplary commonplaces of a different sort, Theodore L. Kassier observes that: "Ultimately, the concern with the *cancionero*, and the work's partial basis on a negative reading of it, suggests a role for late medieval love poetry in the *Celestina* similar to that of the *libros de caballerías* in the *Quijote*" ("*Cancionero* Poetry and the *Celestina*," *Hispanófila* 56 [1976]: 3). Along similar lines, Peter Earle remarks that "it is perhaps not an over-simplification to say that *La Celestina* is to the sentimental novel as Don Quijote is to the chivalric novel. The greatness of *Don Quijote*, Menéndez Pelayo has observed, consists more in what it adds to pre-existent chivalric ideology than in what it satirizes" ("Love Concepts," p. 92). Yet, of course, the type of novelistic, Cervantine undermining of genres that both Kassier and Earle rightly observe as being at issue in *La Celestina* is operative throughout the *novela sentimental* corpus.

15. Gilman, *The Spain of Fernando de Rojas*, p. 383.

16. Of this tremendous vogue Daniel Eisenberg writes: "The romances of chivalry's greatest popularity in Castile coincides nearly with the reign of Charles V (1517–1555). During this time the composition and publication of new romances, and the reprinting of the classics of the genre, flourished as it never had before and never would again. New romances were published at the rate of almost one per year during this period, and there were twelve editions of the *Amadís* and eight of *Palmerín*. It was during this period that many of the romances which were to prove most popular were written: the works of Feliciano de Silva, *Belianís de Grecia*, Part I of the *Espejo de príncipes y cavalleros*" (*Romances of Chivalry in the Spanish Golden Age* [Newark, Del.: Juan de la Cuesta, 1982], pp. 40–41).

17. This shift corroborates Jakobson's perception of the diachronically alternative predominance of greater or lesser referentiality based on his conception of metaphor and metonomy. (See in this regard the discussion on pp. 175 and 209 above.) Moreover, this alternation is, according to Jakobson, operative in other sign systems as well: "A salient example from the history of painting is the manifestly metonymical orientation of cubism, where the object is transformed into a set of synecdoches; the surrealist painters responded with a patently metaphorical attitude" (Roman Jakobson, "The Metaphoric and Metonymic Poles," in *Fundamentals of Language*, ed. Roman Jakobson and Morris Halle [Paris: Mouton, 1971], p. 92).

# BIBLIOGRAPHY

## PRIMARY SOURCES

Alfonso X. *General estoria*. Segunda Parte 1–2. Edited by Antonio G. Solalinde, Lloyd R. Kasten, and Victor R. B. Oelschläeger. Madrid: Consejo Superior de Investigaciones Científicas, 1957–1961.

Alighieri, Dante. *Divina Commedia*. 3 vols. Edited and translated by Charles S. Singleton. Princeton: Princeton University Press, 1970–1975.

———. *De vulgare eloquentia*. Edited by Pier Vincenzo Mengaldo. Padova: Ed. Antenore, 1968.

Aristotle. *Poetics* [*Aristotle's Theory of Poetry and Fine Art*]. Edited by S. H. Butcher. New York: Dover, 1951.

Boccaccio, Giovanni. *Amorous Fiammetta*. Translated by Edward Hutton. Westport, Conn.: Greenwood Press, 1970.

———. *Decameron*. Edited by Cesare Segre. Milan: Mursia, 1966.

———. *The Decameron*. Translated by G. H. McWilliam. Hammondsworth: Penguin, 1972.

———. *Elegia di madonna Fiammetta*. In *Opere di Giovanni Boccaccio*, edited by Cesare Segre. Milan: Mursia, 1966.

Borges, Jorge Luis. *Otras inquisiones*. Buenos Aires: Sur, 1963.

Cervantes, Miguel de. *Don Quijote de la Mancha*. Edited by Martín de Riquer. Barcelona: Ed. Juventud, 1968.

Condestable de Portugal. *Satira de infelice e felice vida*. In *Obras completas do condestável dom Pedro*. Edited by Luís Adão da Fonseca. Lisbon: Fundação Calouste Gulbenkian, 1975.

———. *Satira de felice e infelice vida*. In Vol. 29 of *Opúsculas literaries de los Siglos XIV a XVI*. Edited by Antonio Paz y Mélia. Madrid: Sociedad de Bibliofilos Españoles, 1892.

De Boer, Cornelis, ed. *L'Ovide moralisé*. 5 vols. Amsterdam: Müller, 1915–38.

Flores, Juan de. *Grimalte y Gradissa*. Edited by Pamela Waley. London: Tamesis, 1971.

———. *Grisel y Mirabella*. In *The Novels of Juan de Flores and their European Diffusion*. Edited by Barbara Matulka. New York: Institute of French Studies, 1931.

Gerli, E. Michael, ed. *Triste deleytaçion: An Anonymous Fifteenth Century Castilian Romance*. Washington, D.C.: Georgetown University Press, 1982.

Langbehn-Roland, Regula, ed. *Triste deleytaçion*. Morón: Universidad de Morón, 1983.

Livy. *Titi Livi ab urbe condita*. Edited by R. M. Ogilvie. Oxford: Clarendon, 1974.

Lorris, Guillaume de and Jean de Meun. *Le Roman de la Rose*. 5 vols. Edited by Ernest Langlois. Paris: Société des Ançiens Textes Français, 1922.

———. *The Romance of the Rose*. Translated by Charles Dahlberg. Princeton: Princeton University Press, 1971.

Núñez, Nicolás. *Cárcel de amor*. In *Dos opúsculos isabelinos*. Edited by Keith Whinnom. Exeter: University of Exeter Press, 1979.

———. *Prison of Love (1492) Together with the Continuation by Nicolás Núñez (1496)*. Translated by Keith Whinnom. Edinburgh: Edinburgh University Press, 1979.

Ovid. *Ars amatoria*. Translated by J. H. Mosley. Cambridge: Harvard University Press, 1929.

———. *"Heroides" and "Amores."* Translated by Grant Showerman. Cambridge: Harvard University Press, 1977.

———. *Metamorphoses*. Translated by Frank Justus Miller. Cambridge: Harvard University Press, 1977.

———. *Tristia: Ex Ponto*. Translated by Arthur Leslie Wheller. Cambridge: Harvard University Press, 1965.

Piccolomini, Aeneas Sylvius. *De duobus amantibus historia*. Edited by Josephus Dévay. Budapest: Heislerus, 1903.

———. *The Tale of Two Lovers*. Translated by Flora Grierson. London: Constable, 1929.

Rodríguez del Padrón, Juan. *El Bursario*. In *Obras de Juan Rodríguez del Padrón*, edited by Antonio Paz y Mélia. Madrid: Sociedad de Bibliófilos Españoles, 1884.

———. *El Bursario*. Edited by Pilar Saquero Suárez-Somonte and Tomás González Rolán. Madrid: Universidad Complutense, 1984.

———. *"Siervo libre de amor."* Edited by César Hernández Alonso. Ph.D. diss., Universidad de Valladolid, 1970.

———. *Siervo libre de amor*. Edited by Antonio Prieto. Madrid: Castalia, 1976.

Rojas, Fernando de. *"La Celestina."* 2 vols. Edited by Miguel Marciales. Urbana: University of Illinois Press, 1985.

———. *La Celestina*. Edited by Dorothy Sherman Severin. Madrid: Alianza, 1969.

San Isidro. *Etimologías*. 2 vols. Edited by José Oroz Reto. Madrid: Biblioteca de Autores Cristianos, 1983.

San Pedro, Diego de. *Cárcel de amor*. Edited by Jorge Rubió Balaguer. Barcelona: Gili, 1941.

———. *Obras completas*. Vol. 1, *Tractado de amores de Arnalte y Lucenda* and *Sermón*, edited by Keith Whinnom. Madrid: Castalia, 1973. Vol. 2, *Cárcel de amor*, edited by Keith Whinnom. Madrid: Castalia, 1972. Vol. 3, *Poesías*, edited by Dorothy Sherman Severin and Keith Whinnom. Madrid: Castalia, 1979.

———. *Prison of Love (1492) Together with the Continuation by Nicolás Núñez (1496)*. Translated by Keith Whinnom. Edinburgh: Edinburgh University Press, 1979.

Virgil. *The Aeneid*. Edited by H. R. Fairclough. Cambridge: Harvard University Press, 1974.

———. *The Aeneid*. Translated by Allen Mandlebaum. New York: Bantam, 1971.

## SECONDARY SOURCES

Alatorre, Antonio. *Las "Heroidas" de Ovidio y su huella en las letras españolas.* Mexico City: Universidad Nacional Autónoma de México, 1950.

Allen, Judson Boyce. *The Ethical Poetic of the Later Middle Ages.* Toronto: University of Toronto Press, 1982.

Almansi, Guido. *The Writer as Liar: Narrative Technique in the "Decameron."* London: Routledge and Kegan Paul, 1975.

Altman, Janet Gurkin. *Epistolarity: Approaches to a Form.* Columbus: Ohio State University Press, 1982.

————. "The 'Triple Register': Introduction to Temporal Complexity in the Letter-Novel." *L'Esprit Créateur* 17 (1977): 302–10.

Anderson, William S. "The *Heroides.*" In *Ovid,* edited by J. W. Binnis. London: Routledge and Kegan Paul, 1973.

Andrachuk, Gregory Peter. "A Further Look at the Italian Influence in the *Siervo libre de amor.*" *Journal of Hispanic Philology* 6 (1981–82): 45–56.

————. "On the Missing Third Part of the *Siervo libre de amor.*" *Hispanic Review* 45 (1977): 171–80.

————. "Prosa y poesía en el *Siervo libre de amor.*" In *Actas del sexto congreso internacional de hispanistas,* edited by Alan M. Gordon and Evelyn Rugg, pp. 60–62. Toronto: Asociación Internacional de Hispanistas, 1980.

Asensio, Eugenio. *Poética y realidad en el cancionero peninsular de la edad media.* Madrid: Gredos, 1957.

Ashton, J. R. "Ovid's 'Heroides' as Translated by Alphonso the Wise." Ph.D. diss., University of Wisconsin, 1944.

Badel, Pierre-Yves. *"Le Roman de la Rose" au XIVe siècle: Etude de la réception de l'oeuvre.* Geneva: Droz, 1980.

Bakhtin, Mikhail. *The Dialogic Imagination.* Edited by Michael Holquist. Austin: University of Texas Press, 1981.

Barthes, Roland. *A Lover's Discourse.* Translated by Richard Howard. New York: Hill and Wang, 1978.

Bastianutti, D. L. "La función de la fortuna en la primera novela sentimental española." *Romance Notes* 14 (1972): 394–402.

Benveniste, Emile. *Problems in General Linguistics.* Translated by Mary Elizabeth Meek. Coral Gables: University of Miami Press, 1971.

Bergin, Thomas. *Boccaccio.* New York: Viking Press, 1981.

Berndt-Kelley, Erna Ruth. *Amor, muerte y fortuna el 'La Celestina.'* Madrid: Gredos, 1963.

Bernheimer, Richard. *Wild Men in the Middle Ages.* Cambridge: Harvard University Press, 1952.

Bloch, R. Howard. *Etymologies and Genealogies.* Chicago: University of Chicago Press, 1983.

————. *Medieval French Literature and Law.* Berkeley: University of California Press, 1977.

Bloom, Harold. *The Anxiety of Influence: A Theory of Poetry.* Oxford: Oxford University Press, 1973.

Branca, Vittore. *Boccaccio: The Man and His Works*. Translated by Richard Monges. New York: New York University Press, 1976.

Brownlee, Kevin S. *Poetic Identity in Guillaume de Machaut*. Madison: University of Wisconsin Press, 1984.

Brownlee, Marina S. "The Generic Status of the *Siervo libre de amor*: Rodríguez del Padrón's Reworking of Dante." *Poetics Today* 5 (1984): 629–43.

———. "Imprisoned Discourse in the *Cárcel de amor*." *Romanic Review* 78 (1987): 188–201.

———. "Language and Incest in *Grisel y Mirabella*." *Romanic Review* 79 (1988): 107–28.

Bursill-Hall, R. *Speculative Grammars of the Middle Ages*. Paris: Mouton, 1971.

Cameron, Sharon. *Lyric Time: Dickinson and the Limits of Genre*. Baltimore: Johns Hopkins University Press, 1979.

Castro, Américo. "Incarnation in *Don Quijote*." In *Cervantes Across the Centuries*, edited by Mair J. Benardete and Angel Flores, pp. 136–78. New York: Dryden Press, 1947.

Castro Guisasola, Florentino. *Observaciones sobre las fuentes literarias de "La Celestina."* 1924. Reprint. Madrid: Consejo Superior de Investigaciones Científicas, 1973.

Cerquiglini, Bernard. *La parole médiévale*. Paris: Minuit, 1981.

Cerquiglini, Jacqueline. "Typology of Lyric Manuscripts of the Fourteenth and Fifteenth Centuries with Emphasis on Machaut." Paper delivered at the 1986 NEH Medieval Workshop at Mount Holyoke College, South Hadley, Mass.

Chiarenza, Marguerite Mills. "Hippolytus's Exile: Paradiso xvii, vv. 46–48." *Dante Studies* 84 (1966): 65–68.

Chorpenning, Joseph F. "Rhetoric and Feminism in the *Cárcel de amor*." *Bulletin of Hispanic Studies* 54 (1977): 1–8.

Constable, Giles. *The Letters of Peter the Venerable*. 2 vols. Cambridge: Harvard University Press, 1967.

Constans, Léopold. "Une Traduction française des *Heroïdes* d'Ovide au XIIIe siècle." *Romania* 43 (1914): 177–98.

Corfis, Ivy A. "The *Dispositio* of Diego de San Pedro's *Cárcel de amor*." *Iberomania* 21 (1985): 32–47.

Crescini, Vincenzo. *Contributo agli studi sul Boccaccio con documenti inediti*. Turin: E. Loescher, 1887.

Cummins, J. G. "Pero Guillén de Segovia y el ms. 4144." *Hispanic Review* 41 (1973): 6–32.

Cvitanovič, Dinko. *La novela sentimental española*. Madrid: Prensa Española, 1973.

Dagenais, John. "Juan Rodríguez del Padrón's Translation of the Latin *Bursarii*: New Light on the Meaning of Tra(c)tado." *Journal of Hispanic Philology* 10 (1986): 117–39.

Da Imola, Benvenuto. *Comentum super Dantis Aldigherij "Comoediam."* Edited by J. P. Lacaita. Florence: G. Barbera, 1887.

Damiani, Bruno. "The Didactic Intention of the *Cárcel de amor*." *Hispanófila* 56 (1976): 29–43.

Day, Robert. *Told in Letters*. Ann Arbor: University of Michigan Press, 1966.

De Man, Paul. "Pascal's Allegory of Persuasion." In *Allegory and Representation*, edited by Stephen J. Greenblatt, pp. 1–25. Baltimore: Johns Hopkins University Press, 1981.

Dembowski, Peter F. "Vocabulary of Old French Courtly Lyrics—Difficulties and Hidden Difficulties." *Critical Inquiry* 2 (1976): 763–79.

De Rougement, Denis. *Love in the Western World*. Translated by Montgomery Belgion. Princeton: Princeton University Press, 1983.

Derrida, Jacques. *La carte postale*. Paris: Flammarion, 1980.

———. "La mythologie blanche." *Poétique* 5 (1971): 1–52.

———. *Of Grammatology*. Translated by Gayatri Spivak. Baltimore: Johns Hopkins University Press, 1976.

Deyermond, A. D. "El hombre salvaje en la novela sentimental." *Filología* 10 (1964): 97–111.

———. *A Literary History of Spain*. London: Ernest Benn, 1971.

———. "The Lost Genre of Medieval Spanish Literature." *Hispanic Review* 48 (1975): 231–59.

———. "Las relaciones genéricas de la ficción sentimental española." In *Symposium in honorem Prof. Martín de Riquer*, edited by A. D. Deyermond and Antoni M. Badia i Margarit. Barcelona: Universidad de Barcelona, 1986, pp. 75–92.

Donato, Eugenio. " 'Per selve e boscherecci laberinti': Desire and Narrative Structure in Ariosto's *Orlando Furioso*." *Barroco* 4 (1972): 17–32.

Dörrie, Heinrich. *Der heroische Brief*. Berlin: Walter de Gruyter, 1968.

Dudley, Edward. "Court and Country: The Fusion of Two Images of Love in Juan Rodríguez's *El siervo libre de amor*." *Proceedings of the Modern Language Association* 82 (1967): 117–20.

———. *Structure and Meaning in the Novel of Juan Rodríguez del Padrón: "Siervo libre de amor."* Ph.D. diss., University of Minnesota, 1963.

Dunn, Peter. "Narrator as Character in the *Cárcel de amor*." *Modern Language Notes* 94 (1979): 187–99.

Durán, Armando. *Estructura y técnicas de la novela sentimental y caballeresca*. Madrid: Gredos, 1973.

Durling, Robert. " 'Giovenne donna sotto un verde lauro.' " *Modern Language Notes* 86 (1971): 1–20.

Dutton, Brian. " 'Buen amor': Its Meaning and Uses in Some Medieval Texts." In *"Libro de buen amor" Studies*, edited by G. B. Gybbon-Monypenny, pp. 95–121. London: Tamesis, 1970.

Eakin, Paul John. *Fictions in Autobiography: Studies in the Art of Self-Invention*. Princeton: Princeton University Press, 1985.

Earle, Peter G. "Love Concepts in *La Cárcel de amor* and *La Celestina*." *Hispania* 39 (1956): 92–96.

Eco, Umberto. *A Theory of Semiotics*. Bloomington: Indiana University Press, 1976.

Eisenberg, Daniel. *Romances of Chivalry in the Spanish Golden Age*. Newark, Del.: Juan de la Cuesta, 1982.

Emerson, Caryl. "The Outer Word and Inner Speech: Bakhtin, Vygorsky and the Internalization of Language." *Critical Inquiry* 10 (1983): 245–64.

Faulhaber, Charles. *Latin Rhetorical Theory in Thirteenth and Fourteenth Century Castile*. University of California Publications in Modern Philology, 103. Berkeley: University of California Press, 1972.

Fineman, Joel. "The Structure of Allegorical Desire." In *Allegory and Representation*, edited by Stephen J. Greenblatt, pp. 26–60. Baltimore: Johns Hopkins University Press, 1981.

Fletcher, Angus. *Allegory: The Theory of a Symbolic Mode*. Ithaca: Cornell University Press, 1982.

Foucault, Michel. "What Is an Author?" In *Textual Strategies: Perspectives in Post-Structuralist Criticism*, edited by Josué Harari, pp. 14–60. Ithaca: Cornell University Press, 1979.

Frye, Northrop. "The Nature of Satire." *University of Toronto Quarterly* 14 (1944): 75–89.

———. *The Secular Scripture: A Study of the Structure of Romance*. Cambridge: Harvard University Press, 1976.

Galinsky, G. Karl. *Ovid's "Metamorphoses": An Introduction*. Berkeley: University of California Press, 1975.

Gascón-Vera, Elena. *Don Pedro, Condestable de Portugal*. Madrid: Fundación Universitaria Española, 1979.

Genette, Gérard. *Narrative Discourse: An Essay on Method*. Translated by Jane E. Lewin. Ithaca: Cornell University Press, 1980.

———. *Palimpsestes*. Paris: Seuil, 1982.

Gerli, E. Michael. "Leriano's Libation: Notes on the *Cancionero* Lyric, *Ars moriendi* and the Probable Debt to Boccaccio." *Modern Language Notes* 96 (1981): 414–20.

———. "Metafiction in Spanish Sentimental Romances." In *The Age of the Catholic Monarchs, 1474–1519: Literary Studies in Memory of Keith Whinnom*, edited by Alan Deyermond and Ian Macpherson, pp. 57–63. *Bulletin of Hispanic Studies* (Special Issue). Liverpool: Liverpool University Press, 1989.

———. "Toward a Revaluation of the Constable of Portugal's *Satira de infelice e felice vida*." In *Hispanic Studies in Honor of Alan Deyermond*, edited by John S. Miletich. Madison: Hispanic Seminary of Medieval Studies, 1986.

Ghisalberti, Fausto. "Medieval Biographies of Ovid." *Journal of the Warburg and Courtauld Institutes* 9 (1946): 10–59.

Gilderman, Martin S. *Juan Rodríguez de la Cámara*. Boston: Twayne, 1977.

Gillet, Joseph E. "The Autonomous Character in Spanish and European Literature." *Hispanic Review* 24 (1956): 179–90.

Gilman, Stephen. *The Art of "La Celestina."* Madison: University of Wisconsin Press, 1956.

———. "The Death of Lazarillo de Tormes." *Proceedings of the Modern Language Association* 81 (1966): 149–66.

———. "The Fall of Fortune: From Allegory to Fiction." *Filologia Romanza* 16 (1957): 337–57.

———. *The Spain of Fernando de Rojas: The Intellectual and Social Landscape of "La Celestina."* Princeton: Princeton University Press, 1972.

Girard, René. *Deceit, Desire, and the Novel.* Translated by Yvonne Freccero. Baltimore: Johns Hopkins University Press, 1965.

———. *Violence and the Sacred.* Translated by Patrick Gregory. Baltimore: Johns Hopkins University Press, 1977.

Giudici, Enzo. *Maurice Scève traduttore e narratore: note su "La Deplourable fin de Flamete."* Cassino: Garigliano, 1978.

Greene, Thomas M. "Petrarch and the Humanist Hermeneutic." In *Italian Literature: Roots and Branches,* edited by G. Rimanelli and K. J. Atichity, pp. 201–24. New Haven: Yale University Press, 1976.

Grieve, Patricia E. *Desire and Death in the Spanish Sentimental Romance (1440–1550).* Newark, Del.: Juan de la Cuesta, 1987.

Harvey, Elizabeth D. "Veuntriloquizing Sappho: Ovid, Donne, and the Erotics of the Feminine Voice." *Criticism* 31 (1989): 115–38.

Herrero, Javier. "The Allegorical Structure of the *Siervo libre de amor.*" *Speculum* 55 (1980): 751–64.

Highet, Gilbert. *The Anatomy of Satire.* Princeton: Princeton University Press, 1962.

Hollander, Robert. *Boccaccio's Two Venuses.* New York: Columbia University Press, 1977.

———. "Dante's Use of *Aeneid* in *Inferno* I and II." *Comparative Literature* 20 (1968): 142–56.

———. *Studies in Dante.* Ravenna: Longo, 1980.

Holquist, Michael. "Answering as Authoring: Mikhail Bakhtin's Trans-Linguistics." *Critical Inquiry* 10 (1983): 307–19.

Huizinga, Johan. *The Waning of the Middle Ages.* Translated by F. Hopman. London: E. Arnold, 1927.

Impey, Olga T. "The Literary Emancipation of Juan Rodríguez del Padrón: From the Fictional *Cartas* to the *Siervo libre de amor.*" *Speculum* 55 (1980): 305–16.

———. "Ovid, Alfonso X, and Juan Rodríguez del Padrón: Two Castilian Translations of the *Heroides* and the Beginnings of Spanish Sentimental Prose." *Bulletin of Hispanic Studies* 57 (1980): 283–97.

———. "La poesía y la prosa del *Siervo libre de amor.*" In *Medieval, Renaissance and Folklore Studies in Honor of John Esten Keller,* edited by Joseph R. Jones, pp. 171–87. Newark, Del.: Juan de la Cuesta, 1980.

Jacobson, Howard. *Ovid's "Heroides."* Princeton: Princeton University Press, 1974.

Jakobson, Roman. "The Metaphoric and Metonymic Poles." In *Fundamentals of Language,* edited by Roman Jakobson and Morris Halle, pp. 90–96. Paris: Mouton, 1971.

Jameson, Fredric. *The Political Unconscious: Narrative as a Socially Symbolic Act.* Ithaca: Cornell University Press, 1981.

Jauss, Hans-Robert. "Form und Auffassung der Allegorie in der Tradition der

*Psychomachia* (von Prudentius zum ersten *Romanz de la Rose*)." In *Medium Aevum Vivum: Festschrift für Walter Bulst*, edited by Hans-Robert Jauss and Dieter Schaller, pp. 179–206. Heidelberg: Carl Winter, 1960.

———. *Genèse de la poésie allégorique française au moyen-âge.* Heidelberg: Carl Winter, 1962.

———. *Toward an Aesthetic of Reception.* Translated by Timothy Bahti. Minneapolis: University of Minnesota Press, 1982.

Kany, Charles. *The Beginnings of the Epistolary Novel in France, Italy, and Spain.* Berkeley: University of California Press, 1937.

Kassier, Theodore L. "*Cancionero* Poetry and the *Celestina*: From Metaphor to Reality." *Hispanófila* 56 (1976): 1–28.

Kauffman, Linda S. *Discourses of Desire: Gender, Genre, and Epistolary Fictions.* Ithaca: Cornell University Press, 1986.

Krause, Anna. "El 'tratado' novelístico de Diego de San Pedro." *Bulletin Hispanique* 54 (1952): 245–75.

Kristeva, Julia. *Desire in Language.* Translated by Thomas Gora, Alice Jardine, and Leon S. Roudiez. New York: Columbia University Press, 1980.

Kurtz, Barbara E. "Diego de San Pedro's *Cárcel de amor* and the Tradition of the Allegorical Edifice." *Journal of Hispanic Philology* 8 (1984): 123–38.

Lacan, Jacques. "La lettre volée." *La Psychanalyse* 2 (1956): 1–44.

La Favia, Louis M. "Il primo comento alla *Divina Commedia* in Spagna." *Hispano-Italic Studies* 1 (1976): 1–8.

Lang, H. R. "The So-called *Cancionero de Pero Guillén de Segovia*." *Revue Hispanique* 10 (1908): 51–81.

Langbehn-Roland, Regula. *Zur Interpetation der Romane des Diego de San Pedro.* Heidelberg: Carl Winter, 1970.

Lanham, Richard. *The Motives of Eloquence: Literary Rhetoric in the Renaissance.* New Haven: Yale University Press, 1976.

Lasperas, L. M. "La traduction et ses théories en Espagne au XVe et XVIe siècles." *Revue des langues romanes* 84 (1980): 81–92.

Lázaro Carreter, Fernando. "Sobre el 'modus interpretandi' Alfonsí." *Ibérida* 6 (1961): 57–114.

Lida de Malkiel, María Rosa. *Estudios sobre la literatura del siglo XV.* Madrid: Porrúa, 1977.

———. "La *General estoria*: Notas literarias y filológicas (I)." *Romance Philology* 13 (1959): 111–42.

———. "La *General estoria*: Notas literarias y filológicas (II)." *Romance Philology* 13 (1959): 1–30.

———. "La hipérbole sagrada en la poesía castellana del siglo XV." *Revista de Filología Hispánica* 8 (1946): 121–30.

———. "Juan Rodríguez del Padrón: I. Vida y obras." *Nueva Revista de Filología Hispánica* 6 (1952): 313–51.

———. "Juan Rodríguez del Padrón: II. Influencia." *Nueva Revista de Filología Hispánica* 8 (1954): 1–38.

———. "Juan Rodríguez del Padrón: Adiciones." *Nueva Revista de Filología Hispánica* 14 (1960): 318–21.

————. *La originalidad artística de "La Celestina."* Buenos Aires: Editorial Universitaria de Buenos Aires, 1962.

Macdonald, Inez. "The *Coronación* of Juan de Mena: Poem and Commentary." *Hispanic Review* 7 (1939): 125–44.

Mandrell, James. "Author and Authority in *Cárcel de amor*: The Role of 'El Autor.'" *Journal of Hispanic Philology* 8 (1984): 99–122.

Marciales, Miguel. *Sobre problemas riojanos y celestinescos [Carta al Dr. Stephen Gilman a propósito del libro "The Spain of Fernando de Rojas"].* Mérida: Universidad de los Andes, 1983.

Marcus, Milicent. *An Allegory of Form.* Palo Alto: Anma Libri, 1979.

Martin, Wallace. *Recent Theories of Narrative.* Ithaca: Cornell University Press, 1986.

Martínez Barbieto, Carlos. *Maçías el enamorado y Juan Rodríguez del Padrón: estudio y antología.* Santiago de Compostela: Sociedad de Bibliófilos Gallegos, 1951.

Matulka, Barbara, ed. *The Novels of Juan de Flores and Their European Diffusion: A Study in Comparative Literature.* New York: Institute of French Studies, 1931.

Mazzotta, Giuseppe. *The World at Play in Boccaccio's "Decameron."* Princeton: Princeton University Press, 1986.

Menéndez Pelayo, Marcelino. *Orígenes de la novela.* 4 vols. Madrid: Bally-Ballière, 1905–1915.

Minnis, A. J. *Medieval Theory of Authorship.* London: Scholar Press, 1984.

Miranda, Edelmira E. "Safo en *La Celestina* y en la *Imitación de diversos* de Fray Luis de León." *Boletín de la Academia Argentina de Letras* 7 (1939): 577–84.

Monfrin, Jacques. "Humanisme et traduction au moyen âge." In *L'Humanisme médiévale dans les littératures romanes du XIIe au XIVe siècles,* edited by Anthime Fourrier, pp. 217–46. Paris: Klincksieck, 1964.

Moravia, Alberto. *Man as an End.* Translated by Bernard Wall. New York: Farrar, Strauss and Giroux, 1966.

Moss, Ann. *Ovid in Renaissance France: A Survey of the Latin Editions of Ovid and Commentaries Printed in France before 1600.* London: The Warburg Institute, 1982.

Nepaulsingh, Colbert I. *Towards a History of Literary Composition in Medieval Spain.* Toronto: University of Toronto Press, 1986.

Nielson, William Allen. "The Purgatory of Cruel Beauties." *Romania* 29 (1900): 85–93.

Nordenskiöld, A. E. *Facsimile Atlas to the Early History of Cartography.* Translated by Johan Adolf Ekelöl and Clements R. Markham. Stockholm: P. A. Norstedt, 1889.

Olmstead, Everett Ward. "The Story of *Grisel and Mirabella*." In *Homenaje ofrecido a Menéndez Pidal: Miscelánea de estudios lingüísticos, literarios e históricos.* 2 vols. Madrid: Hernando, 1925.

Ortega y Gasset, José. "Miseria y esplendor de la traducción." In *Obras completas.* 6 vols. Madrid: Revista de Occidente, 1946–47. Vol. 5 (Madrid: Espasa-Calpe, 2a. ed., 1951), pp. 429–49.

Perret, Michèle. "De l'espace romanesque à la matérialité du livre." *Poétique* 50 (1982): 173–82.

Post, Chandler R. *Medieval Spanish Allegory*. Harvard Studies in Comparative Literature, 4. Cambridge: Harvard University Press, 1915.

Pratt, Mary Louise. *Toward a Speech Act Theory of Literary Discourse*. Bloomington: Indiana University Press, 1977.

Prieto, Antonio. *Morfología de la novela*. Barcelona: Ed. Planeta, 1975.

Prince, Gerald. "The Diary-Novel: Notes for the Definition of a Sub-genre." *Neophilologus* 59 (1975): 477–81.

Quadlbauer, F. *Die antike Theorie der "Genera Dicendi" im lateinischen Mittelalter*. Vienna: Böhlaus, 1962.

Quain, A. "The Medieval *Accessus ad Auctores*." *Traditio* 3 (1945): 215–64.

Quilligan, Maureen. *The Language of Allegory: Defining the Genre*. Ithaca: Cornell University Press, 1979.

Reed, Walter L. *An Exemplary History of the Novel: The Quixotic versus the Picaresque*. Chicago: University of Chicago Press, 1981.

Rey, Alfonso. "La primera persona narrativa en Diego de San Pedro." *Bulletin of Hispanic Studies* 58 (1981): 95–102.

Reynier, Gustave. *Le Roman sentimentale avant "L'Astrée."* Paris: Colin, 1908.

Reynolds, L. D., et al., eds. *Texts and Transmissions: A Survey of the Latin Classics*. Oxford: Clarendon Press, 1983.

Rico, Francisco. *Alfonso el sabio y la "General estoria."* Barcelona: Ariel, 1984.

Riquer, Martín de. "*Triste deleytaçión*, novela castellana del siglo XV." *Revista de Filología Española* 40 (1956): 33–65.

Rosbottom, Ronald. "Motifs in Epistolary Fiction: Analysis of a Narrative Subgenre." *L'Esprit Créateur* 17 (1977): 279–301.

Russo, Luigi. *Letture critiche del "Decameron."* Rome: Laterza, 1986.

Samonà, Carmelo. *Studi sul romanzo sentimentale e cortese nella letteratura spagnola del quattrocento*. Rome: Carucci, 1960.

Saussure, Ferdinand de. *Course in General Linguistics*. Translated by W. Baskin. New York: The Philosophical Library, 1959.

Schevill, Rudolph. *Ovid and the Renascence in Spain*. University of California Publications in Modern Philology, 4. Berkeley: University of California Press, 1913.

Searle, John. *Speech Acts: An Essay on the Philosophy of Language*. Cambridge: Cambridge University Press, 1969.

Sedlmayer, Heinrich. *Prolegomena critica ad "Heroides."* Vienna: Gerold, 1878.

Segre, Cesare. "Cronòtopo." In *Logos semantikos: Studia linguistica in Honorem Eugenio Coseriu*, edited by Horst Geckeler, Brigitte Schlieben-Lange, Jürgen Trabant, and Harald Weydt, vol. 1: 157–64. Madrid: Gredos, 1891.

———. *Structures and Time*. Translated by John Meddemmen. Chicago: Chicago University Press, 1979.

———. "What Bakhtin Left Unsaid." In *Romance: Generic Transformation from Chrétien de Troyes to Cervantes*, edited by Kevin Brownlee and Marina Scordilis Brownlee, pp. 23–46. Hanover, N.H.: University Press of New England, 1985.

Severin, Dorothy Sherman. "Is *La Celestina* the First Modern Novel?" *Revista de Estudios Hispánicos* 9 (1982): 205–9.

———. "Structure and Thematic Repetitions in Diego de San Pedro's *Cárcel de amor* and *Arnalte y Lucenda*." *Hispanic Review* 45 (1977): 165–69.

Shell, Marc. *The Economy of Literature*. Baltimore: Johns Hopkins University Press, 1978.

Shoaf, R. A. *Dante, Chaucer, and the Currency of the Word*. Norman, Okla.: Pilgrim Books, 1983.

Shooner, Hughes-V. "Les *Bursarii Ovidianorum* de Guillaume d'Orléans." *Mediaeval Studies* 43 (1981): 405–24.

Sieber, Harry. "The Romance of Chivalry in Spain: From Rodríguez de Montalvo to Cervantes." In *Romance: Generic Transformation from Chrétien de Troyes to Cervantes*, edited by Kevin Brownlee and Marina Scordilis Brownlee, pp. 203–19. Hanover, N.H.: University Press of New England, 1985.

Smarr, Janet L. *Boccaccio and Fiammetta: The Narrator as Lover*. Urbana: University of Illinois Press, 1986.

Stock, Brian. *The Implications of Literacy*. Princeton: Princeton University Press, 1983.

Todorov, Tzvetan. *Mikhail Bakhtin: The Dialogical Principle*. Translated by Wlad Godzich. Minneapolis: University of Minnesota Press, 1984.

———. "Reading as Construction." In *The Reader in the Text*, edited by Susan R. Suleiman and Inge Crossman. Princeton: Princeton University Press, 1980.

Traugott, Elizabeth C. "Generative Semantics and the Concept of Literary Discourse." *Journal of Literary Semantics* 2 (1973): 5–22.

Valbuena Prat, Angel. *Historia de la literatura española*. 2 vols. Barcelona: Gili, 1950.

Van Dyke, Carolyn. *The Fiction of Truth*. Ithaca: Cornell University Press, 1985.

Verducci, Florence. *Ovid's Toyshop of the Heart: "Epistulae Herodium."* Princeton: Princeton University Press, 1985.

Vickers, Nancy J. "Re-membering Dante: Petrarch's 'Chiare, fresche et dolci acque.'" *Modern Language Notes* 96 (1981): 1–11.

Violi, Patrizia. "Letters." In *Discourse and Literature*, edited by Teun Van Dijk, pp. 149–67. Amsterdam: J. Benjamins, 1985.

Waley, Pamela. "*Cárcel de amor* and *Grisel y Mirabella*: A Question of Priority." *Bulletin of Hispanic Studies* 50 (1973): 340–56.

———. "Fiammetta and Panfilo Continued." *Italian Studies* 24 (1969): 15–31.

———. "Juan de Flores y *Tristán de Leonís*." *Hispanófila* 12 (1961): 1–14.

———. "Love and Honour in the *Novelas sentimentales* of Diego de San Pedro and Juan de Flores." *Bulletin of Hispanic Studies* 43 (1966): 253–75.

Wardropper, Bruce W. "Allegory and the Role of 'El Autor' in the *Cárcel de amor*." *Philological Quarterly* 31 (1952): 39–44.

———. "El mundo sentimental de la *Cárcel de amor*." *Revista de Filología Española* 37 (1953): 168–93.

Weinrich, Harald. "Structures narratives du mythe." *Poétique* 1 (1970): 25–34.

Weiss, Julian. "Juan de Mena's *Coronación*: Satire or *Sátira?*" *Journal of Hispanic Philology* 6 (1981–82): 113–38.

Weissberger, Barbara F. "Authors, Characters and Readers in *Grimalte y Gradissa.*" In *Creation and Re-Creation: Experiments in Literary Form in Early Modern Spain. Studies in Honor of Stephen Gilman*, edited by Ronald E. Surtz and Nora Weinerth, pp. 61–76. Newark, Del.: Juan de la Cuesta, 1983.

———. "'Habla el Autor': *L'Elegia di madonna Fiammetta* as a Source for the *Siervo libre de amor.*" *Journal of Hispanic Philology* 4 (1980): 203–36.

Whinnom, Keith. "*Autor* and *Tratado* in the Fifteenth Century: Semantic Latinism or Etymological Trap?" *Bulletin of Hispanic Studies* 59 (1982): 211–18.

———. *Diego de San Pedro.* Boston: Twayne, 1974.

———. "Diego de San Pedro's Stylistic Reform." *Bulletin of Hispanic Studies* 37 (1960): 1–15.

———. "The *Historia de duobus amantibus* of Aeneas Sylvius Piccolomini (Pope Pius II) and the Development of Spanish Golden-Age Fiction." In *Essays on Narrative Fiction in the Iberian Peninsula in Honor of Frank Pierce*, edited by R. B. Tate, pp. 243–55. Oxford: Dolphin, 1982.

———. "Nicolás Núñez's Continuation of the *Cárcel de amor.*" In *Studies in Spanish Literature of the Golden Age Presented to Edward M. Wilson*, edited by R. O. Jones, pp. 357–66. London: Tamesis, 1973.

Wilkinson, L. P. *Ovid Surveyed.* Cambridge: Cambridge University Press, 1962.

Zumthor, Paul. *Essai de poétique médiévale.* Paris: Seuil, 1972.

———. "Narrative and Anti-Narrative: *Le Roman de la Rose.*" *Yale French Studies* 51 (1974): 185–204.

# INDEX